MW01009865

YOU CAN'T EAT FREEDOM

YOU

CAN'T

EAT

FREEDOM

SOUTHERNERS AND SOCIAL JUSTICE
AFTER THE CIVIL RIGHTS MOVEMENT

GRETA DE JONG

THE UNIVERSITY OF NORTH CAROLINA PRESS

Chapel Hill

This book was published with the assistance of the
Fred W. Morrison Fund of the University of North Carolina Press.

© 2016 The University of North Carolina Press
All rights reserved
Manufactured in the United States of America
Set in Charter and Block types
by codeMantra

The University of North Carolina Press has been a member
of the Green Press Initiative since 2003.

Cover illustration: Residents of Mound Bayou, Mississippi, on
their front porch, 1976. © Alex Webb / Magnum Photos.

Library of Congress Cataloging-in-Publication Data
Names: De Jong, Greta, author.
Title: You can't eat freedom : southerners and social justice
after the Civil Rights Movement / Greta de Jong.
Description: Chapel Hill : The University of North Carolina Press,
[2016] | Includes bibliographical references and index.
Identifiers: LCCN 2016014539| ISBN 9781469629308
(cloth : alk. paper) | ISBN 9781469629315 (ebook)
Subjects: LCSH: Southern States—Economic conditions—1945– |
African Americans—Social conditions—1964–1975. | African
Americans—Economic conditions. | Agriculture—Economic
aspects—Southern States. | Southern States—History—1951– |
Migration, Internal—United States—History—20th century.
Classification: LCC HC107.A13 D426 2016 | DDC 331.6/396073076—
dc23 LC record available at http://lccn.loc.gov/2016014539

CONTENTS

Acknowledgments / vii

Abbreviations / xi

Introduction / 1

1. The Man Don't Need Me Anymore:
From Free Labor to Displaced Persons / 18

2. This Is Home: Black Workers' Responses to
Displacement and Out-Migration / 44

3. They Could Make Some Decisions:
The War on Poverty and Community Action / 62

4. Okra Is a Threat: The Low-Income Cooperative Movement / 88

5. OEO Is Finished: Federal Withdrawal
and the Return to States' Rights / 116

6. To Build Something, Where They Are: The Federation of
Southern Cooperatives and Rural Economic Development / 141

7. A World of Despair: Free Enterprise and Its Failures / 174

8. Government Cannot Solve Our Problems:
Legacies of Displacement / 200

Conclusion / 222

Appendix / 227

Notes / 231

Bibliography / 273

Index / 287

MAPS, ILLUSTRATIONS, AND TABLES

MAPS

1. Louisiana Cotton Plantation Region / 7

2. Mississippi Cotton Plantation Region / 8

3. Alabama Cotton Plantation Region / 9

ILLUSTRATIONS

Map prepared by the Citizens' Council accompanying
an article in the *Citizen*, May 1962 / 37

Pamphlet inviting poor people to a conference at the Delta
Ministry's headquarters in Mt. Beulah, January 1966 / 49

Cartoon noting the federal government's shift in focus away from
the War on Poverty to the Vietnam War, November 1967 / 83

Poster encouraging people to form cooperatives, late 1960s / 96

President Richard Nixon meeting with advisers
in the Oval Office, 13 March 1970 / 126

Fund-raising advertisement from an Emergency
Land Fund newsletter, December 1979 / 163

Cartoon on President Ronald Reagan's budget cuts, early 1980s / 180

TABLES

1. Agricultural and nonagricultural employment in
the plantation counties, 1950–1990 / 227

2. Black unemployment and poverty rates in the
plantation counties, 1950–1990 / 229

ACKNOWLEDGMENTS

I am fortunate to be part of an inspiring and supportive academic community at the University of Nevada, Reno, and in the wider field of southern and African American history. My colleagues in the Department of History, the Core Humanities Program, and the Gender, Race, and Identity Program at UNR have been vital allies in my intellectual endeavors, and I am grateful for numerous opportunities I have had to share ideas and receive feedback from them at organized events and in casual conversation. I am especially indebted to Debbie Boehm, Scott Casper, Linda Curcio, Dennis Dworkin, Neal Ferguson, Justin Gifford, Martha Hildreth, Jen Hill, Emily Hobson, Meredith Oda, Daniel Enrique Perez, Elizabeth Raymond, Hugh Shapiro, Charles Tshimanga-Kashama, and Barbara Walker for their astute observations and enthusiastic encouragement of my work. Jenni Baryol and Jodie Helman provided much-appreciated administrative assistance. Research for this book was partially funded by a Junior Faculty Research Grant from UNR and by the John and Marie Noble Endowment for Historical Research.

My mentor and friend Nan Elizabeth Woodruff has continued to offer excellent guidance on matters both scholarly and unscholarly with her inimitable energy and good humor. I owe her everything. Pete Daniel has been another valued adviser whose work on race and labor in the southern plantation economy has strongly influenced my own. Over the years I have participated in various conferences and other forums where I was able to present portions of my research in nascent forms and interact with other scholars in my field who helped hone my analysis. In particular, I would like to thank participants at the Region, Class, and Culture Conference in Memphis (2009) and the War on Poverty Conference at Dartmouth College (2011) for their insightful questions and comments on my papers. V. P. Franklin, Michael Martin, and Annelise Orleck and Lisa Hazirjian edited journals and anthologies where some early articles appeared. Their comments and those of the peer reviewers of those works helped shape the direction of the larger study that became this book. Special thanks also to Annelise Orleck and the other (anonymous) reviewer for the University of North Carolina Press, who carefully read the draft manuscript and whose insights dramatically improved the final version presented here. My editors at UNC Press, Brandon Proia and Mary Carley Caviness, also offered invaluable advice, encouragement, and support as I worked on revising and preparing the manuscript for publication. Nancy Raynor's careful copyediting added clarity and eliminated many mistakes.

I am grateful to the leaders and members of the Federation of Southern Cooperatives for their continuing efforts to bring racial and economic justice to the South in the decades following the civil rights movement and for ensuring the preservation of the organizational records deposited at the Amistad Research Center in New Orleans, which provided much of the archival material used in this book. Thanks especially to Wilbert Guillory and John Zippert, who agreed to be interviewed for my research on the Louisiana freedom struggle some decades ago and who provided information about the southern cooperative movement that helped inspire this project. I had planned to conduct more interviews after completing an initial draft of the manuscript based on the archival research, so that I could direct my questions toward gaps in the record that needed to be filled. However, the project took much longer than expected to complete, and in the meantime many of the older activists fell ill or died, while those who remained involved in the movement tended to be extremely busy. Fortunately, I was able to draw on interviews conducted by scholars Robert Korstad and Neil Boothby that they generously shared online through the Southern Rural Poverty Collection at Duke University, and I am indebted to them and to interviewees John H. Brown Jr., L. C. Dorsey, Leslie W. Dunbar, H. Jack Geiger, John Hatch, F. Ray Marshall, and Charles Prejean for creating these oral histories. I owe a similar debt to Susan Youngblood Ashmore for kindly sending me a copy of the transcript of her interview with Ezra Cunningham.

Many thanks also to the helpful archivists and staff of the depositories I visited during the course of my research: the Special Collections and Archives Department of the Draughon Library at Auburn University, Alabama; the Hill Memorial Library at Louisiana State University; the Wilson Library of the University of North Carolina; the Charles W. Capps Jr. Archives and Museum at Delta State University; the McCain Library and Archives at the University of Southern Mississippi; the Wisconsin Historical Society; the Amistad Research Center and Tulane University Special Collections in New Orleans; the University of Mississippi Archives and Special Collections; the Special Collections Department and the Congressional and Political Research Center of Mississippi State University Libraries; the Rockefeller Archives Center in New York; Special Collections at the Hoole Library of the University of Alabama; and the National Archives in Washington, D.C. Their knowledge, expertise, suggestions, and insights proved invaluable to me during my time in the archives and helped uncover sources that I might not have thought to look at otherwise. I also thank the archivists at the University of Mississippi, the University of Southern Mississippi, and Mississippi State University for their fast responses to my requests for digital copies of the illustrations used in the book.

I could not have completed this book without the love and support offered by my family and nonacademic friends during the decade or more that it took me to write it. My parents, siblings, and nieces back home in New Zealand—Keith, Daphne, Kim, Martin, Maureen, Kris, Lisette, Lucy, Ella, and Rhia—and my genius friend Greg Locke remained close even when they were far away, and they made my trips home fun-filled respites from the stresses of academic life. In Reno, I have enjoyed and learned much from my involvement with the Great Basin Community Food Cooperative as a member-owner and sometimes board member. Watching the co-op grow and adjust to the challenges of expansion while trying to balance economic imperatives with social justice goals offered insight into the difficulties facing the rural southern cooperative movement analyzed in this book. I thank the co-op's leaders and members for their dedication to serving our local community and working to create alternatives to the industrial food system.

ABBREVIATIONS

AFBF	American Farm Bureau Federation
AFDC	Aid to Families with Dependent Children
BDO	Business Development Office
CAA	community action agency
CAP	community action program
CCR	Commission on Civil Rights
CDGM	Child Development Group of Mississippi
CETA	Comprehensive Employment Training Act
COI	Coahoma Opportunities Inc.
CORE	Congress of Racial Equality
CSA	Community Services Administration
DCHHC	Delta Community Hospital and Health Center
DOL	Department of Labor
EDA	Economic Development Administration
ELF	Emergency Land Fund
FES	Federal Extension Service
FmHA	Farmers Home Administration
FSC	Federation of Southern Cooperatives
FSC/LAF	Federation of Southern Cooperatives/Land Assistance Fund
GAO	General Accounting Office
GMVPC	Grand Marie Vegetable Producers Cooperative
HEW	Department of Health, Education, and Welfare
HUD	Department of Housing and Urban Development
LMDDC	Lower Mississippi Delta Development Commission
MBCH	Mound Bayou Community Hospital
MDTA	Manpower Development and Training Act
MFDP	Mississippi Freedom Democratic Party
MPC	Minority Peoples Council on the Tennessee-Tombigbee Waterway Project
NAACP	National Association for the Advancement of Colored People
NBCFC	North Bolivar County Farm Cooperative
NBCHC	North Bolivar County Health Council

NSF	National Sharecroppers Fund
OEO	Office of Economic Opportunity
OMBE	Office of Minority Business Enterprise
OPD	Office of Program Development
PLBA	Panola Land Buyers Association
PPC	Poor People's Corporation
RTRC	Rural Training and Research Center
SCC	Southern Consumers Cooperative
SCDF	Southern Cooperative Development Fund
SCDP	Southern Cooperative Development Program
SCEF	Southern Consumers Education Foundation
SCLC	Southern Christian Leadership Conference
SEASHA	Southeast Alabama Self-Help Association
SEDFRE	Scholarship, Education and Defense Fund for Racial Equality
SEOO	State Economic Opportunity Office
SNCC	Student Nonviolent Coordinating Committee
STAR	Systematic Training and Redevelopment
SWAFCA	Southwest Alabama Farmers Cooperative Association
TDHC	Tufts-Delta Health Center
TTW	Tennessee-Tombigbee Waterway
TTWDA	Tennessee-Tombigbee Waterway Development Authority
USDA	United States Department of Agriculture
VISTA	Volunteers in Service to America
WBFC	West Batesville Farmers Cooperative

YOU CAN'T EAT FREEDOM

INTRODUCTION

In her study of the transition from slavery to free labor in nineteenth-century Maryland, Barbara Fields refers to freedom as a "moving target" that was constantly being redefined in contests over economic and political rights that freedpeople attempted to assert and planters sought to deny.[1] At that time, the meaning of freedom for the nation's working class was being transformed as the rise of industrial capitalism pushed the status of self-reliant property owner out of reach for large numbers of wage earners. Historically, Americans had considered property ownership essential to the enjoyment of liberty and the basis of citizenship in a democratic republic, but when freedpeople and their allies suggested that real freedom required a redistribution of land and resources in the South to ensure economic independence for former slaves, political leaders balked. They believed the future lay in large-scale agriculture, not small farms. If freedpeople and poor white southerners received land that allowed them to live and work on their own terms, who would be left to labor on the plantations, and what would stop propertyless northerners from demanding similar reforms?

By the late nineteenth century, the debate was settled in favor of a more restricted definition of freedom that granted legal and political rights to freedpeople but left most of them dependent on white land-owners for employment. Former slaves were not to become independent small farmers but instead joined white workers as free laborers, selling themselves in the marketplace for the best price they could find. Even those limited gains disappeared after white supremacists regained control of the state governments in the South and the federal government withdrew its presence from the region, leaving black people unprotected against the onslaught of disfranchisement and segregation legislation passed in the 1880s and 1890s. The Jim Crow laws served to limit workers' bargaining power and maintain an ample supply of labor for plantation owners by denying black people access to education, economic opportunities, and the legal system. Most African Americans ended up as sharecroppers, working land owned by white people in return for a portion of the proceeds from the crops they grew each year. Paid only once annually, sharecropping families relied on plantation owners to supply housing, food, clothing, and other necessities throughout the year, the costs of which were deducted from their pay at harvest time.[2]

Until the 1930s, black labor was so cheap in the South that planters had little incentive to mechanize their operations. That began to change during the Great Depression, when the federal government moved to limit production and raise farmers' incomes by paying them to take land out of cultivation. Plantation owners were supposed to retain tenants and sharecroppers on their farms and share the subsidy payments they received from the government with their workers, but loopholes in the legislation enabled many landlords to evade this responsibility. Thousands of families lost their homes and livelihoods when landowners reduced the number of workers they employed and invested their government checks in tractors and other labor-saving technology instead. Agricultural mechanization accelerated during World War II as many black laborers left to work in defense industries, which reduced the supply of workers and raised labor costs, and it received a final push with the rise of the civil rights movement and the threat of black political empowerment in the 1950s and 1960s. In those decades, economic and political considerations drove plantation owners to get rid of their remaining laborers as quickly as possible, leading to mass evictions that displaced hundreds of thousands more people.[3]

The civil rights legislation passed in the mid-1960s freed African Americans from the oppressions of the Jim Crow system during another period of capitalist transformation that threw long-standing assumptions regarding the meaning of citizenship into disarray. Just when white workers had managed to secure a new version of the republican ideal rooted in unionized manufacturing jobs with generous pay and benefits, New Deal social welfare programs that offered a modicum of economic security, and federally subsidized home ownership, the ground shifted again as the nation made the transition to a postindustrial, globalized economy that rendered a good proportion of the labor force obsolete. The black plantation workers who were pushed off the land by the modernization of southern agriculture were not to join the industrial working class in the post–civil rights era. Instead, they were the first to experience the transition from free labor to displaced persons that awaited millions of other workers in this new era of economic restructuring.

Rural black southerners found that equal rights were easier to establish on paper than in practice in communities where their labor was expendable and white racists controlled access to the means of economic survival, including employment, credit, housing, and public assistance. African Americans who ventured to register to vote or participate in elections risked being fired from their jobs, evicted from their homes, denied loans, or cut from welfare rolls. Thousands of others faced unemployment and homelessness as the southern sharecropping system headed into its final death spiral. Black people's economic dependence severely limited their political independence, and civil rights leaders understood that raising black southerners' economic status was a prerequisite to ensuring the other rights they had fought for in the 1960s. For many people, simply obtaining such basic necessities as food and shelter was a more immediate concern than was voting. As Alabama activist Ezra Cunningham explained, "You can't eat freedom. And a ballot is not to be confused with a dollar bill."[4]

Cunningham's insight reflected his and others' long involvement in a struggle for social justice that predated the civil rights movement and continued beyond it. A farm owner and schoolteacher in Monroe County, he quit his teaching job when the superintendent asked him to take the children out of class to pick cotton. He taught farming techniques to black soldiers returning from the war in the 1940s and encouraged African Americans to register to vote in the 1950s. When national civil rights groups came into Alabama at the height of the freedom movement, Cunningham was among the hundreds of local people who participated in demonstrations and voter registration drives that successfully pressured the federal government into outlawing racial discrimination. Activists' struggles did not end there, however. In the decades following passage of the Civil Rights and Voting Rights Acts, Cunningham and other movement veterans worked to draw attention to persistent forms of racial oppression that required more action. Their goals extended beyond desegregation and political participation to encompass measures designed to ensure economic security, including jobs with adequate incomes, affordable housing, and access to medical care. Civil rights and social justice activism merged in various initiatives aimed at asserting economic rights that were needed to solidify the legal and political rights won in the mid-1960s.[5]

Activists' battles for both ballots and dollars faced steep challenges. The economic revolution wrought by mechanization threatened to negate the political revolution brought about by the civil rights movement. In plantation counties where hundreds of sharecropping families were once employed cultivating the cotton and other cash crops that enriched their landlords, human beings gradually disappeared from the fields as tractors, herbicides, and mechanical harvesters took over their jobs. Farm employment in the South declined from 5.6 million to 3.1 million between 1940 and 1960, and another 1.2 million positions were gone by 1969.[6] With these changes came a fundamental shift in the relationship between white and black people. For most of the region's history, the central concern of white landowners was how to force black people to work for them, a problem they solved by restricting economic opportunities and political rights for African Americans in the slavery and Jim Crow eras. In the 1960s, the focus shifted to deciding what to do with workers whose labor was no longer needed—and who could now vote. Just when black southerners seemed poised to take their place as equal citizens in their communities, many of their white neighbors wondered whether there was a place for African Americans at all.

As the new economic order took shape, planters and political leaders argued that the best solution to unemployment was for displaced workers to leave the region and seek work elsewhere. In response, African Americans asserted that they had a right to stay in the communities where they had lived and worked for generations. Both sides understood the political implications of black out-migration from counties where African Americans made up significant voting majorities. As Mississippi activist Lawrence Guyot observed in February 1966, "even if Negroes get registered, we still have to worry about keeping them here." For their part, white leaders viewed out-migration as a way to dilute black political power and avoid the considerable expenditures needed to address the unemployment problem. Robert Patterson, a segregationist who founded the Citizens' Council in 1954 to oppose the civil rights movement, called black Mississippians an "economic and political liability" and stated, "The only thing for the Negro to do is to voluntarily migrate."[7]

This book examines the ideological debates and political struggles that occurred in the cotton plantation regions of Alabama, Mississippi, and Louisiana as residents wrestled with the dilemmas posed by agricultural displacement and black political empowerment after the mid-1960s. I use the terms "displacement" and "displaced worker" in the same way they were used by contemporary observers in the mid-twentieth century: to refer to people employed in agriculture (farm owners, tenants, sharecroppers, and day laborers) who lost their jobs when their labor was no longer needed. Most of these people would also meet the technical definition developed by the Department of Labor's Bureau of Labor Statistics in the mid-1980s (when displacement affected large numbers of industrial workers nationwide) and still in use today: "persons 20 years and over who lost or left jobs because their plant or company closed or moved, there was insufficient work for them to do, or their position or shift was abolished."[8]

Economic restructuring and the passage of civil rights legislation necessitated a renegotiation of social relationships and generated sharp contests over the distribution of power and resources in southern plantation regions. When some activists called for government action to address mass unemployment and poverty, opponents argued that these problems resulted from the normal workings of a free market economy and required no intervention. Casting displacement as a natural phenomenon that was beyond human control absolved planters from responsibility for the crisis, denied any need for redistributive economic policies, and preserved the disparities in wealth produced by generations of exploiting black people's labor. Fierce defenses of free enterprise and limited government replaced Jim Crow laws as a key means of maintaining regional elites' political and economic power. These ideas also informed responses to mass layoffs and labor displacement that occurred on a national scale as the United States made the transition from industrial capitalism to finance capitalism in the late twentieth century. Understanding what happened to black workers in the plantation South therefore helps us make sense of developments that shaped other Americans' experiences in the post–civil rights era.

The three Deep South states examined in this book were notorious for the mistreatment their white residents inflicted on African Americans in the slavery and Jim Crow eras, and they emerged as centers of black political activism in the 1960s. The fertile lands located along floodplains in northern Louisiana and western Mississippi and stretching east through the Alabama Black Belt were home to some of the richest white people and the poorest black people in the nation. As both white and black residents understood, these two facts were connected, for the vast fortunes that planters accumulated rested on denying black laborers a fair share of the wealth they produced. White supremacists in the plantation counties frequently led the way in devising mechanisms for disempowering African Americans that were later adopted throughout the South. In the 1960s, well-publicized events such as the desegregation and voter registration efforts of the Congress of Racial Equality (CORE) in Louisiana, Freedom Summer in Mississippi, and the Selma to Montgomery march in Alabama placed local activists in these states at the forefront of the black freedom movement.[9] Clashes between supporters and opponents of racial equality in this region helped shape other Americans' understanding of the civil rights struggle and its aftermath. The media spotlight and close attention from federal policy makers gave participants on both sides powerful forums for disseminating their contrasting views. Events in these plantation counties strongly influenced national perceptions and responses, making them a logical focus for this study.[10]

This book is informed by, contributes to, and connects several historiographical strains that have emerged in the past two decades. Whereas many accounts of the struggle for racial justice end with the passage of civil rights legislation in the 1960s, more recent scholarship has highlighted the persistence of racism and black political activism in later years. Local community studies by historians Emilye Crosby, Todd Moye, Cynthia Fleming, Hasan Jeffries, and Françoise Hamlin have examined ongoing freedom struggles that continued beyond the civil rights era in such places as Wilcox County, Alabama, and Sunflower County, Mississippi. These works reveal the depth of opposition to black equality that existed in the rural South, the ongoing challenges facing impoverished communities, and continued racial disparities. Complicating the popular notion that the civil rights movement ended racism in the United States, they demonstrate how white supremacists obstructed further progress and perpetuated inequality after the 1960s.[11]

Other scholars have shown how racial ideologies took new forms as overt expressions of bigotry became less acceptable. Joseph Crespino's study of the ways white Mississippians adapted to the end of Jim Crow demonstrates important connections between opposition to racial equality and the rise of the conservative movement in the late twentieth century. Analyses by Kevin Kruse and Matthew Lassiter of white suburbanites' reactions to federal civil rights enforcement provide insight into the ways segregationist arguments evolved into defenses of individual liberty and limited government that seemingly had no racial motivations. Rather than asserting that African Americans were inherently inferior to white people, as they had in the past, opponents of the freedom movement expressed support for integration while resisting every practical means of achieving it on the grounds that these represented a tyrannical use of federal power. Through this process, a form of "colorblind racism" replaced the blatant forms of discrimination of earlier decades. Rejecting the proactive measures that were needed to overcome racial inequality,

6   INTRODUCTION

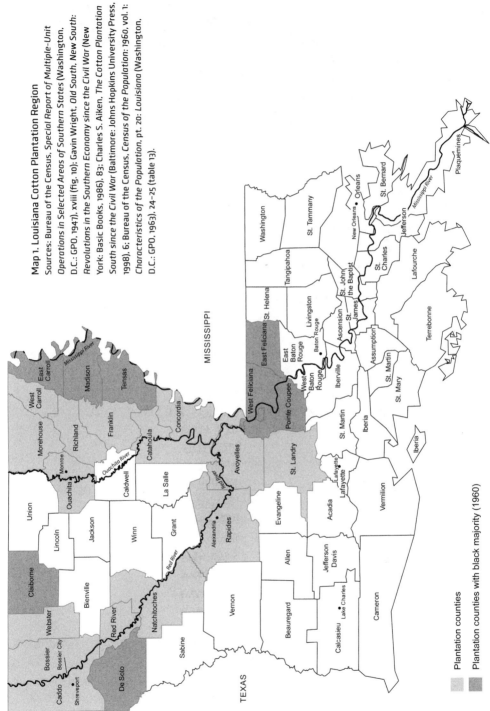

Map 1. Louisiana Cotton Plantation Region

Sources: Bureau of the Census, *Special Report of Multiple-Unit Operations in Selected Areas of Southern States* (Washington, D.C.: GPO, 1941), xviii (fig. 10); Gavin Wright, *Old South, New South: Revolutions in the Southern Economy since the Civil War* (New York: Basic Books, 1986), 83; Charles S. Aiken, *The Cotton Plantation South since the Civil War* (Baltimore: Johns Hopkins University Press, 1998), 6; Bureau of the Census, *Census of the Population: 1960*, vol. 1: *Characteristics of the Population, pt. 20: Louisiana* (Washington, D.C.: GPO, 1963), 24–25 (table 13).

Plantation counties

Plantation counties with black majority (1960)

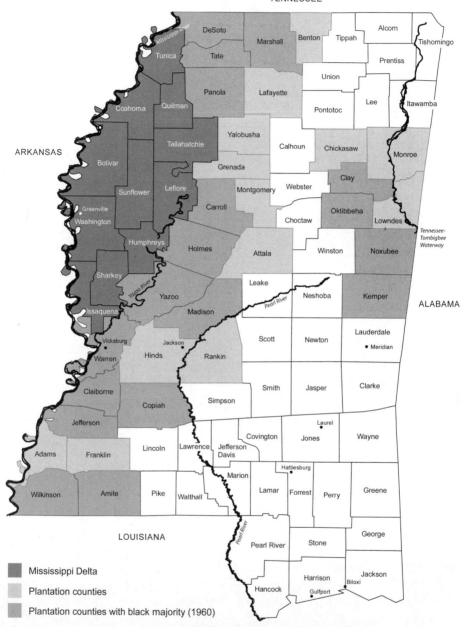

TENNESSEE

ARKANSAS

ALABAMA

LOUISIANA

Mississippi River

DeSoto
Marshall
Benton
Tippah
Alcorn
Tishomingo
Tunica
Tate
Prentiss
Union
Panola
Lafayette
Lee
Itawamba
Coahoma
Quitman
Pontotoc
Yalobusha
Tallahatchie
Calhoun
Chickasaw
Monroe
Bolivar
Grenada
Clay
Sunflower
Leflore
Montgomery
Webster
Greenville
Carroll
Oktibbeha
Washington
Choctaw
Lowndes
Humphreys
Holmes
Attala
Winston
Noxubee
Sharkey
Yazoo River
Leake
Neshoba
Kemper
Issaquena
Yazoo
Pearl River
Madison
Vicksburg
Jackson
Scott
Newton
Lauderdale
Warren
Hinds
Rankin
Meridian
Claiborne
Smith
Jasper
Clarke
Copiah
Simpson
Jefferson
Laurel
Covington
Jones
Wayne
Adams
Franklin
Lincoln
Lawrence
Jefferson Davis
Wilkinson
Amite
Pike
Walthall
Marion
Hattiesburg
Lamar
Forrest
Perry
Greene
Pearl River
George
Pearl River
Stone
Hancock
Harrison
Jackson
Gulfport
Biloxi

Tennessee-Tombigbee Waterway

Mississippi Delta

Plantation counties

Plantation counties with black majority (1960)

Map 2. Mississippi Cotton Plantation Region
Sources: Bureau of the Census, *Special Report of Multiple-Unit Operations in Selected Areas of Southern States* (Washington, D.C.: GPO, 1947), xviii (fig. 10); Gavin Wright, *Old South, New South: Revolutions in the Southern Economy since the Civil War* (New York: Basic Books, 1986), 83; Charles S. Aiken, *The Cotton Plantation South since the Civil War* (Baltimore: Johns Hopkins University Press, 1998), 6; Bureau of the Census, *Census of the Population: 1960*, vol. 1: *Characteristics of the Population*, pt. 26: *Mississippi* (Washington, D.C.: GPO, 1963), 24–25 (table 13).

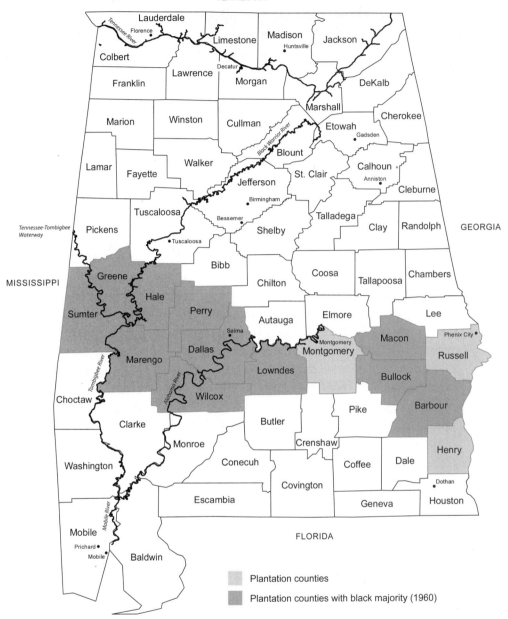

Map 3. Alabama Cotton Plantation Region

Sources: Bureau of the Census, *Special Report of Multiple-Unit Operations in Selected Areas of Southern States* (Washington, D.C.: GPO, 1947), xviii (fig. 10); Gavin Wright, *Old South, New South: Revolutions in the Southern Economy since the Civil War* (New York: Basic Books, 1986), 83; Charles S. Aiken, *The Cotton Plantation South since the Civil War* (Baltimore: Johns Hopkins University Press, 1998), 6; Bureau of the Census, *Census of the Population: 1960*, vol. 1: *Characteristics of the Population*, pt. 2: *Alabama* (Washington, D.C.: GPO, 1963), 24–25 (table 13).

policy makers instead moved to adopt racially neutral approaches that effectively froze existing disparities in place.[12]

Continued racism necessitated continued activism long after the 1960s. Historians such as Thomas Peake, Mark Newman, Stephen Tuck, Chris Danielson, and Timothy Minchin have shown how ongoing pressure from civil rights groups and individual activists was crucial to realizing the rights set out in the Civil Rights and Voting Rights Acts. The National Association for the Advancement of Colored People (NAACP), Southern Christian Leadership Conference (SCLC), and National Urban League all continued to act as important voices for African Americans in the post–civil rights era, drawing attention to persistent discrimination and lobbying Congress on issues relating to racial justice. Although internal conflicts and financial troubles destroyed the Student Nonviolent Coordinating Committee (SNCC) and badly weakened CORE in the late 1960s, small cadres of local activists and a few outside supporters continued the freedom struggle in the communities these groups had helped mobilize earlier in the decade. The Mississippi Freedom Democratic Party (MFDP), Delta Ministry, and Selma Inter-Religious Project were among dozens of organizations that fought to enhance rural black southerners' political and economic rights in the post–civil rights era. The Scholarship, Education and Defense Fund for Racial Equality (SEDFRE), a national organization founded by former CORE members, supported these efforts by providing leadership training and technical assistance to community groups and black elected officials in the 1970s.[13]

In addition to securing equality under the law, a central concern of the freedom movement was economic justice. African Americans did not have access to the same educational and employment opportunities as white Americans during the Jim Crow era, leaving them at a disadvantage even after civil rights legislation outlawed racial discrimination. For these reasons, activists called on the federal government to create employment, provide job training, assist unemployed people, and foster broader economic development in rural southern communities. A small step toward addressing these issues came in 1961 when Congress created the Area Redevelopment Administration to provide aid to distressed areas through grants and loans that encouraged new business development, infrastructure investments, and job training programs. Local political and business leaders prepared the plans and made the decisions that determined how to allocate these resources, however, and they paid little attention to the needs of poor and nonwhite people. When authorization for the agency expired in 1965, its responsibilities passed to the newly established Economic Development Administration (EDA) in the Department of Commerce. Although local governments still initiated projects, federal officials decided which ones to fund and enforced antidiscrimination provisions that regulated use of the money, allowing for more participation by African Americans.[14] Pressure from civil rights activists also helped inspire the federal government's War on Poverty, launched in 1964 with the Economic Opportunity Act. One of several measures aimed at realizing President Lyndon Johnson's vision of a "Great Society" that offered all citizens the same chance of success, the legislation created the Office of Economic Opportunity (OEO) within the executive branch of government and provided for direct federal funding of programs initiated by local community groups, including many that were led by participants in the black freedom movement. Recent scholarship by Annelise Orleck, Susan Youngblood Ashmore, William Clayson, and others has shown that the OEO's community action programs (CAPs) were key sites of contestation in the fight for racial and economic justice, making the War on Poverty an essential element in the story of post-1960s black political activism.[15]

My work brings these historiographical strands together in a regional study emphasizing the centrality of labor displacement in shaping developments in the plantation counties after 1965. Existing accounts tend to treat the changes in southern agriculture as the backdrop or a side note to other events rather than the driving force behind the actions of white supremacists and social justice activists in this period. Leaving these shifts in the political economy unexamined creates the impression that the motivations of those who resisted the freedom struggle were static and aimed at preserving the racial hierarchies created by slavery and Jim Crow.[16] A full understanding of this period requires moving beyond frameworks that examine ongoing struggles over race and rights simply as extensions of earlier conflicts to acknowledge the transformation in class relationships that occurred with the conversion of black southerners from cheap labor to unneeded labor. Presuming that white leaders' goals were unchanging makes the policies they pursued seem like attempts to maintain timeless racial traditions rather than what they really were: a concerted effort, necessitated by new circumstances, to cast off a large population of unemployed and poor people. As this book shows, plantation owners' responses to the civil rights revolution reflected economic and political motivations rooted in the social context of the late twentieth century, not nostalgia for the late nineteenth century. Moreover, the rationalizations they offered foreshadowed a national shift in thinking that occurred as the United States entered a period of economic restructuring that threw millions of people out of work in the 1970s and 1980s. What happened in these rural counties established precedents for the treatment of other Americans whose lives were disrupted by the vicissitudes of the market in later decades.

On the other side, this book challenges the notion that economic marginalization was the inevitable outcome for workers whose labor was no longer needed and that nothing could alter sharecroppers' fate once the forces of agricultural modernization took hold.[17] Rural black southerners were not powerless victims of inexorable processes that were beyond anyone's control. They understood that political decisions rather than inalterable laws of supply and demand created impoverished people and communities. These activists offered innovative solutions to social problems that could have placed the region—and the nation as a whole—on a significantly different trajectory if they had not encountered such strong resistance from opponents. The conflicts that ensued in the plantation counties after the passage of civil rights legislation and their long-term consequences for white as well as black Americans demonstrate how race and class domination act in concert as intertwined and mutually reinforcing systems of oppression. Post-1960s social justice activism reflected participants' awareness of these connections and the need to address them simultaneously through efforts to enhance economic security along with racial equality. The initiatives undertaken in these decades were not futile or insignificant, and they provide useful lessons for citizens seeking to fully realize the unfulfilled promises of the civil rights era.

Chapter 1 of this book describes the extreme hardships facing plantation workers as they made the transition from free labor to displaced persons simultaneously with the rise of the civil rights movement and the demise of Jim Crow. White supremacists responded to black civil rights gains by accelerating the displacement of farm families from the land and blocking efforts to provide alternative means of support for thousands of unemployed people who were left without homes or income. Southern welfare and economic development policies were designed to encourage black out-migration from the region, enabling wealthy white families whose fortunes were built on exploiting black labor to avoid responsibility for those workers once they were no longer needed. At the same time, reducing the number of African Americans living in the plantation counties helped minimize the threat posed by black political empower-ment. By the mid-1960s, these policies had forced hundreds of thousands of African Americans to leave the region and generated rising unemploy-ment and poverty rates for those who remained.

Local activists and their allies from outside the South knew that politi-cal rights alone could not solve these problems. Civil rights legislation did not represent the culmination of their goals but was instead a necessary starting point from which to launch a new phase of the freedom strug-gle focused on securing economic justice. They envisioned a reordering of the region's political economy along lines that ensured a living wage for working people, adequate social supports and retraining programs for the unemployed, a tax system that generated the revenues needed for public investments in education and infrastructure, and opportunities for all citizens to participate in democratic decision making. As outlined in Chapter 2, activists responded to the economic crisis in the rural South by publicizing widespread hunger and poverty and pressuring federal officials to act. African Americans who had lived and worked in the plan-tation counties for generations made it clear that they did not want to leave and argued that they had a right to remain in their home commu-nities instead of being forced to move elsewhere to look for jobs. They proposed alternatives to out-migration that called for increased public expenditures on education, job training, and improved social services for displaced workers. Their lobbying and clear evidence of the misery that resulted from the policies pursued by state and local governments in the plantation regions convinced the federal government to step up antipov-erty efforts.

Chapter 3 examines the impact of the War on Poverty in the planta-tion counties and the threat that it posed to the people in power. Direct access to the OEO's grant-making divisions enabled black residents to bypass racist administrators of state and county offices who had previ-ously controlled access to federal assistance, bringing millions of dollars into impoverished areas. Antipoverty initiatives provided services and job opportunities for poor people, encouraging displaced laborers to stay in the South and work to improve conditions in their communities. In its first few years, the radical potential of the War on Poverty was demon-strated in inventive and effective projects that included early childhood development programs, cooperative farms and businesses, and compre-hensive health services for low-income people. The OEO's mandate to include representatives of the poor in program planning enabled rural black southerners to directly influence the distribution of resources in their communities for the first time in their lives. All of this threatened the interests of regional elites, and they responded by attacking the programs. Opponents used exaggerated (and often fabricated) charges of corruption and mismanagement to paint the War on Poverty as a waste of taxpayer money and undermine public support for the effort. Political pressure and budget cuts weakened the OEO's support for black southerners' rural development projects and generated some bitterness among participants in antipoverty programs. By the end of the 1960s, many activists were disillusioned with government efforts to solve social problems and sought alternative solutions that fostered black autonomy and economic independence.

Contrary to racist perceptions of African Americans as lazy welfare recipients who preferred dependence on government assistance to making a living on their own, black southerners were intensely interested in self-help efforts that enabled them to break free from white control. Chapter 4 examines the rise of the low-income cooperative movement and the opportunities it offered for rural poor people to take charge of their economic destiny. In response to layoffs and evictions, activists formed cooperative enterprises that provided employment to people who lost their jobs because of their political activities. More than just a survival tactic, cooperatives were a crucial part of the freedom struggle in the post–civil rights era. They represented an attempt to establish a measure of economic independence for rural poor people and thus facilitate political participation in a region where many African Americans still feared losing their homes or livelihoods if they tried to challenge the social order. Creating black-owned businesses founded on cooperative principles also demonstrated that alternatives existed to capitalist economic structures that exploited and then discarded black labor. Despite some internal weaknesses and hostility from white supremacists that hindered their effectiveness, cooperatives showed significant promise as a model for alleviating rural poverty. In the late 1960s, activists formed the Federation of Southern Cooperatives (FSC) and secured funding from the OEO and the Ford Foundation to pioneer a comprehensive plan for regional economic development that aimed to establish cooperatives as the path forward to a more equitable and sustainable future for rural poor southerners.

As the cooperative movement emerged and coalesced into the FSC, the national political winds shifted direction when voters elected a more conservative Congress in 1966 and gave the presidency to Republican candidate Richard Nixon in 1968. Chapter 5 describes how the political discourse of the 1970s echoed the sentiments expressed by southern opponents of the civil rights movement and the War on Poverty in the 1960s, tracing changes in federal policy that reflected the growing acceptance of these ideas among government officials and the population at large. Citing the need to halt the trend toward federal intervention in the economy and other areas of American life, Nixon proclaimed an era of "New Federalism" that reduced funding for antipoverty programs and restored control over economic development to state and local governments. These moves neutralized the transformative potential of the War on Poverty and left existing power relations intact, leaving poor people without strong advocates in government or adequate assistance during a decade of rising unemployment and economic distress.

As shown in Chapter 6, Nixon's reversal and the difficulty of securing private funding in a faltering economy hindered the FSC's attempts to expand and build upon the achievements of the low-income cooperative movement. Even so, the organization made significant contributions to the freedom struggle in the post–civil rights era. The services it provided to cooperatives ensured the survival of many black-owned enterprises and encouraged African Americans to remain in rural southern communities instead of migrating away. Its Rural Training and Research Center in Sumter County, Alabama, trained hundreds of cooperative managers and members, providing vital services to small farmers and other rural people who were mostly ignored by federal agricultural agencies. The FSC's activist staff continued the struggles for civil rights and social justice by working to increase black representation in economic development initiatives, encouraging black political participation, and organizing local communities to fight persistent racism. Predictably, these efforts generated resistance from powerful white southerners. In 1979, accusations that the FSC was misusing government grants to fund political activities sparked an eighteen-month-long investigation that disrupted and weakened the organization, despite finding no evidence of wrongdoing. The federation's troubles were compounded in the 1980s with the election of conservative Republican Ronald Reagan to the presidency and an even sharper shift to the right in the national government.

Chapter 7 analyzes the Reagan administration's approaches to social problems and their consequences for rural poor southerners. Seeking to end excessive government interference in the economy, the president and his advisers cut taxes, weakened civil rights enforcement, and reduced funding for social programs that served low-income Americans. Like his political allies in the South, Reagan was convinced that private enterprise and market forces were the most efficient mechanisms for creating wealth and distributing resources. Such policies worked no better in the 1980s than they had before the 1960s, however, and conditions in the plantation counties worsened during this decade. At the end of Reagan's second term, the region was still plagued by unemployment, poverty, inadequate health care, substandard housing, and out-migration. The FSC and other social justice organizations did what they could to alleviate the crisis, but budgetary constraints and the indifference of the nation's political leaders posed massive obstacles to their efforts. Although the FSC survived and continued its work into the twenty-first century, it was never able to complete the social revolution that its founders hoped to bring about in the 1960s.

Chapter 8 examines connections between the experiences of black workers in the rural South and those of other Americans in the late twentieth century. Antigovernment sentiment and extreme individualism of the type promoted by opponents of the freedom struggle made their way into mainstream thinking on the subjects of unemployment and poverty after the 1960s. Like their southern counterparts, white northerners reacted angrily to federal initiatives aimed at integrating their schools and neighborhoods, generating a growing antipathy toward government. Candidates for public office found that opposing federal overreach, calling for cuts in social programs, and blaming poor people for their own problems were effective methods for attracting votes both within and outside the South, even as many Americans faced layoffs and declining job prospects in deindustrializing communities. At the same time, a stagnant economy that seemed impervious to policy makers' efforts to revive it opened space for laissez-faire theorists to promote a more hands-off approach. Economic policy in the 1980s and 1990s emphasized spending cuts, deregulation of businesses, and evisceration of the social safety net rather than attempts to boost demand for goods and services by raising incomes. These decisions threatened Americans' economic security and generated increasing inequality throughout the United States, undermining the purchasing power of consumers and creating a debt crisis that caused the near collapse of global financial institutions in 2008. When the resulting recession threw millions of people out of work, opposition to government intervention in the economy prevented Congress from adopting the kinds of creative solutions to poverty and unemployment that existed in the 1960s. As noted in the Conclusion, however, the FSC's social justice agenda lived on in efforts to support family farms and sustainable agriculture as well as renewed interest in the cooperative business model as an alternative to existing economic structures. The political and ideological struggles examined in earlier chapters of this book thus left lasting legacies on both sides of the debate.

Developments in the rural South after the mid-1960s served as a rehearsal for similar processes that eventually affected other Americans in the era of deindustrialization, globalization, and the rise of finance capitalism at the turn of the twenty-first century. Participants in these struggles raised and tried to answer questions that remained relevant decades later, offering contrasting theories regarding the causes of poverty and inequality, the role of government in the economy, and the ability of free markets or government initiatives to fully attend to human needs. The outcomes had consequences for all the nation's people, not only for African Americans. Examining how residents of the plantation counties adapted to the social transformations that shook their world in the mid-twentieth century and paying attention to the ways that racial, economic, and political concerns intersected with one another enhances our understanding of ongoing debates over how to deal with the displacement of large numbers of workers during periods of economic restructuring.

CHAPTER 1

THE MAN DON'T NEED ME ANYMORE

FROM FREE LABOR TO DISPLACED PERSONS

When President Johnson signed the Voting Rights Act into law on 6 August 1965, he declared it "a triumph for freedom as huge as any victory that has ever been won on any battlefield." The measure outlawed electoral practices that had effectively disfranchised black southerners since the late nineteenth century and allowed the federal government to intervene in jurisdictions that continued to exclude them from political participation. Coming in response to decades of protest that saw supporters of racial equality being arrested, jailed, beaten, and murdered as they struggled to end racism, the new law promised to exorcise the horrors of the Jim Crow era. Johnson was confident that by exercising their right to vote and taking advantage of opportunities opened by the Civil Rights Act passed a year earlier, African Americans could secure their place as equals alongside white Americans in every aspect of their lives. "Through this act, and its enforcement, an important instrument of freedom passes into the hands of millions of our citizens," the president asserted.[1]

On the ground, in the plantation counties that were the main targets of the legislation, civil rights activists saw a somewhat different picture. Edna London registered to vote in West Feliciana Parish, Louisiana, shortly after a federal registrar arrived there in October 1965. In response, the owner of the plantation where she had lived and worked for two decades evicted London and her eleven children. Henry Cummings and Nolan Jones Sr., both elderly black farmers, were also laid off by their landlords after registering, as were Leonard Peck and his wife. By January, twenty-seven families in the parish found themselves without jobs or homes after members had exercised their newly restored rights. Alabama landowner James Minter also retaliated against people who were involved in the freedom movement, firing six tenant farmers on his plantation in Dallas County after they refused to sign over their cotton subsidy checks to him in 1966. Local banks and welfare officials denied the black farmers' requests for loans and other assistance, telling them to "go to Mister James. . . . You don't need it." Meanwhile, in Mississippi, sharecroppers L. C. Dorsey and her husband lost their jobs to machines. "Got kicked off the plantation by an owner who wasn't cruel, but who had a small operation to start with, and who had bought himself a mechanical cotton picker and a combine, and who really had no need for a family," Dorsey explained. "So we were asked to leave."[2] As these workers discovered, securing the political rights and economic opportunities that Johnson described in his speech remained a tough row to hoe, especially when they were losing access to the resources required for the task in the first place.

The Jim Crow system took shape in the context of the shift from slavery to free labor in the nineteenth century and ended during another economic transition that converted thousands of black workers into displaced persons lacking jobs, income, and homes. Southern policy makers' initial response to agricultural displacement was to treat black workers as disposable commodities that could be discarded now that they were no longer needed on the plantations. Most landowners felt little responsibility toward former employees who were now, as one planter put it, "as useless as a mule."[3] Racist beliefs about African Americans' limited capabilities convinced many white southerners that there was no point investing in education or training to prepare black people for other jobs. More important, they feared the increased costs of caring for unemployed people and the even greater expenses that could be incurred if black elected officials gained power and implemented sweeping social reforms. White leaders therefore tried to discourage black political participation and implemented policies designed to force African Americans to migrate away. When civil rights activists accused white southerners of deliberately driving black people out of their states, planters and public officials insisted that displacement and out-migration were natural processes beyond their control. In crafting an analysis that obscured the role of political decisions and absolved themselves from blame, regional elites contributed to a narrative regarding the futility of government action to solve social problems that had significant consequences beyond the 1960s.

———————

Since the 1930s, when the federal government introduced price supports for selected agricultural commodities and incentives for farmers to keep some of their land out of production, plantation owners had been laying off workers, shifting to livestock and alternative crops, and investing in new technologies that dramatically decreased their reliance on cheap black labor. Between 1930 and 1960, cotton acreages in Alabama's plantation region declined by 81 percent, from 881,881 acres to 164,123 acres. Louisiana's cotton parishes saw a decline of 68 percent, from 1.3 million to just over 400,000 acres. In Mississippi, cotton acreages dropped by 59 percent, from 2.9 million in 1930 to 1.2 million in 1960.[4] On land that remained in production, tasks that once employed hundreds of farmhands were increasingly given over to mechanical harvesters and herbicides. Mississippi's landowners harvested 40 percent of their cotton crops mechanically at the start of the 1960s, 76 percent by mid-decade, and 94 percent in 1969. In both Alabama and Louisiana, roughly half the cotton was picked by machines in 1960 and close to 100 percent by the end of the decade.[5]

Planters who had once been obsessed with maintaining the region's large, low-paid, and mostly black agricultural workforce now found they could get along fine without most of these workers. On the Delta and Pine Land Company plantation in Bolivar County, Mississippi, the 1,200 tenant families once employed growing 16,000 acres of cotton dwindled to 510 wage hands tending 7,200 acres with an assortment of tractors, harvesters, and combines. The remaining acres were turned over to other uses. Similarly, Senator James Eastland's plantation in Sunflower County saw a reduction from 600 workers to just 40 by the mid-1960s.[6] Owners of small farms as well as tenants and sharecroppers faced being pushed from the land as mechanization made it harder to compete with larger growers and consolidated more acres into fewer hands. Agricultural employment in Mississippi's plantation counties declined from 190,893 to 35,526 between 1950 and 1970, a loss of 155,367 positions. Farm employment in Alabama's plantation region decreased by 49,111 in the same period, and Louisiana's cotton parishes employed 55,460 fewer people in agriculture in 1970 than they had in 1950. (See Appendix, table 1.)

Although agricultural displacement affected white as well as black people, African Americans suffered disproportionately. Racist administrators of the federal government's farm programs excluded black farmers from forms of assistance that were available to white farmers, such as low-interest loans, training, and technical assistance that could help farm operators to stay on the land. The United States Department of Agriculture (USDA) oversaw millions of dollars in public expenditures on programs designed to improve agricultural efficiency and maintain adequate incomes for landowners, including the Federal Extension Service (FES) and the Farmers Home Administration (FmHA). Their efforts mostly benefited large landowners who could afford to invest in new technologies and received the biggest share of the government's farm subsidies. Plantation owners dominated the local USDA offices and committees that distributed loans and crop allotments in the South, and they routinely denied assistance to black farmers. Investigations by the federal government's Commission on Civil Rights (CCR) conducted in 1965 and 1982 found rampant discrimination by USDA agencies throughout the 1960s and 1970s. The number of black farm operators in the United States declined by 94 percent between 1930 and 1978, compared with a 56 percent decline in the number of white operators. The CCR and other analysts attributed the disparity largely to administrators' failure to operate the nation's farm programs in an equitable manner. One account labeled the USDA the most racist of all federal agencies and observed: "The Department has acted as if it wanted to drive the colored farmers off the land, as if it wanted them to fail."[7]

Racial disparities also affected black southerners' ability to adjust to the changing economy. The inferior education most had received in segregated schools made it difficult for them to find nonagricultural employment. As displaced white workers found jobs in the region's emerging industrial sector, black people languished as underemployed seasonal laborers. In 1964 the average black farm laborer in the South was employed in agriculture for just seventy-seven days a year and worked another twenty-four days doing odd jobs, for an annual income of $503—far below the federal government's official poverty threshold of $3,000 per year for a family of four. Further decreases in cotton crop acreages mandated for participants in the government's subsidy programs in 1965 and passage of a federal minimum wage law for farm labor in 1966 provided landowners with more incentive to reduce the workforce. In the Mississippi Delta, fall harvest man-days of agricultural labor dropped from 756,624 in 1960 to 95,967 in 1966, an 87 percent decline. Secretary of Agriculture Orville Freeman reported feeling "really shocked" by the figures and observed, "That is an enormous dropoff of this kind of employment."[8]

Declining employment opportunities led many African Americans to leave the South in search of work. Approximately 3.2 million black southerners migrated away from their home states between 1950 and 1970, including 455,000 from Alabama, 602,000 from Mississippi, and 261,000 from Louisiana. In November 1965, an article on out-migration from Mississippi that appeared in the *Bolivar County Democrat* noted that for every white person who moved into the state, two white residents moved out, while the ratio for nonwhite people was one to sixteen. "People appear to be one of Mississippi's principal exports," the author stated. A survey of black high school students found that two-thirds of them wanted to leave Mississippi after graduating, citing the lack of economic opportunity and persistent white racism as the top two reasons why. John Brown Jr., a Mississippi native who later became a school-teacher and civil rights activist in Alabama, recalled that it was normal for young people in the town where he grew up to move away after finishing school. "All my brothers and sisters went either to St. Louis or Detroit," he stated. "I'm the only one out of the nine children that did not go north." In Greene County, Alabama, younger black residents shared the same plight and sentiments as their counterparts in Mississippi. According to one report, local employment opportunities were so limited that "for years the high school graduation ceremony has had to be scheduled in the morning so the more impatient graduates can catch the afternoon bus out of the County!"[9]

Plantation counties where black residents had once heavily outnumbered white people saw their African American populations decline significantly in the mid-twentieth century. In the cotton regions that are the focus of this book, the number of majority-black counties fell from fifty-eight in 1930 to forty-three in 1960.[10] Because younger adults were the most likely to migrate away, the population losses particularly affected the percentage of black people of voting age (twenty-one years or older) residing in these areas. Tunica County, Mississippi, saw its 80 percent black voting majority reduced to a voting minority of only 44 percent between 1950 and 1970. Black voters saw their numerical advantage slip away in Carroll, Clay, De Soto, Kemper, Leflore, Panola, Quitman, Tallahatchie, Tate, Washington, and Yazoo Counties as well. Concordia and De Soto Parishes in Louisiana and Dallas and Marengo Counties in Alabama experienced the same fate. The political ramifications for newly enfranchised African Americans seeking to influence elections in counties where white people reliably voted against black candidates were not lost on civil rights activists. Asked why so few young adults were left in his rural community, an older black man asserted: "Son there is a plot here in Alabama by the white folk to run all our young people away so that they can continue to control us at the polls and everywhere else, there is no work or fun for these kids."[11]

Anyone observing conditions in the plantation counties could understand the impulse to leave. Reports on the economic problems and development potential of these regions prepared by the EDA in the mid-1960s documented rampant unemployment, anemic family incomes, substandard housing, inadequate public services, poor health of residents, low education and skill levels of the available workforce, and racial discrimination in rural southern communities. The assessment for Lowndes County, Alabama, noted that its population had declined by 2,600 people between 1950 and 1960, largely because of shifts in the agricultural economy that displaced many workers. Agricultural employment accounted for "the entire loss" of some 2,000 jobs in the county over that decade, most of them held by African Americans. In 1954 the county had 2,132 black farm operators (owners, tenants, and sharecroppers); in 1964 only 886 were left. Other sectors of the economy showed only minor expansion, adding just a few hundred jobs and failing to absorb the large numbers of people leaving the land. Most people in the county, black and white, were poor. Seventy-two percent of families earned less than $3,000 per year and only 3 percent earned more than $10,000. The median number of school years completed was 6.5, compared with the national median of 10.6. Analysts observed that natural resources in the area were not managed well but asserted that the county's most neglected economic asset was "the development of its people." Historically, the cotton planters and cattle farmers who dominated local politics had not needed an educated or skilled workforce. Now that their labor needs had decreased, they showed little interest in investing in social services or economic development, leaving their former employees with few options apart from moving away to look for work.[12]

Reports from many other counties showed the same patterns. Next door to Lowndes, in Wilcox County, the population declined by one-third between 1940 and 1960, dropping from 26,279 to 18,739. Median family income was $1,550, and almost 60 percent of families in the county earned less than poverty level. Nearly one-quarter of residents aged twenty-five years or older had completed less than five years of school. African Americans received education that was "vastly inferior to that available to the local white community," EDA analysts stated. Although county officials pointed with pride to vocational agriculture and industrial training programs offered in the public schools, they denied African Americans access to these programs until the 1960s. Movement toward granting equal opportunities to black residents was "halting and begrudging, with almost all progress being forced on the community through Federal action."[13] A similar picture emerged from descriptions of Sunflower County, Mississippi, where more than 80 percent of the workforce had not even completed elementary school. The out-migration rate was 41 percent, one of the highest in the nation, and median family income for nonwhite residents was $1,126. An article about the county that appeared in the *Southern Patriot* in 1966 reported, "Negroes work in the cotton fields during the season and are idle the rest of the year. They make 30 cents [an] hour in the fields or $2.50 a day in white kitchens. . . . At a recent MFDP meeting which 100 persons attended, three had jobs to go to the next day."[14]

Displaced workers faced multiple obstacles in the search for alternative employment. In many places there were simply no other jobs available. In most of the plantation counties, increases in nonagricultural employment did not keep pace with the losses in agriculture until after the 1970s, and much of the economic diversification that did occur was concentrated in urban areas. (See Appendix, table 1.) The 190,737 nonagricultural jobs created in Mississippi's plantation region between 1930 and 1970 amounted to about half the number needed to replace the 357,783 that disappeared from agriculture in the same period. Newspaper editor Hodding Carter III reported in 1968 that the ratio of job referrals to job placements recorded by the state employment service was 186 to 100 and pointed out that the number of people who found positions was "a drop in the bucket compared to the need."[15] A visitor to Dallas County, Alabama, in the 1950s observed that although some manufacturing jobs were being created as farm employment declined, the pace of industrialization was not enough to absorb most of the people coming off the plantations. The county lost 5,319 agricultural jobs and added only 2,795 nonagricultural jobs between 1950 and 1970. In nearby Wilcox County, both agricultural employment and nonagricultural employment declined in the 1950s, for a total loss of 3,151 jobs. An OEO analyst investigating conditions there in 1968 found that the challenges for job seekers were virtually insurmountable and noted bluntly: "There simply is no industry."[16]

The dearth of opportunities was not because the region lacked non-agricultural resources but because plantation owners and their political allies had long opposed the location of manufacturing plants or other businesses in their communities for fear that competition for labor might force them to pay higher wages to their workers. As the need for farm labor decreased in the mid-twentieth century, some people promoted efforts to diversify the economy and create jobs for surplus workers, but the programs encountered opposition from other residents. In Bolivar County, Mississippi, leaders were concerned with "maintaining a proper balance between agriculture and industry," according to the local Area Development Association. Although a few manufacturing plants were located in the county, reservations regarding further industrial development were expressed by some citizens who thought industrialization was "moving too rapidly." An EDA official reported in 1966 that despite data showing an estimated 80,000 to 90,000 unemployed or underemployed people in the Mississippi Delta, the region was "not among those the Governor thought should receive priority attention." Alabama college professor Theodore James Pinnock noted similar obstacles to economic diversification in his state. In a report on the lack of job prospects for displaced workers in Lowndes County, Pinnock observed: "Decentralization of industries would be the solution but it is doubtful the extent to which the State of Alabama would encourage industries to be located in Lowndes County or any other black belt county for that matter."[17]

African Americans also found their employment prospects limited by overt racism, despite provisions in the Civil Rights Act that banned discrimination in hiring, training, or referring people for jobs. L. C. Dorsey recalled that when she moved to Shelby with her husband after they lost their sharecropping jobs in the mid-1960s, everyone employed in the banks, stores, and the town's two manufacturing plants was white. "There just weren't any jobs for blacks, and that was understood," she stated. "They wouldn't hire you." Employment agencies frequently blocked opportunities for black workers by refusing to recommend them for skilled positions regardless of their qualifications. In selecting workers to participate in federal job training programs, some state employment agencies excluded African Americans, citing a regulation that stated training was to be provided only when there was reasonable expectation of employment. A report prepared by the Department of Labor (DOL) explained, "This Section has been construed by some state officials as calling for non referral of minority group members for training in trades in which minority group members are not now employed." Investigations into more than 200 complaints received in 1967 revealed that employment agencies continued to engage in various forms of discrimination, including misclassifying nonwhite workers, denying access to unemployment insurance, providing inferior services to black communities, maintaining racial wage differentials on training projects, and segregating their facilities.[18]

Businesses that relocated to the South from outside the region did little to improve African Americans' job prospects. Government researchers found that racial discrimination by "recent industrial transplants" contributed to the high unemployment rates in plantation counties and that northern-based corporations often accommodated local practices rather than challenging them. The black newspaper *Louisiana Weekly* reported in 1966 that despite the large number of jobless workers in West Feliciana Parish, the managers of a manufacturing plant there preferred to bus white workers in from Mississippi rather than hire local black people. In Alabama, Bernard Shambray decided to seek a job at the Dan River Mills plant shortly after the Civil Rights Act was passed, hoping that the new law might inspire the company to end its near-total exclusion of black workers. Although he was hired as a trainee weaver, his supervisors routinely assigned him to cleaning and maintenance work instead. Shambray stayed for a while, enduring segregated bathrooms and watching white men being promoted over him, but eventually quit. Sadie Allen, another resident who was familiar with the company's hiring practices, stated, "Most Negroes know they aren't going to be hired for anything but sweeping the floor. . . . So they just don't go out there."[19]

Employers proved adept at circumventing equal opportunity laws and developing rationales for why they could not hire more black people. The most common argument was that they could not find enough qualified black candidates to fill positions, a reasonable excuse given the inferior schooling and lack of advanced training offered to black southerners within the Jim Crow education system. At hearings held by the CCR's Louisiana Advisory Committee in February 1966, the personnel manager for Wyandotte Chemical Corporation stated that black applicants typically failed the tests the company administered to prospective employees. He explained that workers at the plant were handling hazardous materials and needed to think fast during emergencies, so applicants' qualifications and competence were serious matters. Other speakers also argued that it was not racial discrimination by employers that was keeping African Americans out of jobs but the state's failure to adequately prepare black people for skilled work. At the same time, however, some companies were raising the qualifications bar to keep black workers out. Employers concerned about the impact of antidiscrimination laws adopted rigorous examinations to screen out undesirable applicants. It was often unclear how tests measured job-related skills or the ability to perform specific tasks. Questions such as "Do the Beatles have soul?" were reminiscent of the arbitrary quizzes administered to black people by racist southern registrars seeking to prevent them from voting before such practices were outlawed in 1965. One expert labeled such methods a "pseudo-scientific form of prejudice" that aimed to perpetuate racial exclusion.[20]

State and local officials showed little interest in addressing the educational inequities that interfered with African Americans' ability to find jobs. Long after the Supreme Court outlawed segregation in the public schools in 1954, school boards continued to resist the federal government's efforts to force them to provide the same quality of education to black children that they provided to white children. Most school districts simply ignored the law until civil rights activists filed lawsuits and federal courts ordered them to develop desegregation plans. In theory, the "freedom of choice" plans that many districts adopted in the 1960s allowed families to send their children to any school they chose. In practice, white administrators and vigilantes coerced African American parents into keeping their children in inferior, all-black schools. The MFDP called the desegregation plans "hopelessly inadequate" and reported in October 1965 that several families had received death threats for sending their children to white schools. Similar tactics deployed in Louisiana meant that only 1 percent of children there attended desegregated schools in 1967. The *Louisiana Weekly* reported that segregationists were hastily setting up private, all-white institutions to provide alternatives for parents who did not want to send their children to integrated public schools. State and local officials abetted this movement by channeling taxpayer funds to these segregation academies. In the 1965–66 school year, around 11,000 students received grants-in-aid from public coffers to attend private schools that excluded black children.[21]

Southern school districts continued to allocate more resources to predominantly white schools than to black ones, perpetuating African Americans' educational disadvantages. Complaints from Mississippi that officials were misusing federal funds provided under Title I of the Elementary and Secondary Education Act (1965) sparked an investigation by the Department of Health, Education, and Welfare (HEW) in July 1969. The money was supposed to be used for programs to bring "educationally deprived" low-income students up to the level of their more privileged counterparts, but officials instead used it for general purposes and diverted funds to schools that did not need them. According to Rims Barber of the Delta Ministry, administrators forced black principals to sign vouchers for equipment and supplies that their schools never received, and there was no monitoring of where the money went. Barber reported that Title I programs were designed to maintain educational inequality instead of ending it. Most of them were simply "regular programs done at half-speed," such as assigning half the number of books as in a regular class or teaching an algebra course over two years instead of one. These tactics reinforced the education gap between white children and black children under the guise of offering equal opportunity. Local activists believed "remedial" programs amounted to "a conspiracy to keep people uneducated, to keep people in a permanent position of inferiority."[22]

Discriminatory practices extended to the training of adults as well. White community leaders who dominated local planning committees of the Area Redevelopment Administration in the rural South made sure that little of this federal aid reached black people. Some residents vehemently opposed the program as excessive government interference in the economy, and even those who welcomed the assistance were concerned with maintaining the region's race and class hierarchies. As a result, most projects provided low-wage jobs for white laborers and excluded black workers.[23] In January 1962 the Delta Council, a regional organization of planters and business leaders, suspended plans to use redevelopment funds to expand farm machinery training courses in response to "apprehensions concerning possible implications that might result and objections to such a training program" from some of its members. Farm labor organizer H. L. Mitchell identified two powerful and overlapping political interests that opposed this and other efforts: the American Farm Bureau Federation (AFBF), an organization primarily made up of large landowners that was "opposed to any kind of federally financed program which they cannot control," and the segregationist Citizens' Council, which was likely to create "mass hysteria among the population by charging that the training of farm workers is 'integration' of Negroes and whites."[24]

Similar problems afflicted training programs that the federal government tried to promote in economically depressed areas under the Manpower Development and Training Act of 1962 (MDTA), which authorized the DOL and HEW to fund projects to help unemployed and underemployed workers develop new skills. Of the initial seventy projects approved by September 1962, only four were located in the Deep South (two in Mississippi and two in South Carolina).[25] The following year, an NAACP study of MDTA programs in Alabama, Florida, Georgia, and South Carolina found that the projects were segregated, catered mostly to white workers, and offered black participants "training only in menial tasks." A report on black employment in 1965 noted a need to expand MDTA programs and recruit more African American trainees, using federal authority if necessary to overcome local resistance. The Economic Opportunity Act empowered federal officials to initiate programs whether local elites supported them or not, but they continued to face obstruction in some communities. An OEO consultant in Alabama observed in 1967 that the challenge of making job training available to the thousands of workers who needed it was "more complex and confusing when you take into consideration that State and local government officials are not over-anxious to solve the problem." The lack of training opportunities in turn hindered black southerners' ability to secure stable employment. Researchers found that African Americans in a sixteen-county area of rural Alabama studied in May 1968 held only 8 percent of the region's skilled positions and that black nonfarmworkers were concentrated in declining industries that were shedding jobs.[26]

Ejected from their agricultural jobs and shut out of other types of work by discrimination, large numbers of black southerners depended on a sketchy social welfare system that left them precariously balanced between subsistence and starvation. Farm laborers were not covered by the unemployment insurance provisions of the Social Security Act of 1935 and instead relied on underfunded public assistance programs run by state and local governments. These included Old Age Assistance, Aid to the Blind, Aid to the Permanently and Totally Disabled, and Aid to Dependent Children (renamed Aid to Families with Dependent Children [AFDC] in 1962), programs created to help citizens who were not eligible for the more generous pensions and benefits that New Deal reforms provided to the mostly white and male industrial workforce. Some counties offered additional assistance to poor people through the USDA's surplus commodity distribution program, which provided a monthly allotment of free food for needy families. Although the commodities program helped keep people from going hungry, the variety of food items was limited, and the nutritional quality was low. Aware of these problems, Congress voted in 1961 to authorize a pilot program providing poor families with food stamps that were redeemable at local stores and allowed recipients more choice in what they ate. In 1964 the Food Stamp Act made the program permanent, and it gradually replaced surplus commodities distribution as the main source of food assistance available to poor people.[27]

Historians of the nation's social welfare policies have noted the racial and gender biases built into the system. Unlike unemployment insurance coverage, which was funded through workers' payroll taxes and considered an earned benefit by most Americans, the public assistance programs that many nonwhite unemployed people depended on were funded through federal grants and frequently stigmatized as unearned handouts for people who were too lazy to work.[28] Most states excluded able-bodied adults from eligibility on the assumption that they could find jobs. Byzantine regulations and arbitrary decisions by administrators made it difficult for many people who were entitled to aid to receive it. Mississippi plantation worker Ida Mae Lawrence explained that to qualify for surplus commodities after the cotton-picking season ended, "You got to find out how many people you worked for and get them to sign for you as being poor. If they don't feel like signing, like maybe they don't like you for civil rights activities, you don't get commodities. But you still poor, whether the white boss says so or not." Similarly, Jessie Atkins could not understand how welfare officials in Shaw determined her income each month. "I have a boy and he's unable to work as he has a mental condition," she stated. "I gets a check and sometimes its $50 and sometimes its $40. They cuts it like they wants to. . . . And it ain't enough to live on. And we're lacking for food and we're lacking for clothes, and I ain't able to get coal to set to the fire." Another Mississippi resident reported that she received about $22 a month while she was living with her invalid sister, who later died. After she moved in with her daughter's family, her payments were reduced to $18, and then cut to $4 when she began attending civil rights meetings. A granddaughter and her five children who were also living in the home were unable to secure any assistance at all. In January 1966 an MFDP newsletter asserted that injustice in the welfare system was "probably the single most important problem for thousands of people in this state." Other observers could find "no pattern or standard" that determined whether people received assistance in Mississippi, while noting a strong tendency toward "active discouragement by the welfare department of anyone applying for aid."[29]

Welfare policy was a powerful weapon in the hands of racist administrators. Regulations aimed to limit the number of people who qualified for assistance and often targeted African Americans in particular for exclusion. In 1960, Louisiana legislators passed a law that made children born to unmarried mothers ineligible for public assistance, a measure that disproportionately affected poor black families and was widely understood as retaliation against the civil rights movement in the state.[30] Two years later, lawmakers in Mississippi required county welfare departments to report deserting parents to legal authorities, a measure that discouraged many black women whose husbands had migrated away in search of work from applying for aid. A mandate that recipients maintain a "suitable home" for children, a term that case workers defined capriciously to deny assistance to civil rights activists, had a similar effect. In October 1962, a researcher for the state's Department of Public Welfare reported, "We are finding that a large number of ADC [Aid to Dependent Children] applications are being rejected and ADC cases being closed due to the mother not wishing to be reported to the court. Thus the mother either withdraws her application or requests the closure of the case." Of the 325 cases reported to the courts during a three-month period from July to September that year, 305 involved African American families.[31] Like most other Deep South states in the civil rights era, Alabama implemented new rules in June 1964 that disqualified mothers who cohabited with men from receiving assistance, treating the male partners as "substitute fathers" who could presumably support the children of the women they lived with. A study of the law's impact found that it removed 15,000 children from the state's welfare rolls and that out of 498 cases examined in seven counties, 97 percent of the families that lost their benefits were black. As a report on poverty in the rural South noted in 1967, a major reason why so many people lacked basic necessities was that "welfare and food programs . . . are in the hands of people who use them selectively, politically, and with obvious racial considerations in mind."[32]

For those who did manage to qualify for public assistance, state officials set benefits at levels they knew did not provide enough income for people to live on. In 1963 the Alabama Department of Pensions and Security estimated the minimum cost for food, housing, clothing, utilities, and household supplies for a family of four to be $177 per month, but the state's welfare payment to such families was less than half that amount. Mississippi provided its AFDC beneficiaries with only one-third of the income necessary for a minimum level of subsistence. When a Supreme Court ruling in 1968 determined that states could no longer use "man in the house" rules to deny aid to dependent children, Louisiana officials ordered benefits to be cut to accommodate additional enrollees without increasing the budget for public assistance. The state's public welfare commissioner acknowledged that the 10 percent decrease in payments would impose significant hardship on families, since welfare grants were already "far below the level necessary to provide proper food, clothing, shelter and necessities."[33]

Political leaders argued that their states were poor and lacked the money to provide more help to their neediest citizens. At the same time, however, southern states and counties failed to take advantage of millions of dollars in federal aid that was available to fight poverty. In the early 1960s, Congress authorized matching funds to encourage states to enhance their public assistance programs, including provisions for extending AFDC eligibility to two-parent families along with single mothers and guardians. Despite the potential to alleviate suffering among the children of unemployed workers, no southern state participated in this program. The federal government also paid most of the costs for the surplus commodity distribution and food stamp programs in counties that agreed to administer them, yet according to one analyst officials in many rural southern communities were "disinclined to offer a food program for . . . economic reasons, or for political or other reasons."[34] In 1966 only thirty-two of Alabama's sixty-seven counties participated in federal food programs, and only three of the counties with programs were in the state's plantation region. The programs reached just 132,000 of an estimated 1.2 million people living in poverty in the state. Similarly, Mississippi passed up $75 million in federal funds that were available to help feed hungry people.[35]

State and local leaders' lack of interest in programs to assist the poor contrasted with their eager acceptance of federal money that helped regional elites, such as funds for highway construction and levees and the USDA's technical assistance and subsidy programs. Mississippi congressman Thomas Abernethy was a strong critic of social welfare expenditures, yet in his district 1,438 landowners received $28.7 million from the government in 1966. In Bolivar County, the federal government paid 82 percent of the construction costs for a drainage project that cost $3.5 million. The improvements benefited 600 landowners and increased their net income by $500,000. Meanwhile, per capita income for the county's 21,000 black residents was $759, with 72 percent living below poverty level.[36]

The combination of mass unemployment and inadequate social services generated levels of human suffering that Americans were accustomed to seeing in news reports from famine-stricken regions of Africa and Asia, not in their own country. Visitors to the South in the 1960s were shocked by what they saw: rickety shacks with no indoor plumbing; unsanitary outhouses and contaminated wells; open sewers in front of poor people's homes; children with distended bellies and skin lesions indicating nutritional deficiencies; hungry and diseased adults who could barely muster the energy to stand. Activists who canvassed black communities to assess health care needs in Bolivar County, Mississippi, in 1966 found that local residents' concerns were more basic than access to medicine or treatment for disease: their most urgent problem was obtaining enough food. A flurry of studies on the extent of hunger in the United States found that similar conditions existed in many other communities around the nation and that the problem was especially acute in the rural South, largely because officials had failed so miserably to deal with the consequences of agricultural displacement.[37] One investigator described Mississippi's plantation region as "a kind of prison in which live a great group of uneducated, semi-starving people, from whom all but token public support has been withdrawn." An NAACP report on the humanitarian crisis in Mississippi's rural counties was equally harsh. "The Negro has become an unwanted commodity in the Delta," the authors wrote. "Mules can be disposed of humanely. Negroes can't. They are left to rot and starve and die, and no officials within the state seem to care."[38]

Civil rights leaders and many other analysts believed the situation reflected a systematic effort to cut off economic options for African Americans and force them to leave. In 1963, CORE worker Charlotte Devree reported that white supremacists in Mississippi were firing workers, evicting families, cutting off credit, ending job training programs, and denying public assistance as retaliation against black political activism and to encourage out-migration. "The pressures of poverty are being brought to bear to drive out the economically expendable," she wrote. "County and state governments . . . in Mississippi want Negroes out, not there and better off." According to another activist, the mayor of one Delta town threatened black people by telling them, "We're going to see how tight we can make it—it's going to be rough, rougher than you think." After becoming involved in voter registration efforts, L. C. Dorsey spoke with one landowner in Bolivar County who amicably encouraged her to take his tenants down to the registrar's office, then added: "Oh, by the way, now, when you finish with them registering to vote, don't bring them back here. Take them to your plantation." Dorsey considered the economic intimidation to be worse than the physical violence inflicted on people who challenged the system. "Everything that you needed from a match to a doctor, you had to go through these people to get it," she explained. "And they had the power to give it to you or to deny it.

They had the power even to make sure you didn't get it any place else." The intent of evictions and new bans on foraging for food and firewood that some landowners imposed in the 1950s and 1960s seemed clear to Dorsey. The civil rights movement threatened planters' plans for the region, so they "put in place those things that would result in people being starved to death."[39]

Callous actions like these led the Delta Ministry to attribute the mass displacement of agricultural workers not simply to mechanization or cuts in federal cotton allotments but also to "the desire of some people to get rid of the 'Negro problem' by getting rid of Negroes." Another observer echoed that view, arguing that technological advances "provided an excuse and a way for the 'final solution' to the race question. That solution is Negro emigration." Analysts in Alabama reached the same conclusion. A report on developments in Lowndes County in 1966 asserted that "a deliberate policy of eviction, foreclosure, employment blacklisting, and physical harassment" had forced many African Americans to leave. Greene County activist Percy McShan told the CCR: "The whole row now is to get Negroes out of the county." After documenting the lack of interest in industrial development, job training, or antipoverty initiatives among local officials in the state's plantation region, Theodore James Pinnock concluded, "It is obvious that the unwritten plan of the white power structure in the rural counties of Alabama is to make things so economically difficult for the Negro and poor Caucasian that they have no alternative but to leave."[40]

Southern political leaders and many white constituents denied that people were hungry in their states and responded angrily to suggestions that they were deliberately trying to starve African Americans out. Mississippi senators John Stennis and James Eastland called the accusations a "gross libel and slander" and asserted that the reports were "totally untrue." In a letter to his congressman, Charles Jacobs Jr. referred to reports of hungry children as "propaganda" and expressed his fear that this was "the prelude to an all-out effort to flood Mississippi and the other deep South states with federal money and give-away programs for negroes in an effort to keep them in the South." Another Mississippi resident urged state governor Paul Johnson to set up an unbiased commission to investigate the claims, saying, "I know some malnutrition exists among our people, but this commission could prove once and for all the exaggeration of the lies about our state." The director of the Mississippi State Sovereignty Commission, Erle Johnston Jr., responded to inquiries about the situation by assuring correspondents that legislators were concerned for the welfare of all the state's people and that training and vocational programs had been expanded in recent years to help displaced agricultural workers. "We acknowledge the existence of the poor and undernourished, but we vigorously deny that the proportion is any greater than in other states," he wrote.[41]

Analyses undertaken by more neutral observers emphasized that the hunger crisis was real and confirmed suspicions that, even if there were no organized conspiracy to drive African Americans out of the South, most white people preferred to see them leave than expend the considerable amounts of money and other resources needed to enhance access to education, jobs, homes, and health services. In March 1964 the *Houston Post* sent a team of journalists to Mississippi to investigate claims that the state's welfare policies aimed to force African Americans to migrate away. They found that although some reports were exaggerated, many poor people did not get enough to eat. "They are not being starved out," the reporters concluded. "A better way to put it is that they are being 'hungried' out of their state. . . . State Welfare Director Fred A. Ross of Jackson told us he feels the federal government—if it wants to do something constructive—'should rehabilitate the Negroes and relocate them to other parts of the country.'" Another investigator stated that when he first heard people saying that public officials in Mississippi were consciously pursuing policies that aimed to force black people to leave, the idea seemed "beyond belief," but it became "more credible" in light of what he saw with his own eyes during his tour of the plantation counties. In a lengthy article for the *New York Times* titled "It Isn't True That Nobody Starves in America," Robert Sherrill reported that most of the white southerners he spoke to wanted African Americans to disappear. "The same people who were considered 'good ol' darkies' a few years ago are now considered deadwood, hardly worth keeping alive," he explained. "They and their shotgun shanties only clutter the landscape, chafing the consciences and the pocketbooks of the region. Get rid of them."[42]

White residents of the plantation counties understood the financial implications of efforts to ensure a more racially egalitarian society. "The sins of omission of six generations of fathers are now being visited on their sons," Harris Wofford observed in his study of Dallas County, Alabama. One farmer he spoke with acknowledged that African Americans in the county had not received their fair share of public funding for local schools and that equalizing the quality of education was going to be costly.

Though some white people admitted that the situation was their own fault, there was a general feeling that addressing it required expenditures "so enormous that some whites say it would require a lowering of white educational funds—at which they balk." The National Education Association sounded a similar theme in a comprehensive study of Wilcox County that included interviews with white as well as black residents. Its report found that many large landowners were afraid "the Negro majority will obtain control and raise land taxes to finance education and other services. There must be, consequently, many whites who wish to reduce the number of Negroes to a minority; and also who wish to avoid the costs of developing the low-income citizens, both whites and Negroes." White southerners were happy to accept federal aid for industrial and agricultural development that benefited themselves, the investigators pointed out, but "this same South shows little taste for the antipoverty programs of the sixties because it is more anxious to solve its problems through outmigration than it is to improve all of its people." Staff of the EDA's Southeastern Area Office noted that similar sentiments prevailed among the white leadership of Tunica County, Mississippi. A 1967 policy paper reported "a general attitude which encourages the displaced Negro farm laborers to leave the area in an effort to reduce the impact of the human problem" on the county.[43]

The stated goals of southern political leaders and other residents corroborated these analyses. One development official in Mississippi explained that he was only interested in generating jobs for white people, since expanding employment opportunities for everyone would encourage African Americans to remain in the state. In May 1962 the Citizens' Councils of America published a map of the United States in its monthly magazine the *Citizen* showing areas of "surplus" and "deficit" in black population and advocated measures to "expedite volunteer migration of any dissatisfied Negroes from the South" to alleviate the racial tensions resulting from the civil rights movement.[44] In response to the Freedom Rides organized by civil rights activists to desegregate interstate transit, opponents of racial equality arranged "reverse freedom rides" that involved giving African Americans free one-way bus tickets to northern cities in the early 1960s. According to segregationist leader Robert Patterson, black out-migration was the most humane solution to the "race problem." In 1964, senators John Stennis and Richard Russell took this up at the national level by proposing an amendment to the Civil Rights bill that would have established a "Voluntary Racial Relocation

Negro Surplus Or Deficit For Each State

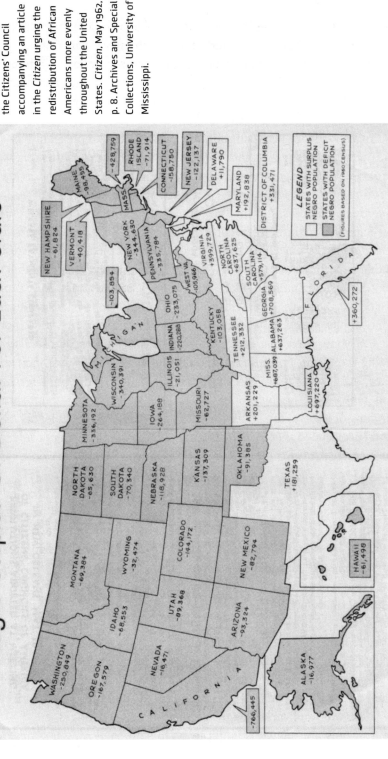

Map prepared by the Citizens' Council accompanying an article in the *Citizen* urging the redistribution of African Americans more evenly throughout the United States. *Citizen*, May 1962, p. 8. Archives and Special Collections, University of Mississippi.

THESE FIGURES BASED ON NATIONAL AVERAGE NEGRO POPULATION

LEGEND
STATES WITH SURPLUS NEGRO POPULATION
STATES WITH DEFICIT NEGRO POPULATION
(FIGURES BASED ON 1960 CENSUS)

WASHINGTON −250,849
OREGON −167,579
IDAHO −68,553
MONTANA −69,384
WYOMING −32,474
NORTH DAKOTA −65,630
SOUTH DAKOTA −70,340
MINNESOTA −336,192
WISCONSIN −340,391
MICHIGAN −103,854
NEW HAMPSHIRE −61,824
VERMONT −40,418
MAINE −98,495
MASS. −428,759
RHODE ISLAND −71,914
NEW YORK −344,630
CONNECTICUT −158,750
PENNSYLVANIA −335,784
NEW JERSEY −122,137
VIRGINIA +399,729
WEST VA. −105,966
OHIO −233,075
INDIANA −220,288
ILLINOIS −21,051
IOWA −264,188
NEBRASKA −118,928
NEVADA −16,471
UTAH −89,368
COLORADO −144,172
NEW MEXICO −82,794
ARIZONA −93,324
CALIFORNIA −766,445
KANSAS −137,309
MISSOURI −62,727
KENTUCKY −103,058
TENNESSEE +212,332
NORTH CAROLINA +637,625
SOUTH CAROLINA +579,114
GEORGIA +708,569
ALABAMA +637,263
MISS. +687,039
ARKANSAS +201,229
LOUISIANA +697,220
OKLAHOMA −91,385
TEXAS +181,259
DELAWARE +11,790
MARYLAND +192,838
DISTRICT OF COLUMBIA +331,471
FLORIDA +360,272
HAWAII −61,498
ALASKA −16,977

Commission" to assist in "the equitable distribution" of white and black residents throughout the United States. Although it was framed as an antipoverty measure, other senators saw the proposal as an attempt to ensure continued white political dominance in the South and shift the costs of dealing with the region's social problems onto other Americans, and the amendment failed to pass.[45]

Correspondence between southern congressional representatives and their constituents reveals the political and economic concerns that were on people's minds. In March 1965, as voting rights legislation made its way through Congress, Shirley Till Russell wrote to Alabama senator John Sparkman to express alarm. She compared the specter of black political participation to "the hell of reconstruction [when] negroes and the federal government did once have complete control over the South." The results of that experiment, she stated, were "so economically disastrous that the South is just beginning to make a recovery." Similarly, Mrs. A. P. Brooks predicted "the rise of a new class of southern state politicians coming into political power on a wave of pie in-the-sky promises of free state money for everyone. Next, the futile attempts to carry out those promises by taxing the farms, business and industry of the South at ever-increasing rates, even while failing to satisfy the demands of the poor for more and more. Then the flight of industry and business from the unbearable burdens of the welfare state." Mississippi Citizens' Council leader Ellett Lawrence echoed these views, warning that property owners could face tax increases of "100%, 200%, or more" if African Americans were elected to public office.[46]

To stave off such disasters, white Mississippian Annie Denman advocated denying jobs to African Americans who were involved in political activism and forcing others to secure permits to work or engage in commerce in the state. "If they want food and clothes, let them go outside Mississippi and Alabama to purchase those things," she wrote. "Let us sting and pinch and drive many into other states before the federal government binds us hand and foot in a corrupt surrender." C. R. Singletary expressed similar sentiments in a letter to Louisiana senator Russell Long: "I really think the best thing the country could do would be to give [black people] a couple of those mid western states and force them to live there and send their overflow back to Africa." Alabama resident Joseph Miller argued that if the Voting Rights Act allowed southern communities "to be taken over and run by negro governors, mayors, judges, etc. . . . the South's only alternative is going to be to stop employing negroes, and force them to emigrate to the industrial centers up North, thus transferring their tremendous burdens of welfare costs, illiteracy, etc. to the citizens up there."[47]

When civil rights activists drew attention to the hardships that economic displacement and persistent racism created for poor black people, some white southerners responded by flatly denying that these problems existed. "The Nigras haven't suffered for the white people," claimed the welfare director in Lowndes County, Alabama. "We've taken good care of them." Similarly, Mississippi's state commissioner of public welfare rejected claims that black residents suffered from any kind of discrimination, noting that 78 percent of families that received AFDC assistance in the state were African American. "Is that racial 'prejudice'—'discrimination'?" he asked, going on to suggest that if black people were not satisfied with this assistance, it would take only a simple majority vote in both houses of the state legislature to eliminate the welfare department. "The white population of Mississippi give, monthly and yearly, *more money*, *goods* and *services* to the members of the Negro race in Mississippi than do the white people of any other state in the United States when the comparable ability to pay taxes is considered," he asserted.[48]

Many people were convinced that unemployed workers received too much rather than too little assistance. Public officials, newspaper editors, and a majority of citizens who wrote to their elected representatives to express their views on this topic were adamant that jobs were plentiful and people could find employment if they looked hard enough. In a newsletter article criticizing the food stamp program, Mississippi congressman Thomas Abernethy argued that the best way to alleviate poverty was through a strong economy free from "wild government spending" that caused inflation and deficits, not welfare handouts. A woman in Alabama scoffed at federal efforts to ensure adequate diets for poor people, stating that "99.8% of the people receiving this aid has never gone hungry a day in their entire life. . . . Some of these people went in brand new cars, air conditioned no less, to pick up their hand-outs." Another Alabama resident wrote to her congressional representative to suggest: "These big wigs from Washington and up North should visit and investigate these so called underprivileged for they live in shacks for the purpose of getting everything they can from the government and welfare. There is not one of them that could not better themselves if they so desired."[49]

Other commentators also attributed poor people's lack of adequate income to their own deficiencies and argued that ample opportunities existed for citizens who were willing to apply themselves. The president of the AFBF noted in 1966, "We have the world's best education system and our dynamic, free-enterprise economy provides an abundance of job opportunities." With such resources at the disposal of every American, he asserted, being poor was inexcusable and reflected "a poverty of the mind and soul—a lack of desire." An economic development plan prepared by the Bolivar County Area Development Association in 1967 recognized that there was a scarcity of jobs in the region and that welfare services were inadequate, but it attributed many problems to poor people's own behavior and ignored the role that centuries of exploitation and discrimination played in shaping social conditions in the Delta. On the subject of dilapidated tenant shacks, for example, the document stated: "Lack of pride is a major problem here." According to the authors, poor people also lacked motivation and were unaware of resources "other than money" that were available to them. In the same vein, the AFBF asserted, "Some poverty exists through no fault of the individual, but much exists because some individuals choose not to take advantage of available jobs, education, and other opportunities." Officials in Louisiana took this emphasis on individual accountability to extremes in their response to reports of widespread hunger among poor people in the state. Welfare commissioner Garland Bonin denied that this had anything to do with policies that restricted access to public assistance programs and kept benefits below subsistence level. In a press release issued in April 1968, Bonin stated that he had contacted local health care providers and welfare workers and found no cases of people going hungry because of lack of food, only some "children who were suffering from malnutrition because of ignorance or neglect of parents." One doctor Bonin spoke with assured him that "if there were anyone starving or malnourished, it was strictly through choice and not poverty."[50]

Some analysts expressed their opposition to antipoverty initiatives in racist terms. Mrs. B. G. Burton, for example, believed African Americans were inherently lazy and immoral. "I don't think anything they can do will make a citizen out of them either," she wrote. "As long as the gov't feeds them, they won't work and as long as each bastard gets an allowance, why work. They have no moral responsibility or care." Roger Samson expressed the same view in a letter to Russell Long: "The niggers don't want to work. They want everything handed out to them on a silver platter, not caring to know the whites worked hard to get what they have." Another of Long's constituents responded to the suggestion that mothers on welfare could not enter the workforce because of the difficulty of finding child care with this comment: "Give one of those big fat mammys a gallon of wine and man with a few dollars and she doesn't need anybody to take care of her kids on Saturday night. . . . I'm for promoting their immigration to Liberia." More genteelly, but still casting black people's racial deficiencies as the core problem, Alabama congressman Bill Nichols argued that government assistance just encouraged "a certain complacency and dependency within the Negro race as opposed to motives of self-help and self-determination that should be instilled in their race at this crucial time."[51]

Another line of argument denied that race had anything to do with the plight of African Americans in the plantation counties or white people's responses. According to these theorists, displacement was the result of natural and inevitable economic forces, and there was nothing anyone could do about it. "We like our Nigras but we can't afford to keep 'em around," explained Alabama newspaper editor Hamner Cobbs. "The county's economy can't take it." In a speech to the New Orleans Rotary Club in 1965, former Louisiana governor Sam Jones addressed concerns about agricultural displacement by noting the greater efficiency of those who remained on the land. "We've reduced our farm operators from 150 thousand to 75 thousand," he acknowledged. "But the 75 thousand farmers farm more land than the 150 thousand used to, and they produce more than twice as much food and fibre. *What's wrong with that?*" Although Jones stated that he would like to see people remain in the state and find employment in other sectors, he understood why many left to find jobs elsewhere. "I don't know how you feel about it, but I'd rather see them do that than have to go on welfare," he told his audience.[52] Federal officials who visited Coahoma County, Mississippi, in 1967 heard similar arguments from leading white residents. Local lawyer Semmes Luckett attributed black out-migration to "the normal laws of supply and demand" and argued that training and job creation efforts only interfered with healthy economic processes that should be allowed to continue. In a radio interview the following year, Luckett stated that he did not see "any true future for the Negro in this community or the white persons in this community" unless at least half of the black population left.[53]

Like Luckett, some observers from outside the region found it difficult to imagine alternative solutions. An article that appeared in *Newsweek* in February 1966 attributed poverty and hunger in the Mississippi Delta to "cruel economic realities that have idled thousands of unskilled Negro farm workers in the state," eliding the racist political decisions that exacerbated these problems. The report framed attempts by unemployed workers and "civil rights zealots" to protest the situation as largely useless and distilled the plight of the region's displaced persons down to one simple fact expressed by an elderly black sharecropper: "The Man don't need me any more."[54]

Whereas *Newsweek*'s account was imbued with a sense of powerlessness and despair, reluctantly accepting the tragedy of the situation, other observers actively opposed taking action to alleviate the misery and suffering taking hold in the nation's economically depressed areas. A critique of the EDA that appeared in a newsletter of the American Taxpayers Association argued that meddling with market forces was unwise. According to the author, some parts of the United States lacked industry and employment opportunities for good reasons: they just did not have the natural resources, trade centers, transportation ease, and labor forces that might encourage businesses to locate there. "The fact that these areas of slow-growth have the problems that they are experiencing is a tacit indication that they are unsuited for efficient production," the article explained. Any improvements achieved through government assistance were artificial and just led to continued dependence of those communities on taxpayer funds. Instead, the government should allow businesses to decide for themselves where and how they could most productively contribute to the economy and not try to channel resources to underdeveloped regions. The AFBF made similar assertions when it set out its own proposed policies for dealing with economic hardship. The organization opposed federal spending to create employment and spur rural development efforts, because this drew resources away from the private sector. The group was also against liberalizing social security programs and expanding unemployment insurance to cover more workers, preferring an emphasis on "individual thrift and personal responsibility" as the solution to social problems.[55]

The emphasis on allowing the market to work its magic conveniently absolved plantation owners and political leaders from responsibility for the social problems created by centuries of racist oppression. In their analysis, the crisis in the South was a naturally occurring phenomenon that no one could control. Social programs and taxes levied to pay for them were a useless and unnecessary form of government intervention in the economy, not a moral obligation to ensure that the people whose lives were disrupted by economic transformations received assistance. There was no collective responsibility to provide for citizens' needs, only personal responsibility. The economy ran itself, and success or failure within the system was determined solely by each individual's own actions. As expressed in some southerners' explanations for what was happening in their states, people chose not to get an education, chose not to work, chose to live in shacks, and even chose to starve.

Toward the end of the 1960s, Mississippi civil rights activist Aaron Shirley pondered the meaning of freedom for black people a century after the end of slavery and in the wake of another reordering of southern society that dramatically altered the relationships between plantation owners and their workers. Shirley told reporters that he sometimes thought enslaved African Americans in the nineteenth century had one significant advantage over the displaced persons he saw struggling daily to secure the basic necessities of life. "In open slavery times human life was of some value," he stated. Masters who spent hundreds or thousands of dollars on their human property at least had an interest in taking care of their enslaved laborers. "But now the black people are no longer on the plantations. There is no feeling of responsibility toward them, no need to help them."[56] Convincing white southerners that justice required them to address the social costs of racism and assist displaced workers was one of the biggest challenges that participants in the freedom struggle faced in the decades after the civil rights movement.

CHAPTER 2

THIS IS HOME

BLACK WORKERS' RESPONSES TO DISPLACEMENT

AND OUT-MIGRATION

In the summer of 1966, black farmer Willie Williams offered a lesson in southern political economy to a reporter from the *Washington Post*. Williams was one of the tenants who James Minter had fired from his 11,000-acre cotton plantation in Dallas County, Alabama, earlier that year. The Minters had owned the land for 135 years, and the black families that tended the crops could trace their ancestry back just as far. "He's one year older than me, Mister James is," Williams stated. "We were raised as children together. His Daddy carried him to school in a horse and buggy every day right by us colored people's houses. . . . I didn't get no higher than second grade. They needed me for the farm. We were working for Mister James to go to school."[1]

Williams and other black southerners could see that white people's wealth was not built solely by individual effort and rested in large part on the work performed by generations of African Americans for little or no pay. For them, justice required more than the formal equality before the law mandated by civil rights legislation. They sought redress of the wrongs inflicted on them by slavery and the Jim Crow system and access to the types of education, jobs, and housing that white Americans enjoyed. After the mid-1960s, participants in the freedom movement continued the struggle against racism by calling for economic reforms that aimed to raise black people's incomes and ensure a decent standard of living for all the region's residents.

Social justice activists did not accept explanations for the agricultural crisis that attributed poverty, hunger, and out-migration to the natural workings of the market. They believed these problems were the result of decisions made by the people in power, whose policies protected the interests of the region's wealthiest residents and neglected the needs of those who were less well off. In the richest nation on earth, in counties with plenty of fertile farmland that produced millions of dollars in profits for its owners, there was no logical reason why people should be starving. The problem was not that the plantation regions were poor and unable to sustain the existing population, they argued, but that resources were not being distributed fairly. To address the imbalance, activists called on the federal government to intervene with direct assistance to displaced workers, improvements in social services and infrastructure, and economic development initiatives to create jobs.

In the late 1960s activists succeeded in convincing many government officials, journalists, and other Americans that southern political leaders were not interested in addressing the extreme economic hardships facing poor black people in their states and would do little to solve the crisis unless they were forced to act by outside pressure. As urban African Americans rebelled against racist oppression in their own communities, policy makers realized the connections between rural poverty and the wave of riots that occurred in cities across the nation between 1964 and 1968. Federal agencies stepped up their efforts to get aid to displaced workers in the South and persuade local officials to cooperate with antipoverty efforts. As a result, food and welfare programs were expanded to reach more people, government agencies paid closer attention to rural problems, and advocates for initiatives to stem out-migration gained allies at both the national and the local levels.

White supremacists' preference for policies that encouraged African Americans to leave the South came up against black people's determination to stay. Many of the people being fired and evicted from the plantations in the 1960s felt deeply attached to the land that they and their ancestors had worked for several centuries. In a letter to President John F. Kennedy expressing concern about the impact of mechanization on farmers in Bolivar County, Mississippi, a resident wrote, "They want more than anything else, to stay here, but they also want a decent living for their families." If it were possible for them to earn enough income, most would choose to remain in the county rather than migrate away. Explaining his reasons for staying in the South when most of his friends and family were leaving, John Brown Jr. stated, "I spent one summer in Detroit and that was enough of Detroit for me." Brown disliked crowded cities and much preferred rural life. "I've always enjoyed the farm," he said. "I love farming. I love to see things grow." Reporters from the *Houston*

Post who visited Mississippi in 1964 recorded similar sentiments from people who, though they were desperately poor, wanted to remain in the state. One man who worked on a cotton plantation for 50 cents an hour told them he did not want to leave and "all he wanted to do was stay home and be able to make a living." Asked why he did not move North like so many other black people, Delta Ministry staffer and native Mississippian John Bradford stated, "My idea is that this is home to me, as I know it, and I think that if the problems here will ever be worked out, then we're going to have to do it." At hearings held by the CCR in Alabama in April 1968, panelists heard testimony from African Americans who were frustrated with the slow pace of change and constant violations of their rights yet emphasized that they wanted to stay. Journalist Paul Good observed in the official account of the proceedings, "Home in the South, for all its poverty and exploitation, contains a familiar ambience, a link to past generations, the feel of belonging to the land despite white assertion that black exists there only through white sufferance."[2]

Aside from a preference for remaining in the places they called home, many rural poor people were not convinced that leaving the South would lead to much improvement in their lives. The war-driven economic boom that generated full employment and ensured jobs for those who moved north in the 1940s had subsided by the 1960s, and manufacturers were closing plants in Detroit, Chicago, and other cities that had once offered hope for a better life. Moreover, African Americans in those cities faced the same obstacles to economic opportunity that existed in the South and found their prospects limited by employment discrimination, inferior schooling, and housing segregation. Informal practices as well as government policies created separate and unequal communities in the urban North that mirrored the oppressions African Americans felt in the rural South, making migration a less-than-satisfactory solution to black southerners' problems. A study of seasonally employed farmworkers in Alabama found that, contrary to the popular belief that cities were inherently more attractive than rural life, small farmers did not want to leave and saw "no future in migrating to the big cities to join the ranks of the unemployed."[3]

Taking such factors into account, some analysts asserted that there were better approaches to the unemployment crisis than encouraging out-migration and that policy makers should instead support programs that enabled displaced workers to remain in their home communities. John Hatch, a social worker and native southerner employed by the Boston

Housing Authority, was convinced that poverty was harder and "more disabling" for African Americans in the North than in the South. People living in the city's public housing projects seemed to lack the social networks and community support that black southerners, however poor, could rely on during times of economic desperation. Hatch eventually chose to leave his job in Boston to work on an antipoverty project in Mississippi, hoping to create "opportunities for community building and developing, so that the choice to stay South would not mean neglect of hopes and dreams." As he explained to an interviewer, "If I thought for a moment that [migrants] were really moving toward a better life, I would not have seen it with the kind of urgency that I did. But my feeling was that this was not occurring." The leaders of Southern Rural Action, an organization formed in 1966 to experiment with new models for regional development, shared Hatch's view. In a proposal to the OEO seeking funds for its efforts, the group noted that attempts to export poor people from the South had proven ineffective and it was time to try something else. Forcing people to move to northern and western cities was "destructive, massively costly, and socially and politically unacceptable," these activists asserted. "The idea that a cycle of readjustment could be achieved in this way, by getting rid of 'surplus people' from Southern agriculture, has proved to be fallacious." Wilkinson County NAACP president James Joliff Jr. concurred. "We must realize that the real answer is to stay here and to make things better," he stated. "Most Negroes run off to Chicago, New Orleans or California, not realizing that they're just going from a small ghetto to a large one. But I wouldn't trade Mississippi for all the tea in China. Sure, there's guys pushing you here, but you just got to push back."[4]

Activists pushed back against pressures on black people to leave by offering financial assistance to laid-off workers, publicizing the human suffering that existed in the plantation regions, and pressuring political leaders to do more to address the crisis. In response to the economic reprisals against African Americans who attempted to vote in the early 1960s, supporters of the civil rights struggle formed Operation Freedom to provide loans and other aid to people who lost their jobs, homes, or access to credit because of their political activities. "A voting Negro population in Mississippi will change this state and eventually the nation, and those who fear the change know it," the Southern Patriot observed. "Economic strangulation is the only weapon strong enough to defeat them; if the people who believe in democracy provide the money to help them defeat this weapon, they will win." In November 1964 the National Student

Association organized the one-day Thanksgiving Fast for Freedom, which raised $34,000 for the Delta Ministry's efforts to get food to hungry people in counties where local officials refused to participate in federal food programs. When some workers at the Andrews Brothers Plantation in Tribbett were evicted after going on strike to demand an eight-hour day and higher wages, the Delta Ministry provided tents, food, and medical care to the families. Assistance from these and other initiatives enabled African Americans who might have had to leave the state to remain in the region and continue to fight for their rights. Civil rights groups and northern donors provided similar aid to local activists in many other communities, and traditions of sharing among rural black southerners also mitigated the effects of economic reprisals. Lawrence Guyot praised local people's persistence, which signaled to white supremacists that it was "no simple matter to dispose of sufficient Negroes to eradicate their potential political strength."[5]

Civil rights workers viewed the decision to leave or to stay as a political one and often described those who remained in the South in heroic terms. Mississippi activist Joseph Wheatley explained, "Relocation is a dirty word to Negroes here in the Delta. The white politicians think it is the social remedy. Our people want to build decent homes and stay here." Sue Geiger made the same point in explaining why local residents opposed a plan to relocate 300 black families to the Gulf Coast area instead of letting them use antipoverty funds to build homes in Washington County. "We see this as a plan to move Negroes to an area where they will have no political power," she stated. "This is their home. We say they have a right to jobs and homes here." In Lowndes County, Alabama, Robert Strickland told a reporter in 1967, "The jack rabbits have stopped running," meaning that "frightened Negroes have left, that those remaining intend to stay put and fight for a better life."[6] Southwest Alabama Self-Help Housing, a group that applied for federal funding to help poor people build their own homes in Lowndes and several other counties, noted that many of the families evicted from the surrounding plantations had left the area, but "others have elected to stay in the county and help solve the problems of their native land. These people deserve the right to be given the chance to be productive citizens in this place of their choosing." A follow-up proposal outlined the organization's history and the tribulations these displaced workers endured after being laid off from their jobs, put out of their homes, and moving into a tent city in 1966: "Sanitation in this tent city was poor and winter's cold was devastating. Yet they remained. They

COME to MT. BEULAH

We want every poor person who wants to <u>organize</u> and <u>fight</u> for a real FREEDOM program to come to the Mount Beulah campus - Delta Ministry headquarters near Edwards -

This FRIDAY - January 28

Let's all get together and plan

How to Get   OUR FOOD

OUR JOBS

OUR FREEDOM !

Bring Blankets,

bedding,

and YOUR NEIGHBORS.

Prepare to stay several days.

If you have no transportation, rides will be

arranged from your area.

Call Jackson 352-9128
or Edwards 852-2622

<u>TO</u> <u>GET</u> <u>TO</u> <u>MT.</u> BEULAH:

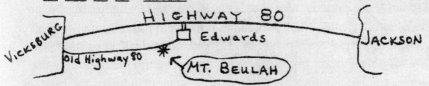

HIGHWAY 80

VICKSBURG

Old Highway 80

Edwards

MT. BEULAH

JACKSON

Exit from Highway 80 at Edwards.

Mt. Beulah Center is 3 miles west of Edwards.

Pamphlet inviting poor people to a conference at the Delta Ministry's headquarters in Mt. Beulah, Mississippi, January 1966. Michael J. Miller Civil Rights Collection, McCain Library and Archives, University of Southern Mississippi.

were threatened by Klansmen and Whites they had once called friends, yet they remained. Sometimes there was little or no food because the families had no adequate jobs after the evictions. Yet they remained. And because these people remained we see as a shining light illuminating the way saying this is America, the Land of the Free."[7]

Asserting that people had a right to live where they chose and not be forced by economic circumstances to move away from their homes directly countered the arguments of those who thought market forces should dictate these decisions. When some activists in Louisiana proposed a program to assist small farmers in St. Landry Parish they noted that this intervention might be deemed useless by some economic theorists but made a case that diversifying into vegetable and livestock production could enable farmers to remain on the land. "Some people and experts would argue that migration is a natural movement and may even be beneficial to an area by removing persons who are un- or underemployed [and use] social services which raises the general tax burden," they acknowledged. Yet out-migration only relocated poverty rather than solving it, as conditions in many of the nation's urban neighborhoods showed. A better alternative was to provide training and loans for farm families to shift into vegetable production, which was labor intensive and, thanks to the region's mild climate, could provide year-round income. This plan was "designed to arrest further migration from St. Landry Parish by helping the existing small farmers to make a better income where they are with what they have." Similarly, the director of a literacy program in Lexington, Mississippi, explained that most black people did not accept that out-migration was a solution to mass unemployment. He told a reporter: "The power structure's idea is to ship 5,000 Negroes out of the Delta and cut down that 2–1 Negro population ratio. Our idea is to bring in more industry and have the federal government supply public works jobs."[8]

To make the case for government action to stem out-migration and for economic policies that enabled rural people to continue living in their home communities, activists drew attention to the failures of the economic system that were on display everywhere in the plantation regions and invited news reporters and government officials to come and see for themselves how free enterprise was working there. New York congressman Joseph Resnick visited Mississippi in November 1965 to meet with members of the MFDP and other local people, who showed him the results of unemployment, evictions, and denial of assistance by the administrators of federal farm programs and welfare agencies. Resnick publicly expressed his concern that none of the state's leaders seemed to care about the plight of thousands of displaced workers who were losing their jobs and homes, and he told a reporter who asked why a representative from New York should concern himself with Mississippi's affairs that black residents lacked anyone to speak for them in Congress. In a letter to Orville Freeman, Resnick stated that planters and local officials were blocking efforts to get food to hungry people and said he was "frightened at the lengths these people will go to keep the Negro from taking his rightful place in American society." Reports of the USDA's inaction and indifference circulated by civil rights groups led more than a dozen of Resnick's congressional colleagues to inquire about the situation, ramping up the pressure on the agency to act.[9]

More publicity came in January 1966, when the MFDP and the Delta Ministry convened the Poor People's Conference at Mt. Beulah. The event drew hundreds of participants from around Mississippi to discuss the problems caused by agricultural displacement and how they could encourage the government to do more. Attendees included Isaac Foster and Ida Mae Lawrence, farm laborers who had participated in the organizing efforts that led to the eviction of workers on the Andrews plantation, along with dozens of others who had lost their livelihoods and had nowhere to go. James Hartfield was unemployed and could not secure any help from welfare officials in Sunflower County, where he lived in a leaky, freezing shack. Viola Wall described the hardships she had faced that winter and how she scratched together an income by "cutting and selling firewood like a man." Ora Wilson, a day laborer and single mother of four who was finding it impossible to support her family by chopping and picking cotton a few weeks of the year, decided to attend the meeting after hearing about it on the radio. "They said it was for poor peoples and, Lord knows, we were poor," she stated. "Ever'body was hungry at that time and we sure was."[10]

After discussing their plight and possible solutions, the unemployed and homeless workers considered occupying Greenville Air Force Base, a disused facility where 300 warm and dry buildings that could be used to house people inexplicably sat empty. Isaac Foster later recalled that almost everyone at the conference supported the plan, but they were also afraid. Then, "Mrs. Ida Mae Lawrence, who ain't afraid of nobody, finally broke out with, 'Dammit, I'm goin'.' All of you too afraid, go home and eat some more greens.'" The MFDP's Unita Blackwell indicated her willingness to join the protest, and the two women convinced Foster to go with them as "the man leader." About fifty people eventually took part in the action, slipping onto the base in the early hours of January 31 with mattresses, blankets, food, and stoves.[11] In a statement calling on President Johnson to provide immediate assistance for people who could not find work and lacked adequate incomes, they explained: "We are here because we are hungry. . . . We are here because we have no jobs. Many of us have been thrown off the plantations where we worked for nothing all of our lives. We don't want charity. We demand our rights to jobs, so that we can do something with our lives and build us a future." In response, federal authorities sent 140 military police to evict the protesters. The families found refuge in the tent city in Tribbett and expressed their intention to find a way to survive in Mississippi, with or without help from their government. Ida Mae Lawrence told reporters that the Johnson administration's decision to evict them from the base showed that political leaders cared more about property than people, causing her to conclude, "There's no way out but to begin your own beginning, whatever way you can."[12]

The Greenville sit-in made national headlines and inspired more visits by reporters, congressional representatives, and government agents to investigate conditions in Mississippi and other southern states. *Newsweek* examined the circumstances that sparked the protest in its article "DP's in the Delta" in February 1966, and a second report in March called displaced workers "the kindling of revolution." An OEO official who visited several Delta counties in late February concurred with this assessment, observing that people were desperate, unable to secure housing or feed their families, and convinced that political leaders did not care if they lived or died. Worried that this might lead to more attempts to seize public or private property and perhaps food riots, he concluded: "Jobs, cash income, food, housing, medical care, education and training programs must reach Negro farm workers as soon as possible." After touring some of the nation's most depressed rural areas in 1967, Orville Freeman reported to President Johnson that he visited "dozens of miserable hovels, South and North, where families live in shocking poverty. . . . It matches in some instances the worst I have seen in less developed countries around the world."[13] In April that year the Senate Labor and Public Welfare Subcommittee on Employment, Manpower and Poverty held hearings in Jackson, Mississippi, that provided a forum for residents to express their grievances and convinced some legislators that more government action was needed to solve the crisis. Following testimony of "malnutrition, unemployment, and actual starving," committee member George Murphy called on the president to declare an emergency and take immediate steps to alleviate the suffering. At the opening of a second set of hearings held in the nation's capital in July, Senator Jacob Javits emphatically rejected the notion that the situation was the result of natural economic forces that people just had to accept. "The United States does have agencies, the United States does have food, the United States does have the money to see that there is no poverty in this country," he asserted.[14]

The publicity campaign put pressure on southern governments and nudged them toward accepting some forms of federal assistance they had previously shunned. After the Delta Ministry provided the USDA with a list of counties in Mississippi that did not have food programs and offered to distribute surplus commodities in those places itself, nine counties agreed to initiate programs, expanding access to 64,000 more people. Southern officials did not want radical civil rights groups coming into their communities and providing services to poor people, and they were equally afraid of federal intervention if they failed to act. The late 1960s saw a gradual increase in the number of rural southern counties that participated in the commodities or food stamp programs as activists and federal officials persuaded, cajoled, or threatened local leaders into accepting them. In March 1966 Mississippi became the first southern state to have food programs in every county. With help from an OEO grant, the state's Department of Public Welfare planned to extend food assistance to half a million more poor people over the next six months. In a letter to congresswoman Edith Green, Orville Freeman explained: "The people of Mississippi do not like programs to come in from the outside. The threat of this program coming in meant that some of the constructive folks were able to convince some of the obstructionist ones that it was to the interest of Mississippi as well as the needy folks that this food be made available."[15] In July 1968 Freeman announced that the USDA planned to make sure that every one of the nation's 1,000 poorest counties had food programs, stating that the agency was prepared to pay for administrative costs and operate programs itself if local governments refused. This initiative extended food assistance to another 4 million poor people nationwide, bringing the total to 10 million by 1970 and extending coverage to all but 22 of the nation's 3,091 counties.[16]

The struggle to address the hunger crisis succeeded in forcing political leaders to accept some responsibility for alleviating economic hardship, but activists knew that simply handing out food to poor people was not enough. A leaflet prepared by the Freedom Information Service explained that the USDA's surplus commodities program was designed for the bene-fit of large agribusinesses, not poor people. Growers produced more than they could sell at profitable margins, so the government purchased the extra food to keep farm incomes at a healthy level. This enabled land-owners to invest in machinery and dispense with human laborers, who then relied on the government's food programs to survive. As the leaf-let noted, the system was an inadequate solution to poverty and invited questions regarding the sanity of the nation's policy makers: "Poor peo-ple ask 'is this the way a Great Society works?' *Without jobs poor people get poorer*. Food only helps them stay alive and poorer longer." Similarly, John Brown Jr. and other community organizers understood that their long-term goal must be to empower people to help themselves. Some-times solving a problem meant pressuring those responsible for creating a problem to fix it, and sometimes it meant mobilizing resources within the community. "Real progress comes when people begin to do some-thing for themselves," Brown stated. "My judgment is that this is what the government, this is what everybody who believes in human development and human dignity should be about."[17]

Just as much as did those who urged poor people to exercise their own initiative and strive for self-reliance, displaced laborers recognized the centrality of work to achieving economic success in the United States. Black southerners' often expressed and deeply held desire for employment contradicted white racists' claims that laziness and a preference for wel-fare handouts explained the high poverty rates in their communities. John Hatch recalled that even when there was no money to pay workers on the project he headed in Mississippi, "there was no shortage of volunteers. . . . The will to better yourself and to become involved and to expend energy. It was abundantly demonstrated." As one black Mississippian empha-sized, "People that are able to work want to work. We don't want welfare. We want work to do, where we can make [a] living for our familys." In a journal entry written in July 1966, Natchez antipoverty worker Marjorie Baroni described a woman she knew who wanted "very much to get off welfare" and could be helped if training programs were expanded to reach more people.[18] Community organizers seeking to set up adult edu-cation classes and job training projects noted that local people responded enthusiastically and that there were not enough spots for everyone who wanted to participate. In April 1967 a meeting held to inform residents in a five-county area of Mississippi about a planned retraining program for agricultural workers drew 1,000 people for 300 available positions.

Health care providers at an OEO-funded clinic in Bolivar County recalled, "People would walk twelve miles and sit in our front yards when we got up in the morning looking for jobs." Similarly, South Delta Community Action Association in Louisiana reported receiving five times as many applicants as there were available employment opportunities in one of its programs.[19]

Federal administrators also observed evidence of the priority African Americans placed on employment. Secretary of Labor Willard Wirtz corrected a Louisiana correspondent's statement that "Negroes want handouts, not jobs," by informing her: "Evidence speaks quite loudly to the contrary. The success of job-training programs proves that the disadvantaged want only a chance to stand on their own two feet. They want the opportunity which will enable them to be financially independent." Officials at the OEO echoed this assertion in their 1968 annual report. "The large majority of poor people entering neighborhood centers in poverty areas every day are there seeking jobs, or training, or information on where to go for employment assistance," they stated. "Decent jobs are basic to ending poverty." The following year, the SCLC's Ralph Abernathy reminded President Nixon's new labor secretary that African Americans were still waiting for meaningful solutions to the unemployment problem. "All we are asking here is that we be given a chance to prove that we are not lazy and be given a chance to add to the productivity of the American system and stop having to take the degrading handouts of welfare," he stated. Reliance on private businesses to generate enough jobs was ineffective, he argued, because the need was so much greater than the capacity of free enterprise alone to meet the demand for employment. Only a "massive Federal Effort" could hope to create the 3 million or more new jobs that were needed to absorb displaced workers.[20]

Although the resources political leaders allocated to antipoverty and job creation initiatives were not enough to solve the unemployment problem, federal officials did attempt to channel more aid to rural southern communities in the late 1960s. The Greenville sit-in led to a flurry of activity as the OEO, DOL, EDA, and USDA worked together and separately to convince poor people that the government was on their side. Within a few weeks of the protest the OEO and the DOL jointly pledged nearly $4 million for adult education and job training programs for 1,000 farmworkers in Coahoma County, Mississippi. Staff from the USDA, Job Corps, and Forest Service met with representatives from the MFDP and the NAACP in March 1966 and assured them that federal agencies were actively seeking ways to address rural poverty through food programs, job training, and literacy classes for displaced workers.[21] The same month, officials at the EDA reported that they were making some progress in extending economic development efforts in Mississippi, quoting an aide to the governor as saying, "This will work now even though it would have been impossible a few months ago." In addition to approving ten training programs in McComb, Greenville, Kosciusko, and Mound Bayou, the EDA worked with the MFDP and the Delta Ministry to promote small businesses and other self-employment opportunities for displaced workers. Officials from both the OEO and the EDA traveled to Mississippi to speak with state and local leaders, informing them about federal programs and encouraging them to work with civic organizations and community activists to alleviate poverty.[22]

Supporters of government intervention cited moral and pragmatic reasons for their position. Jacob Javits compared calls for relocating rural poor people to other parts of the country to initiatives that might be expected in totalitarian nations, not a democracy like the United States. "Population movements 'encouraged' to solve social problems are the greatest interference in private, individual lives, and have historically been the hallmark of tyrannical societies," he stated. Noting the failure of southern segregationists to convince many African Americans to take up offers of free transportation to northern cities, Javits concluded that this proved "the great majority of southern Negroes, just like southern whites, obviously would prefer to live in the area of the Nation in which they were born and have lived." As part of its Poor People's Campaign in 1968, the SCLC outlined the vast disparities in wealth that existed in the nation and questioned whether spending $2 billion a month on the Vietnam War was a defensible use of taxpayers' money when there were people starving at home. Surely, the SCLC suggested, the government could redirect some of these resources to people in need. Noting that poverty severely hindered people's ability to enjoy the rights to "life, liberty, and the pursuit of happiness" promised in the Declaration of Independence, these activists built on earlier arguments in favor of civil rights legislation to make a case for action based on the need to fully realize national ideals.[23]

Other observers highlighted practical reasons for investing resources in distressed communities and argued that failing to do so would cost the nation more in the long run. Texas lawyer and congressman Wright Patman outlined the need for more rural development to address the impact of mechanization and agricultural displacement in an article that was read into the *Congressional Record* in March 1964. Unless something was done, he warned, the nation's rural counties would be "little better than 'poor farms,'" costing taxpayers "billions of dollars in relief payments to support the destitute inhabitants of these economically blighted areas." The movement of displaced workers to urban areas promoted by some economists and business leaders was not an effective solution, both because cities lacked the capacity to absorb all of them and because of the strong attachments most of them felt to their local communities. For these reasons, Patman asserted, "it makes better sense to help rural people develop new opportunities at home. And this can be done through the cooperation of government and people."[24]

Uprisings by poor people in Watts, Harlem, Detroit, and other inner-city communities helped undermine the arguments of those who promoted out-migration as a solution to the South's economic problems. As numerous observers pointed out, this approach did not eliminate poverty but simply moved it from one place to another. Urban riots drew attention to the shared experiences of African Americans in the North and South and the futility of trying to solve problems in the nation's cities without first addressing the mass displacement of rural workers. An analysis prepared by the USDA in October 1966 asserted, "The weed of urban poverty— slums, ghettoes, overcrowding, crime—has its roots in a rural America lacking enough jobs and health and education services—the essentials needed to halt the out-migration of people from country to city." The following month, Assistant Secretary of Commerce Eugene Foley told an audience at the annual conference of the Regional Planning Association that the EDA planned to make more grants and loans available to rural communities in an attempt to alleviate problems created by the influx of southern migrants to northern cities. Officials at the OEO also perceived the rural-urban poverty connection and sought to fund demonstration projects that would "give the government a plan for discouraging out-migration of the poor from the rural area to the urban slums in spite of prophets of doom and gloom about the inevitability of this trend." When Congress made amendments to the Economic Opportunity Act in 1967, it specifically directed the OEO to fund rural programs that provided alternatives to migration and enabled people to become economically self-sufficient in their own communities. Meanwhile, President Johnson's National Advisory Committee on Rural Poverty gave rural development the same moral imperative as civil rights legislation by proclaiming that all Americans had the right to equal economic opportunity regardless of "race, religion, national origin, or place of residence."[25]

White southerners were not monolithically opposed to this idea, and advocates for economic development sometimes managed to gain allies among regional elites and other residents of rural southern counties. "I always thought we had foolish policies to try to encourage blacks to leave the south," recalled native Louisianian and agricultural economist Ray Marshall. "That always struck me as one of the dumbest things we ever tried." Marshall thought a better solution would be to upgrade people's education and skills to prepare them for participation in a changing economy. When EDA representative Wilfred Leland visited Mississippi in December 1965 to impress upon the state's local planning committees that the agency would not grant funds for projects that excluded African Americans from the benefits, he found that, contrary to expectations, some of the people he spoke with welcomed the initiative and expressed their willingness to cooperate. "Those leaders who favor economic expansion in the area (there are some who oppose it) recognize the need to develop and use the potential skills of Negro, Indian, and white workers to meet the labor requirements for such expansion," he stated. He recommended reorganizing the committees to replace reactionaries who resisted such efforts with people who had more progressive leanings. Mississippi state senator A. J. Foster might have been an example of the type of person Leland had in mind. Foster served as executive director for a three-county antipoverty program in the northeastern part of the state and wrote to Orville Freeman in April 1966 to express support for the USDA's efforts to pay more attention to small farmers and displaced workers. Noting that there were half a million people in the area who relied on federal food programs for survival, Foster stated, "A few of these people don't want anything any better, but by and large these are good poor people that want homes and independence just as any other red-blooded American. They will work if given any incentive." Foster cited the success of New Deal programs that loaned money to people to buy land in the 1930s, which produced "educated nice families who are our leading citizens now." Like those earlier generations, the people who were being thrown off the plantations could prosper and make valuable contributions to their communities "if given the proper opportunity and just a little help."[26]

Some of Senator John Sparkman's white constituents in Alabama supported similar solutions to their state's racial and economic problems. Jennie Burrell asked the senator to support fair housing and civil rights legislation pending in Congress so that the legacies of past racism would not haunt future generations, expressing her willingness to pay higher taxes if necessary to carry out the programs. "I do not feel these taxes will be a burden," Burrell wrote. "I feel they will be 'money in the bank,' an *investment* in my children's future and in the future of their country." Claire Benjamin stated that she was looking to Congress to "show the Negro that we are indeed willing to give them a decent beginning and a share in our hope" by enacting a program of guaranteed employment for all workers seeking jobs. Charles Watson also believed Alabama's political leaders should "make a greater effort now to improve the life and rights of the Negro in the state" and urged Sparkman to support antipoverty and job training programs. Similarly, Alabama's director of vocational education urged the senator to vote in favor of legislation providing federal funding for job training and economic development, telling him that it was hard to secure money for these purposes at the state and local levels.[27]

Mounting pressure from activists and the threat of federal intervention in the late 1960s made regional elites more responsive to demands for initiatives aimed at addressing unemployment and out-migration. Governor Paul Johnson in Mississippi warned his constituents that the only way to preserve states' rights was to introduce reforms that demonstrated a commitment to solving social problems. Mississippians could either start doing this themselves or face the prospect of federal agencies doing it for them. In March 1966 the EDA's assistant for intergovernmental relations, William Nagle, reported that the resistance many Mississippians had shown toward economic development efforts was abating and that state officials had invited staff from the agency to help them develop programs for retraining displaced workers. Later the same month, Nagle noted that some white as well as black residents supported the EDA's efforts and held it in high regard. He identified several leading white moderates, including state treasurer William Winter, Greenville mayor Pat Dunne, and Clarksdale plantation owner Andrew Carr, who seemed "genuinely interested in creating jobs and solving unemployment problems for *all* the people of the area." An article in *Business Week* in June 1968 also noticed a change in attitude among legislators and business leaders in Mississippi, quoting Jackson banker Nat Rogers as saying, "In the past, the so-called 'no-never' attitude dominated. We now know that the poor, both white and Negro, must be educated and trained, not only for their own benefit, but for the public at large."[28]

For these and other reasons, the late 1960s saw a slight thawing in white southerners' attitudes toward the War on Poverty. Sometimes this shift was motivated by pure self-interest, as when local political leaders filed applications for federal grants themselves to prevent other organizations from receiving funds and to ensure that they retained control of any money coming into their communities. Southern governors also tried to minimize disruptions to the existing social order by staffing State Economic Opportunity Offices (SEOOs) with people they trusted not to demonstrate independence or mobilize challenges to their own authority. The governors of Louisiana and Mississippi both came under fire in March 1965 for appointing segregationists with little experience or interest in working with poor people to head their state antipoverty offices.[29] Meanwhile, Alabama governor George Wallace frequently interfered with appointments to the boards of directors of programs in his state to prevent people he viewed as too militant from taking part. An OEO report on southern antipoverty initiatives expressed concern that a number of community action agencies (CAAs) were operated by the region's "lily-white political power structures" with "one or two safe Negroes on a board, or parallel Negro subcommittees that meet to approve the minutes of the main board."[30]

At the same time, there was genuine goodwill and willingness on the part of some white southerners to make serious attempts to alleviate poverty. In Wilcox County, Alabama, an investigator found several white business owners who were willing to quietly support the local SCLC branch's efforts to set up a CAA, though they could not be too open about it for fear of retaliation from segregationists. Several of them agreed to serve on the agency's board of directors but did not attend meetings. Camden mayor Reginald Albritton explained, "The whites don't know I'm on the board. If they did, they'd use it against me. It would be pure dynamite for me to go to a meeting." Yet he and the other secret board members wanted to see change come to the community. "The other whites on the board feel as I do that they're (the Negroes) are human beings and need help," the mayor stated. "They'd like to see these programs."[31]

Activists in Mississippi were also not entirely without white allies. L. C. Dorsey recalled that white landowner Ben Walker was "an unusual man who really did not believe in all the nonsense that some of the other plantation owners professed" and that he was one of several local farmers who offered help to the evicted and blacklisted workers from the Andrews plantation in Tribbett. The president of the board of supervisors in Wilkinson County also sympathized with social justice efforts. Writing to OEO director Sargent Shriver in November 1966, he expressed agreement with Shriver's decision to override Governor Johnson's veto of an antipoverty project and stated, "This area needs help real bad. I have been trying hard for some time to bring in an industry to our county but so far I have not had very much luck." Lexington newspaper editor Hazel Brannon Smith castigated opponents of the War on Poverty and called on the state's congressional representatives to support funding for programs that helped poor people. In particular, Smith praised the OEO's Migrant and Seasonal Farm Workers Program for giving displaced farmworkers the chance to retrain for other jobs.[32]

In Coahoma County, Andrew Carr played a key role in setting up the local CAA, Coahoma Opportunities Inc. (COI). Assistant Director Bennie Gooden explained that Carr "opened doors of the power structure. We couldn't get the Board of Supervisors or any local officials to meet with us. He's rich enough, and influential enough, and brave enough not to have to give in to the pressure." Asked what motivated him, Carr stated that he had always believed in equal rights and thought the injustices inflicted on black people threatened social stability in his community. "I've got five children," he said. "I want peace here." Carr's brother Oscar, a banker who was not afraid to anger local segregationists by loaning money to African Americans, also helped secure white leaders' support for the project, telling those who were reluctant to join the effort that the alternative was more federal intervention in their community and an antipoverty program run by black people. In terms that closely resembled the analyses presented by civil rights activists seeking to address the economic legacies of Jim Crow, Andrew Carr told OEO investigators: "The Negro in the Mississippi Delta has never really had help to realize his potential development. You've had help; I've had help; the anti-poverty program is the Negro's chance for help."[33]

Against the arguments of free market proponents who presented out-migration as natural and inevitable, advocates for government intervention asserted that agricultural modernization need not force thousands of people from their homes. Social justice activists viewed the poverty and suffering in rural southern communities as unnecessary and intolerable, defined inaction as an immoral violation of human rights, and proposed alternative solutions that respected displaced workers' desire to stay in the rural counties where they had lived all their lives. By publicizing conditions in the plantation regions, activists convinced federal and southern officials to act and drew some white allies into the cause. At the same time, antipoverty efforts continued to face obstruction from white supremacists. In the late 1960s and early 1970s, the OEO's community action programs emerged as a key battlefield in the struggle for racial equality and economic justice.

CHAPTER 3

THEY COULD MAKE SOME DECISIONS

THE WAR ON POVERTY AND COMMUNITY ACTION

President Johnson's State of the Union address in January 1964 expressed many of the same desires felt by displaced workers in the South: equal treatment under the law, jobs with adequate pay, decent homes, access to education, and economic security for those who were too old or sick to work. Johnson pointed out that as the richest, most powerful nation in the world, the United States surely had the capacity to ensure a comfortable standard of living for all its citizens, but racism and inadequate incomes excluded many people from the opportunities that others took for granted. He promised to wage an "unconditional war on poverty" and listed a slew of proposals that aimed to resolve the problem: enacting youth job programs, revamping the unemployment insurance system, extending coverage of the federal minimum wage to more workers, broadening access to food stamps, increasing funding for education, investing in infrastructure, ensuring affordable housing, and providing health care for the elderly.[1] Many of these ideas made their way into the Economic Opportunity Act that Congress passed later that year. Along with the array of new programs to assist poor people, the legislation's provision for a special office within the government charged with solving poverty raised hopes that the administration was serious about eliminating the inequities that Johnson targeted in his speech.

In its first few years of existence, the Office of Economic Opportunity acted as an ally in the freedom struggle, helping activists to bypass the racist political structures that hindered black southerners' access to federal programs. During this phase, the agency fostered a variety of innovative projects, including the early childhood development program Head Start, self-help housing initiatives that offered training and employment to poor people as they built their own homes, and comprehensive neighborhood health centers that addressed the social and environmental causes of illness in addition to providing medical care to low-income communities.

Antipoverty programs that provided services and job opportunities for poor people encouraged displaced plantation workers to stay in the South and work to improve conditions in their communities instead of migrating away. At the same time, the OEO's mandate to include poor people themselves in planning and operating programs enabled rural black southerners to directly influence the distribution of resources in their towns and counties, threatening to destabilize long-standing race and class hierarchies.

The War on Poverty undermined the tight control that white landowners and business leaders had maintained over their communities, and they responded by attacking and obstructing antipoverty efforts. Opponents of government intervention to solve economic problems publicized instances of mismanagement and corruption to support their argument that the programs were a waste of taxpayer money. Racist rhetoric and Klan violence discouraged participation by poor white people and created the perception that Great Society initiatives only benefited African Americans. As the decade progressed, the War on Poverty increasingly competed with the war in Vietnam for attention and resources. These factors all contributed to a growing reluctance among citizens and their representatives in Congress to spend money on social programs. Within a few years of promising to end poverty and ensure an equal chance of economic success for all Americans, the Johnson administration backed down on this commitment. Political pressure and budget cuts in the late 1960s weakened the strong support that the OEO had previously given to grassroots social justice organizations, generating suspicion and bitterness toward the government among participants in antipoverty projects. By the end of the decade, African Americans were coming to see that they could not rely on national political leaders to support their struggles any more than they could depend on state or local politicians.

Southern political leaders' indifferent response to economic problems in the early 1960s convinced many analysts that federal action was needed to address unemployment and poverty in the region. The framers of the Economic Opportunity Act understood that leaving control of government programs in the hands of white elites meant that black southerners were unlikely to benefit from them, and they included measures designed to bypass local governments and get resources directly into the hands of poor people. As the legislation made its way through Congress, some representatives wanted to include provisions that preserved states' rights by allowing governors to review and veto plans for CAPs. The suggestion drew an exasperated response from Washington senator Warren Magnuson. "Some charge 'leave it to the local communities,'" he stated. "Where do they think the problems have existed? And where do they think action has been lacking, or lagging?" Senator Robert F. Kennedy also asserted that a departure from previous approaches was necessary, noting the inadequacies of existing public assistance programs and the general sense of powerlessness among beneficiaries. Kennedy praised measures that involved poor people in designing antipoverty programs, stating that this gave them "a real voice in their institutions." The *Louisiana Weekly* suggested that by providing a direct line to federal resources and a way around the discriminatory practices of local officials, the new law could have an even more transformative effect on black southerners than civil rights legislation.[2]

The War on Poverty did not aim merely to provide social services but also to empower poor people to change their communities for the better. An important aspect of the provisions for setting up CAPs was that they allowed for private nonprofit groups as well as public entities to seek designation as CAAs and receive OEO funding. This enabled civil rights groups and other organizations to propose projects of their own in places where local political leaders failed to act, and it also meant they could hire people with limited education who were typically shut out of government positions because of civil service regulations.[3] The first CAAs to form in many rural southern communities were extensions of the black freedom movement, organized and operated by the same people who were involved in desegregation and voter registration efforts. The Child Development Group of Mississippi (CDGM), which received a grant to operate a Head Start program in summer 1965, was headquartered at the Delta Ministry's facilities in Mt. Beulah and included numerous veterans of the civil rights movement on its staff. Unita Blackwell and L. C. Dorsey both led efforts to establish Head Start centers in their local communities. Dorsey called antipoverty work "a continuation of the civil rights movement," noting that the skills used to teach people "how to make the system work for them, how to go to the Welfare Department with records and demand your rights, [and] how to go to elected officials and get things done in your community" were the same as those she learned registering people to vote. Holmes County activist Bernice Johnson recalled community centers being used for Head Start during the day and MFDP meetings at night, and participants across the state were members of other groups such as the NAACP, SNCC, and CORE as well. In Lowndes County, Alabama, civil rights leaders Robert Strickland, John Hulett, Frank Miles Jr., and Lillian McGill were all involved in initiating antipoverty programs. An OEO official found significant overlap in the membership of local civil rights organizations and the county's CAA board and noted that participants viewed these as part of the same struggle for social justice.[4]

These activists understood that economic and political progress for black southerners were closely entwined. As Lillian McGill explained, "We could win [elections] in this county if the poverty program gets enough people out of poverty so they can be independent when they go to the polls." L. C. Dorsey thought the War on Poverty "freed a lot of black folks and poor whites from a strangle hold economy that just didn't let you live, or barely let you live. We went to work for wages that we never dreamed you could earn in Mississippi, and people were freed for the first time from a system that really controlled you through the threat of starvation." Similarly, a paper prepared for CORE volunteers in Louisiana in June 1965 highlighted the potential for real challenges to existing conditions that could emerge out of poor people's participation in Great Society initiatives. "One might say that in any parish in Louisiana it is a political step for a Negro Headstart program even to exist," the author noted. "Placed in this perspective one can readily see the political value of Headstart as an instrument to build up confidence in the Negro community." A group of observers who visited a Head Start program in Concordia Parish later that year concluded that it was working in exactly that way. More than 500 local black people were employed by the project, and there was a growing sense among participants that they could do things to improve their own lives and broader social conditions.[5]

In Bolivar County, Mississippi, two related antipoverty projects emerged that provided examples of what rural poor people could achieve with a little outside help. The county was the second poorest in the nation, with a median annual income less than $1,000 per year. The unemployment rate for black workers was in the double digits, and many families lived in substandard housing lacking adequate plumbing or access to clean drinking water. Sixty out of every 1,000 black babies died within a year after being born, a rate that was three times the national average and comparable with those in the most impoverished developing nations of the world. Surveying conditions in this plantation region in the summer of 1964, H. Jack Geiger of the Medical Committee for Human Rights realized that "one didn't have to go to Africa, Southeast Asia, or Latin America to find poverty. There was a third world within the United States."[6]

Geiger worked with fellow activist Count Gibson of Tufts Medical School in Boston to propose building a health center in the all-black town of Mound Bayou to offer free treatment and preventive care to poor people in the community. The project aimed to go beyond traditional approaches to health care and attack the root causes of disease instead of merely treating problems after they developed. This meant addressing a wide range of social problems, including poverty, unemployment, housing, sanitation, inadequate education, and political powerlessness, all of which prevented poor people from leading healthy and productive lives. In their application for OEO funding, Geiger and Gibson argued that a comprehensive approach to health care that treated the whole community, not just individual patients, could be "a route to social, economic, and political change" in the region. Over opposition from white doctors and political leaders in Mississippi, the OEO agreed to provide a grant of $1.5 million for the construction and operation of a comprehensive health center to serve a population of 14,000 poor people in Bolivar and several neighboring counties.[7]

The Tufts-Delta Health Center (TDHC) opened in Mound Bayou in November 1967, housed initially in a temporary clinic and moving into a newly constructed, modern facility in December 1968. The project combined direct treatment for illnesses with efforts to create a healthier environment by improving sanitation systems, digging ditches and wells, fitting fly screens, and repairing the ramshackle houses that many poor people inhabited. Health center nurses visited the homes of all new patients to assess the needs of entire households and help families address problems in their physical surroundings that contributed to ill health. "We ask where the family's water comes from, where the outhouse is located, how many people live in the building (usually one or two rooms), and if they have any income," nurse obstetrician Stella Simpson explained. "Then we make referrals to the various departments, including sanitation, so they can remedy existing problems."[8]

In addition to treating roughly 200 people a day at the clinic or in their homes, the TDHC offered adult education classes, provided technical training, and created dozens of jobs that were filled by local people. Many of these employees were former plantation workers who had received very limited formal education. The health center helped them earn high school diplomas or attend college, taught them new skills, and opened avenues to successful careers in nursing, nutrition, social work, environmental health, office management, administration, and other areas. L. C. Dorsey found employment at the center as an outreach worker, took evening classes to earn her high school diploma, and went on to complete a Ph.D. at the State University of New York at Stony Brook. Nurse's aide Irene Williams later recalled how working at the center changed her life. Williams grew up in a sharecropping family in Round Lake, east of Mound Bayou. After dropping out of school in the fifth grade to work in the cotton fields, she married young and went to work with her husband on a white man's farm. Eventually the couple bought some land in Mound Bayou and built their own home there using lumber salvaged from condemned houses, but with seven children to support they still struggled financially. Soon after the center opened Williams secured a trainee position at the clinic that paid fifty dollars a week and opened up a new world of opportunity. "It was wonderful," she stated. "I was able to raise my children half decent, give them some of the things I never would have been able to give them. . . . I couldn't have done that without [the TDHC], and I'm thankful."[9]

The TDHC's record of job creation and hiring from within the community was much better than those of many private enterprises that located in the rural South. In 1969 twenty-one of the center's twenty-six nursing staff were local people.[10] A year later the TDHC had approximately 200 employees, including 180 from Bolivar County. Some of the workers had previously been subsisting on food stamps or the surplus commodities program and were now earning good incomes as managers of the health center's own supplemental food programs. According to Jack Geiger, as TDHC training programs prepared more people for employment, "local residents filled more and more of the health center jobs, used their salaries to build decent homes and send their children to college, and taught us all lessons about resilience in the face of adversity."[11]

The TDHC also empowered local residents to shape the future of their community by encouraging them to develop and implement ideas of their own. The first phases of the project began before the clinic opened and involved canvassing the service area to determine residents' health care needs. Organizers and local volunteers visited rural people's homes and invited them to mass meetings where they could discuss their concerns and help shape the development of the health center. It soon became clear from these conversations that although access to medical treatment was important, certain more basic needs must be met before poor people could achieve better health. Staff members reported that at a meeting in

Rosedale, one woman expressed "thanks to Tufts, God and the Government" but told them "if we wished to get to the cause of sickness as we had said, we should look at the inadequate food supply which she felt to be a big cause." Around 3,000 people in the service population were malnourished, and doctors saw some patients who were "slowly starving to death."[12] The TDHC responded to the problem by stocking food in its pharmacy and giving out prescriptions for groceries that were filled by local stores, explaining to OEO officials who questioned these practices that people were hungry, and the treatment for hunger was food. These measures offered immediate relief for some families, but an idea for a more long-term solution came from local residents: give these agricultural workers access to land, and they could grow food to feed themselves. Tufts-Delta organizer John Hatch explained, "People did not view commodities as the solution and wondered why the government wanted to ship food into Mississippi when they knew how to grow it, were living on top of the richest soil in the world and did not mind working."[13]

With help from some black farmers who provided land and equipment, donations from northern supporters, and additional funds raised through fish fries and barbecues, 900 of the county's poorest families joined together to form the North Bolivar County Farm Cooperative (NBCFC) in April 1967. The project received an additional boost when the OEO approved a $150,000 grant as part of its effort to encourage demonstration programs that experimented with innovative solutions to poverty. In the spring and summer of 1968, the NBCFC employed roughly 250 members growing vegetables for $4 in cash plus $6 in food credit per day. The remaining members purchased food from the cooperative at discounted prices. The NBCFC produced more than a million pounds of food in its first season and effectively solved the hunger problem in Bolivar County.[14]

Not content to be just another food program dependent on government funding, participants researched food-processing and marketing possibilities with the goal of becoming a self-sustaining enterprise. A Ford Foundation grant in 1969 enabled them to buy more land, expanding the cooperative's growing space to 500 acres. That year the NBCFC provided employment for more than 300 families and produced enough vegetables to supply its members and seven local hot lunch programs for senior citizens and school children, along with some surplus produce that was sold in New Orleans and Detroit. The co-op also built an office building and storage shed, held workshops, and sent staff members to economic development conferences that explored the future of vegetable production in the Delta. A progress report for 1969 stated, "Our first goal was to help people out of malnutrition. We have done it. Now we are moving to help people out of poverty, which is what caused the malnutrition. . . . We are strong and still growing. We have the future potential for economic independence."[15]

The TDHC fostered political as well as economic autonomy by encouraging local residents to take an active part in planning and administering its programs. Residents in the towns and hamlets within the target area chose representatives to serve on local health associations whose members met regularly to decide how to address the needs of their constituents. Stella Simpson reported in October 1968: "Each little community in the area now has a well organized group who sort of takes charge of the little things such as finding someone who will drive patients to the clinic from their particular area and getting a house or other building as a place from which to dispense clothes and where we can hold screening and prenatal clinics." By February 1970 ten local health associations had been organized, comprising a total membership of 2,835 people. Delegates from each of these groups also served on the area-wide North Bolivar County Health Council (NBCHC), an advisory board to the TDHC. Organizers deliberately placed as many projects and decisions as possible in the hands of the council rather than health center staff to enable local residents to gain managerial experience. The long-term goal was for the NBCHC to gradually take on more responsibilities and eventually assume control over the project.[16]

Participation in the health associations offered rural poor people opportunities to express their views, engage in democratic decision making, and envision alternatives to the social structures that created the problems they were working to solve. In some cases attempts to address the root causes of poverty and illness led to direct confrontations with the people in power. When several clients reported that the white woman in charge of the local post office had made them wait several days before giving them their welfare checks, TDHC staff filed a complaint that resulted in her dismissal.[17] In August 1970 a group of residents in Rosedale organized a boycott of white-owned stores and sent a letter to the mayor demanding better water and sewage systems, housing code enforcement, streetlights, and paved roads in the black neighborhood, along with more hiring of African Americans by the municipal government and private businesses. The NBCHC endorsed the boycott and urged members of each local health association to donate funds to help sustain it. Health association members also engaged in voter registration activities, as did many staff members when they were off work. One of the TDHC's local trainees, Johnny Todd, later became the first black mayor of Rosedale. Whereas some critics viewed such activities as deviating from the TDHC's health care mission, participants in the project saw connections between political structures and social conditions in their communities. They attributed the poor health of black residents to the neglect of their needs by existing officeholders, and they sought to replace the people in power with elected officials more responsive to their concerns. Consequently, Jack Geiger observed, "there was a real translation of community organization out of this project into political leadership."[18]

In addition to challenging the authority of the white men who dominated most of the county's local governments, TDHC participants upset power relations within the black community in Mound Bayou and the surrounding countryside. Much like their white counterparts in other parts of the state, the black professionals and business leaders who made up the town's political elite held rural poor people in low regard, viewing them as unintelligent, incompetent, and largely responsible for their own poverty. Nor were they above exploiting the region's plantation workers for their own ends. Two poorly run fraternal hospitals existed in Mound Bayou before the arrival of the TDHC, chiefly for the purpose of extracting contributions from members in return for substandard service. According to one resident, these entities resembled the town as a whole in being "just a business run by some Black people to rob other Black people."[19] Most poor people struggled to pay the fees charged by the hospitals, and when state legislators passed new regulations in the 1950s that required thousands of dollars in renovations, the hospitals themselves were pushed to the brink of bankruptcy. In conjunction with its grant to establish the TDHC, the OEO provided funds that enabled the fraternal hospitals to merge and form the Mound Bayou Community Hospital (MBCH) in 1967. The MBCH was supposed to provide free hospital treatment that complemented the TDHC's outpatient services, but the hospital did not always hold up its end of the deal. Stella Simpson and other observers reported that MBCH administrators sometimes denied admission to patients, charged others for services that were paid for by the OEO grant, and used the hospital to enrich themselves rather than providing health care to poor people. Resentful of the competition posed by the TDHC and alarmed by the growing assertiveness of its rural poor clientele, Mound Bayou leaders sought to limit the health center's disruptive potential by pressuring the OEO to turn control of the project over to themselves.[20] The situation in

Mound Bayou exposed the class dimensions of conflicts that manifested as racial tensions in other southern communities. More than just attempts to preserve white supremacy, opposition to antipoverty initiatives were also aimed at maintaining economic structures that enabled some people to become wealthy at the expense of others.

Throughout the plantation regions, the transformative effects of the War on Poverty were increasingly evident. The employment opportunities that CAPs generated gave former sharecroppers who had previously been shunned by private employers a chance to prove that they were capable of acquiring the skills needed to perform tasks other than picking cotton, with results that often surprised people who had been skeptical of the value of these programs. In 1967 an engineer in Coahoma County who worked with two ten-man crews of trainees from COI wrote to the CAA's director to praise its achievements. After admitting to initially having "misgivings about certain aspects of the so-called poverty program," he explained how the dedication, competence, and production record of COI's trainees caused a shift in his thinking. "The 'Operation Main Stream' Program is one which I can heartily endorse based on the experience we have had with our work crews," he wrote. "In my opinion, it is an extremely worthwhile program giving suitable and dignified employment to those who obviously want to work. The work accomplished by these crews is in turn an asset and enhancement to the communities in which they live." Similarly, the board of supervisors in Chickasaw County, Mississippi, emphasized the positive effects of its local Neighborhood Youth Corps, stating, "This program has made a great impact on our county from both an economical and cultural stand point. A great majority of these enrollees have been taken off the welfare rolls and are making a livelihood for themselves."[21]

Participants in antipoverty programs developed other useful skills in addition to training for specific jobs. Coahoma Opportunities Inc. offered a broad range of services, including Head Start and adult education programs, legal counseling, small business development assistance, and a credit union that provided low-cost financial services and freed poor people from dependence on local loan sharks. A program that served 459 people in Wilcox County, Alabama, focused on "reading, writing, communicative skill, consumer education, availability of helpful agencies within their reach and individual worth and dignity," according to project director Thomas Threadgill. Classes that taught basic math, accounting, and financial management enabled people to better navigate the economic system and avoid exploitative credit arrangements that enticed them to borrow money at high interest rates. Threadgill reported that families that had been "trapped in debt for years" were now paying some of it off, and people who had marked their signatures with an X all their lives were "now able, with dignity, to sign their names." Another CAP in rural Alabama helped seasonal farmworkers secure places in an MDTA project and transfer into higher-paying jobs after completing their training, encouraged tenants and landowners to work together in repairing substandard housing, and increased voter registration among participants in the program from 47 percent to 90 percent.[22]

The War on Poverty's impact went beyond improvements in the lives of individual participants to encompass entire communities. In Wilcox County, investigators noted that employment for sixty people made possible by an OEO grant of $302,081 meant that $20,000 in wages and salaries was injected into the local economy every month. When the money spent for supplies and services was factored in, they estimated the impact on the area's businesses to be $50,000 a month. Staff of the TDHC in Mississippi used their OEO grant money as leverage to enhance banking services in the area. After letting it be known that they had $2 million a year to deposit in a local bank that was willing to establish a branch in Mound Bayou, hire African Americans as tellers, and make loans in a nondiscriminatory manner, they found an eager taker in the Bank of Bolivar County. Described by Jack Geiger as the "smallest, previously most racist bank in the region," its owners nonetheless jumped at the offer because "whatever kind of trouble they had with black they didn't have with green." Similarly, evaluators of COI in Coahoma County observed that local businesses benefited from workers' upgraded skills, and the presence of a more highly trained labor force could help recruit industries to the area. In Greenville, Mississippi, a local zipper manufacturing plant snapped up all fifty-nine graduates of one training program as soon as they graduated in March 1966, reflecting the demand for skilled labor. Some analysts highlighted the return on taxpayers' dollars as additional justification for the government's investments in antipoverty programs. According to one study, for every dollar spent on a high school equivalency education program that helped migrant and seasonal farmworkers secure better jobs, participants returned $1.96 in federal taxes to the national treasury and saved the government $2.73 in expenditures on welfare and other social services.[23]

Along with the economic benefits, observers noted significant social benefits that resulted from the War on Poverty. Citizens who had previously felt neglected and shut out of mainstream institutions found their voices and became active, engaged members of their communities. Unita Blackwell explained that through inclusion in their local CAPs, "people learned coming off the plantations that they could make some decisions.... They learned that they could argue with one another and try to reason and found out they could make some decisions for themselves." The OEO reported in May 1968 that more than half of the employees in CAPs nationwide were "non-professional residents of the areas served—who were poor until employed." In addition, more than 51,000 people from low-income target populations served on CAP boards and advisory committees, helping to set policy and determine priorities.[24]

Poor people's ideas and expertise not only shaped the direction of OEO programs but also influenced more traditional government bureaucracies. The DOL, the USDA, HEW, and the Department of Housing and Urban Development (HUD) all altered some of their policies to make it easier for people with limited education and income to qualify for loans, job training, housing assistance, food programs, and other forms of federal aid. Community action also pushed state and local agencies to better meet the needs of poor residents. In Coahoma County, the late 1960s saw the inclusion of a nonwhite representative on the local welfare board and the drafting of an economic development plan that paid some attention to poor people's concerns. The county's Chamber of Commerce and a few banks and stores also made efforts to include or hire black people. The OEO reported in 1969 that studies by several outside research firms showed CAPs were "a significant factor in bringing about improvements in public employment services, public schools, public welfare agencies, and major private welfare agencies."[25]

In some communities CAPs helped white and black residents to bridge the racial divide. A visit to an adult education program run by Systematic Training and Redevelopment (STAR) in Mississippi led an OEO consultant to predict that it would go a long way toward alleviating white racism in the region. "Caucasian students I talked to all reported the same feelings: Initially wary of their first experience in an integrated situation, they became rapidly enthusiastic members of their classes, devoted to their teachers, and reported feeling a real kinship with their fellow students, regardless of color," he wrote.[26] One STAR worker reported seeing the sheriff of a small rural town chatting amicably on the street with two black women that he now worked with in the program and calling two white women over to meet them. This example of friendly interracial interaction was "the kind of thing that had never been seen in that town before." Administrators of Mid-State Opportunity, Inc., another Mississippi CAA, also emphasized how antipoverty efforts fostered interracial cooperation around the state. Previously, there had been little communication between white and black Mississippians, but OEO rules stipulating that all segments of society be included in planning and implementing programs forced people to cooperate. "The public is now accepting leaders of both races working and planning together," they stated, citing this as a laudable achievement of the War on Poverty. A federal investigator who surveyed fifteen southern communities and interviewed more than one hundred people for a report to the Senate Appropriations Committee in 1967 reached the same conclusion. "The progress which has been made in the past two years in racial harmony through anti-poverty programs in the Southeastern area of the country is almost unbelievable," he wrote. "There appears to be not only general acceptance of the antipoverty programs in Mississippi among the poor and Negro, but by business and a substantial segment of the white community."[27]

As this report suggested, some opponents of the War on Poverty changed their minds once they saw the programs in action. In Lowndes County, Alabama, the positive impact of payroll checks and stipends associated with a retraining program for displaced workers circulating through the local economy opened residents' eyes to the benefits of the project and established "a limited line of communication between the white community and the Negroes," according to one account. By 1968, some plantation owners in the area who had earlier threatened tenant families with eviction were now encouraging them to participate in antipoverty programs.[28] Administrators of similar efforts in Lexington, Mississippi, reported that the success of their early initiatives convinced some white residents to support projects they had previously opposed. The community now had a CAA and an MDTA program, the local courthouse was integrated, and white and black citizens were "communicating for the first time in 150 years." The directors of CAPs in Bolivar and Sunflower Counties told an OEO analyst in June 1967 that when they first started the programs, "the idea of OEO was not at all accepted." Now, however, most people were pleased with the CAPs and more were "being won over as time goes by."[29]

Antipoverty programs demonstrated that there were viable alternatives to policies that simply discarded displaced agricultural workers or wrote off rural southern communities as unsalvageable. The realization that there were other options offered hope to poor black people and encouraged more of them to stay in the plantation counties rather than leave to seek jobs elsewhere. A handout explaining the purpose of the TDHC for local residents stated that its goal was to "penetrate the environmental circumstances which dictate to Negroes of Bolivar County the following message: '*Die or get out.*' We hope to change this to '*Live* and let live, fully *here* in your HOME."[30] After losing 14 percent of its black population in the 1950s and another 18 percent in the 1960s, the rate of out-migration from the county slowed to 8 percent in the 1970s. As Jack Geiger explained to a Senate subcommittee, the project transformed the outlook of people who previously "had no reason to hope or dream." The TDHC and NBCFC demonstrated that change was possible and inspired multiple locally initiated projects addressing a wide range of problems. An OEO investigator noticed similar life-changing effects on participants in antipoverty programs in Wilcox County, Alabama. "For the first time in their lives, the Negroes of Wilcox County have something that they can call their own . . . something to help them exert their role in their society," he wrote. "That's what the anti-poverty program has done for them."[31]

Not everyone looked on these developments with the same enthusiasm shown by participants, administrators, and federal officials involved in the War on Poverty. Opponents of antipoverty programs viewed them as a waste of taxpayer money that undermined individualism and encouraged dependence on government. Mississippi newspaper columnist Thurman Sensing doubted that many poor people were being helped and maintained that a better way to solve social problems was by "giving free rein to the initiative and incentive of the individual citizen under the free enterprise system." The AFBF also dismissed the effectiveness of antipoverty programs and stated that they "led to confusion, waste, and duplication of effort and have contributed to inflation and concentration of power in the federal government." Plantation owner Leon Bramlett, who served for a while on the board of COI but resigned along with two other board members in November 1965, told an OEO investigator that antipoverty programs destroyed participants' individual initiative and that "Negroes all over the Delta are taking the attitude that the world owes them a living." Bramlett believed the programs were based on a "Robin Hood philosophy of taking from the provident to sustain the improvident" that bordered on socialism. A couple in Alabama expressed similar views in a letter to John Sparkman, informing him that they needed no help from the government and asking him to oppose expansions of the welfare state that threatened to destroy Americans' property rights. Like many white southerners, they viewed the poverty problem and federal initiatives to address it in racial terms that pictured the people who benefited from government programs as black and those who paid for them as white. "We still have our pride, and are willing to do honest work to pay for the services we need," they stated. "But the negro is not."[32]

The racial overtones that imbued many criticisms reflected significant overlap between segregationists and opponents of the War on Poverty. Alabama congressman George Andrews viewed the Economic Opportunity Act as "nothing but another vehicle to be used to promote integration" and pledged to do all that he could to prevent it from passing. Thomas Abernethy also suspected the Johnson administration's motives, telling a constituent that antipoverty money was being sent to Mississippi "for the purpose of financing and expanding" the civil rights movement. In 1966 an article in the *New York Times* noted that racist resistance to any program that offered equal access to black as well as white residents was one reason why southern governments were slow to apply for federal funds. Complaints by white citizens about the War on Poverty were frequently peppered with derogatory references to African Americans that cast them as lazy, promiscuous, illiterate, and lacking initiative. Objecting to the use of taxpayer funds to rehabilitate low-income neighborhoods in Monroe, Louisiana, Mrs. N. E. Roberts asserted, "Most of those Negroes are already on 'welfare'—getting more in their welfare checks, for doing nothing, (mostly bringing illegitimate children into the world for the State to support) than some of us old folks are receiving—having worked and tried to earn our keep." In Tunica County, Mississippi, journalist Neil Maxwell recorded similar sentiments expressed by local white residents who resented a job training program for displaced workers. One woman told him African Americans did not deserve any sympathy because they preferred to live on welfare. Plantation owner R. I. Abbey agreed. "They don't want to get ahead; just want to sit and rock," he stated.[33]

Some opponents of the War on Poverty used tactics that were similar to those they had deployed earlier against the civil rights movement. An anonymous flyer distributed to antipoverty workers in Mississippi warned them not to "mix with the niggers by teaching in nigger schools" and urged these "white trash scum traitors" to leave the area. White supremacists terrorized participants and torched a school that was being used for summer Head Start classes in Louisiana as well. Three churches associated with antipoverty projects in Lowndes County, Alabama, were also burned down.[34] In Wilcox County, black people who were involved in setting up the local CAA suffered economic reprisals. "Formerly sympathetic banks are now refusing additional loans presumably because of the participation of these people in voting rights and poverty committee activities," an OEO official reported. In 1967 a "summary of accomplishments and disappointments" concerning a seven-county project in rural Alabama listed several incidents of harassment and stated that in every community participants "were subjected to some intimidation from extremist groups."[35]

Segregationist opposition and the dangers faced by antipoverty program staff, boards of directors, and enrollees made it difficult to involve white southerners in the projects. A common refrain from administrators was that it was virtually impossible to meet the OEO's requirement that programs be integrated because white people refused to participate. In July 1965, African Americans working to initiate a CAP in Mississippi reported that they had tried to get support from local political and business leaders with no success. "Seemingly the white people don't want to work with the negroes to work out this program, but we want to work with them, but to no avail," they wrote. Antipoverty workers in Wilcox County also encountered problems convincing local white residents to support their efforts and ended up hiring white people from outside the region so that the project would not be staffed entirely by black people. The scarcity of white Alabamians willing to get involved was such that one man, Francis X. Walter of the Selma Inter-Religious Project, served on four different CAP boards in his area and shouldered a disproportionate responsibility for ensuring their eligibility for funding. As one black resident put it, "Francis integrates all our boards."[36]

Even poor white people who stood to benefit from antipoverty programs were reluctant to participate. A survey conducted by a CAA in Alabama to prepare for a Head Start program located 1,004 black children but only 20 white children interested in registering. South Delta Community Action Association was even less successful with its Head Start initiative in Concordia Parish, Louisiana. "In spite of extensive recruitment efforts," the group admitted in a report to the OEO, "it was not possible to enroll any white children in the program." In Mississippi, CDGM staff encountered one white boy who came to the Head Start center in Rose Hill several days in a row but was caught and reprimanded each time by relatives who did not want him to be there. When the center's director visited the family's home to ask why they would not allow him to attend the program, the boy's grandmother said it was because Head Start was "for the colored children." Many people who would have liked to participate were afraid to do so because they feared negative reactions from white supremacists in their communities. Visitors to Wilcox County, Alabama, observed that although its antipoverty programs were open to all, no white people applied for inclusion. One person they interviewed told them: "I have heard a white say to another that he wished he could go to the poverty school. The power structure not only denies the Negro, but the poor whites are being handicapped because of the few whites who have money."[37]

In some communities where county governments or school boards initiated projects, administrators deliberately discouraged white participation to ensure programs were not integrated. In 1967 the OEO's civil rights coordinator for the Southeast region, Robert Saunders, recommended denying an application for a Head Start program from school administrators in Chickasaw County, Mississippi, because they had made no effort to include white children. Superintendent Murphy Lowther explained that he only submitted the application because some local black people asked him to do it. "The applicant's attitude is that the program is only for Negroes and that he is doing them a special favor by applying," Saunders reported. The board of supervisors in Leflore County also lost funding for its Head Start program because of the failure to integrate. Administrators located all the centers in black schools and did no recruitment in white communities, then claimed that white families were just not interested. Yet when the OEO sent a representative to see if he could find some white people to participate, he managed to recruit the first ten families he spoke with.[38] Saunders observed that political leaders in the South portrayed antipoverty projects as black programs to imply that supporting the War on Poverty meant supporting civil rights, and "they never tell their poor white constituents that the programs are aimed to help all of the poor people in the community." By the late 1960s the perception that antipoverty programs helped only African Americans was so pervasive that the *Baltimore Sun* outlined plans for a self-help housing project in Wilcox County under the headline "All-Negro City Set in Alabama." In fact, an OEO official explained, the project was open to poor white as well as black people, the racial composition of the one hundred families that had expressed interest was unknown, the staff was integrated, and the board that screened applications from potential participants included four white members.[39]

Reports of waste and corruption publicized by opponents of antipoverty programs also frequently departed from reality. The War on Poverty was not devoid of problems such as misuse of federal funds, staff misconduct, or bureaucratic bungling, but unsympathetic observers presented relatively minor cases of mismanagement as if they were nefarious conspiracies to bankrupt the nation and turn it over to black political domination. Mississippi congressional representative John Bell Williams called the War on Poverty "the most colossal and collectively crooked raid on the treasury in this nation's history," charging that it benefited only "self-seeking politicians and poverty bureaucrats" who were using taxpayers' money to buy votes and reward supporters with jobs. Edwin Strickland of the Alabama Legislative Commission to Preserve the Peace accused the OEO of "using persons of questionable background and character to administer its radical programs" and channeling funds to "white-hating 'black power' groups" that aimed to take over the South's plantation counties. Thurman Sensing also believed the War on Poverty was a vehicle for political agitation and argued that efforts to help "residents of slum areas" meant "the productive citizen is penalized in order to confer privileges on the non-productive citizens." In a similar vein, an article by Vant Neff in the *Bolivar County Democrat* linked antipoverty projects to political corruption and urban riots. "Tell your Congressman *your* opinion," Neff exhorted readers. "After all, the War on Poverty is wasting *your* money!"[40]

Citizen watchdogs often did inform political leaders when they saw or heard about dubious expenditures in antipoverty programs. Thomas Herren wrote to George Andrews in August 1967 to complain, "Many of the poverty programs are being administered by negroes, ignorant and inexperienced, who are actually teaching the overthrow of the government. . . . All poverty programs and other schemes to spend the taxpayers money dreamed up by do-gooders should be carefully examined—and cut to the bone." A resident of Alabama who noticed the color logo on envelopes mailed out by a CAA in Wetumpka sent one to Congressman Bill Nichols with a note saying, "Seems to me this is mighty fancy stationery and that the 'pore folks' could be helped more if less sophisticated printing were used." Similarly, constituent John Morrow wrote to John Sparkman after seeing a group of Job Corps trainees boarding a plane to suggest that cheaper means of transportation could have been used. Sparkman passed the complaint on to Sargent Shriver, who explained that the OEO used the most cost-effective methods available and that air travel was sometimes cheapest when other expenses associated with bus or rail travel, such as meals and accommodation, were taken into account.[41]

The OEO's director and staff frequently felt compelled to correct misinformation about the agency's activities. In 1967 Shriver wrote to Louisiana congressman John Rarick to express concern that Rarick had inserted "numerous factual errors and misleading statements" into the *Congressional Record*, including claims that an OEO grantee in Lafayette had never been audited, employed subversives who hated America, and failed to properly justify or document its expenses. All these statements were false. An internal document titled "Myths and Facts about OEO" armed staffers with arguments and statistics for refuting critics, including some helpful comparisons between the amounts Americans spent each year on alcohol ($12.9 billion), tobacco ($4.3 billion), and OEO programs (about $1.5 billion). The size of the agency, with its staff of 2,600 administrators in Washington and regional offices across the nation, was tiny compared with other federal bureaucracies such as the Small Business Administration (twice the size of OEO) or the Department of Defense (500 times the size of OEO). "If you abolished OEO, fired every employee, closed down every program, the taxpayer would pay one and a half cent less on his tax dollar," the document stated. Contrary to the popular belief that the Job Corps spent $25,000 to $50,000 per year for each trainee, the actual cost was $7,000. Moreover, this was money invested, not wasted, because when trainees moved off the unemployment rolls and into jobs, their higher earnings were recycled back into the economy in the form of consumer spending and the tax dollars they repaid to the government.[42]

Outside evaluations of the OEO's activities confirmed that the agency provided valuable services to poor people and contributed to the economic well-being of the nation as a whole. At the direction of Congress, the National Advisory Council on Economic Opportunity conducted an extensive study of antipoverty efforts based on hundreds of OEO reports, research studies by independent agencies, congressional hearings and committee studies, and comments solicited from state and local officials as well as private organizations representing diverse political leanings, from the Chamber of Commerce to the Citizens Crusade Against Poverty. Although its report was not due until 1968, the council released an interim statement summarizing some of its early findings in August 1967 because of members' concerns that growing criticism and talk of abolishing the OEO threatened to destroy what they had found to be an innovative and effective means of fighting poverty.[43] Rather than extending traditional welfare services through more government "handouts," as some critics claimed, OEO programs fostered empowerment and independence by involving poor people in solving their own problems. The council's draft report in January 1968 stated that this approach appeared to be working and praised CAPs in particular. The main problem was not that billions of dollars of taxpayers' money was being wasted but that Congress was fighting "a limited, not an unconditional, war on poverty" that reached only 6 million of the nation's 30 million poor people.[44]

In 1969 the federal government's General Accounting Office (GAO) reached similar conclusions based on fourteen months of studying OEO programs. Its report stated that despite some administrative problems, these initiatives were contributing usefully to the decline in poverty rates and that their effectiveness was hindered by uncertain funding as well as conflicts with state and local officials and other federal agencies. Staff at the OEO viewed the findings as largely positive and pointed out that the GAO found no widespread corruption in antipoverty programs or any evidence to support opponents' fears that federal money was being used to fund revolutionary activity by black power groups. Justice Department officials confirmed that allegations of rampant corruption in OEO programs were unfounded. "While there are a substantial number of matters and cases in the Department arising out of these programs, the number of really significant ones is limited," the attorney general's office reported.[45]

The OEO's achievements notwithstanding, a growing number of Americans became convinced that the War on Poverty was a waste of money. Hundreds of people wrote to the president, congressional representatives, and the OEO itself to express this view, revealing what one analyst called "a startling social attitude and a degree of gullibility influenced by a conservative if not reactionary press." President Johnson's escalation of American involvement in the Vietnam War provided an additional rationale for limiting government spending on social programs. In response to a constituent urging him to vote against continued funding for the OEO and other Great Society initiatives in 1966, Thomas Abernethy agreed and indicated his fear that these programs were draining resources from the military conflict. John Stennis also thought that ensuring victory in Vietnam was more important than solving poverty in the United States. In an address to state legislators in Mississippi, Stennis stated that the war "should be the first order of business throughout Washington" and that "those Great Society programs with the billions that they are gulping down, should be relegated to the rear." The *New York Times* reported that annual spending on defense was $54 billion and projected to rise by $6 billion per year between 1965 and 1967, raising questions about whether the nation could afford to wage both the War on Poverty and the war in Vietnam.[46] Although proponents of antipoverty efforts argued that these should take priority, policy makers ultimately gave precedence to the defense budget. Even the president's commitment to the Great Society waned as discord over his foreign and domestic policies grew within the United States. In December 1966 Johnson told an aide that many people associated the War on Poverty with black people and antiwar "Commies" whose demands that funds be redirected from Vietnam to domestic programs seemed unpatriotic to other Americans. In this climate, requesting too much money for social spending could add to the backlash and risk killing the initiatives.[47]

In the late 1960s lawmakers moved to limit appropriations for the War on Poverty and passed amendments to the Economic Opportunity Act that deradicalized antipoverty programs. Concerned that political activism by CAP participants and conflicts between CAAs and local governments were undermining public support for the programs, the Johnson administration included measures that gave state and local governments a bigger role in antipoverty efforts when it submitted a revised bill to Congress for reauthorization in 1967. The final version of the legislation gave local officials the power to designate which agencies or organizations could operate programs in their communities and mandated that representation on CAP boards be balanced evenly among public officials, poor people, and community groups. Antipoverty workers were also forbidden to engage in political activity or encourage protests and demonstrations while they were on the job. Fearing for their agency's survival, OEO staff became much less willing to champion grassroots organizations that challenged traditional power relationships. In a report on the CAA in Wilcox County, Alabama, in January 1968, Al From stated that it was performing well but warned that the influence of local civil rights activists needed to be curtailed. In an election year with critics such as George Wallace ready to "blast OEO's activities" at every turn, the agency could not risk "money collected at its centers going to subsidize persons engaged in partisan political activities whether they be Republican, Democrat or Black Panther."[48]

Budget cuts as well as political concerns limited the effectiveness of antipoverty efforts in the later part of the decade. For fiscal year 1967, Congress voted to allocate $1.6 billion to OEO programs, $150 million less

Cartoon by Vic Runtz noting the federal government's shift in focus
away from the War on Poverty to the Vietnam War in the late 1960s.
Bangor Daily News, 8 November 1967. AAEC Editorial Cartoons Collection,
McCain Library and Archives, University of Southern Mississippi.

than the president initially requested. Although lawmakers later approved an additional appropriation of $75 million, many programs lost funding and had to be discontinued. In January 1968 Sargent Shriver reported to the president that Congress's failure to adequately fund the OEO necessitated the closing of 23 Job Corps centers, exclusion of 13,000 children from full-year Head Start programs, and the loss of 170,000 positions in the Neighborhood Youth Corps, among other cuts.[49] The OEO also came under pressure from the Bureau of the Budget to decrease the number of CAAs operating around the nation to a maximum of 900, about half the number that the agency was funding in 1968. The process of merging or defunding existing CAAs and refusing to fund new ones left many communities without programs, and the number of OEO field staff was reduced to levels that were not adequate to serve the CAAs that remained. A black Vietnam War veteran on leave in Alabama wrote to President Johnson to protest the cuts, stating, "The saddest thing about it is that the program calls for so little money for so many people. So much more is needed and yet Washington cut down on even that small amount to appease the Southern racists."[50] At the end of the decade the GAO reported that Head Start programs reached only one in three of those eligible to participate, and the Neighborhood Youth Corps only 6 percent. As one analyst concluded in 1970, there really was no "war" on poverty, "just a continuing series of skirmishes sorely compromised by limited resources. . . . Within two years of launching the Economic Opportunity Act it was clear that neither the nation, Congress nor the President were prepared to extend increasing financial resources to that War, and certainly not to Community Action Programs."[51]

Inadequately funded to begin with, annual battles over appropriations and the constant threat of budget cuts made it difficult for programs to function effectively or engage in long-term planning. In December 1966, with no guarantee of continued OEO support after its current contract expired, STAR administrators in Mississippi expressed concerns that some of the CAA's most dedicated and competent staff members might begin looking elsewhere for work. The director of COI reported in March 1967: "'Have you got the money yet?' is the question that has replaced 'How are you?' as most widely used in this community." As testimony to local residents' determination and organization, they continued with their plans despite delays and uncertainty of funding and managed to have a job training project up and running less than two weeks after the OEO finally approved it. Other groups were not so lucky. Unable to tell participants the exact starting date of an education program for seasonal farmworkers in Alabama, administrators found that many prospective trainees eventually gave up and migrated away to look for work. The reduced level of funding that did come through made it necessary to cut the number of centers in operation down to two, which made it hard for people who lacked transportation to attend classes. In May 1969, Jack Geiger told a Senate subcommittee that only a profound commitment to social justice kept many of the TDHC's employees working for the Mississippi health center. One local staff member likened the situation to the "short-rations" system on the plantations that "never let you look ahead or get ahead." Similarly, the National Advisory Council on Economic Opportunity's assessment of the War on Poverty noted, "Uncertainty of funds has a crippling effect on CAAs. They are admonished to plan, develop, coordinate, and evaluate. But . . . it is difficult to employ staff when there is no assurance of a relatively permanent job. It is difficult to contract with other agencies for the operation of component projects when there is no assurance of funds for financing."[52]

Politically motivated attacks on programs that threatened the traditional social order also interfered with antipoverty efforts. In Mississippi, the CDGM operated its Head Start program for just eight days before John Stennis accused its administrators of mishandling federal funds and demanded an investigation. Participants and many sympathetic observers believed Stennis's real motivation was to close down a program that was being run by African Americans and encouraged poor black people to believe they could aspire to more than a lifetime of low-wage labor or dependence on welfare. When the OEO caved to Stennis's pressure to cut off funding to the project, civil rights organizations and other supporters mobilized to defend it. Their counterpressure persuaded Sargent Shriver to temporarily restore funds, but fears that Stennis might use his position on the Senate Appropriations Committee to destroy the OEO caused federal officials to turn the Head Start programs over to Mississippi Action for Progress, a biracial group of middle-class moderates, in August 1966. The new administrators did not encourage poor people to take an active part in running the centers and tended to do things "to and for" participants instead of letting them make decisions for themselves.[53]

The CDGM's fate was not uncommon. Many of the most effective antipoverty programs across the South fell victim to similar misconduct charges and investigations that, if they did not destroy programs completely, circumscribed efforts to challenge injustice. In 1966 George

Wallace delayed funding for adult education and retraining programs for seasonal farmworkers proposed by the Lowndes County Christian Movement for Human Rights by charging that the organization was promoting black power ideology. The OEO looked into the matter, found nothing untoward, and eventually released the grant money, but it imposed conditions aimed at curbing the group's political activities and its close association with the local civil rights movement. Several activist board members voluntarily resigned their positions so as not to invite further trouble for the CAA.[54] The OEO faced increasing scrutiny from congressional representatives under pressure from their constituents in the late 1960s, along with numerous requests to investigate programs. In 1970 the Mississippi Council on Human Relations outlined the familiar pattern afflicting CAPs that proved too successful in empowering poor people: "Funds are withheld and the program closes for an indefinite period, or it operates on a volunteer basis. An investigation by a federal agency follows. The program usually is refunded with a number of senseless conditions that only create busy work and divert time and energy away from the Poor."[55]

These problems cast doubt on the federal government's reliability as an ally in poor people's struggles for justice. In June 1966, a participant in a conference at Mt. Beulah called to discuss possibilities for organizing rural black southerners to form cooperatives reported that most of the attendees opposed seeking OEO funds "as this would limit our freedom to do anything useful, relevant or meaningful." Francis X. Walter reported similar feelings of disillusionment among participants in antipoverty programs in Lowndes and Wilcox Counties in Alabama while they waited for the OEO to release the grant money being held up by Governor Wallace's black power charges. Robert Saunders argued in a 1967 memorandum that opponents' obstruction of antipoverty projects was laying the ground for riots in southern cities. Recent violence in Jackson, Mississippi, he noted, was perpetrated by black youths who saw "no future for themselves and know few friends." The following year, the chairman of the CCR's Alabama advisory committee asserted that after years of having their hopes raised and crushed, African Americans were wary of federal promises to ensure fairness or equality. "The black people of Alabama don't believe these words and they told us so in countless meetings across this State," he stated. "We say it is a serious thing when people have lost faith in their Government."[56]

The War on Poverty began with high hopes and examples of what poor people could achieve when they were empowered to devise their own solutions to the problems in their communities. However, opponents of antipoverty programs undermined their effectiveness and generated negative publicity that turned many Americans against these projects. Social justice efforts also lost some powerful allies as policy makers gave priority to fighting communism overseas rather than to ending poverty at home. The OEO's increasing reluctance to support truly transformative initiatives disappointed many activists and caused them to doubt the wisdom of relying on the federal government for help. Although they continued to pressure political leaders to allocate more money and resources to the War on Poverty, they also sought ways to enhance black autonomy and economic dependence through forming cooperatives and black-owned businesses.

CHAPTER 4

OKRA IS A THREAT

THE LOW-INCOME COOPERATIVE MOVEMENT

In a telegram to President Johnson, spokesmen for the hundreds of people who gathered at the Poor People's Conference at Mt. Beulah in January 1966 noted the government's inadequate response to agricultural displacement and asserted: "We see that we will have to solve our own problems. . . . We don't want charity. We are willing to work for ourselves if given a chance."[1] Expanding and improving access to federal programs in the South through the War on Poverty were important achievements, but the long-term goal of most participants in the freedom movement was to foster black autonomy. As they saw it, reliance on outside assistance only perpetuated poor people's dependence and ensnared them in a new plantation system. Like the landowners who evicted their tenants for registering to vote, federal officials could cut funding for social programs if they perceived participants as unruly or undeserving. For these reasons, many black southerners turned to projects that offered possibilities for economic independence and the ability to control their own affairs.

Pooling resources in cooperatives and self-help efforts became the focus for many activists as they sought solutions to black people's economic problems. Long-standing traditions of mutualism among rural poor southerners made community-owned businesses a logical choice and placed them within a lineage of creative responses to capitalist deficiencies dating back to the 1840s. The first cooperatives were formed in nineteenth-century England by a group of weavers in Rochdale who lost their jobs and were blocked from employment after an unsuccessful strike. Together they established a grocery store that they owned and operated collectively, later branching into other activities, including grain mills, bakeries, and warehouses. The core principles promulgated by the Rochdale pioneers inspired and guided cooperative businesses all over the world in later decades. Unlike traditional capitalist enterprises, cooperatives were owned and democratically controlled by their members.

Rather than seeking to enrich individuals or shareholders by maximizing profits above all other concerns, cooperatives aimed to generate social benefits as well as income for participants.[2]

Cooperative enterprises became testing grounds for innovative solutions to labor displacement in the rural South. In some counties, cooperatives revitalized struggling communities, bringing in new sources of income and allowing their member-owners to allocate their earnings as they saw fit instead of seeing the money expropriated by cheating landlords. Creating profitable, self-sustaining, employment-generating businesses demonstrated that there were other choices aside from outmigration and raised hopes for a better future for African Americans in the region. As with other projects that threatened the interests or preferred policies of regional elites, cooperatives faced sustained and sometimes violent opposition from planters, business leaders, and elected officials. Significant potential, along with enormous obstacles, became evident as cooperative efforts coalesced, received support from federal officials, and faced concerted attempts by white supremacists to destroy them.

The low-income cooperative movement emerged from and complemented the civil rights movement. Civil rights workers responded to economic reprisals against local people by helping them to organize cooperatively owned small businesses that produced handcrafted clothing, bags, and other items for purchase by supporters of the freedom struggle. Farmers' cooperatives also formed in some communities as a way to provide employment for displaced agricultural workers and assist struggling small farmers. Ezra Cunningham recalled, "You would have these meetings to decide what in the heck we were going to do with these people that had been kicked off the land. Then you got to talk to them a little bit too. So the general idea was that they did not want to go to Chicago, Detroit, all that . . . they wanted to still farm." In July 1963, CORE staff member Nanette Sachs reported that several cooperatives had formed in Mississippi "to counter-act economic pressure exerted by the white community" and predicted the growth of this trend.[3]

The immediate purpose of these efforts was to assist families who had lost their homes and income. However, cooperatives were also a way for people to declare economic independence and facilitate the continuation of the freedom movement. As one activist explained, "People are not free to act politically in their own interest when political actions can result in the loss of whatever small income they have. . . . Cooperatives represent an important step in demonstrating to poor people, and to the rest of the nation, that poor people are capable of earning a decent living and of establishing their economic and political integrity and independence."[4]

In September 1963, CORE enlisted help from the National Sharecroppers Fund (NSF) for a project aimed at encouraging these activities. Reports from Mississippi indicated a need for someone to specialize in helping black people organize cooperatives, learn about federal farm programs, and secure funding from government agencies that were concerned with rural economic development. Activists proposed to hire a rural field-worker to focus on this task. The rural specialist could teach people how to take advantage of various types of aid that were available, such as farm loans and technical assistance, rural housing loans, and job training programs. In addition to meeting immediate needs, the goal was to nurture local leaders and encourage them to seek out "longer-range economic aid—in setting up new factories and new businesses—that is available through government and private programs."[5] In May 1964, CORE hired James Mays for the position. A former teacher and self-employed farmer who had worked with the SCLC and SNCC in Georgia, Mays was familiar with agricultural policies and had successfully secured federal assistance for his own operation. Mays received training and support from the NSF and an advisory board that put him in contact with civil rights workers in Mississippi. Over the next few months Mays worked with other activists to explain the government's agricultural programs to black farmers and help them apply for assistance, pressure local officials of USDA agencies to stop discriminating against African Americans, and encourage people to form cooperatives.[6]

The West Batesville Farmers Cooperative (WBFC) in Panola County was one result of these efforts. Mays worked with members of the local voters' league and other activists to organize the group after black farmers unsuccessfully tried to pressure the local white man who usually purchased their okra crops to raise the price he paid them from 4 cents to 8 cents a pound. By 1966 the WBFC had 120 members who marketed their okra collectively to buyers in Memphis and Chicago. At the cooperative's price of 5 cents per pound, okra brought in an average of $360 an acre to farmers during the twelve-week growing season, and members planned to diversify into other vegetable crops to provide income during the fall. The cooperative also secured loans from the FmHA and the OEO to buy trucks and machinery for use by members. For many activists the psychological impact of the WBFC's success was just as important as its economic impact. Co-op president Robert Miles observed that before the farmers organized, "The white man made us think we couldn't do anything for ourselves. He made us think we were stupid, and we went along with him." Participation in the cooperative increased black farmers' confidence in their own abilities and gave them the freedom to make their own decisions. Shortly after its founding, the white landowner who had refused to pay members more for their crops told co-op secretary Bob James, "You know, you're doing this all the hard way, you know that don't you?" James replied, "Mr. Jacobs, we might be doing it the hard way, but we're the ones who is doing it."[7]

J. T. Williams, a mechanic who took a cut in pay to work for a sewing cooperative in Canton, Mississippi, expressed similar sentiments. Although he was earning less money, he said, "There's no hollering and screaming at you. . . . People here know about how to treat you." The Madison County Sewing Firm was founded by a group of women who were tired of being exploited and abused by white employers. Co-op president Maggie Douglass recalled, "People was working for white people and thought that was the only thing they could do. When we realized we could do something for ourselves, we really became involved." Civil rights workers helped the women find markets in northern cities, and a manufacturer in New York sent them some sewing machines so they could employ more workers. After the group secured a contract to make children's clothing for the CDGM, local interest in the cooperative increased. Job applications poured in from domestic workers seeking to escape from white people's kitchens. People who had been fired for civil rights activity received first preference for positions, and women who were having trouble supporting their families on low wages received priority after that. Members earned $30 a week and agreed to have $6.50 a week deducted from their paychecks to help pay for rent and utilities on the co-op's building. They also participated in all decisions about dividing or spending the profits. The chance to determine how to use the income they generated was a new experience for these women, as was the ability to participate in the freedom movement without fear of losing their jobs. "By their own account, the women feel freer than they did before about civil rights activities," one report stated. Almost half of the workers had enrolled their children in previously all-white schools, and many were active in the MFDP.[8]

The connections between African Americans' economic and political struggles were evident in other projects as well. As part of its response to the mass evictions of plantation workers who went on strike for higher wages in 1965, the Delta Ministry provided emergency shelter and assistance but also sought a more long-range solution by helping the workers to form a woodworking cooperative named Freedomcrafts. The co-op began by producing nativity sets and later expanded to include groups in four other communities, making candy and ceramics as well as wood products under the Freedomcrafts label. Freedomcrafts Candy, located in Edwards, was a direct response to the powerlessness black people felt within an economic system dominated by white racists. Tired of being shut out of employment opportunities in the town, local residents "looked for ways to become employers themselves," finding the solution in the candy cooperative.[9]

The Delta Ministry went on to establish Freedom City, a cooperative community that provided homes and employment to displaced people in Washington County. Many of the families had participated in the Greenville Air Force Base sit-in and had no homes to go to after being removed from the base. The Delta Ministry housed them for several months at Mt. Beulah and worked with the group to locate and purchase a tract of land just south of Greenville with money loaned by a northern donor. In July 1966, one hundred people moved into prefabricated homes that they had erected at the site. Their plans included farming the land, building a school, operating adult literacy and training programs, and establishing small handcraft and manufacturing enterprises with the goal of becoming self-sustaining. As Ida Mae Lawrence explained: "We asked president Johnson what side was he on, the poor folks or the millionaires. And he sent his air police with his answer. There ain't no room for the poor people in this world society. We gotta declare our independence, and build something of our own."[10]

Though the idea of creating cooperative enterprises held great appeal, most rural black people lacked the capital and other resources they needed to get started. In the spring of 1965 SNCC worker Jesse Morris set out to solve this problem by soliciting donations from northern supporters to create a revolving fund that black Mississippians could draw on to establish new businesses. After raising several thousand dollars, Morris and other activists created the Poor People's Corporation (PPC) to provide "financial assistance to initiate and sustain self-help projects of a cooperative nature that are designed to offset some of the effects of poverty." Membership was open to all poor people, with dues set at 25 cents per year. Groups of ten or more people chartered by the state as cooperatives or corporations could apply for interest-free loans with flexible repayment schedules to start small businesses, farm cooperatives, and housing projects.[11]

On 29 August the PPC held its first meeting to decide how to distribute the $5,000 its supporters had raised in the past few months. "Softly and sometimes inarticulately, spokesmen talked of their enterprises and asked for grants of $400, $1,000—nothing very large," wrote Elizabeth Sutherland in an article for the *Nation*. "They passed around sample goods while members of the audience asked detailed questions about production and marketing. It was easy to invoke nightmare visions of bad management and laughable bookkeeping, but people were going to learn by doing, and that was something the white boss had never encouraged." After discussing the potential benefits of each project and modifying some of the loan requests to stretch the available funds as far as possible, members agreed to provide funds to seven groups. The Madison County Sewing Firm in Canton received money to purchase industrial sewing machines; three leatherworking cooperatives left with several hundred dollars each to buy equipment and materials; and a group of women in McComb secured start-up funds to establish a sewing cooperative modeled on the one in Canton. A furniture-manufacturing cooperative in McComb also received assistance, along with a group in Winstonville that requested help to start a cooperative supermarket.[12]

The PPC met again in December and voted to grant funds totaling almost $3,000 to six new cooperatives. A small staff based in Jackson provided advice, support, and training to co-op members, and another office in New York helped with fund-raising, purchasing supplies, and marketing. By March 1967 the PPC had retail outlets in New York, Detroit, and Jackson, and it sold items to thousands more customers by mail order. Although some PPC-funded enterprises failed to survive for longer than a few months, twelve producer co-ops and one marketing co-op remained in business in July 1968. The organization had an overall membership of roughly 1,000 people, its catalog mailing list had grown to 65,000 addresses, and it had added 3 new stores in Massachusetts, Ohio, and Wisconsin. Workers in many PPC cooperatives earned higher incomes than they had in previous jobs. According to *New York Times* reporter Phillip Wiggins, the PPC was "an important vehicle for providing economic independence from whites for a growing number of poverty-beset Negroes."[13]

Activists in Alabama also perceived the potential of cooperatives. After the passage of civil rights legislation in the mid-1960s, a coalition of church groups and civil rights organizations formed the Selma Inter-Religious Project "to continue the relationship established between these groups and the people of Selma and Black Belt Alabama." The group's early efforts focused on providing assistance to African Americans who suffered economic reprisals for exercising their right to vote and connecting poor people to organizations that could help them. Its members helped set up the Freedom Quilting Bee, a handcraft cooperative in Wilcox County that produced quilts, baskets, and pottery. The Southern Regional Council provided a small grant, and a New Orleans–based Catholic charity sent a volunteer to provide advice and technical assistance to the cooperative's 150 participants. In summer 1966 the group sold 125 quilts for $3,200 at an auction in New York. At its first annual meeting in April 1967, the co-op reported a gross income of $10,158 and paid out $8,200 to its members. The *Alabama Council Bulletin* reported: "This organization is providing an income and more importantly an outlet for the energies and talents of persons previously denied decent wages, self-expression and recognition as a 'worthy' member of society."[14]

At around the same time, black women in Greene and Hale Counties who had worked as domestics or seasonal farm laborers responded creatively to mechanization and evictions that left many of them with no income. They began making clothing in their homes and selling their items collectively in the community, but they found they rarely made enough money to cover costs. In 1967 they incorporated as a cooperative and borrowed $2,000 from a local bank to set up a small sewing factory in Greensboro. Lewis Black, a local activist who had worked with SNCC and CORE along with serving as the NSF's state representative in Alabama, helped the women gain a contract with a garment manufacturer in New York that provided year-round employment. The group also offered a training program for other people who were interested in sewing for a living. Over the next decade, the Greene-Hale Sewing Cooperative made useful contributions to the local economy, employing a workforce of forty people and paying out more than $100,000 in wages annually during its peak production period in the mid-1970s.[15]

One of the most ambitious projects to take shape in the early days of the cooperative movement was the Southwest Alabama Farmers Cooperative Association (SWAFCA). With help from Ezra Cunningham, Lewis Black, and SCLC activists Albert Turner and Shirley Mesher, black people in the plantation counties began meeting in 1966 to discuss ways to respond to the economic and political forces that were pushing them off the land. They decided to start a program to help small farmers convert from cotton to vegetable farming and to form a cooperative to purchase supplies and market their products collectively. As part of a larger vision aimed at improving the lives of all rural poor people in the area, they planned to develop a range of social development programs, including adult literacy classes, recreational facilities, health care services, and consumer education. Many of the group's founders were older people who had participated in the demonstrations and protest marches that led to passage of the Voting Rights Act in 1965. In the second half of the decade, their biggest concern was losing their children in the exodus of black southerners to northern cities. Rather than encouraging young people to move away, they stated, "We want to be able to leave them evidence of hope for farming and good reasons for staying on the land and in the South."[16]

A survey of farmers identified more than 700 people who were willing to support the project, and in January 1967 SWAFCA was officially incorporated to serve farmers in ten counties (Choctaw, Dallas, Greene, Hale, Lowndes, Marengo, Monroe, Perry, Sumter, and Wilcox). Members elected two people from each county to serve on the board of directors, and the volunteers who had been working with the group continued to offer advice and assistance. After approaching dozens of government agencies and private organizations for funding and technical support, SWAFCA secured several small loans to buy fertilizer and seeds at reduced prices for its members.[17] Opposition from white politicians and business leaders delayed processing of a request for OEO assistance, but in May 1967 the agency approved a demonstration grant to SWAFCA. Federal officials justified the expenditure by highlighting the connections between rural and urban poverty and the potential for southern self-help projects to alleviate social problems in the nation's cities. By funding SWAFCA, the OEO aimed to test the cooperative model as a tool for fighting poverty and stemming out-migration from the rural South.[18]

Like their counterparts in Mississippi and Alabama, activists in Louisiana were also interested in exploring the potential of cooperatives to address the economic problems of rural poor people. John Zippert stepped from the civil rights movement into a lifelong career with the cooperative movement by helping black sweet potato farmers in St. Landry Parish to organize against the large growers and processors who had exploited them for decades. A white northerner from New York, Zippert participated in the Selma protests in March 1965 and volunteered

Poster created by the Office of Economic Opportunity encouraging people
to form cooperatives in the 1960s. Records of the Community Services Administration,
381-PX-3, RG 381, National Archives.

for CORE's Louisiana project that summer. In addition to encouraging voter registration and desegregation, participants met with local people to find out what issues were most important to them. Among black farmers in St. Landry, Zippert learned, the biggest problems were USDA discrimination and getting a fair price for their crops. "The people didn't say 'We want a cooperative,'" he later recalled. "They said 'We want some kind of organization that we would set up to market our own sweet potatoes.' Well after a good bit of study it seemed like the cooperative way was the best way to do that." Zippert spent the second half of 1965 meeting with farmers, researching how to set up and operate cooperatives, and locating resources that were available to support the effort. Within a few months of its founding in February 1966, the Grand Marie Vegetable Producers Cooperative (GMVPC) secured funding from SEDFRE, the OEO, and the FmHA to purchase buildings and equipment that allowed members to store, prepare, and market their crops themselves. The price farmers earned for each crate of potatoes tripled, and the cooperative also initiated an education program to increase poor people's participation in federal farm and antipoverty programs.[19]

Zippert's work in Louisiana brought him into contact with A. J. McKnight, a black Catholic priest who had been working to spread cooperative ideals and practices among his parishioners since the early 1960s. A native of Brooklyn, New York, who belonged to the Holy Ghost Fathers religious order, McKnight was assigned to serve as assistant pastor of a church in Lafayette, Louisiana, in 1953. McKnight challenged segregation in the church and worked with local black leaders to desegregate the University of Southwestern Louisiana before being transferred to Vermilion Parish in 1957. The poverty, illiteracy, and hopelessness he saw among residents of his new parish inspired him to seek ways to help them develop the confidence and skills they needed to achieve economic independence. McKnight saw this as a prerequisite for political power. "There is a close connection between economic control and political participation, for those who control the financial processes of a region also control the politics," he observed. "The poor, in acquiring economic prestige, acquire a greater voice in politics and a freer rein to exercise their civil rights." After studying cooperative principles at St. Francis University in Nova Scotia in the summer of 1960, McKnight returned to the parish and persuaded each member of his church to contribute five dollars toward setting up a buying cooperative. Parishioners used the money to buy food and other grocery items at wholesale prices and stored them in the church basement. Volunteers served as storekeepers, selling the items for a few cents more than they cost but at much lower prices than people paid at retail outlets. Members divided the profits from the sales among themselves at the end of each year.[20]

McKnight learned that successful organization of a community required paying attention to people's felt needs and that "working with poor people . . . sooner or later those needs will lead to economics." Conversations with his parishioners convinced him that cooperatively owned and operated credit unions could help solve some of their financial problems by providing a place for them to save their money and to borrow funds at reasonable interest rates. McKnight assisted people in several communities to set up federally chartered credit unions in the early 1960s. Finding the effectiveness of the enterprises limited by their small size and the poverty of their members, participants decided to form a statewide investment cooperative, Southern Consumers Cooperative (SCC), which was formally incorporated in 1964. The organization set up a loan company to help capitalize new black businesses and founded the Acadian Delight Bakery in Lake Charles with help from a $25,000 OEO grant.[21] Acadian Delight fruitcake became a popular delicacy among social justice supporters in the second half of the 1960s. In a letter to the National Student Association aimed at publicizing the cakes, John Zippert recalled the organization's earlier assistance to starving Mississippians. "Some of those recipients have now turned to self-help programs like Southern Consumers bakery which the college students in the North can now support by eating and purchasing as a gift item, our fruitcakes and candy," he stated. By 1968 the bakery had accumulated assets valued at $135,000 and planned to begin nationwide marketing and distribution of its fruitcakes.[22]

Southern Consumers Cooperative supported several other black-owned enterprises, including a gas station, a shrimp fishing business, and farmers' cooperatives like the GMVPC. After first meeting McKnight and several of his staff when they came to an early organizational meeting of the sweet potato cooperative, Zippert formed a close relationship with the group as they worked together to strengthen the co-op and help the farmers secure federal assistance. In December 1967, television crews filmed Secretary of Agriculture Orville Freeman buying GMVPC sweet potatoes at a supermarket in Washington, D.C., to celebrate the group's first shipment of produce to a major city. The publicity led to increased interest from buyers, and within a month the cooperative had sold the remainder of its sweet potatoes.[23]

In the course of developing SCC, McKnight and his supporters also created a nonprofit subsidiary, Southern Consumers Education Foundation (SCEF), to foster cooperative principles and help instill these in the movement's participants. Since joining SCEF was required before people were allowed to purchase shares in SCC, the membership of the two organizations was essentially the same. As well as providing educational services to cooperatives, SCEF secured millions of dollars in OEO funds over the next few years to operate Head Start and other antipoverty programs in several Louisiana parishes. As McKnight noted, SCC's experience in community organizing and the credibility it had built among local poor people placed it in a favorable position to take advantage of the War on Poverty. McKnight also made his first foray into raising funds from private sources to secure a small foundation grant so that SCEF could employ a full-time secretary.[24] The expertise that McKnight and other SCC leaders had acquired by the mid-1960s placed them at the forefront of developments that eventually extended the cooperative movement throughout the South.

In summer 1966, representatives from about twenty cooperatives and credit unions in Alabama, Louisiana, Mississippi, and Tennessee met at the Delta Ministry's Mt. Beulah headquarters to explore ways to coordinate and strengthen their efforts. They decided to develop a grant proposal for an initiative to support cooperative enterprises and request funding for the project from the Ford Foundation. A continuing committee that included A. J. McKnight and John Zippert worked on the plan for several months, and they eventually drafted an outline for the Southern Cooperative Development Program (SCDP), an initiative to provide loans, education, and technical assistance to low-income cooperatives. The goal was to demonstrate that, with a little help, poor people could create businesses that would generate jobs, income, and economic development in the rural South.[25] In September 1967 the Ford Foundation awarded SCEF a two-year $578,000 grant to administer the SCDP in fifteen communities in the four states represented at the Mt. Beulah meeting. The grant provided for a $75,000 revolving loan fund to help capitalize cooperative businesses and money to hire field-workers to assist local people in forming cooperatives. Advisers from the state land grant colleges, federal agencies, and the United States Cooperative League as well as SCEF would also provide training and technical assistance to participants in the cooperatives. In addition, the project aimed to develop local leadership and encourage poor people to take advantage of government resources that were available to fight poverty.[26]

McKnight directed the program, and Zippert served as its assistant director. The SCDP's field organizers were mostly local black people who were veterans of the civil rights and cooperative movements. Former CORE volunteer Bruce Baines, local activist David Noflin, and the GMVPC's Wilbert Guillory were among those who worked for the SCDP in Louisiana. Robert Miles of the WBFC joined the organizing effort in Mississippi. The SCDP's Alabama staff included Albert Turner and Ezra Cunningham of SWAFCA and Mildred Black from the Greene-Hale Sewing Cooperative. After receiving three weeks of training in Abbeville, Louisiana, field staff returned to their communities to share what they had learned. Cunningham recalled that the training the group received "really helped me. . . . And I came back and worked hard with SWAFCA and the Quilting Bee and put together other little groups." In October 1967 the Hinds County MFDP chapter publicized the presence of SCDP field representatives working in Jackson and rural areas of the county, stating that they were there to assess poor people's needs and help local residents develop ways of solving their own problems.[27]

A report on the SCDP's progress six weeks later outlined the support it provided to existing groups as well as efforts to encourage new cooperatives to form. The field-workers in Jackson helped residents form a buying club so they no longer had to pay the inflated prices charged at white-owned grocery stores, and they also assisted people with welfare, housing, and consumer complaints. Other staff in Mississippi provided management assistance to the WBFC, facilitated the expansion of a small buying club in Greenwood into a cooperatively owned supermarket, and helped members of the Miss-Lou Farmers Cooperative (comprised of farmers from four Mississippi counties and one Louisiana parish) to market their cucumbers and sweet potatoes. Organizers in Alabama assisted SWAFCA to overcome some management problems and expand its programs to include training farmers for livestock production, initiating self-help housing projects, and establishing buying clubs in its ten-county area. They also met with the leaders of the Southeast Alabama Self-Help Association (SEASHA), a group headed by John Brown Jr. that grew out of a tutorial program sponsored by Tuskegee Institute, to explore possibilities for feeder pig and vegetable production by small farmers in the area. In Louisiana, an organizer worked with the local voters' league in Madison Parish to set up a credit union, while SCDP staff in the southwestern part of the state worked on membership education for SCC, encouraging local people to patronize cooperative businesses and to start new projects.

In the course of these activities, field staff identified problems that needed to be overcome and potential areas of development for the cooperative movement, such as finding markets for products, improving rural housing, and helping small farmers to make better use of their land.[28]

Like other social justice activists, SCDP staff saw connections between the economic and the political empowerment of black Americans. "The removal of Negroes from land ownership in the South is part of a conscious policy to destroy the political power of the black vote," they observed. Cooperatives could keep small farmers in business and also address the problems of unemployment, poor housing, and lack of training opportunities for displaced workers, encouraging people to stay in the South. "Many of the communities where we are working have black majorities now in population and voter registration," the report continued. "This will make it possible to have a coordinated political and economic program in these communities." As one example, organizers mentioned Holmes County, Mississippi, as "a demonstration site with outstanding potential" because of its 76 percent black population, strong MFDP chapter, and the presence of a black cotton-ginning cooperative that was created as part of a New Deal project in the 1930s. "If an industry could be attracted to the area and a workers co-op formed this would create an economic security, power and independence to complement the county's political program," the report stated.[29]

Opponents of the freedom struggle also perceived these links. Cooperatives often encountered hostility from landowners, politicians, and business leaders who feared them both as economic competitors and as potential sources of black political empowerment. Some local administrators of USDA agencies refused their services to black farmers' organizations in Mississippi, and in November 1964 James Mays reported that arsonists had burned down two churches where "the only meeting that were held there was the Farmers League meeting." According to Mays, the church burnings helped unify rather than deter the black community. "The fact that the churches were never harmed when large meeting were held at the churches for religious services make the people know that the white community fears civil and economical organization much more than they fear larger groups praying," he stated.[30]

Like the civil rights workers of the early 1960s, people who participated in the cooperative movement did so at risk to their lives. White supremacists regularly shot into Robert Miles's home in Panola County until some of his neighbors began taking turns guarding the house so that the family could get some sleep. Wilbert Guillory endured similar attacks on his house in Louisiana because of his involvement in the GMVPC. Such stories were "a grim reminder of the conditions under which Negro farmers of the deep South are struggling," an NSF fund-raising letter stated. "This is the price their families must frequently pay when they dare to organize a cooperative or credit union which will allow them to earn the incomes they must have to remain in farming." As John Zippert observed in a letter requesting assistance for the GMVPC, "In 1969 for a Black sharecropper to bring his sweet potatoes to Grand Marie is as dangerous and heroic an act as it was for a Black man to register to vote in these same counties five years ago."[31]

Opponents also mobilized their considerable economic and political power against the cooperative movement. In October 1965 a PPC organizer reported difficulty "finding a landlord who will rent space for the people to work" along with other "harassing frustrations" that hindered her efforts. The organizers of Mississippi Fish Equity, a catfish-raising cooperative in Clay County, experienced similar problems. According to co-op leader Clifton Whitley, the group's first application for OEO funding was turned down in March 1968 after local FES staff complained about the project to the state's congressional delegation. The cooperative obtained support from church groups and foundations instead, but when they tried to purchase land they found that prices suddenly jumped from $200 to $500 an acre. Members spread a rumor that they had found an absentee landowner willing to sell to them, which helped convince a local man to change his mind and sell them a place for $350 an acre. The cooperative refused to pay similarly inflated charges for having fish ponds dug. Instead, members researched how to do it and dug the ponds themselves. Local store owners also tried to sabotage the co-op by doubling their usual charges for farm supplies. In response, co-op leaders purchased a truck and shopped in other communities where they were unknown until local businesses lowered their prices. The group's determination and ingenuity failed to impress its white neighbors, whose reactions were generally dismissive. The owner of a competing catfish operation predicted the cooperative's failure, saying, "I don't think those people have that type of get up and go about them."[32]

Cooperatives in Louisiana also encountered hostility from local residents. White leaders denounced A. J. McKnight and petitioned church leaders to transfer him out of the state. In May 1964 McKnight's superiors tried to discourage his increasing involvement in the cooperative movement by reassigning him to Lake Charles, seventy miles from his core base of support. They seemed unaware that by this time Lake Charles had the second largest number of SCC members in the state. McKnight simply transferred the Acadian Delight bakery project, then in its initial phases of development, to his new home. After SCC received OEO funds to expand the bakery, the leaders of the Holy Ghost Fathers in Rome overruled his American supervisors to grant him more time to work with cooperatives. In January 1965 McKnight was assigned to a small church near Lafayette that made few demands on his time, allowing him to work "part-time as a pastor and full-time in the Cooperative Movement."[33]

McKnight's enemies failed to oust the activist priest, but other kinds of harassment continued. A Citizens' Council newsletter ridiculed SCC's antipoverty efforts by publishing a recipe for a "Poverty Fruit Cake" that included "Dough from Taxpayers," "Sugar from the Politicians," "1/2 baked ideas," "1 Gullible Public" and similar ingredients, along with instructions to "Stir the gullible public to a frenzy. Soak the nuts in cheap wine. Mix all light and dark ingredients to a mulatto blend. Baste with Sargent Shriver. Heat quickly and serve while the odor is strong." The local newspaper reported regularly and negatively on the activities of SCC and SCEF, culminating in a front-page story on 7 December 1966 headlined, "Communists Infiltrate Poverty Program." The story prompted an investigation and several days of hearings held by the Louisiana Un-American Activities Committee in March 1967, which failed to uncover any communist involvement in the programs. Several weeks later the sheriff and district attorney raided SCC's office in Lafayette and confiscated its records. Civil rights lawyers could not dissuade a local federal judge from allowing the district attorney to keep the documents and audit SCC and SCEF. One year later, the records were "quietly returned" with no finding of any wrongdoing, but according to McKnight the anticommunist hearings and the audit did irreparable damage to SCC. "The membership confidence in the Cooperative was badly shaken," he recalled. "New investment flow from the membership, which averaged more than fifteen thousand dollars a month, dissipated. Southern Consumers Cooperative never fully recovered from that attack."[34]

The GMVPC drew similar fire from opponents. Many landlords refused to allow their tenants to join, and a group of white farmers who seemed interested in participating during the organizational phase later broke away and formed their own cooperative. The white group's leader, Frank Melancon, was a wealthy grower and shipper who employed black workers on his farm and aspired to the position of manager of the GMVPC. Other members were reluctant to place a white man in charge of the cooperative, especially since one of the main purposes of the GMVPC was to allow black people to make decisions for themselves. As one newsletter put it, "We small sweet potato farmers been going to the shippers back door for too many years—now we want a co-op so we can go in the front door, a door we built for ourselves." Melancon also clashed with John Zippert, whose ideas about how to operate the cooperative sometimes conflicted with Melancon's views on what constituted sound business practices. After the co-op's organizing committee voted against a proposal to purchase a cannery that had been pushed by the white members, Melancon and most of the seventy farmers he had signed up left the GMVPC. They formed a rival cooperative in Acadia Parish, secured a $98,000 loan from the FmHA, and proceeded to compete directly with the GMVPC.[35]

In contrast to their willing support for Melancon's cooperative, local and regional FmHA officials delayed processing of the GMVPC's request for a loan for several months. The long wait for funds to purchase facilities and equipment caused severe hardship for the cooperative. In June and July 1966, as farmers' sweet potatoes ripened rapidly in the fields, the GMVPC scrambled to obtain funds from other sources so that members could harvest the crops before they spoiled. A $5,000 emergency loan from SEDFRE and some additional help from the Aaron E. Norman Foundation came just in time to save the cooperative, according to GMVPC president Joseph Lee Marlbrough.[36] This near-death experience shook many members' confidence, however, and the cooperative continued to be plagued by problems. The GMVPC had no money to pay farmers when they brought their potatoes to the co-op, so members had to wait until the potatoes had been washed, graded, and shipped to a broker in Lafayette before they were reimbursed. The broker was often slow to pay the cooperative, leading to corresponding delays in payments to farmers. The GMVPC fared little better when it tried shipping produce directly to northern buyers. Several companies went out of business without paying for the crops they purchased from the co-op. John Zippert summed up the GMVPC's experience in a letter to SEDFRE director Marvin Rich: "We have had every sort of obstacle, bureaucratic delay, intimidation, mechanical difficulties and disappointment sent our way."[37]

The strongest and most organized resistance to black cooperatives came from white supremacists in Alabama. After SWAFCA applied for a $503,460 grant from the OEO in January 1967, dozens of opponents including local and state officials, businesspeople, antipoverty agency heads, the Alabama congressional delegation, and a few black leaders joined a chorus of protest aimed at preventing the federal government from funding the organization. State senator Walter Givhan and others claimed that Shirley Mesher was a communist seeking to organize a movement of black farmers to overthrow the government, citing as evidence that Mesher was "most secretive about her personal background" and had no visible source of income and her methods showed "extensive training in the field or organization."[38] The president of Whitfield Pickle Company in Montgomery expressed concern that federal funds would be used to "control this Negro vote as a bloc and they will vote to the disadvantage of private enterprise and excessive taxation of established business." Black lawyer Orzell Billingsley Jr. warned the OEO that SWAFCA relied "too heavily on those who do not seem to have any leadership potential to develop and ignores and drives way those leaders of stability" (like himself). Selma mayor Joe Smitherman and other city officials listed racial violence, disillusionment with community action, mistrust of elected officials, and the disintegration of the state Democratic Party as some of the dire consequences that could result from funding SWAFCA. They proposed submitting an alternative proposal through the Dallas-Selma Community Action Agency instead.[39] The leaders of the Little River Community Action Program in Monroe County attacked both SWAFCA and the Dallas-Selma plan, arguing that SWAFCA's programs would only create "confusion [and] disorganization" and stating that they would not cooperate with any outside group that tried to operate in the county. Early in April both of Alabama's senators and four of its House representatives met with OEO officials for three hours in an attempt to dissuade them from supporting SWAFCA.[40]

On the other side, social justice activists mobilized to put pressure on the OEO to fund the cooperative. The Leadership Conference on Civil Rights, the NAACP, and the American Friends Service Committee were among dozens of organizations that supported SWAFCA, and the OEO heard directly from prominent black leaders, including A. Phillip Randolph, Martin Luther King Jr., and Roy Wilkins. The CCR and officials charged with enforcing antidiscrimination regulations in government programs also joined the effort. Francis X. Walter outlined the real motives behind opposition to SWAFCA in an article for the Selma Inter-Religious Project's April newsletter: the co-op would force processing companies to pay black farmers more for their crops; it would encourage black people to stay in the region instead of migrating away; and, unlike the funds that went to the existing CAAs, the money SWAFCA received from the OEO would be beyond white people's control. "Yes Lord, we're subversive, vegetables are subversive Lord," he wrote. "Okra is a threat. . . . Whitfield Pickle Company done admitted it had to raise its cucumber price from 5 to 6 cents a pound 'cause of us. They signed with us Lord, then Mr. Whitfield took off with Mayor Smitherman to Washington to bust us up." According to Walter, SWAFCA interfered with white supremacists' efforts to turn Alabama into "a land rolling in pasture, forested with pulp wood, empty of Negroes."[41]

The fight to fund SWAFCA deployed the same methods and structure that activists had used to stave off similar attacks on the CDGM in Mississippi a few months earlier. Supporters wrote and called their congressional representatives, and SWAFCA members traveled to Washington to argue their case before federal officials. After hearing the arguments on both sides, on 11 May 1967 the OEO announced a grant of $399,967 to SWAFCA—roughly $100,000 less than the group's original request. Opponents had convinced the OEO not to fund non-farm-related portions of the proposal to avoid competition between SWAFCA and the local CAAs. In a letter explaining the OEO's decision, deputy director Bertrand Harding attempted to reassure white Alabamians that the agency was not funding a black revolution. A thorough check into the backgrounds of SWAFCA organizers and board members had found no evidence of communist connections or other subversive tendencies, and the OEO's grant conditions required SWAFCA to take active measures to encourage white farmers to join. Contrary to opponents' accusations that the cooperative had been organized in a secretive manner, SWAFCA had held open meetings throughout its organizational phase and invited local extension agents, federal officials, and agricultural specialists from Tuskegee and Auburn Universities to attend. The OEO was confident that the grant would be put to good use and serve as a useful demonstration experiment "in our efforts to assist poor farmers to help themselves."[42]

The OEO's compromise and its arguments justifying the funding failed to appease SWAFCA's opponents, and the co-op encountered further obstruction when it tried to secure funding from other federal agencies. In October 1967 SWAFCA applied for a loan of $852,000 from the FmHA to expand its services to farmers, construct processing facilities, and enable members to borrow operating funds from the cooperative. The FmHA expressed willingness to provide $450,000 to begin the expansion and promised to "make every effort" to increase its support for the cooperative later if necessary. Upon learning of the FmHA's plans, Congressman Bill Nichols wrote to Orville Freeman in protest, citing concerns about wasteful government spending, the project's lack of economic feasibility, and duplication of services that were already provided by the USDA.[43] Nichols met with Freeman personally in March 1968 to reiterate these arguments, and other Alabama representatives also registered their opposition. Meanwhile, SWAFCA leaders and OEO officials who supported the loan request worked to convince the FmHA that $450,000 was not enough to ensure survival of the cooperative. Since the money was to come from Economic Opportunity Loan funds that had been delegated to the FmHA by the OEO, they argued, the agriculture officials should fully fund SWAFCA "as a test and demonstration" of their commitment to rural antipoverty efforts.[44]

On 14 March the FmHA approved a loan for $850,000 to SWAFCA, but the contract imposed stringent conditions that seemed designed to take control of the organization away from its members and transfer key decisions to USDA officials in Alabama. Consultants and OEO staff who examined the agreement found that many of its stipulations conflicted with both normal FmHA rules and sound business practices. One provision confined the cooperative to selling in the processing market and prohibited sales in the more profitable fresh produce market, and another prevented SWAFCA from making loans with repayment periods longer than thirty days. The agreement also required the co-op to secure FmHA approval for all expenditures of the loan funds and to gain permission to borrow money from other sources. Under these conditions, local FmHA staff who had already demonstrated their hostility toward SWAFCA could easily paralyze or destroy the cooperative. Moreover, OEO analysts noted, such close supervision would defeat the purpose of their own agency's demonstration grant, which was supposed to test the effectiveness of cooperatives owned and operated by poor people themselves. "It is not a question of whether FHA can run a marketing co-op, but whether SWAFCA can," they pointed out.[45]

The cooperative's leaders refused to sign the agreement. Although they were willing to accept some guidance from the FmHA, they would not trade members' "new hope of economic independence for a Federal loan."[46] Co-op president William Harrison and manager Calvin Orsborn wrote to Orville Freeman on 13 May explaining their objections to the contract and asking him to review the conditions set by the FmHA. While they understood that some restrictions were necessary for the federal government to protect its financial interest and welcomed any assistance the FmHA could provide, they emphasized that this must be done in a way that preserved the ability of co-op members to make decisions for themselves. Harrison and Orsborn also expressed sensitivity to the difficulties Freeman faced in supporting SWAFCA and sought to boost the agriculture secretary's resolve. "We recognize the political pressures on the Department of Agriculture not to make a loan to a predominantly black Cooperative, such as ours, in the State of Alabama," they said. "But we feel that SWAFCA, open to all poor farmers, offers a real chance for self-improvement on a pay-as-you-go basis to many who have never had this opportunity before."[47]

The letter elicited a favorable response from the USDA's top officials. After agency heads indicated their willingness to modify the terms of the agreement, eight SWAFCA representatives traveled to Washington, D.C., to meet with Freeman and Assistant Secretary John Baker. During seventeen hours of negotiations, the farmers described local FmHA agents' history of discrimination against black Alabamians and previous efforts to undermine the cooperative, eventually convincing federal officials to delete most of the loan restrictions. The result was an agreement that gave SWAFCA considerable autonomy to manage its own affairs and to deal directly with USDA staff in Washington instead of the county supervisors in Alabama. According to SWAFCA attorney Stanley Zimmerman, the new contract was "a real victory for low-income farm co-ops."[48]

Despite making allies at the federal level, SWAFCA remained under attack in its own state. On 14 March, the same day the FmHA made its original loan offer, Bill Nichols wrote to Alabama congressman George Andrews asking him to use his authority as chairman of a House subcommittee on legislative appropriations to demand an audit of SWAFCA by the GAO. Andrews promptly complied, and Nichols cited the GAO audit in a telegram aimed at blocking additional funding that SWAFCA managed to secure from the EDA in May. Nichols asked the agency to delay its decision until the audit was complete. "GAO is having difficulty in obtaining information from SWAFCA," he claimed. "Also, state and regional Economic Development Administration offices should have been consulted before making this grant." An EDA official responded saying that, to his knowledge, SWAFCA was cooperating fully with the GAO investigation and that the EDA had consulted with its area office in Huntsville, Alabama, before making its decision. As further reassurance to the congressman, he explained that the contract with SWAFCA required the cooperative to submit monthly progress reports and provide receipts for its expenditures, thus safeguarding taxpayers' money.[49]

As Alabama's political leaders battled federal officials in Washington, the state's landowners and business leaders tried to sabotage SWAFCA at the local level. Large growers refused to lease land to black farmers who wanted to grow crops for SWAFCA. Processing companies also shunned doing business with the co-op and announced they would contract only with individual farmers. When a SWAFCA representative managed to sell some turnip greens to a local supermarket, the buyer warned him that he should always tell people the crops were his own because no one would purchase produce if they knew it came from the cooperative. The difficulties of finding sales outlets within Alabama forced SWAFCA to ship its products out of state, which created logistical problems and cut into its profits. Some local drivers hired to transport the vegetables deliberately turned off the refrigeration in their trucks and allowed the produce to spoil. After attacking SWAFCA for its lack of integration during the effort to block the OEO grant, opponents ensured that it remained a mostly black organization by discouraging white participation. The cooperative lost a capable white horticultural expert it employed in 1967 "in part because his wife was unable to bear the social ostracism visited on them by the Selma white community."[50]

Opponents also tried to undermine support for SWAFCA among the people it aimed to serve. In June 1968 the consulting firm employed by the OEO to conduct monthly evaluations of SWAFCA's progress reported that after a meeting between the field staff and USDA experts aimed at improving grading practices, an assistant county agent who misunderstood part of the discussion told his supervisor that SWAFCA was buying only the less valuable larger cucumbers from farmers and throwing out the more desirable small ones. "This story has since been spread as an example of SWAFCA's lack of business acumen," the analysts stated. "Insofar as we can determine, there is no truth in it." The same report noted that Whitfield Pickle Company had introduced some "unusual" grading practices of its own that year, accepting cucumbers that it normally would have rejected. Sometimes the company's buying stations did this only for a few days before reverting to their regular standards—just long enough to create suspicions that SWAFCA was cheating its members when it subjected them to conventional grading procedures. One farmer who brought 500 pounds of cucumbers to a SWAFCA station for sorting later took his rejected items to a Whitfield station, where he received more for the substandard produce than SWAFCA had paid for the cucumbers it accepted. "Whatever the purpose [of Whitfield's actions] may have been," the report stated, "the result was to embarrass SWAFCA."[51]

Local newspapers joined the effort to discredit the cooperative, often distorting facts or relating inaccurate information to question its legitimacy. During the furor over the OEO grant in March 1967, the *Selma Times Journal* argued that "any underwriting or award of funds to the SWAFCA would be the same as the OEO underwriting the Black Panthers or Black Muslims in an extension of their influence." After the cooperative received its grant, news media spread false rumors that SWAFCA had caused members' crops to spoil by using faulty equipment and that it had sent grading machines to places with no electricity.[52] In March 1968 a report by James Free in the *Birmingham News* suggested that congressional representatives had been trying unsuccessfully for months to obtain copies of SWAFCA's financial records so they could check its expenditures of federal funds. In reality, as editorial writer Jerry Hornsby found when he was working on a follow-up story, the records were easily available upon request from the OEO, and members of the state's congressional delegation had only recently asked for them. The newspaper refused to print Hornsby's story correcting Free's account, and Hornsby resigned in protest.[53] Later that month state news media loudly publicized the arrest of SWAFCA field representative Percy Johnson for allegedly growing marijuana on his property. An OEO staff member looking into the incident reported: "Johnson, a 61-year old Negro, has denied any knowledge of the marijuana. In view of the political implications, the possibility of a plant cannot be ruled out."[54]

Attempts to obstruct SWAFCA's operations continued through the late 1960s. Governor Albert Brewer vetoed a second OEO grant of $595,751 awarded in June 1968, arguing that the cooperative did not broadly represent the community where it was active, that the OEO had bypassed him when it approved the grant, and that the GAO audit placed SWAFCA under suspicion. The OEO responded by stating that SWAFCA was meant to serve low-income farmers in Alabama, not the entire community; that it had given Brewer the required thirty days to review the grant before approving it; and that GAO audits of federally funded programs were routine and did not necessarily imply any wrongdoing.[55] After the agency overrode the governor's veto, Joe Smitherman accused SWAFCA of misusing federal funds and obtained a court injunction preventing the cooperative from spending any of the $1.5 million in grants and loans it had received from the OEO and the FmHA until the GAO audit was complete. On 30 October SWAFCA filed suit in federal court to lift the injunction and demand an end to "harassment and intimidation" by state and local officials. At the OEO's request, the Department of Justice issued an injunction against Smitherman's injunction, but the legal problems delayed SWAFCA's hiring of new staff to conduct surveys of members' crop production estimates and interfered with its planning.[56]

Not all of SWAFCA's problems were the result of external hostility. Mismanagement and divisions among the participants themselves also weakened the organization and provided ammunition for its critics. According to one observer, SWAFCA's inexperienced board members sometimes exceeded their policy-making role and interfered with the activities of the staff, which created confusion and delays in day-to-day operations. Calvin Orsborn had other business interests that prevented him from managing the cooperative full-time, and he often failed to carry out directives from the board. Outside consultants conducting an evaluation in May 1968 found that Orsborn was rarely "available and actually on the SWAFCA grounds" and that he was unable to provide important information that they requested. Other problems highlighted in the report included poor record keeping, delays in getting supplies and equipment, and hesitancy among the members to fully support the cooperative. Many farmers were "hedging their bets on SWAFCA's still dubious future" by signing contracts with Whitfield and other processing companies as well as SWAFCA.[57]

Tension between Orsborn and board members finally resulted in his dismissal in June 1968. Six weeks later SWAFCA discovered that the former manager had embezzled funds from the cooperative. Since December 1967, Orsborn had transferred $75,000 of the federal funds he administered into a private bank account and withdrawn $14,000 of the money for his personal use. Board members only discovered the theft after the bank accidentally sent an account statement to SWAFCA instead of to Orsborn. The co-op recovered most of the money and threatened to sue the bank for allowing the transactions without proper authorization from the board. An OEO official concluded that SWAFCA was not to blame for the situation and acted quickly to correct it, but the incident was widely publicized and seemed to lend substance to accusations that the group was misusing taxpayers' money. The GAO mentioned the stolen funds in a preliminary report issued to Alabama congressmen in October 1968, copies of which "mysteriously" made their way to state newspaper offices despite the GAO's warning not to disclose the contents of the document. An article in the *Montgomery Advertiser* on 6 November implied that the incident cast doubt on the integrity of the entire organization, noting that the GAO's audit had been hindered by the disorganized state of SWAFCA's financial records, the theft of some papers, and the difficulty of obtaining information from Orsborn. Congressman Nichols was quoted as saying he could not understand "why the OEO would want to continue to pour money into SWAFCA after this report."[58]

The GAO's final report, issued in January 1969, found no evidence that SWAFCA had misappropriated federal funds. However, it criticized SWAFCA's lax accounting practices, reiterated many of the management problems observed by earlier evaluators, and made several recommendations for improvement. As the GAO observed, Orsborn's failings were "a significant factor contributing to the weaknesses in program activities." Under the leadership of new manager William Harrison, SWAFCA implemented substantial reforms. A Selma accounting firm helped the cooperative to develop more efficient accounting and inventory systems, and in accordance with the conditions of its second OEO grant, SWAFCA submitted monthly financial reports to federal officials. The cooperative also enlisted SEDFRE's assistance in training participants at all levels to better understand their roles. In January 1969 SEDFRE and SCDP staff held a series of workshops for SWAFCA's board, staff, and members to improve their knowledge of cooperative principles, develop greater commitment to the organization, and enhance their communication skills.[59]

Internal divisions, inexperience, and management problems affected many of the other low-income cooperatives as well. After visiting several groups in Alabama in December 1966, John Zippert concluded that most of the new businesses were likely to fail unless they received sustained and coordinated assistance. One group in Hale County "seemed to lack any clear analysis of what common problems brought them together to form a co-op business except a sort of 'close ended hopelessness.'" Overcoming the challenges of organizing production, locating markets, and keeping accurate financial records was a major undertaking. Zippert acknowledged, "We have set ourselves no easy task if we expect to organize poor farmers in the Black Belt cooperatively." Similarly, a report on progress at one of the PPC's sewing enterprises in December 1968 stated that the last few months had been "a trying and confusing period." Many workers seemed interested only in having a job, and their appreciation for what it took to successfully operate a collectively owned and managed business was limited. There was a lot of friction among participants, and the quality of the items they produced was uneven. Despite having more autonomy, money remained tight for both individual members and the co-op as a whole. Poverty and frustration were taking their toll, making continued commitment to the cooperative doubtful.[60]

The NBCFC in Mississippi also suffered from dissension among members and declining support for the cooperative after its first few years. In 1969 a proposal to build a cannery so that the co-op could move into producing processed food generated disagreements among board members and other participants that eventually killed the idea. After L. C. Dorsey took over as project director in October that year, she encountered some hostility from male members who resisted her authority. Dorsey tried to win them over by working with them in the fields, but they remained suspicious of her ability to run the cooperative. Eventually she suggested replacing the cooperative's manager, John Brown. As much as the director and everyone else in the NBCFC liked and respected Brown, Dorsey worried that inadequate crop planning, record keeping, and equipment maintenance were hindering the cooperative's progress. Most board members could not bring themselves to fire Brown, and they voted against Dorsey's advice. When an OEO consultant later made the same suggestion, the board supported it by a narrow vote that badly split the group.[61]

In addition to the divisions among the cooperative's leaders, tensions existed between its field laborers and managerial staff. The people whose job it was to pick vegetables in the heat of a Mississippi summer often resented those who directed operations from the comfort of their offices. The NBCFC came up against a problem that commonly afflicted the low-income farm cooperatives: the intense dislike that many black southerners had developed toward agricultural labor. Although a major goal of the cooperatives was to enable African Americans to remain on the land, not everyone felt drawn to farming as a vocation. Younger people, especially, preferred other occupations if given the chance. Some NBCFC participants seemed to view the cooperative as just another plantation that exploited them rather than an opportunity to work for themselves. Just like white landowners during the slavery and Jim Crow eras, the NBCFC endured theft, negligence, and poorly performed work at the hands of its employees.[62] Delta Ministry staff member Thelma Barnes reported a similar situation at nearby Freedom City in 1967. The farm manager devoted only limited time to the project, and much of the cooperative's equipment needed repair because of inadequate maintenance.

Unlike USDA administrators in Alabama, the local county agent had been supportive and helpful. "The real problem is the people just don't like to farm," Barnes concluded.[63]

Cooperatives also faced obstacles that resulted unavoidably from the limited resources available to rural poor people. A fundamental problem for all these organizations was the lack of operating capital. Traditional sources of credit were either reluctant to loan money to such high-risk enterprises or deliberately withheld funds in an effort to destroy them. Even the most financially sound cooperatives found it hard to borrow money. Southern Consumers Cooperative, for example, could not convince local banks in Louisiana to loan it $5,000 even though it owned property valued at $30,000 to use as collateral. The inability to secure financing from the private sector forced most cooperatives to rely on government and foundation funds that were often inadequate and came with restrictions on their use, interfering with the goal of achieving economic independence. In 1967 Jake Ayers identified insufficient capital as a key factor preventing Freedomcrafts in Mississippi from becoming a thriving business. The cooperative's carved nativity sets sold well, and it had recently decided to diversify into other wood products, but lack of money meant it could only afford to make items that were ordered and paid for thirty days in advance. According to Ayers, these limitations lost the cooperative a considerable amount of business and limited its ability to become self-sustaining.[64]

Another challenge faced by many cooperatives was their members' lack of education and business skills. The Jim Crow school system had left most rural black southerners with only an elementary education, and many older people could barely read or write. Calvin Orsborn pointed to this when he was taken to task over the state of SWAFCA's financial records just before he was fired. According to the minutes of a board meeting held in June 1968, Orsborn argued in his defense that "our project is experimental and we are somewhat prohibited by OEO from hiring people of a certain caliber and we cannot compare the system that this infant organization has to that of [other organizations] for we are working with grassroots people and this program is designed for such." Trainers who worked with the cooperative's board of directors in 1969 found that some members' limited education and lack of confidence hindered their ability to make decisions, while others were too proud to admit deficiencies in their own expertise and pushed the cooperative into taking unwise actions as a result.[65]

Local African Americans with business or management experience were hard to find. When people who did have some training came in to assist cooperatives, the results were not always to strengthen the enterprise. Arrogance or an inability to acknowledge that poor people had valuable contributions to make to an organization could obstruct the efforts of otherwise competent and well-intentioned managers. For their part, poor people often suspected that outsiders' real motives were to exploit rather than to help them. People from outside the community who volunteered or took jobs with low-income cooperatives needed special skills of their own to work effectively with participants. As the Freedom Quilting Bee's advisory committee pointed out when it sought candidates for the position of cooperative manager, applicants needed to demonstrate more than just the ability to develop work plans, keep accounts, and handle correspondence. The job also required "the patience and humility necessary to live and work among the poor." Recruiting middle-class black or white people to help was a necessary short-term measure, but as one analyst noted, the real solution was to train local residents to take over these responsibilities themselves. Unless poor people gained control of their own organizations, power would remain with "those who can manipulate, those who can exploit, those who can wheel and deal and the poor will never be involved, only duped."[66]

The early experiments with black economic empowerment in the 1960s demonstrated both the potential and the challenges facing the cooperative movement. Rural poor people were intensely interested in projects that promised to enhance their financial security and political freedom. Dedicated activists from within and outside the South whose organizing techniques were honed in the civil rights movement had shown their willingness to further the struggle for social justice. Federal officials also seemed supportive of the effort, at least for the time being. But the rise of the low-income cooperatives and the threat they posed to existing economic structures provoked a commensurate response from powerful opponents. In addition, the movement exposed the difficulties inherent in efforts to create businesses that were owned and operated by people with limited finances and expertise. John Zippert's prediction that the cooperative movement had set itself "no easy task" was borne out in later decades as activists attempted to ensure the long-term survival of these projects, even as the nation's political climate became increasingly hostile to their efforts.

CHAPTER 5

OEO IS FINISHED

FEDERAL WITHDRAWAL AND THE RETURN TO STATES' RIGHTS

Already wavering in the late 1960s, the federal government's commitment to antipoverty initiatives weakened further over the course of the next decade as political leaders who were less disposed toward these types of investments gained dominance in the White House and Congress. Voters who were unhappy with the Johnson administration's support for civil rights initiatives and attempts to address the deeper legacies of racism defected from the Democratic Party and began casting their votes for Republican candidates instead. A shared interest in limiting the federal government's influence in their lives and communities drew segregationists together with conservative business leaders concerned for the future of free enterprise, and Republican Party leaders were not above exploiting racism to encourage southern Democrats to vote for them. Social justice activists watched with dismay as the party that was founded by antislavery activists a century earlier embraced opponents of black equality and morphed into the new party of white supremacy in the post–civil rights era.

Under the administration of President Richard Nixon and his successor, Gerald Ford, federal officials withdrew support for antipoverty projects and efforts to empower black Americans. Attempts to ensure a more equitable distribution of the nation's wealth stalled as Nixon pared back the OEO and restored control over many programs to state and local governments. Supporters of the War on Poverty fought these policies and managed to preserve some core initiatives, but at the end of the 1970s the dream of a Great Society that offered all citizens the same opportunities for education, employment, and economic security remained far out of reach. Increasingly, political leaders eschewed government intervention on behalf of disadvantaged communities in favor of approaches that allowed private enterprise and market forces to determine the distribution of resources, with results that did not bode well for rural black southerners.

The civil rights movement and social turmoil of the 1960s precipitated a realignment of southern and national politics in the late twentieth century. Angered by the Democratic Party's support for the black freedom movement and resentful of federal meddling in the region, many white southerners turned to Republican candidates whose policies seemed less likely to overturn the existing social order. Lifelong Democrats expressed disgust at attempts to force integration on the South and threatened to switch their allegiance if these trends continued. In a letter to George Andrews in 1963, constituent A. Q. Weaver self-identified as a "firm Democrat" but warned, "based on present administration actions unless there are some drastic changes, it will be necessary for me to vote otherwise in the coming elections." After passage of the Voting Rights Act in 1965, G. M. Ogle informed John Sparkman: "I have always been a Democrat and my Dad was, but I am afraid I will have to go Republican after I see the way things is going. I do hope we have some one in the White House that will [say] no to our nigger loving Pres. before he gives Washington to his pet Negros." Louisiana resident Martha Kilgore expressed both the racial and economic concerns that motived many people to switch their party allegiance when she complained about the effects of antipoverty programs on black people's work ethic. "I must protest the 'Great Society' of President Johnson," she exclaimed in a letter to Russell Long. "Do you realize that I cannot hire a negro day worker from the Louisiana employment service, & have not had one referred to me in months? . . . When they will not work, we are really headed for socialism—Please do something *right now* before I take the stump for the Republicans."[1]

Disaffected Democrats found a champion in the outspoken segregationist George Wallace, who challenged Lyndon Johnson for the party's presidential nomination in 1964. Wallace strongly opposed civil rights legislation and warned white Americans that it threatened individual liberties, along with their jobs, schools, and neighborhoods. In his view, the new laws forced employers to hire black people over white applicants, undermined private property rights, and eliminated business owners' ability to choose their own clientele, all of which represented an alarming concentration of power in the national government. Reelecting President

Johnson would mean a further erosion of fundamental rights, Wallace argued, whereas a vote for him would "let the people in Washington know that we want them to leave our homes, schools, jobs, business and farms alone." Although Wallace withdrew from the race in July, his unexpectedly strong showing in early primary elections indicated that his message resonated with many voters.[2]

Divisions within the Democratic Party deeply concerned some white southerners. Noting that Republicans were beginning to win over more voters in Mississippi, the editors of the *Jackson Clarion-Ledger* urged Democrats to unite behind Paul Johnson in the state's gubernatorial election of 1963. Republicans were playing a dangerous game that could lead to "minority control of the state by splitting the white, conservative majority," they claimed. Mississippi state senator William Alexander also warned of a potentially disastrous split among white voters that could ultimately be self-defeating. If the Republican Party gained strength in the South, he argued, it would mean the end of the one-party system that underpinned the region's race and class hierarchies. "We do not need two parties and we cannot afford two parties," he asserted. "It splits the conservatives to such an extent that the negroes and/or [labor] or both could gobble us up."[3]

Democratic leaders were unable to prevent defections, and many eventually joined the exodus to the Republican Party themselves. Senator Strom Thurmond of South Carolina, a prominent segregationist, left the Democratic Party in September 1964 to support Republican presidential candidate Barry Goldwater, whose campaign emphasized the need to restore limited government and roundly criticized Johnson's civil rights and social welfare initiatives. Thurmond praised Goldwater for resisting "the liberal, left-wing, socialist establishment in this country—even in his own party—in order to stand by his convictions as to the meaning and intent of the founding fathers." Goldwater carried all five Deep South states in the election and secured 27 million votes nationwide, giving hope to some white supremacists that the Republican Party could lead the country back from the precipice of racial equality.[4] Observers noted that Goldwater's supporters included many people who were hostile toward the civil rights movement and who were gaining influence in the state party organizations, giving them a racist tinge. While some in the party's liberal wing expressed distaste for these developments, other Republican leaders welcomed or actively courted disaffected white racists, viewing them as a key source of support that could help them regain political dominance over the nation. Republican National Committee head William Miller acknowledged that racism was helping the party to win elections but asked, "Why shouldn't we take advantage of it? The Democrats have been getting away with it for years."[5]

Recent scholarship on the Republican Party's "southern strategy" has noted that racial anxieties were not the only factor that lay behind the political conversion of white southerners in the late twentieth century.[6] Religious beliefs, reactions against federal overreach, and a commitment to defending free enterprise against encroachments by the welfare state undoubtedly motivated many voters. Yet the region's racialized class structure and social relationships made it difficult to disentangle these concerns from fundamental assumptions about black people that influenced white people's thinking on other issues. Segregationists cited the Bible to rationalize the racial hierarchies that they fought to preserve and argued that exposing white schoolchildren to black southerners' inferior cultural values violated their Christian faith. Defenders of individual rights against federal tyranny focused particularly on the enforcement of civil rights laws, warning that attempts to integrate schools and neighborhoods were among the first steps in a slide toward dictatorship that included outlawing prayer in schools and regulating gun ownership, among other dangers. Criticisms of government efforts to address economic inequality frequently conflated poor people with African Americans, reflecting racist beliefs that attributed these disparities to black people's inherent deficiencies, not class oppression.

Racial themes intersected with social, political, and economic concerns in opponents' reactions against government policy. An issue of a newsletter titled *Christian Conservative Communique* that circulated in Mississippi in May 1965 was entirely devoted to attacking civil rights legislation, interracialism, and antipoverty programs and referred to two white women who were working for racial equality in Rankin County as "Disciples of Satan." Similarly, the proliferation of private, all-white Christian academies in the 1960s and 1970s was not simply an assertion of parents' right to decide where to send their children to school but also reflected the connections between these families' religious beliefs and their belief in white supremacy. Among the lessons taught in such schools, according to one student, were that "the Supreme Court is under Communist control and that integration is a plot made up by Communists and Jews." The Mississippi Council on Human Relations observed in 1971, "One of the more outrageous myths developing around the mushrooming private 'academy' movement is that these racist institutions are really *okay*, more or less like parochial school." The nickname applied by local residents to a private school in Starkville—"Bigot High"—showed that few people were deceived by the "whitewash propaganda."[7]

Between the mid-1960s and early 1970s, opponents of black equality learned to moderate their rhetoric and cast racist agendas in terms that had broader appeal, focusing on the need to protect constitutional principles, property rights, and American ideals. In 1966, for instance, Thomas Abernethy touted a 100 percent voting record rating from Americans for Constitutional Action by explaining that it meant he had "consistently voted against Civil Rights, the War on Poverty . . . and other Great Society programs that have resulted in inflation, violence and a dangerous trend toward socialist dictatorship." When he was honored by the same organization five years later, the news release announcing the award deployed more neutral language, emphasizing Abernethy's devotion to "individual rights, law and order, a sound dollar and a growing economy." Senator Russell Long's staff also suggested avoiding open professions of racism in a planned speech to the National Association of Real Estate Boards. A proposed outline for the speech advised him to "emphasize that you are not a racist" and to explain that his opposition to legislation banning discrimination in housing stemmed from his belief that it undermined the rights of white and black homeowners alike. White Louisianian Henry Brisbay adopted a similar tactic in a letter to Strom Thurmond opposing the use of busing to integrate the nation's public schools. After stating that integration aimed to "bring about the mass-hybridization of American society—the goal of Liberalism," Brisbay attempted to soften the reference to miscegenation by framing his opposition to busing as a commitment to liberty: "The President should be reminded that freemen have risen before to quell intolerance and tyranny. They will do so again. A large part of the resistance to forced-busing no doubt is racial—but basically the issue is freedom." In the same vein, Citizens' Council leaders linked school desegregation with other examples of excessive government interference in people's lives, calling the Supreme Court's decision in *Brown v. Board of Education* a violation of the Constitution and urging readers to write to Congress to oppose government regulations that threatened their rights.[8]

The ideas expressed in the *Citizen* during the transition from Jim Crow to the post–civil rights era provide a window into the trajectory of white supremacist beliefs and rhetoric. In the early 1960s the publication's editors and contributors attacked civil rights activists for generating "racial chaos, friction and sectional division in our nation," advocated "voluntary repatriation" of black citizens to Africa, and asserted that integrated schools were a bad idea because black children were "less adequately endowed with native intelligence" than white children.[9] In the 1970s, the magazine included fewer rants about the threat that desegregation posed to American civilization but plenty of articles focusing on liberal coddling of welfare recipients and criminals, who were almost always depicted as black.[10] A regular feature deceptively titled "Random Glances at the News" in fact singled out stories of violence, mayhem, and fraud involving African American miscreants, headlined with titles such as "Negroes Rob Hospital," "Chapel Hill Coeds Raped," and "19 Nabbed for Fraud in Food Stamp, Aid Cases." A story that appeared in November 1972 criticized HUD for buying and leasing apartments, renting them to "racially-mixed occupants from the slums," and providing residents with modern luxuries that middle-class homeowners could not afford. Toward the end of the decade, a spokesman for the Citizens' Council enumerated the public policies that the group opposed, demonstrating the way its segregationist, antigovernment agenda had evolved since the 1950s. Beginning with the *Brown* decision, the list went on to name the Civil Rights and Voting Rights Acts, "forced busing . . . reverse discrimination in employment . . . welfare and food stamps . . . subsidized housing . . . [and] gun controls."[11]

As reflected in the Citizens' Council's attacks on social welfare programs, racist assumptions underlay many voters' reactions against government intervention in the economy. That white Americans made up the majority of citizens living below the poverty line did not prevent many people from seeing black when they heard "poor." When the SCLC organized the interracial Poor People's March on Washington in 1968 that included people of all ethnic backgrounds, Mississippi resident James Perkins interpreted it as just another unreasonable demand from African Americans. "How long do you think this country can support the minority race economically?" he asked. "Will Congress pass a bill to give the Negro a certain amount of money each year? What are the possibilities of getting states rights back in controlling the riots, civil rights and gun control?" Robert Griffin complained to Bill Nichols that antipoverty programs in Lowndes County, Alabama, had done nothing to solve poverty and only encouraged dependence on government handouts. Griffin viewed OEO and CAA staff as "nothing but paid agitators," and he ridiculed the agencies' emphasis on including poor people as planners and administrators of the programs. If the local people in this majority-black county were "capable of managing multi-million dollar projects, they wouldn't be poor in the first place," he argued. Mississippian W. C. Watson suggested a much simpler solution to poverty in a letter to Thomas Abernethy: the removal of African Americans from the United States. Watson was sure that once the black people were gone, the nation would "enter a period of prosperity, with less crime, never before known to mankind." Abernethy concurred with his constituent in a response that stated, "You are right that the best and only solution is to return the negroes to Africa."[12]

Racializing poverty enabled voters to ignore systemic injustice and conditioned them to accept arguments that promoted a hands-off approach to the problem. At the same time, concerns about an overbearing federal government reinforced the appeal of laissez-faire economic theories. In its policy proposals for 1967 and 1968, the AFBF blamed antipoverty programs for concentrating power at the national level and called on Congress to abolish the OEO. According to its leaders, lower taxes and other incentives for private employers were more effective ways to solve joblessness than programs targeted at poor people. Critical of public expenditures that endangered the nation's financial health and lacking trust in Washington planners, the AFBF advocated returning control over rural development initiatives to state and local governments for more efficient administration. Additionally, the group opposed using artificial means such as "loans, grants, or tax credits" to encourage economic activity, arguing that development should be left to natural forces such as location and resources. "Hasty and ill-considered action to dedicate tax resources to this purpose may result in their wasteful and uneconomic use, and would be particularly unwise in light of the current federal budgetary situation," it warned. Alabama congressman Walter Flowers expressed similar concerns about an expansive, overspending government in an article he wrote for the *Greene County Democrat* in February 1970. Flowers explained his vote against what he considered excessive appropriations for federal bureaucracies by citing concerns about inflation and calling for more fiscal responsibility on the part of the nation's political leaders. "The American people have grown tired of the Federal Government expending day after day through creation of new agency after agency and new programs on top of old programs," he stated.[13]

Similar arguments against antipoverty efforts made their way into national political campaigns. In 1968 vice presidential candidate Spiro

Agnew attacked the War on Poverty for fostering corruption and funding the activities of radical revolutionaries, promising that Republicans would abolish the OEO's community action initiatives if elected. For his part, Richard Nixon denounced Democratic presidential candidate Hubert Humphrey's proposals for increasing federal assistance to poor people as a plan that would "drain the Federal treasury to soothe the public conscience [and] leave untapped the greatest reservoir of neglected resources in America today: The energies and the spirit of the American people themselves." The party platform that year promised major revisions to welfare and poverty programs to discourage dependence on government assistance, promoted state and local control over federally funded programs, and asserted that the key to job growth lay in unleashing free enterprise. An OEO memo on candidates' use of antipoverty programs as a campaign issue noted that Republican strategists had targeted seven Democratic challengers in the congressional elections who were former OEO employees. Party operatives seemed intent on framing the races as "a choice between Republican responsible government and continued Democratic wasteful spending."[14]

Although political candidates in the late 1960s generally avoided blatantly racist rhetoric, such campaign issues as crime, welfare, education, and housing policy remained racially charged. When George Wallace made a second bid for the presidency in 1968, this time running as the leader of the newly created American Independent Party, he no longer swore to defend segregation and instead focused on halting federal violations of people's constitutional rights. Nonetheless, supporters understood the real threat he aimed to combat was black people. As one observer noted, "He can use all the other issues—law and order, running your own schools, protecting property rights—and never mention race. But people will know he's telling them, 'A nigger's trying to get your job, trying to move into your neighborhood.'"[15]

Richard Nixon appealed to this same demographic by promising to crack down on crime and rein in government. Although Nixon denied that he was using coded racism and carefully framed these issues as problems that affected everyone, he still came across as a milder version of Wallace. Asked to explain what law and order meant, one white man replied, "Get the niggers. Nothing else." If voters like these were truly concerned about criminal activity, Hubert Humphrey's tough (and successful) stance against organized crime in Minneapolis during his tenure as mayor of the city in the 1940s might have garnered him more support than Nixon, whose record in this area was nonexistent. Yet in polls asking voters which candidate would do the best job of enforcing the nation's laws, Nixon won with 36 percent, Wallace came in second with 26 percent, and Humphrey trailed in third place with 23 percent.[16] Like poverty, crime had a black face in the minds of many Americans. Candidates' references to increasing lawlessness conjured images of riots and street muggings, not activities such as embezzlement, political corruption, or flouting court orders to desegregate public education.

After Nixon won the election, social justice activists expressed some anxiety over the shift in leadership. The minutes of a Delta Ministry meeting held in March 1969 noted that there was "a lot of apprehension on the part of a lot of people, especially in the South, as to where the priorities for the new administration exist. . . . There is no indication that how Black people feel about economic development in Mississippi is going to be heard by the Nixon Administration." Over the next year, as the president backtracked on civil rights enforcement and attempted to nominate racist ultraconservatives to the Supreme Court, Nixon faced growing criticism from African Americans. In July 1970 one NAACP leader called Nixon the first president since Woodrow Wilson who could be characterized as "anti-Negro." Similarly, after three months of trying to persuade the president to meet with them, members of the Congressional Black Caucus concluded that Nixon's snub as well as his inaction on issues that concerned them indicated his "apathy not only toward black people—but toward all poor Americans." The president's disengagement from efforts to ensure equality generated protests from some white southerners as well. A woman who described herself as a native white Mississippian and a Republican decided to switch her allegiance to the Democratic Party after Nixon spoke out in opposition to busing. She believed the administration's policies were reversing progress toward racial justice in the United States and explained to John Stennis: "I felt it immoral to continue to support a man who, through word and action, undergirds the lowest and basest instincts in man—bigotry and self interest at the expense of his fellow human beings."[17]

Nixon and his staff denied charges that they were unconcerned with problems such as unemployment, poverty, and racism, insisting that they were trying to make government services more efficient by eliminating wasteful spending and duplication. They also wanted to return control over programs to the local level and alleviate some of the tensions that resulted when federal initiatives bypassed state and county governments.

The National Governors' Conference, the National League of Cities, and other organizations representing nonfederal elected officials frequently complained about inefficiencies and miscommunication that frustrated their members' efforts to serve their local communities. At their annual conference in 1967, the nation's governors called on the Johnson administration to ensure state participation in any new federal assistance initiatives and suggested that some existing programs could be replaced by block grants that allowed for "greater efficiency, economy and local determination." Meanwhile, local officials wanted control over federal funds taken out of the hands of people they thought were poorly suited to administering programs and restored to "responsible people" like themselves.[18]

In a televised speech delivered on 8 August 1969, Nixon announced that it was time to reverse trends toward the centralization of power in the federal government that began with the New Deal reforms in the 1930s and continued with the Great Society initiatives of the 1960s. "After a third of a century of power flowing from the people and the states to Washington it is time for a new federalism in which power, funds and responsibility will flow from Washington to the states and to the people," he asserted. The president proposed to replace existing manpower training programs with a more flexible system that returned responsibility for these efforts to state and local governments, enabling federal money to "follow the demands of labor and industry, and flow into those programs that people most want and most need." Under a new revenue-sharing plan, a portion of federal income taxes were to be returned to the states with minimal restrictions on how they could be used and with the stipulation that some of the funds be passed to local governments to spend as they liked. Nixon also promised an extensive overhaul of the OEO to transform it into a "laboratory agency" that tested new approaches to solving social problems and then spun successful programs off to other federal departments to administer.[19]

Although the administration framed the changes as setting a bold new direction, undertaken with the same pioneering spirit and commitment to success as the nation's space program, to other observers they seemed like a return to the failed policies of the past. The OEO's acting deputy director Robert Perrin recalled the debates over federal versus state authority that occurred when the agency was first created and expressed concerns over allowing state governments more control over antipoverty programs. "OEO is sometimes accused of having an 'Alabama syndrome'— that is, basing our view of all 50 states on how Alabama might subvert

President Richard Nixon meeting with advisers in the Oval Office,
13 March 1970. White House Photo Office Collection (Nixon Administration),
NLNP-WHPO-MPF-3144 (04A), National Archives.

antipoverty programs if it got control," he acknowledged. Nonetheless, Perrin explained, the agency's past experience with governors in the North as well as the South gave its staff good reasons to be suspicious. Similarly, the National Urban League worried that past forms of discrimination by state employment agency personnel would be revived if federal jobs programs were transferred to the states. Regional CAP directors echoed these fears at a meeting held in February 1971. After learning that under Nixon's revenue-sharing plan manpower training funds would be chan- neled through state governors and mayors instead of being given directly to CAAs, several attendees wondered about the inequitable impact this might have. "How do you protect the masses of Mississippi in Revenue Sharing, since it is almost impossible to do so under present programs?" one regional director asked. Leaders of the low-income cooperative move- ment were equally apprehensive, noting that there were no guarantees that these funds would reach nonwhite populations. Louisiana activist Gerald LaBrie predicted that revenue sharing would be "highly disadvan- tageous to Blacks, where there is no Black political representation, espe- cially on a local level."[20]

Federal budget tightening also raised concerns for the future of anti-poverty efforts during the Nixon era. Job training, youth programs, economic development, and education all suffered from funding cuts, placing assistance further out of reach for many people. After reviewing the appropriations bill for the DOL, HEW, and other departments concerned with social welfare for fiscal year 1970, an administrator in the Louisiana Department of Employment Security expressed dismay that Congress had once again failed to accommodate rising joblessness and the increasing need for services. "This constant program retrenchment . . . results in a constant decrease in the volume of service we are able to provide the citizenry of this state," he stated. Leaders of the NBCFC in Bolivar County feared that funding cuts could jeopardize the project's momentum and "cause irreparable damage to the spirits of a people who were just beginning to believe that the government was seriously interested in helping to improve their conditions."[21] Federal administrators sympathized, but they could do nothing to alleviate such concerns. The OEO's assistant director Frank Carlucci explained that the agency simply lacked the resources to fund services for every community that needed help. In 1970 the OEO reduced the amount of money its CAAs could spend on local initiatives from $358 million to $333 million and introduced new evaluation methods to weed out underperforming agencies. Out of the first sixteen CAAs to come under review, only two were refunded. Eight agencies were defunded, and decisions on the other six were still pending when Carlucci reported on these efforts to a congressional committee in December. In the meantime, the uncertain future of threatened programs caused untold headaches for OEO field staff, CAA employees, and poor people. Regional directors complained that regardless of defunding and refunding outcomes, these episodes inevitably resulted in "wrecking or harming" antipoverty efforts.[22]

Uncertainty over OEO policy and funding undermined the Nixon administration's stated goal of encouraging innovation and raised questions about its true motivations. A staffer in the Office of Program Development (OPD) reported in January 1970 that Nixon's reorganization of the agency had left it paralyzed. "No grants and contracts are moving," he wrote in a memorandum to the OEO's new director, Donald Rumsfeld. "A few existing projects are starting to lay off staff because of actual or expected delays in refunding—more will do so in the immediate future. . . . At present, we are confronted with an absence of clear signals as to what program directions you feel OPD should take and a bright red light on OPD initiatives." A year later, Jack Geiger wrote to TDHC director Andrew James to warn him to expect significant cuts in funding for the Mississippi project, adding that the government was no longer interested in empowering poor people to solve their own problems. Instead, federal officials were "much more concerned with the routine, efficient and businesslike operation of the programs it funds—i.e., back to the usual deal of just providing services *for* people . . . and much less concerned about developing people's capacity to do it themselves."[23]

Poor people's self-help efforts faced even greater challenges when, in January 1973, the Nixon administration announced plans to abolish the OEO by ending federal funding of CAPs and transferring the agency's remaining functions to other government departments. According to the president, some CAPs had proven useless, and those that were successful should be funded by state and local governments. Nixon then appointed Howard Phillips, a Harvard graduate who helped found the conservative student organization Young Americans for Freedom in the early 1960s, as acting director of the OEO, dismaying supporters of antipoverty efforts. Phillips was openly antagonistic toward the OEO's original mission, telling reporters that it was founded on "a Marxist notion . . . that the poor should be treated as a class apart" and that it needed to get out of the business of "politicizing the poor." Ending federal support for CAPs and allowing local officials to decide whether to continue the programs was part of the Nixon administration's plan to "return social decision-making to private citizens and to public officials who are electorally accountable," he explained.[24]

For the next two years, chaos reigned at the OEO as Phillips attempted to fulfill his mandate to dismantle the agency while opponents challenged the legality of his appointment and actions. Later accounts of this period in the agency's history described it as a time of corruption, confusion, and overall lack of leadership that crippled antipoverty efforts. During Phillips's tenure, "staff vacancies were not filled, program decisions were not made, and field operations were virtually halted," according to one analyst. Another recalled that the agency became "the dumping ground for political appointments and payoffs," headed by administrators who had little concern for poor people.[25] Meanwhile, lawsuits filed by OEO employees, community groups, and several senators noted that Phillips's appointment was never submitted to the Senate for confirmation and that Nixon's plan to parcel out agency functions violated restrictions on the delegation of programs imposed by Congress during a long and bitter fight to reauthorize the OEO in 1971. A federal district appeals court issued the final ruling in these cases in June 1973, ordering that Phillips be removed from office and asserting that the president could not abolish the OEO without congressional approval. Conflicts over the future of the OEO continued, and when the agency's legislative authorization expired on 30 June 1974 with political leaders still debating what to do, its supporters in Congress had to use continuing resolutions to extend funding on a quarterly basis.[26]

Finally, in January 1975, Congress passed the Head Start, Economic Opportunity and Community Partnership Act to reorganize administration of federal antipoverty programs. The legislation created a watered-down version of the OEO, the Community Services Administration (CSA), and transferred its programs to the new entity. Like the OEO, the CSA was an independent agency within the executive branch of the government. Congress also allowed for continued funding of CAPs and a few other niche programs, and it authorized the CSA to establish and fund community development corporations to encourage business enterprise among low-income people. The CSA never operated with the same energy, creativity, or resources that characterized the OEO in its heyday, however. Its $500 million annual budget was less than a quarter of the funding Congress had provided for the OEO during its peak in the late 1960s. A spokesman for the agency told a reporter in 1980, "We don't even call it a War on Poverty any more. The antipoverty campaign has never recovered from Nixon."[27]

The president's push to transfer administration of programs to other government departments also undermined antipoverty efforts in the 1970s. The OEO already had some experience with this before Nixon was elected, and upon learning that the president planned to spin off more OEO functions to other departments, several staffers pointed out that this had not always worked out well. In the past, wrote Gerson Green, the receiving agencies had "bastardized the programs to a point where they are not recognizable in terms of their original intent. The Departments appear to be able to emasculate programs with impunity." When responsibility for rural loan programs was delegated to the FmHA, one observer noted, the new administrators' "conception of who the program was to be aimed at and how it was to be operated . . . differed radically from OEO's."[28] The agency seemed more interested in funding recreational facilities for wealthy residents and tourists than in fulfilling Congress's intent to enable rural poor people to buy homes or establish farms and businesses. The FmHA's record of discrimination against black farmers continued unabated, discouraging many from applying for assistance. Farmworkers' organizations reported that the DOL was equally bad at operating programs for poor people and that they felt "generally ignored, circumvented or rejected by various officials within the Department." Transferring antipoverty programs to traditional federal bureaucracies such as the USDA, DOL, and HEW weakened their effectiveness and ignored the reasons the OEO was created in the first place: to provide an independent voice for poor people within the government and address needs that other departments were failing to meet.[29]

The OEO's advocacy role was further eroded as the Nixon administration moved to give state and local governments more power over how they spent federal funds. In January 1970, Nixon's Presidential Task Force on Rural Development recommended redesigning federal programs to "preserve and strengthen our decentralized system of government" by passing responsibility for addressing community needs back to elected officials in towns, counties, and states. Supporters of decentralization placed significant faith in local officials to step up and help solve problems in their communities. Donald Rumsfeld explained the administration's position by emphasizing that the OEO was "only a very small part of the nation's effort to deal with the problems of the poor. Other federal departments, state governments, local governments, and the private sector have important roles to play." During his tenure the OEO spent considerable staff time and resources on improving relationships with state governors, local governments, and mayors. Regional directors were instructed to make forging positive relationships with local officials a high priority, new guidelines required CAAs to work more closely with SEOOs to avoid bypassing governors' authority, and SEOOs were empowered to play a bigger role in overseeing and evaluating programs.[30] Between 1969 and 1971, the budget allocated for SEOOs almost doubled, from $6.8 million to $12.5 million, reflecting the new emphasis on encouraging state and local government participation in antipoverty efforts. In May 1973 the DOL reported that it planned to allocate about 70 percent of the following year's $1.34 billion budget for manpower training and economic opportunity initiatives to states and localities, which would have "maximum discretion" to operate programs without having to deal with federal bureaucracies. Later that year, President Nixon signed the Comprehensive Employment Training Act (CETA) into law, which replaced the MDTA and some sections of the Economic Opportunity Act.

Rather than granting funds to the roughly 10,000 public and private organizations that administered employment training programs under the old system, the DOL now would work through a much smaller number of state and local government sponsors to plan and operate programs according to local needs.[31]

Hopes that these changes would encourage local political leaders to accept responsibility for addressing social problems in their communities were not always realized. Delta Ministry staff who reviewed revenue-sharing expenditures in Mississippi in the first six months of 1973 found that programs serving poor people received a minimal portion of the funds. Participants in an economic development conference sponsored by SEDFRE the same year shared similar stories from their own states, and the general conclusion was that government resources were bypassing the needs of nonwhite Americans.[32] Activist Danny Mitchell noted, "One of the strongest tools we had throughout the civil rights movement in the South was federal money and the jobs that went with it. It made black people independent because control of their existence was moved outside the white racist power structure. . . . Reorganization means a shift from black to white control. And in Mississippi white control means white racism."[33]

Other studies confirmed these assessments, finding that only about 3 percent of revenue-sharing funds went toward providing social services and that local governments spent the bulk of the money on basic functions such as police and fire departments. With inflation driving up the costs of providing these services, directing federal money to mundane purposes saved state and local governments from raising taxes on constituents, effectively transforming antipoverty funds into another subsidy for wealthier citizens. In 1975 the Southeast Region Equal Opportunity Association sent a resolution to the president and the heads of eleven federal agencies that outlined the ways revenue sharing had set back progress toward eliminating poverty and racial inequality. The lack of designated funding to address poor people's needs, inadequate monitoring to ensure an equitable distribution of federal money, and the reduced role for CAAs threatened to reverse the gains made in the 1960s, according to the association. Its leaders called on the government to increase appropriations for agencies and programs that specifically served poor people, allow CAAs to sponsor job training projects under CETA, and install monitors in every locality that received revenue-sharing funds to guard against discrimination. Senators Hubert Humphrey and Dick Clark also expressed concern about the deterioration in job training and employment place-ment services to rural poor communities, urging Secretary of Labor John Dunlop to direct more CETA resources to these areas.[34]

A report on CETA's impact on former OEO programs designed to help the children of migrant and seasonal agricultural workers to prepare for alternative careers suggested that there were good reasons to question the wisdom of decentralization. Under amendments to the Economic Opportunity Act passed in 1967, the OEO administered twenty-two high school equivalency and college assistance programs to recruit, train, and find employment for young people from rural poor families. The initia-tives were hugely successful and the OEO was planning to expand them before they were transferred to the DOL in 1973. Under the DOL the pro-grams continued to demonstrate their effectiveness in launching stu-dents into more promising jobs, with one study indicating that the costs of operating them were returned to the federal treasury in the form of increased tax revenues. After CETA came into effect, the DOL reallocated the funds for these programs to state and local governments and directed the CAAs and other organizations that had previously operated them to apply to those entities for continued funding. Most of the applications were rejected, however. Instead of enhancing the delivery of services, the report concluded, decentralization was likely to mean the elimination of successful programs.[35]

An analysis of CETA's implementation in four rural southern counties reiterated these concerns. Echoing what EDA analysts had found in the plantation counties in the 1960s, researchers reported continued oppo-sition to economic development efforts and resistance to helping unem-ployed people. Local officials frequently used job training slots for political purposes, and many of them did not "share the views of those who have written CETA with regard to the importance of serving racial minorities and the economically disadvantaged." Administrators' ideological biases compounded other limitations imposed by the lack of resources and expertise. "The plain fact is that most rural governments are incapable of administering human resource programs," the report concluded.[36]

The shifts in federal policy threatened to undermine some of the most promising grassroots projects the OEO had funded in the 1960s. William Harrison submitted a progress report for SWAFCA in July 1972 that faulted the OEO for leaving the cooperative in financial limbo and hinder-ing its operations. Lack of money for equipment repairs resulted in some produce spoilage, and the technical assistance that the agency provided through northern-based consulting firms that had no understanding of local conditions was largely useless. Harrison believed low-income cooperatives were on their way to proving themselves as viable enterprises that could ultimately become self-sustaining until the OEO's change in direction undermined them. He and others wondered whether federal officials really wanted these businesses to succeed or if they were "simply waiting for cooperatives to 'wither on the vine' so that they will simply write them (cooperatives) off as bad experiences with the Black community."[37]

Policy makers' increasing interest in evaluating the effectiveness of antipoverty programs and guarding against misuse of taxpayer money led to closer monitoring that hindered rather than improved operations. After its successful first year, the NBCFC hired a Clarksdale accounting firm to conduct an audit as required by OEO rules. The accountants dragged the audit on from May until December 1969, claiming that the cooperative's bookkeeping practices caused the delay. According to L. C. Dorsey, receipts were available for every expenditure, and no money was misused, but the NBCFC's nonstandard system combined with the accountants' racial prejudices convinced the auditors that "sacred accounting procedures were being broken and that the blacks were stealing." Meanwhile, the OEO withheld the grant it had approved for the co-op's second year until completion of the audit, which would have killed the project in its infancy if Tufts University had not stepped in with a $100,000 loan. The OEO allowed a second audit to be conducted by Boston accountants Prendergast, Creelman and Hill, which found no misuse of funds and helped improve the NBCFC's accounting system. Brenton Creelman later observed that the federal government could have been more helpful by providing better technical assistance instead of encouraging the NBCFC to hire expensive professionals from the private sector, "some of whom acted worse than carpetbaggers after the Civil War in the way they exploited the co-op."[38]

The NBCFC had a similar experience with Continental Allied, a consulting firm foisted on them by the OEO to conduct a feasibility study before the agency would decide whether to fund a cannery project aimed at strengthening the co-op's ability to become self-sustaining. Rejecting the idea of building a large, modern facility as the NBCFC initially proposed, the consultants instead recommended funding a smaller, more labor intensive plant that could generate more jobs. Some NBCFC members interpreted this as indicating that the OEO and its consultants doubted rural poor people's ability to run a more complex business enterprise. At a meeting held in August 1969 to discuss the project, John Hatch accused OEO representative Rudy Frank of wanting the cooperative to "think small, obsolete, and humble." Hatch preferred a larger operation that would create a diverse range of jobs in addition to hand labor and encourage young people to stay in Bolivar County by providing skilled work.[39] After sending Continental Allied's proposal to experts at three different universities and receiving a unanimous verdict that it made no sense, the co-op's board of directors rejected the plan. Despite spending thousands more dollars on consulting fees, NBCFC leaders could not reach agreement on how to proceed, and they eventually abandoned the cannery idea in 1972.[40] *Boston Globe* reporter Herbert Black noted that federal officials' refusal to support the NBCFC's more ambitious cannery plan, along with the amount of money that was wasted on "private consultants, architects, advisors of all types who came in at $100 a day," left the co-op unable to survive on its own after the OEO grants ran out. Instead, the government "spawned a kind of WPA project that supplied work for a time, that provided vegetables on a subsidized basis, that raised the living level of the people for a time, and then walked away." Jack Geiger eventually concluded that federal officials had no real interest in fostering black economic autonomy. "It became clear to us particularly through the experience of the farm co-op, that the government and society in general were willing to support palliative interventions of all of these kinds but drew the line at capital creation and capital involvement," he stated.[41]

Bolivar County's other grassroots empowerment experiment, the TDHC, also felt the effects of the federal government's shift in direction. In the late 1960s, Mound Bayou political leaders used Nixon's New Federalism and administrators' emphasis on local autonomy to push for a merger of the TDHC and MBCH that shifted control over the project to themselves, drawing on black power rhetoric to argue that white institutions such as Tufts University should not be allowed to dominate projects that served black communities. Health center staff suspected that Mayor Earl Lucas and his supporters were more interested in using federally funded jobs for patronage purposes than addressing poor people's needs. One nurse who had worked at both facilities observed, "Lucas and [Owen] Brooks and those people hate the rural Black poor people and are full of prejudice against them. I myself heard them call them 'niggers' and 'slaves' over and over. The way they kept trying to take the health center over was to yell that *they* were the Black leaders (only none of the poor people ever chose them) and to pretend that the health center was 'white outsiders' and to go to OEO every month and demand a 'merger' of the health center and hospital."[42]

In April 1971 the OEO ordered the two facilities to merge into a new entity, Delta Community Hospital and Health Center (DCHHC). The merger curtailed the role that poor people had previously played in planning and implementing services through the TDHC's neighborhood health councils and undermined the project's effectiveness. A board comprised mostly of politicians and business leaders parceled out jobs to family members and friends and showed little interest in preserving the innovative programs pioneered by the TDHC. The DCHHC also suffered from funding cuts that limited the services it could offer. After responsibility for the nation's neighborhood health centers passed from the OEO to HEW in 1973, federal officials cut $2.2 million from the DCHHC's annual budget, forcing administrators to end supplemental programs such as meals for the aged, home nursing care, and the environmental health unit.[43] Former TDHC director Richard Polk commented on how much the political context had changed since the mid-1960s: "We used to be able to rely on our friends in Washington, I mean, we had a direct line to the source of power and there were people in OEO who really cared about programs like ours. But OEO is finished and we can count on the Nixon administration to begin channeling everything away from the people and back to the politicians."[44]

In the mid-1970s the Center for Community Change, an organization that had a decade of experience providing technical assistance to community groups, assessed the impact of the federal government's retreat from the War on Poverty. Approximately 26 million Americans representing 12 percent of the population still lived below poverty level. Eight years of indifferent and sometimes hostile treatment from the Nixon and Ford administrations left antipoverty agencies "in a state of uncertainty, lethargy and, to a certain extent, ineffectualness." Many CAA directors seemed more interested in getting along with elected officials in their communities and maintaining the status quo than with bringing about social change. The transformative potential of earlier days was gone, and shifting funding decisions to the state and local levels left the allocation of resources in the hands of political leaders who had "little concern and interest in the needs of poor and minority people." Echoing these findings, a study of social welfare services in the rural South reported that administrators made it difficult for people to receive aid and that many local residents expressed contempt toward welfare recipients, who were perceived as undeserving freeloaders. In 1978 analysts found general dissatisfaction with the government's social services programs among the broader American population. Political leaders complained about bureaucracy and inflexibility, community organizations cited lack of participation in decision making by poor people, and citizens who used the programs hated the complex eligibility requirements and inconsistent service.[45] In the decade after Nixon had taken office, all the problems the War on Poverty tried to address had returned.

There was a return to business as usual in the broader arena of rural economic development as well. The Rural Development Act of 1972 restored the centrality of the USDA in this area, giving the agency primary responsibility for coordinating rural programs. The legislation also altered the definition of rural areas for some purposes to make cities with up to 50,000 people eligible for industrial and business loans, expanded the uses of and eligibility for rural loans, and encouraged joint projects between government agencies and private businesses. These measures shifted attention and resources away from rural poor communities. Although the act included some provisions for assisting small farmers, funding was insufficient, and the money was channeled through state extension services and land grant colleges. According to Ezra Cunningham, agricultural programs housed in universities were no help to the farm families he worked with because the academics who ran them could not get past their preconceived notions regarding the future of American agriculture. "We were developing something that as far as they were concerned was no good," he stated. "They said small farmers can't make it under no terms. Don't even try." Cooperative leader Woodrow Keown explained the deficiencies of the legislation in a statement to the Senate Subcommittee on Rural Development in 1975. "Assistance to traditional institutions which have not in the past adequately served poor Black family farmers in the South will not help to remedy the present problems of our members," he stated. "The provisions of the Rural Development Act are just not fully reaching the smallest and most needy farmers."[46]

Policy makers were not as interested in enhancing economic opportunities and stemming out-migration from the plantation regions as they had been earlier. Support for displaced workers' struggle to stay in their home communities waned among administrators of federal programs as some analysts questioned the wisdom and feasibility of this approach. Even as others in the OEO were embracing cooperatives and other self-help initiatives as promising solutions to poverty in the late 1960s, Research Director Robert Levine responded to a draft proposal for a project designed to create jobs in rural areas by noting that it was unlikely to provide employment for everyone, so part of the focus should be "preparation for mobility." A year later the president's Council of Economic Advisers also suggested that mobility must be part of the solution to rural problems, adding that it was too expensive for the government to provide jobs for all workers and that doing so could cause inflation.[47]

Early in President Nixon's first term, a White House subcommittee on internal migration that included representatives from the USDA, OEO, EDA, and HUD discussed the ways government policies affected economic activity and the movement of people to and from different regions. Noting that migration could have both positive and negative effects, the group debated how the government could direct population flows to maximize the positive aspects of mobility. "We should not discourage migration but encourage the proper direction of it," stated one official. A report prepared by a smaller working group of subcommittee members two weeks later outlined the various merits of a "worst first" approach (directing resources to the most severely depressed communities), a "growth centers" approach (focusing on communities that had the most development potential), and allowing economic development to be dictated by market forces alone. After deeming the first option too difficult and concluding that the third option was impossible because government decisions always affected the economy even when this was not intended, the report advocated the growth centers solution as the one with the best hope of success. In December 1970, OEO staffer Lynn Daft discerned the outlines of an emerging consensus that had significant ramifications for the agency's rural poor constituents. Rather than trying to save communities that were experiencing the highest rates of unemployment and poverty, the government was moving toward focusing its efforts on a select group of towns and cities based on recent growth trends and proximity to severely depressed areas. Jobless workers on the periphery would gravitate toward these regional growth centers, encouraged by new employment opportunities and pushed by the lack of alternatives in their home communities.[48]

Although proponents saw growth centers as a happy medium between costly efforts to develop rural poor communities and allowing outmigration to add to the stresses facing northern cities, others interpreted this approach as a form of abandonment. Delta Ministry staff noted in

January 1973 that in Mississippi, if such plans were adopted, resources would be directed to mostly white college towns such as Oxford, Starkville, and Hattiesburg while predominantly black areas in the south-western part of the state remained undeveloped. "A similar fate is in store for other Black Belt areas of the south," they warned.[49] In February 1974 the Nixon administration added to these fears when it submitted a proposal for an economic adjustment plan to Congress that questioned the effectiveness of federal assistance to depressed rural areas. Although the authors advocated early action to prevent communities that were faced with structural unemployment from sliding into permanent decline, they believed it was too late to save places that were already impoverished. Federal intervention there would run counter to the prevailing economic trends and require "massive government assistance to overcome or minimize the impact of market forces." An analysis of the administration's proposal prepared by economist John B. Mitrisin observed that it relied on "out-migration from some depressed areas" as the solution to persistent unemployment. The idea that these communities might have some intrinsic value that could not be measured in dollars was overridden in these policy makers' minds by "economic logic" and their underlying assumption that market forces, not political decisions, explained migration from rural to urban places.[50]

The administration's preference for allowing free markets and free enterprise to solve social problems was also reflected in Nixon's decision to create the Office of Minority Business Enterprise (OMBE), a new agency within the Department of Commerce designed to encourage non-white Americans to set up their own businesses. The OMBE's administrators showed little interest in working with rural communities, however, and its efforts in the South focused on urban centers such as Atlanta, New Orleans, and Dallas.[51] The emphasis on fostering private business also narrowed the scope of antipoverty efforts from the community to the individual level, making them less likely to garner the broad base of support that was evident in OEO-sponsored projects such as the TDHC. An OEO background paper noted that Secretary of Commerce Maurice Stans interpreted economic development to mean "the expansion of income producing activity, aimed at growth in output and in income and employment. It is not, in his judgment, oriented toward upgrading the general welfare of the region." Rather than investing in education or infrastructure in hopes that this would lure industry to an area, Stans believed industry must be attracted first and the rest would follow. Like the proponents of growth centers and the architects of Nixon's economic adjustment plan, Stans favored a reassessment of efforts to assist severely depressed communities, suggesting that it was first "necessary to judge whether the lagging area can in fact be rebuilt."[52]

As with other initiatives, the government's financial commitment to minority business enterprise was far below what was needed. The frustrated president of a black-owned planning and design company wrote to federal officials in February 1971 to complain that, despite completing the process for becoming a certified minority business enterprise at the administration's invitation, the firm had received no contracts for work with federal agencies. When Nixon announced later that year that he was requesting $100 million for the program over the next two years, *Black Enterprise* editor Pat Patterson pointed out that this was only one-tenth of the $1 billion that the president's own advisory council recommended for black economic development. A successful effort to encourage government departments to deposit funds in minority-owned banks resulted in deposits exceeding $80 million by the end of 1972, but budget reductions later undercut this achievement. As a Treasury official explained in April 1973, more than half of the funds were contributed by the OEO, HUD, and the DOL's Manpower Administration, agencies that were now being targeted for trimming.[53]

Assessing the impact of the OMBE's efforts toward the end of the decade, an EDA analyst noted they were not comprehensive enough to deal with the interrelated problems of institutionalized racism and economic distress facing black communities. "The existence of profitable business is a necessary but not sufficient condition for economic development," the report stated, contrasting the "trickle down" approach of encouraging entrepreneurial activity in hopes that this would increase employment opportunities with the "trickle up" approach of investing in job creation that generated higher incomes, more demand for goods and services, and attendant business opportunities.[54] Whereas supporters of limited government hoped that unleashing private enterprise would generate enough economic growth to make continued federal action unnecessary, the evidence suggested that the success of private enterprise could not be separated from public investment.

The Nixon administration's pivot away from Great Society initiatives that had used the power and resources of the federal government to solve social problems dramatically altered the prospects for addressing inequities that lingered after the passage of civil rights legislation. Although the president and his advisers asserted that they wanted to end racism and poverty just as badly as their predecessors and were simply going about it in a different way, the shift in direction was detrimental to these goals. Reorganizing the OEO, decentralizing programs, and cutting funding for social investments disrupted what little progress had been made in the 1960s and worsened conditions in rural poor communities. While Nixon may have shared with social justice activists the ultimate goal of fostering economic independence for poor black people, his failure to recognize the need for a substantial jump-start from government made this objective much harder to achieve. As participants in the low-income cooperative movement continued to assert, solutions to poverty and unemployment would not come cheaply and required greater commitments of resources than the nation's leaders seemed willing to give.

CHAPTER 6

TO BUILD SOMETHING, WHERE THEY ARE

THE FEDERATION OF SOUTHERN COOPERATIVES AND

RURAL ECONOMIC DEVELOPMENT

As the actions of federal officials threatened to negate earlier achievements by shifting responsibility for solving rural poverty back to local officials and private sector actors, participants in the low-income cooperative movement moved to coordinate their efforts more effectively and continued to craft their own solutions. The Federation of Southern Cooperatives brought the disparate groups that had been forming in Alabama, Louisiana, and Mississippi together into an umbrella organization that promoted cooperative enterprise, provided training and financial assistance, advised members, lobbied for changes in federal policy, and secured funding for the movement from government agencies and private foundations. Initially hoping to gain support for a comprehensive rural development plan to revitalize the plantation regions and put displaced workers on a path toward economic self-sufficiency, cooperative leaders found they were operating in a very different political context than had existed earlier. Federal officials were less willing to aid cooperative efforts, and tight economic times made it difficult to secure the needed resources, even from sympathetic supporters of the movement in the 1970s.

At the same time, the FSC's determination to ensure that African Americans retained control over their own projects and the disillusionment generated by the federal government's fading commitment to the War on Poverty created tensions between the organization and potential funding sources. Early assistance from the OEO and the Ford Foundation enabled the federation to experiment with the cooperative model and demonstrate its promise for improving the lives of rural poor people, but when the FSC tried to secure funding to expand on this work, it encountered resistance from those who claimed to share its mission. The resulting conflicts and FSC leaders' reluctance to scale back their agenda to please financial backers cost the organization a considerable amount of support, leaving it struggling to raise funds and serve its members. Continued attempts by opponents to obstruct the cooperative movement also hindered the federation's efforts. Despite these difficulties, the FSC acted as an effective vehicle through which thousands of rural black southerners secured adequate incomes, job training, decent homes, and political representation for themselves and their children in the post–civil rights era.

By the late 1960s, cooperative organizers had acquired considerable experience in helping poor people establish successful business enterprises, along with a keen sense of how fragile these new self-help organizations were. Multiple obstacles threatened the long-term survival of cooperatives, including financial insecurity, the limited business acumen of members, internal suspicion and mistrust, and external hostility from opponents. The SCDP's efforts to provide loans, technical assistance, and training to cooperatives in four states addressed some of these problems, but it was too small to meet the needs of the growing cooperative movement. The program's creators understood from the start the necessity for a larger organization that could combine poor black southerners' resources on a region-wide basis.

In February 1967 representatives from twenty groups met in Atlanta, Georgia, to form the Federation of Southern Cooperatives as a central service organization to meet the financial, educational, and technical needs of low-income cooperatives. The federation was officially chartered a few months later to operate in the District of Columbia and eleven southern states: Alabama, Arkansas, Florida, Georgia, Kentucky, Louisiana, Mississippi, Missouri, Oklahoma, Tennessee, and Texas. After opening an office in Atlanta in 1968 and securing several small foundation grants, the FSC began providing services to twenty-two member cooperatives. A research and technical assistance grant from the OEO enabled it to expand operations, and by January 1969 it had grown to fifty members.[1]

Headed by SCC's Charles Prejean, the FSC worked closely with A. J. McKnight's group in the states where activities of the two organizations overlapped. Prejean was born and raised in Lafayette, Louisiana, one generation removed from sharecropping. The poverty of his parents and grandparents deeply disturbed him, especially since they worked so hard for so little reward. As he watched his grandfather age and give up his farm labor job, Prejean was saddened that the old man "had nothing really left in life. . . . It seemed as if there was a person who had worked all his life and his value to society was as a worker. Once that value was no longer there he did not seem to have a place in society. I didn't want that to happen to me or anybody else." Prejean entered a Catholic seminary at the age of 13 with the idea of working for social justice in his rural community, but left after completing his high school training because he thought he could make a better contribution as a layperson. He met McKnight as a teenager when the priest was stationed in Lafayette in the 1950s and became involved in cooperative organizing and civil rights work under the older man's mentorship. After completing college and working as a teacher for two years, Prejean went to work full-time for SCC, focusing on outreach and helping people set up credit unions.[2]

Other FSC organizers had similar activist backgrounds. According to Prejean, civil rights leadership and cooperative leadership overlapped in many rural southern communities, and local chapters of the NAACP, SCLC, SNCC, and CORE always included people who were interested in economic development as well as desegregation and voter registration. Late in 1969, with SCEF's Ford Foundation grant due to expire in a few months, the FSC absorbed the SCDP's programs and staff. John Zippert, Mildred and Lewis Black, Ezra Cunningham, and other activists who had gained their initial organizing experiences on civil rights projects continued their participation in the freedom struggle through the FSC. As the federation explained in one of its annual reports, the cooperative movement was poor people's "economic response to the Civil Rights Movement," working to capitalize on and supplement the legal and political rights black southerners had won in the mid-1960s. To Prejean, cooperatives were the obvious solution to the dilemmas confronting poor people in the region. "It just makes so much sense," he stated. "If a community is experiencing common problems with little resources, it seemed to us it made so much sense to pool resources and use them to satisfy a common need."[3]

Providing the expertise and resources needed for hundreds of existing and aspiring low-income cooperatives was a huge project. The FSC attempted to beg, cajole, and shame federal agencies and private foundations into providing the millions of dollars required to overcome the lingering effects of racism in the South, but its work was never adequately supported. The direction of national politics in the 1970s was not conducive to the continuation of innovative solutions to rural poverty that had been possible in earlier years. Poor black people lost a key ally in their struggles for economic justice as Nixon set about reorganizing the OEO and returned control over federal programs to the states and traditional government departments. Beset by the costs of the Vietnam War and anguished by the sluggish economy, political leaders were in no mood to receive requests for significant expenditures to help African Americans, even if they supported the FSC's goals of enabling black self-help and autonomy. Along with CAPs and other Great Society projects, cooperatives faced an uncertain future and indifference from government officials in the decades after the 1960s.

Trends toward greater belt-tightening were also evident in the foundation world. In 1969 Congress moved to more closely regulate tax-exempt philanthropic organizations in an attempt to prevent wealthy Americans from using them as tax havens. Although there had been some instances of abuse that were legitimate cause for concern, the reforms proposed by the House Ways and Means Committee in May risked crippling the ability of the nation's charitable institutions to fund activities aimed at solving social problems. Some of the proposed changes, such as a ban on efforts to "influence" elections or government policy, seemed motivated by a desire to cut off support for voter registration and other forms of civil rights activism that were encouraged by the Ford Foundation, the Rockefeller Brothers Fund, and other liberal groups. Although protests from the philanthropic community convinced legislators to modify the bill, the final version of the Tax Reform Act of 1969 had the effect of reducing the amount of foundation funds that were available and limiting their use.[4]

From the start, then, the FSC operated in an economic and political climate that did not favor an expansion of social programs or attempts to empower poor black people to take control of their lives and communities. The small amounts of money the FSC did manage to secure from government or private sources often came with strings attached that restricted spending on vitally needed services. In July 1968 Charles Prejean told a Field Foundation executive that grants from two other foundations did not allow for emergency loans to struggling cooperatives, despite the emphasis the FSC had put on this in its grant requests. Although the FSC had used some of its general support funds to make a few loans, requests for assistance exceeded its ability to help its members. For the most part the organization was limited to providing accounting assistance and researching new products and markets—activities that would be useless if the cooperatives failed for lack of funds. "The response to the Federation has been great," Prejean wrote, "but I am beginning to become frustrated because we have resources to help with so few of the problems of cooperatives."[5]

Activists estimated the credit needs of existing cooperatives at $2 million and pointed out that much more money would be needed if the movement continued its rapid growth. With traditional lending agencies refusing to make loans to poor people's enterprises, the FSC approached the OEO and the Ford Foundation for help in forming a special development bank to serve the low-income cooperatives. At a meeting on 18 January 1969 the OEO agreed to provide $500,000 that the FSC could use to meet the capital needs of its members, and the Ford Foundation made a tentative commitment to invest in the new cooperative bank, contingent on a feasibility study. The EDA contributed $100,000 to the project to cover administrative costs, and several other foundations, unions, and churches also expressed their willingness to invest in the venture. Participants agreed to allow the cooperatives to have controlling ownership of the bank and to define its mission as serving "human needs, with financial criteria no more limiting than necessary to the viability of the institution as one which can attract the capital needed for eventual self-sufficiency."[6]

The end result of these efforts was the creation of the Southern Cooperative Development Fund (SCDF), a for-profit corporation presided over by A. J. McKnight, late in 1969. Using part of the OEO grant to guarantee a return of at least 50 cents on the dollar, McKnight and his staff secured $1 million from foundation and insurance company investors over the next two years. Cooperatives could request loans from the fund through the FSC's state representatives, who helped them gather the information and documentation necessary to file an application. To join the SCDF, cooperatives purchased voting shares in the fund at $100 each, based on the size of their memberships. Borrowing money from the fund required the purchase of additional shares worth 5 percent of the amount of the loan. The interest rate on loans was 10 percent annually on the unpaid balance, with the possibility of interest subsidies that could lower the rate to 6 percent for cooperatives needing additional assistance. By the mid-1970s the SCDF had made loans totaling almost $3 million to its members, and the combined assets of the fund and its subsidiaries had increased to $8 million.[7]

The SCDF acted as a financing agency to the cooperative movement while the FSC provided technical assistance. To join the FSC, cooperatives had to be made up primarily of poor people, be incorporated entities, and pay annual membership dues. Membership in both the member cooperatives and the FSC was open to all people regardless of race. The FSC's staff was interracial, but most of the cooperatives were all black. As Charles Prejean explained, the racial imbalance existed because most white southerners were "reluctant to join with blacks at this point in time." Although the FSC's immediate priority was to help the struggling new cooperatives succeed as self-sustaining business enterprises, its long-range goal was to create an economic and political base for black southerners to enable them to tackle such broader social problems as housing, health care, and jobs. By pooling their resources, people with little money or expertise of their own could gain more power over their lives and create alternatives to a marginal existence as unneeded labor.[8]

In April 1969 the FSC reported on some of the results of this approach after its first year of operation. The farmers' cooperatives had purchased 9,000 tons of fertilizer at significant savings for their members. Participation in several gift shows in New York had generated orders for the handcraft enterprises. A $2,000 loan to the Greene-Hale Sewing Cooperative enabled the group to buy new machines and move into a bigger building, and the FSC also provided training to the co-op's manager, staff, and board. Thirteen other member cooperatives benefited from FSC loans and grants totaling $332,240. The organization's research efforts identified promising new products and markets, and it was developing a library of educational materials to help with training and technical support. It was a promising start, but much more remained to be done. The executive director's report stated, "Although the efforts were 100%, they still only scratch the surface of the problems that are confronting us. The cooperative approach to problem solving calls not only for an adjustment to the evils of the present institutions, but for substitutions in some cases." The theme of the 1969 annual meeting, "Another Way for Us," reflected the FSC's belief that building alternative social structures was both possible and necessary to meet the needs of its constituents.[9]

The government and foundation grants that sustained the FSC through this early phase were intended to help the organization to experiment with the cooperative model while developing a comprehensive program for rural development in the South. Drawing on its experiences with the member cooperatives, the FSC developed a five-year plan with an estimated cost of $6 million per year and submitted it to the Ford Foundation, the OEO, and several other funding sources in May 1969. None of the agencies were willing to invest the entire amount requested, and at the suggestion of Ford program staff the FSC rewrote the proposal and parceled out its various components to different organizations. The Ford Foundation agreed to provide $750,000 for services to a small number of agricultural cooperatives, and the OEO supplied a $500,000 grant to support the handcraft, credit union, and consumer cooperatives.[10] Though the funds were only a fraction of what was needed, the FSC hoped to gain further support once it had demonstrated the viability of its approach.

Over the next two years, the sixteen farmers' cooperatives covered by the Ford grant benefited from an intensive training program designed to improve the business skills of their managers and members, and the FSC hired a marketing specialist to link them to potential customers such as chain stores, food-processing companies, minority-owned businesses, and buying clubs. Field staff showed farmers how to improve crop yields and diversify into livestock production to supplement their incomes. The FSC's purchasing program saved farmers money on supplies, with a collective reduction in spending of $68,000 on fertilizer alone. In 1971 the cooperatives made a total of $1,240,000 in sales and paid out $745,000 to farmers and harvest workers. In its report to the Ford Foundation in October, the FSC stated that its models had produced "viable business operations generating significant incomes for small farmers who had previously been written off by most conservative, conventional, unimaginative, theoretical economists."[11]

In some respects the FSC acted as a substitute for federal agricultural agencies that had long ignored the needs of rural poor southerners, black and white. Despite new regulations banning racial discrimination, administrators of USDA programs continued to neglect black farmers or provide inferior service. The FES, the FmHA, and the state land grant colleges whose research departments focused on aiding large agribusinesses showed scant interest in assisting low-income cooperatives and sometimes actively obstructed them. The FSC and its members faced roadblocks everywhere they turned for help. Charles Prejean reported in 1970 that even the federally capitalized Bank for Cooperatives "will not touch us because we are poor and high risk." Faced with this lack of support from the agencies that were supposed to serve rural people, the FSC was compelled to develop its own research programs, create its own financial institutions, and hire its own specialists in accounting, marketing, horticulture, and other fields.[12]

After successfully operating a training program for small farmers that taught new techniques and management skills to 1,285 operators in seven states in 1971, the FSC began planning for the construction of a permanent agricultural demonstration and training center in Sumter County, Alabama. The goal was to experiment with activities such as cattle production, feeder pigs, catfish farming, row crops, and vegetable production using irrigation and greenhouses to show farmers how to maximize the use of small amounts of land. In addition, the FSC planned to initiate manufacturing projects at the site to provide jobs and training in furniture making, metal stamping, and electronics. To critics who charged that the project duplicated services already provided by the USDA, the FSC responded: "Show us the USDA sponsored facilities that are responsive to the needs of small farmers; show us the facilities that are disseminating information useful to the small farmer in a form and context he can understand; show us the facilities that are oriented toward providing techniques and training to small farmers in enterprises that can produce new income for their families."[13]

With the OEO grant and assistance from several small foundations, the federation continued its work with nonagricultural cooperatives. In Alabama, the FSC experimented with using the cooperative model to promote an integrated approach to antipoverty efforts and economic development by helping a group of displaced farmworkers to initiate self-help housing and other projects. In 1967 tenant families on a plantation in Sumter County who had asked their landlord for their share of cotton allotment payments were forced off the land after he leased their plots to a paper mill company in retaliation. Some of the families moved north, but NAACP and SCDP activists encouraged most of them to stay by providing temporary accommodation and other assistance. Forty families joined together to form the Panola Land Buyers Association (PLBA), and with Lewis Black's help they located some land for sale in their home county. As John Zippert noted, it was rare to find white people in Alabama who were willing to sell land to African Americans. The owner of this particular tract was engaged in a feud with local elites and viewed selling it to a black group as an act of revenge.[14] After three years of legal battles the PLBA finally gained title to 1,164 acres of land near Epes and applied for a cooperative housing loan from the FmHA. The PLBA also allowed the FSC to locate its Rural Training and Research Center (RTRC) at the site. Within a year of the purchase the federation had built offices, classrooms, dormitories, an auditorium, and a cafeteria at the center, along with greenhouses and barns for its demonstration projects. In September 1971 the FSC's program staff relocated to the facility so that they could more easily serve members.[15]

By 1972 the FSC had grown to 110 member organizations serving approximately 30,000 families. Its cooperatives were engaged in diverse enterprises ranging from handcrafts and bakeries to metal stamping and concrete brick manufacturing. The membership also included 20 coop- erative stores and buying clubs with 4,000 participants in seven states. "Co-ops have meant survival to poor people in the rural South," the FSC reported. "They have helped people to use the resources they have—land, labor, native intelligence to build something, where they are. . . . People can taste the freedom in this, and are willing to take on the responsibilities and the blessing that come with this choice." Charles Prejean expressed his belief that FSC members were building a base for self-sufficiency and preparing rural poor southerners to participate in broader economic opportunities becoming available in the region. As some former oppo- nents of the movement were starting to realize, these developments prom- ised to benefit many other people apart from African Americans. Prejean noted that once cooperatives began making purchases from white-owned businesses, those enterprises began to grow, and more white southerners could see the value of the FSC's work.[16]

Responses from the FSC's rural poor constituents were positive as well. After one meeting where members voted to allow annual dues to be set on a sliding scale depending on how much people were able to pay, Prejean observed that while this might not provide much income, "it does indicate that our members are willing to support the Federation as much as they are able." Sumter County resident Lillie Dunn Johnson described how her life was changed after an FSC field-worker came to her house in 1974 and asked if she wanted to learn to crochet. "At 61 years of age, being Black, old, and poor, I had nothing to do and no-where to go," she stated. "The training not only cured my illness, it changed my way of thinking, my way of meeting people, my way of living." Organizers' civil rights back- grounds, their willingness to live and work in the region's most impover- ished counties, and their focus on empowering people to solve their own problems instead of telling them what to do earned them deep respect from participants. In an evaluation of a three-week training session for NBCFC members, Mississippian John Perkins expressed his appreciation for the FSC's approach. "I feel that the Federation staff was really beauti- ful in its preparation and presentation of the training session," he wrote. "John Zippert, Jim Jones, and Ralph Paige did a superb job in bringing about awareness within the membership. Their skills and dedications are unquestionable." Federation staff reciprocated such feelings in expres- sions of appreciation for the cooperatives and families they worked for. In a letter to the Milestone Farmers Cooperative following a meeting with its members early in 1973, FSC marketing director George Paris praised the group's enthusiasm and stated that he was "very impressed by the interest and participation of your cooperative members."[17]

In addition to directly assisting cooperatives, the federation opened up other opportunities for local people that led to fulfilling careers in the movement. Ben Burkett grew up on a farm near Petal, Mississippi, during the civil rights era, earned a degree in agriculture from Alcorn State University in the early 1970s, and originally planned to follow others of his generation to Chicago or Detroit. When his father became ill he stayed to help tend the land, earning a good income until cotton and soybean prices dropped at the end of the decade. With many small farmers facing bankruptcy, Burkett and several other landowners formed the Indian Springs Farmers Co-op to purchase equipment together. The FSC helped them to incorporate formally and supported the farmers as they switched to growing vegetables and located markets for their produce. Burkett remained in farming for the rest of his life while also serving as state coordinator for the federation's Mississippi cooperatives. He helped develop more co-ops there and in other states and traveled internationally with other FSC staff to exchange ideas and techniques with farmers in Africa, Asia, Europe, and the Middle East. Through his work with the FSC and as president of the National Family Farm Coalition, Burkett established a reputation as an innovator and mentor to other farmers, promoting sustainable farming techniques and the right of all people to adequate, nutritious food.[18]

Melbah McAfee was another Mississippi native who found her calling in working for the federation. McAfee's parents grew vegetables and raised livestock on forty acres of land in Rankin County, where she developed a lifelong love for farming and a desire to advocate on behalf of family farmers. In 1972 she took a job as the FSC's director of consumer cooperatives, moved to the training center at Epes, and spent the next three decades in various roles with the organization that allowed her to work on empowering rural communities through cooperative leadership development. McAfee helped form more than twenty-five co-ops in Mississippi and Louisiana, trained boards and members in cooperative principles, lobbied to bring affordable housing to low-income areas, and inspired others with her passion for social justice.[19]

Burkett's and McAfee's experiences were not unique. The FSC employed hundreds of local people from the communities it served, giving many of them their first experience in professional or skilled work. Some of these trainees stayed with the federation for decades, while others went on to become elected officials, government workers, teachers, lawyers, social workers, bank managers, and business leaders. These activists spread the federation's ideals into other arenas, advancing the freedom struggle through their participation in mainstream institutions and as leaders of their towns, cities, and states.[20]

Foundation staff, government officials, and other outside observers recognized the FSC's contributions to improving conditions in the rural South. Cooperative movement sage Jerry Voorhis praised the FSC at the 1971 annual meeting of the American Institute of Cooperatives for "doing a job of outstanding importance" in its efforts to help rural poor people stay on the land instead of migrating to northern cities. The Field Foundation's Leslie Dunbar informed Charles Prejean: "All of us at Field are greatly impressed by what the Federation has accomplished, and by the spirit in which and through which it has been done." A program adviser in the manpower training division of HEW who had helped secure funding for a project to train cooperative managers lauded FSC staff for their "competence, perseverance, and dedication to the cause of social equality and economic progress" and predicted that FSC programs would become "one of our most significant manpower efforts for their effect on the economy of numerous rural hamlets." Buoyed by such expressions of support, the FSC announced in its 1972 annual report: "*We have arrived.* . . . Our 1971–72 fiscal year . . . marked the beginning of our acceptance at the local, state and national levels as 'the' beacon for rural economic development."[21]

Despite its record of achievement, the FSC still struggled to get financing for its activities. The Ford Foundation's cautious approach and the lack of confidence in poor people's abilities shown by some of its staff frustrated Charles Prejean to the point where he admitted to becoming "very obnoxious, hallucinatory and unreasonable" in his communications with the organization. Many people at the foundation held the FSC in high regard, but they had to balance their desire to support the cooperative movement against other groups' demands for the limited social investment funds that Ford gave out each year. Other Ford staff members expressed skepticism about the viability of the low-income cooperatives or worried that the FSC's goal of fostering black self-sufficiency could undermine efforts to alter established institutions and make them more responsive to African Americans' needs. A summary of one staff meeting where these concerns were discussed in February 1969 concluded that the FSC could potentially play a leading role in rural development efforts, but it was too early to tell. The consensus was that Ford should "go slowly before knighting any one group with the authority and resources to orchestrate the southern cooperative movement."[22]

Ford's wait-and-see attitude made little sense to Prejean and others at the FSC. These activists had worked closely with rural poor people since the early 1960s. They knew which approaches worked and which did not, and they had identified the kinds of support and resources that were necessary for the cooperatives to succeed. Yet no one seemed willing to provide those resources, and without adequate funding it was difficult to prove the long-term viability of the projects. As Prejean put it, "We said we could prove to you that we can make a cake if we had the ingredients necessary to make that cake. You said, make a cake, then we will give you the ingredients."[23]

In 1971, believing that its work with the selected sample of cooperatives in the earlier grant had demonstrated the value of its programs, the FSC submitted a proposal asking for $3 million over three years. Once again foundation staff decided that the amount was too high and suggested rewriting the proposal to request $500,000 for one year. A disappointed Prejean told Ford staffer Bryant George: "We have written you a proposal reflecting the needs of the constituency of the Federation. . . . We have no intentions of writing another proposal." To Prejean, Ford's efforts to direct the FSC's work typified the misguided paternalism of white liberals who believed they knew what was best for black people. Rather than expecting the FSC to conform to the Ford Foundation's expectations, he suggested, administrators should embrace the chance to support programs that black people developed themselves.[24] Prejean worried that partial funding for projects was almost as damaging to the cooperative movement as no funds at all. When poor people's hopes were raised but they failed to receive the resources they needed to succeed, their confidence was shaken and they became discouraged. Support from people outside the movement was also jeopardized when cooperatives that could not secure the loans, staff, or advisers they needed did not perform as well as they might have. Far from helping the cooperative movement to succeed, the Ford Foundation and other funding agencies were setting it up to fail.

Prejean outlined these concerns in a letter to foundation president McGeorge Bundy appealing the program staff's decision. He explained that Ford's refusal to make a long-term commitment to the FSC had made it difficult for the Federation to recruit horticulturalists, economists, accountants, and other specialists it needed to provide technical support to its members. Highly trained workers who could command better salaries elsewhere were reluctant to join an organization whose funding and future were uncertain. The FSC could take the $500,000 Ford offered, but it was not enough to ensure success. Consequently, Prejean predicted, "Ford and other FSC funding sources will become more dissatisfied because we have not made these businesses self-sustaining operations. And it will not be important that we were given the wrong ingredients to achieve their desired results."[25]

A. J. McKnight expressed similar views to foundation vice president Mitchell Sviridoff. The FSC's work was vital to the success of the SCDF, McKnight stated, because it provided the assistance needed for cooperatives to become viable and repay their SCDF loans. He explained: "We have learned from previous experience that it does not suffice merely to loan money to the low income cooperatives. The loan must be supported with technical assistance, involving management, marketing and accounting assistance." Inadequately funding the FSC risked placing the SCDF loans in danger. As McKnight pointed out, Ford had helped create the SCDF to provide credit to fledgling cooperatives, with the hope that once they became viable businesses they could qualify for loans from traditional financial institutions. He warned, "Without the supportive technical assistance during this period from the Federation of Southern Cooperatives to the cooperatives this objective will not be realizable."[26]

Ford insisted that it could not increase the amount of the money it had offered or promise continued support to the FSC after the one-year grant expired. McGeorge Bundy blamed budget restrictions and the foundation's annual funding cycle, noting that a three-year grant to the FSC would have to come out of one year's budget, which would leave other organizations that were just as worthy of support unfunded. "We cannot pretend that we are making enough money available to make all of the cooperative endeavors work in the rural South," he admitted, "but we want to continue to do what we can until resources of appropriate scale are made available." Although Prejean continued to harbor reservations, the FSC's board of directors decided that partial funding was better than nothing. Prejean submitted a revised proposal in July 1971, and Ford agreed to fund the FSC's activities for another year.[27]

The FSC's relationship with the OEO was plagued by the same problems it encountered with the Ford Foundation: inadequate and uncertain funding, skepticism regarding the viability of low-income cooperatives, and bureaucratic interference that hindered more than it helped the movement. After using its research and technical assistance grant to expand its staff and operations, the FSC applied for another $1.3 million to support an array of programs, including marketing assistance, health services, field training, and education for its members. Doubling the size of the previous year's grant seemed like a reasonable request given the larger number of cooperatives the FSC now served, and activists also wanted to move beyond forming cooperatives to address broad social needs in rural southern communities. The OEO had itself increased the burden on the FSC's support services by encouraging the development of cooperatives through its community action and rural assistance programs, then referring groups to the federation for help. Like the Ford Foundation, however, the OEO asked the FSC to scale down its ambitions and reduce its request to $500,000. According to Prejean, the decision had nothing to do with the FSC's record, and OEO staff did not question the importance of its activities. "The reason that they give us is not that we deserve a cut, or that our proposal is not worthy of full consideration but that the Nixon Administration folks are cutting everyone so that they can support their own programs," he stated.[28]

The reticence of both the Ford Foundation and the federal government grew partly from doubts that the low-income cooperatives could succeed. Even as some officials lent strong support to the movement, others expressed their belief that the unconventional economic models proposed by participants were doomed to fail. According to OEO staffer Elmer J. Moore, American agriculture was "a private enterprise industry" unsuited for cooperatives, and small farms only ensured poverty for those who lived on them. Moore's colleague Joseph Kershaw expressed amazement that "the idea of putting people back on the land simply refuses to die in this town in the face of 100 years of history where just the opposite has been taking place." He argued that the federal government could better address rural poverty by making "the inevitable transition away from the land less painful." Similarly, a two-year study funded by the Ford Foundation from 1969 to 1971 concluded that the cooperatives were unlikely to ever become self-sustaining. The need for some form of outside assistance was a permanent feature, not a temporary condition, and according to these authors the only entities capable of providing it were the existing USDA agencies. They suggested that the foundation's energies might be better expended on pressuring the FES to provide more assistance to cooperatives than funding the FSC. "Unless the help of U. S. D. A. is enlisted, the situation is hopeless," they wrote. "Any attempts to duplicate its services strike us as unrealistic, however desirable they might be if U. S. D. A. proved to be unresponsive."[29]

These types of analyses, reflecting profound ignorance of the southern political economy and the racist history of federal agricultural agencies, elicited furious responses from the FSC. Charles Prejean condemned the "vicious racist attacks" of the Ford-funded evaluators and told Bryant George: "If Ford must use this document to determine the credibility of the Federation and the credibility of Black people, and if Ford must use this to further conclude that we still come short of being human beings, then it has betrayed its commitment to humanity and has misused its responsibilities as a philanthropical organization." To overcome the reservations of federal officials, the FSC pointed to successful examples of cooperative efforts in Europe, Asia, and Africa in addition to New Deal–era experiments in the United States to demonstrate the long-term viability of its projects. As the FSC's southern rural project director William H. Peace III noted, cooperative members themselves were as keenly interested in self-sufficiency as outside funding agencies were in seeing them become so. Yet, he argued, the FSC could legitimately ask, "Why should we have to become self-dependent?" Taxpayers' money paid for USDA services to the nation's giant agribusinesses, yet the government demanded that poor people who benefited from the FSC's programs pay for these themselves.[30] Moreover, the corporate farms that some analysts held up as models of business efficiency were not self-sustaining. Without the millions of dollars in government subsidies that large growers received under the Agricultural Adjustment Act, these enterprises were no more viable than the low-income cooperatives.

The FSC's staff and members considered that they had established a strong record of achievement and demonstrated the effectiveness of cooperatives in combating rural poverty and out-migration. They had done this in spite of the limitations imposed by inadequate finances, restrictions on the use of grant money, and bureaucratic meddling from people whose own expertise was limited. The doubts expressed by foundation and federal officials, their reluctance to fully support the cooperative movement, and their efforts to steer the FSC toward meeting their own agendas instead of serving rural black southerners generated resentment and caused some people within the movement to wonder what these agencies' real motives were. In May 1970, for example, after the OEO's southeast regional office refused to fund a management training proposal that it had encouraged FSC members to develop, Charles Prejean wrote, "It is inhuman to encourage poor people by promising them assistance that never comes. . . . But maybe we don't have a poverty program that is designed to help the poor. Maybe it's only called a poverty program whose main responsibility is to lie to people and maintain the affluent in lucrative job positions."[31]

Such suspicions emerged again in August 1971, when the OEO announced its intent to conduct an evaluation of the cooperatives it had funded over the past five years as part of a plan to develop "a more effective rural cooperative program." The agency chose a Massachusetts consulting firm that had no experience with cooperatives or rural development to carry out the study over fourteen months at a cost of $360,000. Officials then invited cooperative leaders to submit suggestions regarding the design and direction of the study. In the context of their past experiences with federal agencies and recent cuts in OEO programs, Prejean and many others concluded that the real reason for the evaluation was to provide a rationale for defunding cooperatives. John Brown Jr. urged FSC members to "unite in opposing this 'Bull shit.' They can spend the money, but they *cannot* have a valid study without our cooperation." Brown noted that many cooperatives had received only one or two years of funding from the OEO and some, like SEASHA, had recently had their grants cut significantly. Often, he claimed, the OEO had provided no support at all, "just criticisms, confusion and other practices designed to create failure." In Brown's view, the OEO had already decided to withdraw federal assistance to cooperatives and the study was aimed at justifying this action. He argued that this money could be better spent by giving it directly to cooperatives to help them become self-sufficient.[32]

The FSC and SCDF both opposed the evaluation, as did SEASHA, SWAFCA, and three smaller cooperatives that were slated for inclusion. The cooperative directors called on supporters of the movement in Congress to pressure OEO officials to abandon the study and prepared a position paper outlining their objections. "Already this movement has been studied, monitored, and evaluated to death," they stated. "We have spelled out our needs to our government incessantly. We have written countless proposals asking for assistance. We have either been ignored completely or given crumbs." In a letter to Senator Hubert Humphrey, William H. Peace III emphasized the hopes for a better future that cooperatives had given rural poor southerners. "The cooperative as viewed by our people is not welfare, a hand-out, or somebody else doing it for you. . . . It is self determination, decision making, and participatory democracy in action. And it is the way to a better life for many of the people in our region." What the cooperatives needed now, Peace argued, was not more scrutiny but the "support and commitment on the part of OEO and others for the low-income cooperative movement."[33]

Federal officials attempted to assure cooperative leaders that the evaluation aimed to strengthen the movement, not destroy it. Office of Program Development director Carol Khosrovi pointed out that recent amendments to the Economic Opportunity Act provided for federal funding of cooperatives as "on-going, operational projects." She argued that FSC members could provide federal administrators with valuable information about how to help cooperatives succeed. After a meeting with cooperative directors in November failed to convince them of the study's potential value, Khosrovi and OEO chief Phillip Sanchez reiterated that the agency's goal was not to attack the cooperative movement or justify withdrawing support. They encouraged cooperative leaders to help design and interpret the study, saying, "We offer this not as an accommodation but as a sincere effort to improve our service to the rural poor."[34]

These expressions of federal goodwill eventually won over A. J. McKnight, who stated his willingness to allow the SCDF to participate in the study in December. Several other cooperatives also changed their position, and those with SCDF loans were included by extension whether they wanted to be or not. The FSC remained adamant in its opposition, however. Its staff referred OEO officials to research done by agricultural economists Roosevelt Steptoe, Ray Marshall, and Lamond Godwin that already provided much of the information the agency claimed to need regarding the problems facing low-income cooperatives and potential solutions. Charles Prejean insisted nothing could be gained from further studies, and that even if the evaluation yielded favorable conclusions, there was no guarantee the federal government would continue to fund cooperatives.[35] With the FSC's membership facing more pressing needs and the financial future uncertain, Prejean noted, its leaders could not in good conscience support the OEO's diversion of hundreds of millions of dollars toward another wasteful evaluation. In a strongly worded letter to Sanchez, the FSC director again expressed his organization's refusal to participate. "We will not cooperate with the study and will do all in our power to prevent 'white folks from making other white folk (white consultant firms)' rich at Black people's expense," he stated. Prejean expressed the same views to Khosrovi, threatening to do everything he could to discredit the study if it went ahead. According to Prejean, the FSC's board, staff, and members were prepared to face whatever consequences resulted from this action, including the loss of OEO funds.[36]

As expected, the OEO retaliated by refusing to consider a proposal for refunding the FSC after its grant expired in June. At the same time, the FSC encountered renewed problems in its relationship with the Ford Foundation. In March 1972 foundation staff urged the FSC and SCDF to merge under the leadership of A. J. McKnight, with a single office located in either Atlanta or New Orleans instead of the three bases currently representing the cooperative movement in Lafayette, Epes, and Atlanta. As McKnight understood it, the request was more like an ultimatum, with Ford threatening to cut off funding for the FSC unless Prejean agreed to step down as director. Prejean refused and, with the support of his staff, proposed to move the SCDF headquarters to Epes instead. McKnight was unwilling to give up leadership of the SCDF, however, and his staff did not want to relocate. In April he suggested to Prejean that they work to preserve things as they were, with both men doing what they thought was best for their respective organizations while trying to coordinate their efforts whenever possible.[37]

The mutual hostility between Prejean and Ford executives intensified when Bryant George sought the FSC's cooperation in a "formal evaluation" of its programs. According to George, a comprehensive assessment had not been undertaken since Ford first began to support the cooperative movement, and the foundation planned to remedy this in 1972. Two men who were "very sympathetic to the Cooperative Movement" were hired as evaluators, but they received an icy response when they attempted to obtain information from the FSC. On 26 April George warned Prejean that failure to cooperate with the evaluation would make it impossible for Ford to continue funding the organization. Although he admitted that allowing the evaluation to go forward would not necessarily guarantee funding either, George assured Prejean that Ford had "a strong and continuing program interest in the cooperative movement."[38]

As was the case with the OEO, some cooperative leaders suspected that the Ford Foundation's expressions of support masked a hidden agenda aimed at destroying the movement. Lewis Black noted that Ford and the cooperatives had enjoyed a good working relationship until Bryant George began pushing for a merger of the FSC and SCDF. Motivated by his hatred for Prejean, George had succeeded in turning Ford executives as well as other funding sources against the FSC and convinced McKnight that he should take overall leadership over the cooperatives. "What is the real purpose for Bryant George and Ford Foundation creating all of this disharmony between McKnight and Charles Prejean?" Black wondered. In a letter to George informing him that cooperative leaders had rejected the idea of a merger but were drawing up plans for closer coordination between their organizations, Prejean stated that they all knew this was unacceptable to Ford but they could not allow outsiders to control the course of the cooperative movement. The FSC had tried to demonstrate that even though rural black southerners might be poor and uneducated, they could develop solutions to complex problems if granted the right resources. The Ford Foundation was apparently unconvinced that poor people could successfully guide their own economic advancement despite evidence the FSC had provided to the contrary. "Send your consultants down, Bryant," Prejean urged, "and let them reinforce your opinion of us, if that is what you need to support your final argument against us."[39]

On 15 June 1972 Mitchell Sviridoff informed Prejean that Ford could no longer continue its support for the FSC because of a "basic, conscientious disagreement on policy." The FSC wanted to serve all 110 of its member cooperatives despite the strain this placed on resources and the massive amounts of money required, while the Ford Foundation preferred to concentrate its funds on a small number of cooperatives to serve as models for rural development. Foundation executives had decided their best course was to "assist organizations whose goals are more in line with the scale of operation that it is possible for us to undertake." Sviridoff offered the FSC $90,000 for July and August to help it adjust to the loss of Ford Foundation funds and added, "Our negative decision was not based on a feeling that the program of Federation of Southern Cooperatives lacks merit; clearly, the Federation of Southern Cooperatives is an important force in the lives of the thousands of individuals in the Coops it serves."[40]

Reflecting on Ford's decision some decades later, Prejean acknowledged some fundamental differences in the way the foundation and the FSC viewed social problems. Not entirely convinced that cooperatives were viable and working with limited funds, Ford executives seemed overwhelmed by the scale of the problem and feared a future where the FSC just kept returning and asking them for money. Therefore, they asked the FSC to limit its assistance to the most successful co-ops and essentially abandon the rest. For the FSC's members, Ford's approach was out of the question. "I just couldn't see how they had the right to tell people to scale down their needs," Prejean stated. Moreover, it would be difficult to develop objective criteria to determine which co-ops to help, and doing so would only divide the movement. As Prejean explained, "We had not come into the organization in that way. Everybody had legitimate needs and everybody's efforts would be supported and fought for."[41]

The FSC's determination to pursue its own rural development agenda rather than adjusting its programs to fit the wishes of its two biggest financial supporters cost the organization millions of dollars in funding. Internal discord over the SCDF's decision to cooperate with the OEO study further weakened the cooperative movement. Yet participants refused to allow the movement to die. The FSC survived the next two years by cutting back operations and seeking smaller grants from other foundations and government agencies as well as church groups to enable it to continue to provide a basic level of service to its members.[42] A grant from HEW allowed the staff in Alabama to work with local people on plans to create a Black Belt Community Health Center modeled on the TDHC in Mississippi, and the DOL provided funds to train 490 people in the technical, administrative, and business skills they needed to improve the management of their cooperatives. In 1973 the FSC secured a contract from the OMBE to provide technical assistance and loan packaging services to small business entrepreneurs in seven states. Staff of its business development offices (BDOs) located in rural towns such as Tallulah, Louisiana, helped secure 114 loans totaling $10 million as well as 50 procurement contracts worth $1,741,017 in the first year of the program. The FSC also initiated two projects aimed at generating income and decreasing its dependence on outside funds. PanSco, Inc. was chartered as a for-profit subsidiary that began by operating a gift shop and laundromat at the RTRC in Epes and investigating other potential business ventures that could produce revenue for the organization. The FSC's Forty Acres and a Mule Fund had a similar purpose, aiming to solicit donations for an investment fund. Thus, although money remained tight, the FSC managed to maintain its core services to cooperatives and branched into new areas. In March 1974 Charles Prejean reported that despite the difficulties created by the funding situation, the federation remained "steadfast in our determination to make the rural South a place for Blacks to live and earn a decent livelihood."[43]

The FSC continued to act as a leading advocate for rural poor southerners in the second half of the 1970s, often blending its economic and social development programs with political activism. The struggle to ensure that African Americans and other nonwhite residents received their fair share of the jobs and business opportunities created by the Tennessee-Tombigbee Waterway (TTW) project was an example of this approach. Originally proposed by a group of congressmen from the Tombigbee Valley in the 1940s, construction of the 234-mile waterway was delayed for several decades amid concerns about its cost effectiveness.[44] In the 1960s the War on Poverty provided additional leverage to supporters of the project, who emphasized its potential to revitalize the economically depressed counties that lined its planned route from Mississippi's northern border with Tennessee to the Warrior-Tombigbee Waterway in western Alabama. In 1967 the conservative business leaders who made up the Tennessee-Tombigbee Waterway Development Authority (TTWDA) appropriated the arguments of social justice activists in their appeal for federal funds. "Sociologists have long recognized that a deprived people can be assisted more effectively in their home environment than by uprooting them," they stated. The TTW would create jobs and other economic opportunities for the region's impoverished inhabitants and encourage them to stay in the area instead of migrating to cities that could not absorb them. "Considering the amount of money spent yearly in the Tennessee-Tombigbee region on welfare funds and economic assistance," the TTWDA concluded, "the question must be posed: Is NOT building the Tennessee-Tombigbee Waterway actually a SAVINGS?" Congress provided $500,000 for planning and design of the project, and construction began in 1972.[45]

Despite its expressed concern for the plight of rural poor people, the TTWDA showed little interest in including them as participants or beneficiaries of the project. The first construction contract, for building a dam at Gainesville, Alabama, went to an Oklahoma company that brought in workers from outside the region instead of hiring local people. In November 1973 John Zippert and several other activists staged a demonstration at the dam site to demand equal opportunity for nonwhite workers and more hiring of people from the Gainesville area. In response, company executives invited them to help recruit local people for training and jobs on the project. The FSC agreed to develop a plan to help meet the company's labor needs and began a major outreach effort in the communities along the TTW to educate people about the project and the opportunities that were available.[46]

In January 1974 the FSC hosted the first People's Conference on the Tennessee-Tombigbee Waterway at its training center in Epes. Lamond Godwin told the gathering of more than 200 community leaders from Alabama, Mississippi, and Tennessee: "We have had successful struggles against slavery, for civil rights, for political power; now the struggle is for economic development." He noted that the TTWDA had no African Americans among its thirty-one members or its staff and warned that continued racial discrimination was likely unless black people took action. Conference participants also learned that in addition to the exclusion of nonwhite workers from jobs on the project, government officials were using eminent domain to purchase property from black landowners at less than market value. They voted to create the Minority Peoples Council on the Tennessee-Tombigbee Waterway Project (MPC), chaired by the FSC's Wendell Paris, to monitor developments on the waterway and ensure that local people's voices were heard. The MPC's goals included the employment of nonwhite workers in all phases of the project, representation on planning boards, minority business development and ownership along the waterway, assistance to black farmers to help them retain and develop their land, and raising citizen awareness of the project and its impact.[47]

Staff of the Emergency Land Fund (ELF), an organization formed in 1971 to help black farmers remain on the land, worked closely with FSC leaders in the MPC coalition. Founded by black economist and social justice activist Robert Browne, ELF raised hundreds of thousands of dollars from churches and private donors to save black-owned farms that were threatened by tax sales. The group's assistance bought time for owners to pay their taxes and prevented the loss of 1,498 acres in the first year of the program. Staff members also worked to combat what one of them called "chicanery bordering on the illegal" that frequently transferred black land into the hands of unscrupulous lenders and speculators. Recognizing that economic development and rising land values along the waterway were likely to intensify these problems, ELF developed a list of black landowners in the affected counties and offered legal assistance to help them resist pressures to sell property to the government or private developers.[48]

In the two years following its initial meeting, the MPC published and distributed an informational pamphlet titled "The People's Guide to the TTW," sponsored a workshop for black contractors interested in gaining work on the waterway, pressured the TTWDA to include black representatives on decision-making bodies related to the project, lobbied to increase nonwhite employment on waterway construction, and secured cooperation from the International Union of Operating Engineers for a program to recruit, train, and place black workers in TTW jobs. The FSC's RTRC provided the venue for training approximately 3,000 people

KEEP YOUR ROOTS WITH E.L.F.

THE EMERGENCY LAND
FUND COMES TO YOUR
RESCUE TO ASSIST
WITH THE
PROBLEMS OF
BLACK LAND
OWNERSHIP

Graphic by MICHAEL WATSON (JSU)

Black Sweat & Blood is in it...
Save Black Owned Land!

The Emergency Land Fund's (ELF) land saving efforts are directly related to the amount of contributions the organization receives from those who support its work. ELF cannot engage in its land saving efforts without these contributions. With them, ELF becomes a viable and effective land saving force.

With land, black families can retain the dignity of economic independence. Without land they have nowhere to go but to the cities that cannot absorb them nor provide warm houses or decent, adequate paying jobs.

Your tax deductible gift will ensure the continuation and expansion of our efforts to prevent a vital way of life from becoming extinct. Won't you please join us?

WE NEED YOUR HELP!

EMERGENCY LAND FUND, 564 Lee Street, S.W.,
Atlanta, Georgia 30310
Please find my tax deductible contribution of $ _____

Name

Address

City　　　　　　　State　　　　　　　Zip

Cut out and mail with your contribution

Fund-raising advertisement from an Emergency Land Fund newsletter encouraging African Americans to retain ownership of their farms. *40 Acres and a Mule*, December 1979, p. 8. David R. Bowen Collection, Congressional and Political Research Center, Mississippi State University Libraries.

in skilled trades that included carpentry, masonry, and heavy equipment maintenance to prepare them for employment on the project. Like its cooperative development efforts, the federation's TTW initiatives opened up economic opportunities that encouraged African Americans to stay in the region and, in some cases, lured migrants back to the South. James E. James, a twenty-one-year-old Alabamian who had moved to Boston in the late 1960s, decided to return after hearing about the FSC's training program. "I was a janitor at the South Boston Army Base, and shortly after I came home for a visit, I heard about the Epes training center," he told *Ebony* magazine. "The opportunity to learn a trade and to join the union caused me to move back home."[49]

The MPC also took action to ensure that black workers were employed on the TTW once they were trained. Hiring policies in the initial phases of waterway construction were guided by a federal affirmative action plan that aimed for 20 percent minority participation in a region where African Americans were 40 percent of the population. The MPC developed an alternative proposal that aimed for 40 percent minority hiring by 1977 and secured support for the plan from unions, contractors, and community groups.[50] Federal agencies were reluctant to endorse the plan, but continued pressure from MPC activists eventually led the DOL's Office of Federal Contract Compliance Programs to impose a new TTW project plan on contractors that extended to both federal and nonfederal construction projects in thirty counties in Alabama and Mississippi. Described by Lamond Godwin as "the most inclusive area-wide affirmative action plan ever issued" by a government agency, the measure called for 19 percent employment of nonwhite workers immediately in all thirty counties, to be increased to 30 percent by 1980.[51] Although this goal was never fully achieved, in 1983 contractors reported an overall minority employment rate ranging from 23 to 27 percent during the past five years of construction. An article in *Mainstream Mississippi* noted, "A number of unprecedented programs and activities undertaken on the Tenn-Tom project have ensured that local people, particularly the disadvantaged, do benefit to the maximum extent possible from the job and business opportunities from the waterway construction." One observer attributed this largely to the FSC and its allies, calling the federation "the single most important voice and advocate for minorities on the Tennessee-Tombigbee Waterway." Two years later, after completion of the waterway, the MPC's contribution to ensuring broad participation was recognized at a dedication ceremony in Columbus.[52]

The effort to secure a place for rural poor people in the TTW led the FSC to widen the scope of its activities beyond support for cooperatives. Activists understood the importance of nonfarm employment opportunities to the rural economy, and in the second half of the 1970s the FSC supplemented earlier programs aimed at helping black farmers stay on the land with training programs designed to enable people to make the transition to jobs on the TTW and other industries outside agriculture. In 1975 the FSC applied for CETA funds to operate an outreach, referral, and work experience program and to develop a resource team to craft a long-range training and employment strategy for the TTW region. Federal officials rejected the proposal, but the FSC secured support from other organizations to proceed with parts of the project. The FSC worked with a local union to create an eight-month-long training program for fifty heavy equipment operators, and two-thirds of the trainees went on to find jobs on the TTW. Foundation grants funded the research portion of the plan, which identified other skills in which workers could be trained and employed locally. As Charles Prejean noted, such work was essential to fulfilling the promise to reduce poverty, unemployment, and out-migration from the TTW impact area, which had been highlighted by its supporters when they were lobbying for federal appropriations. "We have yet to see or feel these 're-development benefits' claimed for the project," he wrote in 1976. "This is mainly because the emphasis thus far has been on the physical development of the project and not the human resource development and training needed to involve indigenous, disadvantaged and minority people in the TTW."[53]

Despite the need to do more, the political conservatism and economic austerity of the 1970s were not conducive to expansion or initiation of new projects, and the FSC had problems just continuing some of its existing programs. The success of the business development efforts supported by the OMBE was jeopardized when federal officials ordered the program to decentralize in 1974, forcing each of the FSC's BDOs to seek refunding from regional offices of the federal agency. The FSC's business packager Ramon Tyson detected an urban bias in regional administrators' plans to close the BDO in Tallulah, Louisiana, and open one in Monroe (population 80,000) instead. Black businesses and cooperatives in Madison Parish and seven other rural parishes served by the Tallulah BDO lost a valuable resource as a result of the decision.[54]

In April 1975 the OMBE terminated its contract with the FSC and announced plans to fund state OMBE offices in Mississippi, Alabama, and Georgia instead. Seven of the eleven BDOs the FSC had administered received funding from the regional office in Atlanta, but the others were unable to continue operations. The diversion of funds from nonprofit organizations like the FSC to state offices controlled by southern governors worried Prejean and other activists. State officials' past history of neglect of rural poor people hardly inspired confidence, and recent studies of the ways administrators in Mississippi and Alabama chose to spend federal money showed that economic development efforts were concentrated in areas with predominantly white populations. "We are concerned with what may be an overall trend in OMBE to consign and direct precious flexible Federal resources to state governments who have historically shown little interest in the problems and need for development of business enterprises within the Black community," Prejean wrote in a letter to Congressman Parren Mitchell.[55]

The experience with the OMBE typified the FSC's relationship with the federal government during the Nixon and Ford administrations. Funding was scant and uncertain, bureaucratic rules and restrictions limited the effectiveness of the few programs that were funded, and agency officials expressed little interest in supporting the cooperative movement.[56] The election of Democratic president Jimmy Carter in 1976 was a welcome change, and the FSC's prospects brightened a little with the appointment of several long-time friends to key positions. Secretary of Labor Ray Marshall was the son of a tenant farmer and a southern liberal who understood the root causes of rural poverty, including the role that racism played in the problem. Like FSC leaders, Marshall believed cooperatives could provide poor people with the economic independence they needed to mobilize politically and transform power relationships in the South. Additionally, new leadership at the FmHA resulted in policies that aimed to improve services to rural poor people, increase the proportion of loan funds granted to African Americans, and foster better cooperation with nonprofit groups such as the FSC.[57]

Another promising development came when administration officials successfully pushed for passage of the National Consumer Cooperative Bank Act, which aimed to support consumer cooperatives and included provisions to create a self-help development fund for low-income cooperatives. Speaking in favor of the legislation before a Senate subcommittee in January 1978, Assistant Treasury Secretary Robert C. Altman stated, "Consumer cooperatives in blighted urban and underdeveloped rural areas may offer one of the best prospects for economic development or redevelopment there." The new bank was eventually capitalized with $300 million for loans to cooperatives, and another $75 million was allocated to the Office of Self-Help and Technical Assistance to serve low-income cooperatives. In his 1980 budget, President Carter requested $12 million to invest in community development credit unions.[58]

The FSC benefited directly from federal agencies' renewed willingness to fund its rural development efforts during the Carter years. In 1977 the CSA provided assistance to the FSC for the first time since the fight over the OEO evaluation in 1972, partially funding an energy conservation and renewable energy conversion program for small farmers. Even before the energy crisis of the 1970s, FSC staff had perceived the potential economic and environmental benefits of encouraging farmers to reduce their consumption of expensive fossil fuels. The CSA grant enabled them to develop demonstration projects, such as solar greenhouses, windmills, and alternative crop production methods, and to teach members how to switch from traditional to energy-conserving farming methods. The DOL provided $172,585 in CETA funds for a housing rehabilitation program operated by the FSC in cooperation with local governments in Greene County and the towns of Forkland and Boligee in Alabama. The funds were used to employ a project director and two housing construction crews, each comprising a building supervisor, loan packager, and five CETA trainees. Together the two groups worked to repair sixty substandard homes inhabited by farmworkers and other rural poor people. The FSC was also approved as a national sponsor for the Volunteers in Service to America (VISTA) program, enabling it to recruit one hundred local volunteers from among its member groups as well as ten national volunteers to be based in the southeastern states. By August 1978 the FSC had managed to secure close to $2 million in support of its programs from the federal government.[59]

Although conditions imposed by both federal and foundation grants prohibited the FSC from directly engaging in political activities, its goal of economic empowerment for black southerners was inextricably linked to that of political empowerment. Cooperative businesses provided alternatives to migration and encouraged African Americans to stay in the South, helping maintain black voting majorities in the plantation counties. Moreover, cooperative organizing fostered political organizing in the communities where the FSC was active and helped black candidates win local elections. As Ezra Cunningham explained, cooperatives were a central element in the post-1960s freedom movement. "We accomplished the fact that [black people] stayed," he stated. "Then we also accomplished the other fact that we did some things politically and civically. . . . I really think that SWAFCA had more to do with the political advancement than the Alabama Democratic Conference, the Alabama New South Coalition, and all of these other things."[60]

These connections were also evident in Tallulah, Louisiana. The FSC helped set up a credit union there in October 1969, providing money to hire a bookkeeper and two field-workers to train members. The credit union in turn contributed to the success of a newly established cooperative store, with many credit union members buying shares in the store. According to the FSC, the credit union and cooperative were part of a "general awakening by Black people to control the political and economic destiny of their own communities. A number of Blacks have been elected to public office in Tallulah as part of the same movement which promoted the growth of the credit union and consumer store." In July 1974 the local governments of Tallulah and two other communities served by the FSC (Waterproof and Lake Providence) came under black control for the first time. Tallulah mayor Adell Williams credited the FSC's BDO staff in Louisiana with boosting black business development in the region, participating in community events and organizations, and encouraging town officials to form a local development corporation to initiate new projects. With assistance from the FSC and government agencies, he stated, "we will meet the task in front of us of making Tallulah a better place to live for all its citizens."[61]

The FSC's presence and the new forms of activism it generated worried conservative southerners who feared the consequences of black political power. From the beginning, the FSC had endured constant criticism and attacks aimed at weakening or destroying the organization. Of the eleven states included in its initial OEO grant in 1968, only Georgia gave immediate and unconditional approval for the FSC to operate there. The governors of Alabama, Arkansas, Missouri, and Tennessee vetoed the grant, and officials in Louisiana and South Carolina imposed restrictions that forced FSC staff to gain approval from their SEOOs before initiating projects. The remaining four states neither approved nor vetoed the grant, allowing it to go into effect after the thirty-day veto period expired.[62]

The hostility of state and local officials toward the organization often hindered the FSC's work. The DOL's southeast regional office delayed approval of an FSC management training grant for two years despite federal officials' support for the project. To Charles Prejean, the reasons for the delay were obvious: "We are primarily a Black organization trying to deal with problems of the poor. To fund us would mean an admission of neglect to the Black and poor of the Southeast region."[63] After asking the FSC to rewrite and resubmit its proposal four times, late in 1971 the DOL finally accepted a version that was essentially the same as the original proposal. "We honestly believe that they did this to discourage us," Prejean stated.[64]

Similar obstructionism plagued the PLBA's attempts to build homes for its members on the tract of land it shared with the FSC in Sumter County, delaying completion of the project for a decade. The PLBA filed its initial application for a rural cooperative housing loan from the FmHA in November 1971. After battling multiple obstacles that included the skepticism of local and state FmHA officials, an eight-month moratorium on low-income housing loans imposed by President Nixon in 1973, the Alabama Water Improvement Commission's "arbitrary and capricious" refusal to approve the proposed water and sewage system for the site, prolonged negotiations with the Sumter County water authority to include the project in new water services planned for rural residents, and a last-minute investigation by the USDA's Office of the Inspector General just as final approval from the FmHA was pending in November 1979, forty families finally moved into newly constructed homes and rental units at the PLBA's Wendy Hills subdivision early in 1981.[65]

The strongest opposition to the FSC came from white leaders in Alabama, home to the RTRC and the largest concentration of federation staff. Many of the people who occupied the trailer homes and dormitories at the Epes site were veterans of the civil rights movement. Although they were not allowed to use their work time or resources for political activities, Charles Prejean admitted that FSC staff had "a strong identity with, and continue to support activities in, the areas of racial equality and social justice." White residents of Sumter County thus noticed a marked increase in black voter registration, candidates running for office, and the general level of assertiveness shown by African Americans in their community in the 1970s. Many of them found the changes difficult to accept. The transition to an all-black government in neighboring Greene County was an example of the threat posed to elite white families accustomed to dominating the political and economic structures of the Black Belt. *Livingston Home Record* editor John Neel asserted: "Nobody wants what happened in Greene County to happen here." Yet opponents of black political empowerment proved unable to stop it. African Americans voted in large numbers in the 1976 elections, and white incumbents only narrowly defeated their black challengers. In 1978 black candidates won two seats on the five-member board of education.[66]

White political leaders in Sumter County were convinced that the source of all their problems was the FSC. Rumors of corruption, nepotism, mismanagement, and the training of armed black revolutionaries at the RTRC circulated among local residents, and the *Home Record* denounced "government-funded activism." In May 1979 more than one hundred white people met at the Cotton Patch restaurant in Greene County to discuss the situation. The group included John Neel, I. Drayton Pruitt (a lawyer who had tried to block the sale of land to the PLBA), local officials Sam Massengill and Joe Steagall, state legislator Preston Minus, Congressman Richard Shelby, and staff representatives of Alabama senators Howell Heflin and Donald Stewart. Participants shared stories they had heard about the misuse of federal funds and other illegal activities at the RTRC and agreed that the FSC should be investigated. Pruitt, Massengill, and Steagall then sent a formal letter of complaint to Shelby, who forwarded it to the GAO. The GAO reported in September that its preliminary inquiries had uncovered nothing to suggest that an investigation was warranted, pointing out that the inspectors general of the federal agencies that funded FSC activities could investigate further if they wanted to. John Zippert explained to supporters who asked for information about the GAO inquiry that the FSC had done nothing wrong and that the complaint was a response to a recent school boycott and other activities by local black people aimed at improving conditions in the public schools. Although some federation staff participated in these activities, they did so on their own time and no FSC funds were used. "Basically, we feel this investigation has been motivated as a harassment tactic by local racist Alabama officials against FSC," he stated. "We consider this investigation merely another of many occupational hazards for organizations genuinely committed to assisting poor people in a process of community change and development in America."[67]

The GAO probe did not satisfy the FSC's opponents, and more "occupational hazards" followed. J. R. Brooks, the United States attorney for Alabama's Northern District, convened a grand jury to further investigate the FSC. On 31 December 1979 FBI agents acting on behalf of the jury served Charles Prejean with a subpoena demanding that he turn over "any and all documents in connection with federal funding of the Federation of Southern Cooperatives and its affiliated cooperatives" for the period from 1976 to 1979. The agents refused to provide information regarding specific allegations against the FSC or its employees, and the organization's legal counsel advised Prejean not to comply until the FBI explained the reason for the request. As one Mississippi lawyer who had worked with the FSC for several years noted, the government's subpoena was unusually sweeping. "It reflects a 'witch hunt,'" he wrote in a letter to his senator. "No one has been identified as a target, the nature of any alleged wrong-doing is unknown, and the requested information is so broad that every transaction must be under investigation."[68] Prejean explained that the FSC was willing to cooperate with inquiries into specific individuals or activities, but not with what seemed to be "a deliberate attempt on the part of the F. B. I. and the U. S. Attorney's office to debilitate and destroy the entire organization, without giving any reason or basis for their action." He pointed out that the recent GAO audit had found no misuse of federal funds, suggesting that political motivations rather than legitimate concerns lay behind the grand jury investigation.[69]

In February 1980 the grand jury issued a second subpoena with more precise wording but still no explanation of what the investigation was about. The FSC shipped twenty-two boxes of material to Birmingham, including grant proposals, reports, documentation of work done, and payroll records relating to its administration of federal programs. For the next eighteen months FBI agents pored over the documents and interviewed some 200 people in five states about FSC activities. Charles Prejean and John Zippert were called to testify before the grand jury several times in an atmosphere that Zippert described as an "inquisition."[70] Agents also examined the private banking records of some employees, and the Internal Revenue Service "coincidentally" audited ten staff members during the investigation. The prolonged proceedings damaged the FSC's reputation as well as its ability to operate, and the visits from federal agents intimidated many members. In December, Prejean reported that rumors of pending fraud convictions had turned even some PLBA families against the FSC. The financial costs of the investigation were also significant, with government agencies and foundations refusing to fund FSC projects until the investigation was over. Prejean estimated that the inquiry cost the organization more than $1 million in lost grants and $70,000 in legal fees.[71] The vague nature of several more subpoenas demanding more records and J. R. Brooks's continued refusal to make specific charges against the FSC reinforced Prejean's view that the investigation was a politically motivated attack designed to destroy the cooperative movement. "Since the formal legal abolition of 'Jim Crow-ism' one finds its 'de facto' re-emergence in more subtle and perhaps more dangerous forms," he observed. "In the case of FSC, it seems as if a more institutional approach is being used to frustrate and to nullify our rural Black socio-economic initiatives."[72]

Prejean was not alone in this assessment. In a letter to Attorney General Benjamin Civiletti, seven foundation executives who were familiar with the FSC's work expressed concern about the FBI's harassment of an organ-ization that had never given them cause to question its use of the grants they had awarded. "While we hesitate to label this FBI investigation and grand jury probe 'political' in nature, the chain of events which preceded it does raise questions," they stated. In January 1981 attorney Howard Moore Jr. called on Brooks to investigate the Cotton Patch conspirators for violating the FSC's civil rights.[73] John Paul Dalsimer, a Pennsylvania accountant who visited the FBI offices in Birmingham to find out why the investigation was taking so long, reported that the agents assigned to examine the FSC records were annoyed by the task and viewed it as a waste of their time. The delays resulted in part from the agents' unfamil-iarity with the FSC's accounting system and the disorganized arrange-ment of some of the documents, which made invoices and checks difficult to trace. Had the FSC been more forthcoming in supplying needed infor-mation, one agent stated, the investigation would not have dragged on for so long. Yet Dalsimer also suggested that the FSC's suspicious attitude and its reluctance to fully cooperate were justified. In a private note to Moore left out of his official report, the accountant stated, "It does appear the entire investigation is prompted by an attempt to cause organization-ally harm and embarrassment to the Federation. With no suggestion of any specific illegal actions it seems something is wrong with the system and certainly the examination of all the Federation's books and records allow for a possible 'fishing expedition.'"[74]

Throughout the investigation FSC supporters wrote to their sena-tors, congressional representatives, and federal officials urging them to order an end to the inquiry. Civil rights leaders joined with foundation heads to form the National Committee in Support of Community Based Organizations in September 1980 to publicize the FSC's troubles and put pressure on the Justice Department to either charge someone with a crime or drop the case. Prejean and Field Foundation chairman Leslie Dunbar later credited the group with forcing the FSC's enemies to rethink their tactics. "They realized that we were not going to roll over, that we would eventually sue to get this thing settled, and that *they* would be subpoenaed, *they* would have to go to court, *they* would have to give testimony under oath," Prejean stated. Without this mobilization of support, Dunbar speculated, the grand jury might have issued an indictment on flimsy evidence, which would have been followed by a trial and acquittal for lack of proof. In the process, "all political debts would have been paid and the Federation made virtually bankrupt and destroyed." Instead, J. R. Brooks ended the inquiry on 20 May 1981, stating that after analyzing the material supplied by the FSC and information from other sources, he had concluded that "the conduct of the persons under scrutiny does not warrant prosecution by this office."[75] The verdict came as small consolation to the FSC, which faced the task of rebuilding its reputation and finances in a climate of continued hostility to its work.

Emerging out of black southerners' struggles for equality and economic justice in the 1960s, the FSC came into existence at a time when the national commitment to those ideals was waning and political leaders were turning away from the interventionist approaches of the civil rights era. In this context, the organization's demands for millions of dollars in public investments in rural poor communities met with skepticism or outright rejection, placing limits on its achievements. Nonetheless, the assistance it provided to black cooperatives and self-help efforts, along with the political activism it generated, helped sustain the struggle for social justice in the plantation counties. Families that might have left the land and migrated away saw other alternatives and instead chose to stay, becoming active participants in the electoral process and reform efforts. As the concerted efforts of opponents to destroy the organization suggested, the FSC's activities threatened existing power relationships and had the potential to significantly improve conditions for rural poor people. When foundations and federal officials failed to provide the resources needed to solidify and expand on these achievements in the 1970s, they missed an important opportunity to support innovative models for dealing with the consequences of labor displacement. Instead, antigovernment sentiment and faith in market forces gained wide acceptance among Americans and stymied efforts to forge effective solutions to social problems in the late twentieth century.

CHAPTER 7

A WORLD OF DESPAIR

FREE ENTERPRISE AND ITS FAILURES

The FSC limped into the 1980s badly weakened by the damage that resulted from the grand jury investigation, only to see people who were just as hostile and more powerful than its opponents in the South take control of the federal government. Economic recession, inflation, and disillusionment with the Carter administration drew voters to conservative Republican Ronald Reagan, who won the presidency on promises to reduce taxes and rein in "big government." Over the next decade, Reagan and his advisers completed the counterrevolution against social justice movements begun in the 1970s, prescribing cuts in federal programs as the solution to poverty and implementing policies that favored the nation's wealthiest citizens over poorer people. Government support for the FSC's programs all but disappeared, forcing it to rely on much smaller infusions of funds from members, foundations, churches, and other nonprofit groups. The FSC and other organizations continued their work with rural poor people, but the comprehensive and coordinated approach to regional development that activists had dreamed of implementing in the 1970s remained far from being realized.

Economic policy in the 1980s and 1990s reflected growing skepticism that government action could generate prosperity and an emphasis on private sector solutions to social problems. Although some southern communities were able to attract new businesses by offering tax breaks, subsidies, and other incentives, economic growth largely bypassed the plantation counties. Cuts in social services only exacerbated the hardships imposed on residents of places where there were no jobs. A brief period of renewed interest in addressing these problems in the late 1980s quickly faded amid constraints imposed by federal deficits and lack of faith in the government's capacity for the task. By the turn of the century, some communities resembled ghost towns, abandoned by residents who saw little hope for the future and felt compelled to move elsewhere in pursuit of a better life.

Although the FSC's support for cooperatives and other rural development efforts helped improve the lives of those who were touched by them, they reached only a fraction of the region's impoverished people. The same was true of government antipoverty programs, which remained badly underfunded during the Carter years despite the hopes raised by the return of a Democrat to the White House. New CSA director Graciela Olivarez was a more competent administrator than those who had managed the agency in the Nixon era, but without adequate appropriations from Congress there was little she could do to tackle persistent poverty in the rural South. One of Olivarez's early initiatives, a joint effort with the USDA to sponsor five regional conferences on the plight of small farmers, seemed unlikely to expose any new information that was not already known to the groups that had been working with rural people for the past decade.[1] As social justice activists pointed out repeatedly, more action rather than more studying was needed, but it was hard to convince other Americans of this in the climate of belt-tightening and disillusionment with federal intervention that took hold in the 1970s.

Toward the end of the decade, rampant inflation displaced most other concerns as the major issue of the day. Some economists and policy makers blamed costly social programs for the problem, undercutting support for Great Society initiatives. Inflation had multiple causes, including excessive borrowing by corporations and consumers, federal spending on the Vietnam War as well as the War on Poverty, and spikes in the price of oil that rippled through the economy and raised the cost of food, housing, transportation, and consumer items. Ignoring the complexity of the situation, many Americans fixated on government profligacy as the culprit and promoted reduced public spending as the cure. Hard times and greater competition for resources fostered a less generous mood than had existed a decade earlier among the general public, as middle-class people began to suspect that federal efforts to aid poor people came at some sacrifice to themselves. Author Bernard Sloan suggested in *Newsweek* that the nation needed to "reconsider which of our citizens are entitled to first claim on our resources. In our haste to better the lives of the lowest economic level of our society, we have betrayed another, far larger and more deserving group. People who have worked hard, paid their taxes, contributed to the country. Shouldn't their needs be met first?"[2]

Budget-conscious policy makers argued that with the economy in recession and inflation creating hardships for millions of middle-class Americans as well as poor families, the nation could not afford the same level of support for antipoverty initiatives that existed in the past. As some observers noted, however, the problem was not so much limited funds as misguided priorities. Social justice activists had little doubt that the Great Society was fully achievable if the nation only applied the same level of determination and financing in this area that it accorded to other ambitious projects, such as exploring space or defeating the Soviet Union in the Cold War. Civil rights leader Charles Evers asserted that ensuring access to decent jobs, education, homes, and health care simply required political leaders to decide that this was a worthwhile goal and then to direct resources to that end. In 1977 representatives for the nation's CAA administrators recommended adding another $100 million to President Carter's budget request for the CSA, noting that this was a minuscule sum compared with the $22 billion spent on B-1 bombers and Trident submarines. Journalist Dorothy Gilliam also questioned whether the problem was really a lack of money or simply a lack of political will, observing in the *Washington Post* that austerity was "easily used as an excuse for subverting equality; blacks are too expensive, say the neoconservatives."[3]

Advocates for investing in social programs could not convince policy makers to revive this approach, even though rising unemployment endangered the financial security of increasing numbers of people. The Rural Coalition reported in its March 1980 newsletter that "the fever to balance the federal budget has completely swept the Congress," threatening to make things worse for low-income Americans. In its effort to curb inflation by cutting spending, Congress targeted programs that were essential for helping poor people cope with the higher costs of food, housing, and other necessities. "The burden of balancing the budget is about to fall on those who can least afford it, hitting them with a double whammy of less help and higher costs," the group warned. At the same time, the Carter administration's commitment to dealing with rural poverty seemed to be waning. In July 1980 an assessment of the president's rural policy initiatives noted that although some of his ideas were promising, he requested no new funding for implementation, and even the easiest step of appointing an advisory council was not completed. As one observer stated, "When the Carter rural policy came up against the Carter budget, it wasn't hard to tell which one lost."[4]

The political consensus that the nation could no longer afford costly antipoverty initiatives left intact the racial and economic disparities that social justice activists had tried to address in the 1960s. Almost a decade after passage of the Voting Rights Act, Mississippi's SEOO reported that even though the state experienced unprecedented economic growth between 1966 and 1973, 31 percent of families still lived in poverty, and twenty-six counties had poverty rates of 45 percent or higher. In 1977 the Mississippi Council on Human Relations noted that Mississippi still had the highest number of poor children in the country and that welfare aid remained far below what families needed to survive ($60 per month for a family of four, when the cost of basic necessities was estimated at $252). In May of that year, on the tenth anniversary of the Field Foundation's investigation into the Mississippi hunger crisis, the foundation once again sent a team of doctors into the state to see if conditions had improved. Although the doctors reported that children enrolled in Head Start programs were doing well, inadequate funding meant that many eligible families could not participate. Among those who were left out, observers saw many of the same problems the original team described in 1967: listlessness, sores, infections, and other signs of malnutrition. Restrictive welfare policies and decisions made by local administrators excluded many families from receiving food stamps and other assistance, with the result that roughly two-thirds of poor people who were eligible for aid failed to receive it.[5]

Rather than inspiring action, as had happened in the 1960s, for many Americans such reports only confirmed the futility of government efforts to solve social problems. The prevailing view was that the War on Poverty had failed and that its main achievement was to undermine the independent spirit that made the United States great. In July 1978 the director of the Alabama Development Office, Robert "Red" Bamberg, lampooned federal antipoverty efforts in his response to a question about what he planned to do after he stepped down from the post the following year: "I've got it all figured out. I'm going back to the farm, start drawing Social Security, get on the food stamp program, have them hot lunches delivered to me every day, have one of them vans pick me up and take me to town to the liquor store, in fact, I may get me a federal consultant to come down from Washington with a grant to teach me how to hunt and fish. I've had to work for a living all my life and I never learned how to do either one of them." An assessment of "15 years of 'Great Society' spending" that appeared in *U.S. News and World Report* in June 1980 noted that despite billions of dollars spent to solve poverty and racial inequality, both problems remained, and some black people were "worse off than before Johnson's programs were enacted." The article implied that the government had expended massive amounts of money on "scores of big and costly federal programs" that had virtually no impact. Similarly, William Raspberry argued in the *Washington Post* that the "poverty industry," estimated to be costing $20 billion per year, was essentially a subsidized employment program for "middle-income people who study, count, analyze, chart, graph, fold, staple, and, occasionally, mutilate the poor."[6] Neither author distinguished between the early, often successful innovations of the War on Poverty and the evisceration of programs that occurred later on, nor did they mention that expenditures on these initiatives were consistently far below what was needed for them to work effectively.

Disillusionment with government extended even to people who had once viewed federal action as a force for justice. Whereas antigovernment sentiment among white Americans stemmed from their belief that federal officials were meddling too much, among black Americans the loss of confidence came from the sense that government had abandoned them. In the 1972 presidential election, several black civil rights leaders expressed their frustration by switching their allegiance from the Democratic Party to support Richard Nixon's campaign. Floyd McKissick of CORE argued that Democrats took African Americans for granted and engaging in two-party politics was the only way for black people to gain attention from either party. Similarly, Charles Evers refused to support Jimmy Carter for president in 1976 and endorsed Ronald Reagan in 1980, arguing that Reagan's economic agenda offered the best chance of improving conditions for black Americans. Reagan's emphasis on private enterprise as the key to economic recovery fit well with Evers's own record of business entrepreneurship and his belief that no power could ever flow to individuals or the freedom movement as a whole through programs that made people dependent on their government. Evers urged African Americans to set up small businesses in every possible sector, explaining, "Black folks have got to get ready because nobody is going to do anything for us."[7]

Reagan supporters were outliers in the civil rights community. Most activists viewed the candidate as a retrograde ultraconservative whose ideas about racial justice and social policy bore an uncomfortable resemblance to those of southern white supremacists. As governor of California in the late 1960s, Reagan opposed civil rights legislation and federal enforcement efforts as violations of private property rights, denigrated student protesters, and attacked antipoverty programs. In a speech asserting that "government does nothing as well or as economically as the private sector of the economy," Reagan argued that trying to solve unemployment through "government planning" was futile and only made things worse.[8] Like George Wallace, Reagan portrayed federal efforts to ensure racial equality as a threat to Americans' liberties, asserting that parents had the right to choose which schools their children attended and labeling affirmative action programs as "reverse discrimination." Wallace later commented on the similarities, observing: "I talked about the Supreme Court usurpation of power, I talked about the big central government. . . . Reagan got elected . . . by saying those very same things I said way back yonder when I ran for the presidency myself." Wallace and other southern politicians who needed black votes to get elected had by that time renounced their earlier commitment to segregation, and Reagan strongly denied that he was seeking to perpetuate racial discrimination. Nonetheless, unrepentant racists fully perceived how Reagan's agenda meshed with their own. The Ku Klux Klan endorsed Reagan during his 1980 election campaign, and the Citizens' Council praised his opposition to the "forced busing of school children to achieve arbitrary racial quotas" as well as his plans to eliminate "waste, fraud and extravagance in welfare, subsidized housing and other programs."[9]

Like his conservative counterparts in the South, Reagan believed market forces were the most efficient distributors of resources and attributed economic inequality to individual behavior. A small segment of the population who were truly unable to work might need government assistance, he acknowledged, but most people receiving aid should be encouraged to go out and find jobs. Echoing the sentiments of those who thought Mississippi's poverty problem in the 1960s stemmed from laziness or other character deficiencies, Reagan suggested to an interviewer on ABC's *Good Morning America* that people living in the streets in urban poor neighborhoods were "homeless, you might say, by choice." By cutting social programs designed to help low-income families, Reagan attempted to force people to rely less on government and more on their own initiative. Slashing taxes also aimed to shrink government by depriving Congress of the ability to adequately fund regulatory agencies that interfered with private businesses or to revive the interventionist policies of past administrations.[10]

Cartoon by Eldon Pletcher on President Ronald Reagan's budget cuts in the early 1980s.
New Orleans Times-Picayune, n.d. [ca. 1981–84]. AAEC Editorial Cartoons Collection,
McCain Library and Archives, University of Southern Mississippi. © 2014 NOLA Media Group,
LLC. All rights reserved. Used with permission of the *Times-Picayune* and NOLA.com.

With assistance from the Republican majority in the Senate and
southern Democrats who provided the necessary votes in the House,
Congress passed a budget in August 1981 that reduced government
spending by $140 billion over the next three years, mostly by target-
ing programs that served poor people. One provision imposing tighter
eligibility requirements for public assistance meant that an estimated
687,000 families faced having their benefits reduced or eliminated
entirely. Food and nutrition programs also suffered substantial cuts,
ending assistance to 1 million people, and changes to Medicaid meant
700,000 children no longer had access to affordable health care. Public housing and rental subsidies for low-income families were cut by
$12 billion. In a move that seemed to contradict the goal of moving
unemployed people into jobs, the legislation abolished the public service employment provisions of CETA and reduced funding for other
aspects of the program by 20 percent, eliminating 300,000 positions

and making it more difficult for displaced workers to retrain for new careers.[11]

Civil rights and social justice activists noted the disproportionate impact that cuts in social services and job training programs were likely to have on black Americans. The Commission on Civil Rights expressed concerns that the administration was eliminating or scaling back several key programs designed to address the legacies of past discrimination by enhancing economic opportunities for nonwhite citizens, including the EDA, HUD, CSA, and community health centers. Additionally, commission members worried that budget cuts would weaken civil rights enforcement and that funding community development programs through block grants to the states without adequate monitoring of how the money was spent also threatened progress toward racial equality. The Mississippi State Conference of the NAACP observed that the black community felt "under siege" by the administration's positions on issues affecting African Americans, and the FSC was equally critical. Charles Prejean asserted that the president seemed "determined to set back the hands of time and the recent social and economic gains that Blacks have made."[12]

Even the self-described conservatives who administered Alabama's Department of Pensions and Security questioned the wisdom of Reagan's approach in a statement they prepared in August 1983. Although they shared the president's desire to foster individual responsibility and curb federal spending, they felt bound to point out that reducing benefits for welfare recipients was misguided. "The administration's proposal assumes jobs are available but these persons simply won't work," they stated. "This is not an accurate description of the situation in Alabama." Most people would happily take jobs if they could be found; the problem was there were no jobs. The document cited unemployment rates for several Black Belt counties that ranged from 15 to 20 percent and asserted that forcing more people into the job market by cutting benefits "doesn't recognize the realities in our poorest counties." Although tighter eligibility requirements reduced the state's welfare caseload from 63,000 families to 55,000, requests for assistance from local charities increased by 40 percent, suggesting that problems were being shifted, not solved.[13] Moreover, the nonprofit organizations that many poor people now turned to for aid were themselves being undermined by federal budget cuts. The Alabama Coalition Against Hunger, for example, lost 65 percent of its budget and had to lay off most of its staff when Reagan eliminated the CSA in October 1981. Although state and local governments continued to fund many CAAs and programs, the loss of the federal agency was felt deeply by those who remembered its earlier role in the War on Poverty, both symbolically and financially. A survey of thirty-four social service projects conducted by the National Council of Churches found that they expected their aggregate funding to decline from $12 million to $6 million in 1982, and no one knew how to make up the shortfall. "We cannot eradicate hunger without Government participation in the programs," one church leader observed.[14]

As in his overall economic policy, Reagan's approach to the problems confronting rural Americans emphasized private enterprise as the key to creating wealth and jobs and reduced the role of the federal government. A DOL information sheet set out four themes that guided the administration's approach: shifting control of resources to state and local governments, encouraging grantees to seek nonfederal funding for programs, increasing private sector involvement, and reducing federal regulation. Secretary of Labor Raymond Donovan expressed confidence that these measures would "materially enhance our ability to address rural development problems," but others who were familiar with past moves in this direction during the Nixon and Carter years were not so sure. Gerald Hambleton, a journalist and local official in Rapides Parish, Louisiana, wrote to Russell Long in April 1983 to urge him to oppose plans to shift more responsibility for rural development to the states. Twenty years of observing how governments worked in the region had convinced him that Reagan's proposals would be "the death knell to much needed assistance to the 'truly needy'" and that limiting federal oversight rarely made programs more efficient. As with Nixon's New Federalism in the 1970s, Reagan's conversion of more funds into block grants meant that money currently being used to improve living conditions and services in rural poor communities could easily be diverted "to maintain courthouses, pay policemen, and run other programs with a more powerful constituency." As well as depriving low-income people of their share of resources, Hambleton noted, this dynamic reinforced taxpayers' erroneous belief that local governments could continue to provide basic services even as constituents repeatedly voted down the tax increases needed to pay for them.[15]

Reliance on private sector investment left rural communities at a disadvantage in the competition for industry. Few entrepreneurs wanted to build factories or establish businesses in plantation counties lacking adequate schools, health care, transportation, and communication networks, and researchers documented persistent racial inequities in the geographic distribution of economic development in the South. A report prepared by a regional coalition of southern governors in 1986 noted that the economic boom that was bringing more high-tech industries, skilled jobs, and northern migrants to some parts of the region largely bypassed its poorest communities. "The sunshine on the Sunbelt has proved to be a narrow beam of light, brightening futures along the Atlantic Seaboard, and in large cities, but skipping over many small towns and rural areas," the authors stated. "The decade's widely publicized new jobs at higher pay have been largely claimed by educated, urban, and middle-class Southerners." Although per capita income in the region had reached 88 percent of the national average, millions of southerners remained mired in poverty and were "not being retrained for the next century's technical and service careers."[16]

In a study of development patterns in four states, including Alabama and Mississippi, sociologist Glenna Colclough found that industry and employment growth were "more likely for predominantly white counties and losses more likely for counties having large black populations." Without outside support, she predicted, rural black communities would "continue to be shunned by employers." The director of Alabama's Industrial Development Training Institute acknowledged that companies were reluctant to locate in the state's plantation regions. "A company is not going to buy a bunch of social problems," he stated. "Sure, some companies have said that they don't want to locate in an area with a majority-black population or a black political structure. Anybody who tells you differently is lying."[17] Despite some growth in the number of nonagricultural jobs between 1970 and 1990, black unemployment rates in all the counties that are the focus of this book increased during these decades. Poverty rates for black families declined steadily until the 1980s, then stagnated or began to rise again in the wake of cuts to social services. The average poverty rate in each state's plantation region in 1990 was more than 40 percent. (See Appendix, tables 1 and 2.)

The situation became more dire as free trade agreements promoted by Presidents Carter and Reagan opened new opportunities overseas for American businesses. Industries such as textiles and apparel that made up a significant portion of the southern manufacturing sector in the mid-twentieth century were susceptible to the lure of cheaper labor overseas, which threatened the job security and employment conditions of many factory workers. Newer transplants in the post–1960s decades also proved to be unstable prospects. Southern counties and towns that successfully lured manufacturers to relocate in the region often saw their new prizes pick up and leave for Latin America or Asia within a decade of arrival. In 1981, bicycle manufacturer Schwinn shifted its plant from Chicago to Greenville, Mississippi, but ten years later moved its operations to Taiwan. Greenville leaders also managed to persuade Boeing to build an aircraft repair facility there in 1985, offering the company $20 million in corporate subsidies. Four years later, Boeing left as well. William Harrison of the SCDF reported that St. Landry Parish, Louisiana, had significantly diversified its economy to include manufacturing, wholesale, and retail services in the 1960s and 1970s, but job losses numbering in the thousands raised the unemployment rate from 7 percent to 17 percent by the mid-1980s. International competition made it harder for local governments in the rural South to attract businesses to their communities despite their willingness, as one politician expressed it, to do "anything short of illegal" to help investors. Many feared that further cuts in federal assistance for rural development would worsen the situation. By one estimate, employment in southern manufacturing was projected to decline by 14 percent by the end of the century.[18]

At a conference held to examine social conditions in the Mississippi Delta in 1988, former Mississippi governor William Winter described some of the consequences of federal policies that seemed indifferent to the unique challenges facing the region's rural poor residents. The flight of capital overseas eroded the economic base, and local people lacked the resources to create businesses of their own. Deregulation of the transportation industry left many rural communities without bus, rail, or air service and increased their isolation from the economic mainstream. Health services also deteriorated, leaving infant mortality rates in the Delta at "Third World levels." Out-migration was rising again as people left to seek better opportunities in larger southern cities. "The movement out of the rural areas for the last two years has been the greatest in thirty years," Winter reported. Other observers noted that policy makers appeared to have little idea of what it was like to live in rural America and that social welfare programs were designed with urban areas in mind. Reforms aimed at helping people to move from public assistance to private employment might work in some cities where jobs, transportation, and child care services were widely available, but they failed miserably and only increased poor people's hardships in rural southern communities lacking these things.[19]

FREE ENTERPRISE AND ITS FAILURES

Federal policy shifts added to the burdens faced by the FSC and other social justice organizations as they struggled to continue their work in the late twentieth century. A summary of a meeting of FSC state coordinators shortly after Reagan took office listed several job training, energy, and housing programs that would likely be cut and warned that the organization faced a 40 percent reduction in federal funds for the coming year. The following month, the director of the federation's CETA program wrote to employees in Alabama to explain that he could not guarantee the continuation of the project and suggested they prepare for the possibility that it could end "without ample notification."[20] Uncertain funding also threatened operations at the Black Belt Community Health Center. A plan to provide dental care to rural poor people by partnering with West Alabama Health Services had to be postponed after the president's budget proposals endangered the future of community health centers. John Zippert reported in December: "The rapid shift of the Reagan Budget away from human resource development priorities has caused great hardship to the Federation, its constituent member cooperatives and poor people in rural communities struggling to help themselves."[21]

The FSC's annual report for 1980–81 summarized the damage caused by cutbacks, program eliminations, and the termination of federal contracts that occurred during Reagan's first year in office. Programs that had enabled state coordinators to secure millions of dollars for manpower development and training, community outreach, and technical assistance for cooperatives between 1977 and 1980 were abruptly canceled. The federation was able to enroll just forty VISTA volunteers, down significantly from previous years when enrollment numbered in the hundreds. Almost all support the organization had received from the CSA, CETA, and HUD disappeared. Some of this funding was theoretically still available through block grants sent to the states, but the FSC's hopes for benefiting from this process were "tempered with a knowledge of our past history of dealing with state agencies from a community based organizational perspective." In addition, Reagan tried to abolish the National Consumer Cooperative Bank created during the Carter administration. Although the effort failed, he did succeed in eliminating authority and funding for Title II, the provision allowing for credit and technical assistance to the FSC's low-income constituents.[22]

Faced with a reduction in federal funding from $2 million in 1980–81 to $200,000 in 1981–82, the FSC developed plans to raise an annual basic budget of $1 million though membership fees, charging for services, and donations. Despite receiving support from some state and local governments, foundations, and the National Council of Churches, Prejean reported in September 1983 that the FSC had been forced to make significant reductions in its staff and programs. "Our enemies in the power structure who couldn't beat us through intimidation, investigations and racist attacks will rejoice in our dismemberment—through public and private neglect of the concerns and issues we raise and represent," he wrote. The loss of services, economic hardship, internal divisions, and general discouragement led to the demise of several FSC cooperatives during this decade, including the NBCFC and SWAFCA.[23]

Cooperative organizers struggled along on paltry budgets, maintaining their commitment to the cause despite the restraints interfering with their mission. Melbah McAfee reported from Mississippi: "Although we don't have any money, the enthusiasm is high!" Monthly meetings of the state association of cooperatives drew regular attendance, youth programs were going well, and co-op representatives planned to meet with the governor's staff to "get into the Block Grant process." The FSC also worked with other like-minded groups to consolidate precious resources and facilitate their collective efforts for social justice. As one staff member explained, the budget-cutting trends of the late 1970s and 1980s made it much harder for community-based organizations to secure federal grants, necessitating cooperation and new approaches. Government agencies were increasingly entering into interagency agreements aimed at coordinating their efforts and eliminating duplication, and following their example could enhance organizations' chances of being funded.[24]

In 1978 the FSC, ELF, and the SCDF's Southern Development Foundation joined together to form the Consortium for the Development of the Rural Southeast after each of them was turned down separately for DOL funding. Reapplying together as a consortium, the three groups persuaded the DOL to back a technical assistance program for farmworkers and small farmers that provided training in livestock and vegetable production, cooperative education, farm management, and marketing. Project director Karl Wright reported two years later that participants raised their farm incomes by amounts ranging from $300 to $1,200 and that he expected this to increase once their livestock began to produce steady returns. The Southern Rural Alliance was another collaborative venture with other organizations working on rural development, comprised of the FSC, ELF, the Southern Regional Council, the Voter Education Project, and the southeast regional office of the American Civil Liberties

Union. John Zippert stated in a fund-raising letter that they planned to pursue a joint strategy in fifty majority-black counties with the goal of assisting "local Black political activities and linking these to community development efforts."[25]

Building on their positive experience of working together, FSC and ELF leaders began meeting in 1981 to discuss closer collaboration and an eventual merger. Both groups served the same rural poor constituencies and shared similar goals: economic justice, racial equality, and stemming black land losses and out-migration through programs that enhanced the viability of small family farms. In November, John Zippert laid out plans for creating a membership- and constituency-based organization that would support the preservation and maintenance of black-owned farms; further the growth of cooperatives, credit unions, and other self-help initiatives; foster black political empowerment; and build on social development efforts in housing, health care, and education. After several years of fund-raising and building support for the idea through existing cooperatives, farmers' organizations, and civil rights groups, the FSC and ELF consolidated into the Federation of Southern Cooperatives/ Land Assistance Fund (FSC/LAF) in 1985. The same year, Charles Prejean stepped down as the federation's executive director, turning the position over to Ralph Paige, a member of the Georgia field staff who had directed the organization's VISTA program. Zippert reported in November that although the Reagan administration's "onslaught against poor people and their community controlled organizations" had inflicted considerable damage, the organization maintained a membership of 75 cooperative groups and 20,000 member families, including 10,000 small farmers organized into 30 agricultural cooperatives. Zippert hoped the combined resources of the FSC/LAF would help black farmers to resist foreclosures, partition sales, tax liens, and other pressures that were forcing many of them from the land.[26]

These organizers built on their earlier work and engaged in a broad range of activities designed to improve living conditions and encourage political participation in the rural South. Cooperative development continued, increasing the number of farmers participating in the FSC/LAF network to 15,000 by 1991. Both the cooperatives and individual farmers benefited from research and technical assistance that helped them to craft business plans, develop joint purchasing and marketing strategies, secure loans, and identify new income opportunities. A rural-to-urban marketing initiative connected family farmers to urban consumers and secured subsidies for participants in federal food programs to enable them to buy fresh produce, generating $2.5 million in sales for member co-ops and enhancing access to nutritious food for low-income communities.[27] The FSC/LAF also continued efforts begun in the 1970s to encourage a shift to organic farming methods and greater use of renewable energy sources, despite the elimination of federal funding for such programs in the Reagan era. The Mississippi cooperatives received support from the state government to train 120 family farmers in sustainable techniques, enabling them to experiment with a variety of vegetables and work toward reconditioning their soil with compost and nutrient-replenishing cover crops. "Produce quality and yields were improved over vegetables grown with chemicals," according to a project report, and some of the farmers later applied what they had learned to growing culinary and medicinal herbs. Sales outlets for the produce included a regular stall at the French Market in New Orleans and several inner-city churches as well as supermarkets and restaurants.[28]

Land retention efforts included an education and referral service for black landowners, legal assistance, and workshops that armed families with the knowledge and resources they needed to protect their farms. In addition to racist discrimination in federal farm programs, black land-ownership was threatened by the high number of farmers who died without making formal wills, leaving their land to be divided among surviving family members. Over generations, and combined with the dispersal of rural southerners through out-migration, multiple heirs could end up with claims to ever smaller parcels of land, some of them without even realizing it. Such land, called "heirs property," could not be sold or used as collateral for loans unless the family living and working on it could obtain quitclaims from all the other heirs. As well as hindering owners' ability to obtain credit to operate or expand their farms, heirs property was susceptible to loss through partition sales that were triggered when one heir's interest in the land was sold and the buyer demanded that this interest be partitioned from the rest. If the land could not be easily subdivided, a court could then order the entire tract to be sold and the proceeds distributed among the heirs. Many black farms were also lost through tax sales after the operators died and the heirs failed to continue paying property taxes.[29]

Concerned by what one activist described as "legally sanctioned, forced sales of property," the FSC/LAF worked to raise black farmers' awareness of the pitfalls of heirs property and helped them take the legal steps needed to preserve ownership. As Ralph Paige explained, "The land has given us independence; the chance to register and vote; the opportunity to make a living and form co-ops; a way of life and a livelihood. We will never sell out this heritage and birthright."[30] A series of workshops reaching 550 farmers in Alabama and Georgia in the mid-1980s focused on topics such as estate planning, avoiding tax problems, financing, and dealing with lenders. Activists also built up a network of lawyers, appraisers, and surveyors who were sympathetic to the movement and willing to offer assistance to farmers throughout the Southeast. Volunteers within and outside the region contacted and organized heirs to educate them on the issue and urge them not to force partition sales. These efforts helped save 1,200 acres of black-owned land in 1984–85, and a more expansive program a few years later preserved an estimated 80,800 acres. Although black farmers continued to lose land nationwide, the FSC/LAF was able to significantly reduce the number and acreage of lost farms in the counties it reached.[31]

Political advocacy on behalf of rural black southerners complemented the FSC/LAF's cooperative development and land retention programs. Activists organized conferences of black farmers to gather input for the 1985 farm bill and forwarded policy recommendations to the USDA. When the agency established a special task force to look into the problems facing African American farmers in the wake of a CCR report attributing black land losses to racial discrimination in federal farm programs, the FSC/LAF sent representatives to testify at hearings and meet with agriculture officials in Washington. Its proposals for more outreach, training, and technical support for small farmers prompted the USDA to award the organization a $99,930 contract to work with black farmers in Mississippi and South Carolina.[32] Drawing on its constituency's firsthand knowledge of rural problems and working with other progressive groups concerned for the future of family farms, the FSC/LAF proposed legislation that included measures such as parity prices, environmental stewardship, restrictions on corporate agriculture, restoring funding for the food stamp and child nutrition programs, and affirmative action for nonwhite farmers. Activists managed to get some of these provisions included in the Food, Agriculture, Conservation, and Trade Act of 1990, which authorized outreach and assistance programs for socially disadvantaged farmers, allocations for community-based organizations with experience working in this field, and initiatives to increase the number of FmHA loans to nonwhite landowners. This achievement was undermined, however, by an atmosphere of "budget crisis and huge deficits" that prevented Congress from adequately funding the new programs.[33]

Within the limits imposed by financial constraints, the FSC/LAF continued to foster broader economic development efforts that benefited nonfarm residents as well, most notably through its rural housing initiatives. Extension of the sewage system at the Wendy Hills community in Sumter County allowed for construction of twenty new units, and the Alabama state association developed eleven acres of land in Marion for low-income housing. PanSco Construction, a small company that grew out of the FSC/LAF's efforts to generate its own income, provided employment opportunities and contributed to housing rehabilitation, new construction, and renovation of member cooperatives' facilities.[34] In conjunction with the PLBA Housing Development Corporation, housing advocates secured FmHA loans that financed a thirty-unit apartment complex in Greensboro and twenty-six apartments in Eutaw. In 1989 these efforts were recognized with national and international awards for excellence in low-income housing development, along with a $25,000 grant from the Federal National Mortgage Association to further the FSC/LAF's housing programs. The organization also helped individual families to secure home loans and lobbied for changes in housing policies to encourage more construction of affordable housing by private contractors.[35]

As the hard work of maintaining and organizing black voting majorities finally began to pay off in the election of more African Americans to political office in the late 1970s and 1980s, the FSC/LAF worked with newly progressive local governments to improve conditions for rural poor people. The Greene County Commission and the black-controlled municipal governments of Memphis and McMullens in Pickens County, Alabama, cooperated on efforts to enhance employment opportunities for African Americans and ensure maximum use of minority contractors on federally subsidized construction projects. In 1984 Charles Prejean reported with some satisfaction that the white political leaders in Sumter County who initiated the FBI's destructive investigation of the FSC had been replaced by black elected officials. With its strong ties to civil rights and social justice activists, the new county commission was able to draw on some powerful expertise to help plan community development strategies.[36] Both the Greene County and Sumter County governments provided financial support for the FSC/LAF's work and advocated for state funding of its programs. There was also growing acceptance of the organization's activities by formerly hostile state legislators. The FSC/LAF received $100,000 from the Alabama state budget in 1985, and the governor's office in Mississippi provided some money for farmer training programs in 1987. Additionally, state contracts funded VISTA volunteers in Alabama, Florida, Georgia, Mississippi, and South Carolina.[37]

A quarter century after its emergence from the social activism of the 1960s, the FSC/LAF could reflect proudly on its achievements. "For two dozen years, the Federation/LAF has worked with diligence, determination, discipline and dedication to help thousands of low and moderate income families in our membership to realize and hold fast to their dreams of land ownership, cooperative economic development and community change," its 1990–91 annual report noted.[38] Participants in its programs benefited from increased economic opportunities, improved housing and social services, access to education and training, political empowerment, and the sense of pride that came from building something of their own. At the same time, the past decade had seen the solidification of a national government that was "blind to the problems of poor, Black and rural people in this country," leaving many rural communities in a state of decay. Extreme poverty, unemployment, ill health, underfunded schools, substandard housing, and racial segregation remained the defining features of the South's plantation regions.[39] With its limited budget and small staff, the FSC/LAF could not hope to tackle these problems on anything like the scale that was needed to solve them. The situation required federal intervention and a renewed national commitment to addressing economic inequality.

Persistent poverty in the rural South inspired Congress to establish the Lower Mississippi Delta Development Commission (LMDDC) in October 1988 to study the economic and social needs of a 214-county area in the seven states bordering the river between southern Illinois and New Orleans. Chaired by Arkansas governor Bill Clinton, the commission spent the next eighteen months holding public hearings and meeting with political, business, and community leaders throughout the region.[40] Members frequently heard testimony indicating that some places had seen little change since the 1960s. Participants at a hearing held in Monroe, Louisiana, in January 1990 described the dehumanizing conditions that relegated undereducated and unemployed residents to "a world of despair" characterized by inadequate incomes, illiteracy, boredom, drug and alcohol abuse, crime, and broken families. The root cause of these problems, they asserted, was a lack of jobs, yet local administrators of public assistance programs acted as though the fault lay in poor people themselves. "They treat the people in the Welfare Office who go to get welfare as subhuman people," Joseph George stated, going on to express anger with officials who told people to go and find themselves jobs that paid $7 an hour so that they could support their families: "They're not giving $7.00 an hour jobs out to black men in Monroe, Louisiana, see. They're not giving them out."[41] According to Floyd Gray, welfare regulations that denied aid to two-parent homes continued to force unemployed men to leave their families so that their wives and children could receive assistance. The underfunded public school system failed to adequately prepare young people for skilled work, leading many to resort to selling drugs or other illegal activities to earn income. Those who managed to avoid incarceration ended up warehoused in public housing projects with no prospects for a better life. "In basically the black community, those people who live in project houses have been put there just like cattle," Gray told commissioners.[42]

The LMDDC also heard from black business owners whose attempts to secure a living and contribute to the economic development of their communities through private enterprise remained circumscribed by racism. Berton Cowan, the owner of a small musical instrument store in Greenwood, Mississippi, stated at a hearing held in Itta Bena that his business was growing and he felt ready to expand, but he was unable to secure a loan for this purpose from local banks. The most they would offer was a $1,500 operating loan, despite being presented with clear evidence that the store was a viable investment prospect. Cowan noted that there were few black loan officers in Mississippi and wondered why that was, since banks were regulated and subject to equal employment opportunity laws. If the banks hired more African Americans, he suggested, black business owners might be more likely to secure loans. Another problem was that black entrepreneurs were subject to closer scrutiny from state and federal tax enforcers, according to Cowan. "I can't think of a single small, black business in the Leflore County area which has not been audited by the tax commission and, as a result of that, many have actually gone out of business," he stated.[43] Donald Britton related similar problems at the commission's hearing in Monroe. African Americans made up 40 percent of Louisiana's population, but black businesses received less than 5 percent of the millions of dollars in state contracts awarded each year. Despite affirmative action policies designed to ensure that nonwhite contractors received their fair share, administrators retained a large amount of discretion, which they used to reject bids from black businesses even when they were lower than those submitted by white contractors. Britton was equally disappointed by the Small Business Administration, which he said mostly gave black applicants "a run-around or loaned them enough money to guarantee failure."[44]

Some of those who testified at LMDDC hearings attributed the lack of progress to the policies pursued since the 1970s and argued that the federal government needed to take a more active role in the region. Robert Wagner, the director of a regional planning agency covering several Louisiana parishes, noted that "most of the basic tools of economic development at the federal level have been abolished over the past few years," and local governments lacked the resources to step into the void. Programs offered by the EDA and FmHA had helped stimulate rural economies in the 1960s and early 1970s, but this "began to decline in the '80s as these programs were eliminated." Wagner hoped the commission's work would reenergize efforts to improve conditions in the Delta through new forms of federal assistance "of a scope and magnitude which will create an impact on our problems in a realistic way."[45] Similarly, FES staff in Tensas Parish described the impact of funding cuts on their work with black farmers and youths. Elvadis Fields Jr. told commissioners that the parish's population had declined from 13,000 to 8,000 in the three decades he had lived there, and the number of black farmers had dropped from 112 to 27. He and others in the community wanted to raise funds to build a livestock center and farmers' market, but the parish lacked money, and state funds available through block grants mostly went to communities with more industries.[46]

Inequities created by farm policies that favored large agribusinesses over family farmers were also highlighted at the hearings. James Hendrix expressed concerns about a shift in USDA services away from hands-on work with farmers and a greater reliance on agricultural research conducted at universities by people who had no real understanding of rural communities.[47] Wilbert Guillory, who had helped form the GMVPC in St. Landry Parish and now served as an agricultural specialist for the Southern Development Foundation while successfully managing his own vegetable farm, noted that small farmers had been "overlooked for many years," but his own experiences over the past several decades had shown that these enterprises could be viable with the right kind of support. There was great potential in vegetable and milk production if the FES and other agricultural agencies would step up to provide the needed guidance to farmers. "When you move from soybean and cotton and corn," Guillory explained, "you have to treat it almost like you treat a little baby. You have to be there at all time when it's needed. . . . But it can be very productive, and you can have very happy families doing it." Currently, however, federal agricultural assistance amounted to "one young man that work with the whole parish. . . . The Extension Service is so limited with the personnel that they have that it's no way, and they are still cutting them."[48]

Other analysts critiqued misguided development policies and offered suggestions for new approaches that were reminiscent of those pioneered by the early cooperative movement. Bob Kochtitzky, the director of a non-profit organization in Jackson, Mississippi, asserted that the state needed to discard the "Toyota Plant Syndrome" that attempted to attract invest-ment from outside and focus on developing local people and resources instead. Kochtitzky proposed several models for creating alternative economies that kept and circulated money within the region instead of enriching multinational corporations, including cooperative businesses, noncash systems for exchanging goods and services, and community-supported agriculture allowing consumers to contract directly with local farmers to purchase their entire food needs for the year.[49] Agricultural economist Dewitt Jones argued that "human capital" was a more power-ful driver of economic prosperity than natural resources and represented the Delta's most important untapped asset. Local governments' obsession with luring industry through tax concessions and other incentives had proven counterproductive, leaving many communities worse off than before. "We have seen the industries come in; they use up the tax incen-tives, then they move away," he stated. A smarter way to use development funds was to provide assistance to small businesses and entrepreneurs who provided local services and created jobs that could not be out-sourced. Louisiana's secretary of economic development Arnold Lincove also argued that progress was impossible without more investment in education, retraining programs, and other human services. Additionally, he stated, "Enduring improvement will not take place unless the grass roots are involved in the process. That is, unless the people of the area are given the opportunity to exercise self-determination and self-reliance."[50]

Commissioners listened with interest to the various descriptions and analyses of problems offered by local residents and occasionally responded supportively to suggestions for reform. Commissioner Webb Franklin, for example, concurred with Wilbert Guillory that providing more assistance to small farmers could contribute fruitfully to regional development and assured him that these ideas would be included as recommendations in the LMDDC's final report. The idea that luring industry through tax incentives should not be a priority of state and local governments elicited a more skeptical response, with one commissioner raising concerns that this could place them at a "competitive disadvantage" in relation to other communities that continued to provide tax breaks.[51] In advising hearing attendees to make fuller use of existing programs and funding streams, some members of the LMDDC ignored the challenges posed by decades of budget cuts and decentralization that had reduced the amount of aid available to a trickle and made it more difficult for rural poor communities to secure their share. There were also a few commissioners, such as presidential appointee John C. Shepherd, who suggested that poverty was a behavioral rather than a structural problem. At the hearing in Itta Bena, Rufus McLain of Quitman County Delta Foundation described the devastating effects of joblessness, school segregation, and funding cuts that eliminated needed social services in his community, ending his testimony by noting the high teen pregnancy rate and the need for family planning education. After McLain had finished, Shepherd honed in on the last point. "Rufus," he asked, "what do you think we can do about that teenage pregnancy? . . . The answer to this problem is the key to solving everything, isn't it?"[52]

After completing its studies, the commission produced a ten-year economic development plan to improve education, health care, and infrastructure in the region. In his letter submitting the report to the president in May 1990, Bill Clinton called it "a Handbook for Action—one that can turn the Delta and its 8.3 million people into full partners in America's exciting future, full participants in the changing global economy." In four sections covering "human capital development," natural resources, the role of private enterprise, and environmental sustainability, the commission made more than 400 recommendations aimed at encouraging renewed investments from all levels of government as well as private sector and nonprofit actors. In emphasizing the need for integrated, comprehensive approaches focused on addressing human needs, the report echoed arguments that social justice activists had been making for the past three decades. Some of the commission's specific proposals could have been taken from CAP grant applications or the FSC's action programs in the 1960s and 1970s. Suggestions for improving medical care by shifting more money toward preventive services were reminiscent of the TDHC's holistic approach to addressing health problems. Recommendations for research and technical assistance programs to help small farmers diversify into alternative crops and experiment with organic farming were among the other progressive ideas that made it into the report, along with advice for supporting local businesses and entrepreneurship by creating a regional development bank. The commission also advocated expanding Head Start to enable more families to share in its proven benefits.[53] Such proposals were testament to the persistence of grassroots activism in pursuit of a fairer distribution of regional resources after the 1960s despite the discouraging political climate.

Missing from the commission's report, however, was any sense that federal action might be needed to directly create jobs. That task was left to the private sector, encouraged by policies to promote business investment, improve infrastructure, and develop the local labor force through better schools and training programs to upgrade workers' skills. Some analysts were skeptical that these initiatives alone were enough to place the Delta on a more prosperous path, and in any case most of them were never implemented. Reagan's tax cuts had left the federal government with a huge deficit, making lawmakers reluctant to appropriate the necessary funds. As one observer noted, "Congress showed little interest in pushing for any recommendations that would cost money." Federal legislators rejected a proposal to finance a Lower Mississippi Delta Development Center in Memphis to coordinate development efforts in the region, and attempts to maintain the office through state funding also encountered difficulties stemming from tight budgets. Once again it seemed that government officials had raised hopes that they were interested in helping to alleviate rural poverty, only to back off providing the needed resources. Mississippi resident L. G. Brooks told a reporter in July 1991 that the commission's work—and the $3 million it spent studying the Delta—seemed pointless. "They could have been feeding people with those millions," he said. "You don't have to study no problem. Just drive down Highway 61 and see. If there's no jobs and nobody working, if the factory's closed, if the big boys ain't sending nothing to us—what can we do?"[54]

Even after being elected president, Bill Clinton could not convince Congress to take meaningful action and showed scant interest in the region himself until late in his second term. When the president embarked on a "poverty tour" through the Delta and other economically distressed regions in 1999, James Brosnan observed in the *Memphis Commercial Appeal* that it seemed "a little late" and noted the limited impact of government initiatives undertaken during his administration. As in earlier

FREE ENTERPRISE AND ITS FAILURES

decades, part of the problem was opposition from southern political leaders who opposed antipoverty efforts and did not want to see an expanded federal presence in the region. Mississippi governor Kirk Fordice criticized proposals to create a Delta regional development agency modeled on the Appalachian Regional Commission because it might draw resources away from Appalachia and redirect them to the Delta. "Translation: taking from whites to give to blacks," Brosnan explained. The state's two senators, Trent Lott and Thad Cochran, also expressed reservations. Eventually Congress gave its approval and President George W. Bush signed legislation creating the Delta Regional Authority in 2001, but its effectiveness was hampered by restrictions designed to prevent it from turning into "an out-of-control federal agency." Legislators also added 20 counties in Alabama to the original 214 counties included in the LMDDC study, bringing the number of people served to 9 million. As always, funding was inadequate and channeled toward projects that benefited businesses rather than direct assistance to poor people. Over the next seven years administrators disbursed $63 million in grants throughout the eight states in their jurisdiction, mostly for improvements in infrastructure.[55]

These measures failed to slow the job losses in manufacturing or to create the dynamic, high-skill economy and well-paid workforce that the LMDDC outlined in its final report. Even if unemployed people had received the education and training necessary to adjust to global restructuring in the late twentieth century, this would not necessarily have ensured higher incomes or more job security. For many skilled as well as unskilled people, globalization became a "race to the bottom" that forced them to compete with the far lower wages paid to their counterparts in developing nations or displaced them entirely with new technologies that could perform ever more sophisticated tasks. Software engineers, data entry operators, accountants, and customer service representatives found that their jobs could be just as easily outsourced as those of factory operatives once improvements in computing and telecommunications made it possible for companies to automate such work or assign it to other people around the world. The college-educated workers who initially benefited from the rise of the Sunbelt's burgeoning service and finance sectors ultimately found that they too were vulnerable to layoffs and joblessness.[56] Middle-class white southerners were therefore not immune from the processes that had afflicted black plantation workers in earlier decades and that most of them had chosen to ignore, secure in their belief that hard work and individual initiative were all they needed to succeed within the free enterprise system.

At the turn of the twenty-first century, conditions in the rural South seemed almost as dire as they were in the 1960s. Reporters who visited Lake Providence, Louisiana, in 2002 found a town that was "dwindling away," as one resident put it, unable to withstand persistent unemployment, poverty, and out-migration. "I don't see anything coming," local barber F. C. Davis stated. "Social Security and welfare are the two biggest things around." A woman who had previously left and returned to Lake Providence to take care of her aging parents stated that she planned to leave again as soon as she could. Now that both parents had died, she had no reason to stay, and the town held out little hope of a better life any time in the future. "It's gotten worser and worser over the last 15–16 years," she said. "There used to be a few more little jobs here and there. There's nothing to do but grow old and die."[57]

Journalist Roland Klose wrote a similar account focusing on some rural counties in Mississippi in 2009. The last manufacturing plant in Sharkey County had closed down earlier in the year, and the area's few remaining farmers were also struggling. There and elsewhere, poverty and joblessness rates were in the double digits, and people were migrating away by the thousands. In the first decade of the new century, eleven counties in the Yazoo River Delta region collectively lost 28,158 inhabitants, representing 10 percent of the population. "Vacant storefronts and abandoned trailers are as common as fields of cotton and soybeans," Klose wrote, evoking a landscape of neglected buildings that, like the local labor force, were no longer needed. Although some residents refused to believe all hope was lost and continued to advocate economic development, other observers thought investing more resources in the region was useless. Retired economics professor and Delta researcher David Ciscel argued that rural counties had lost so many people and were left with such inadequate workforces that no companies could be expected to locate in these places in future. "It's probably time to recognize that economic development in many rural counties is hopeless," he told Klose. "Yes, we should care about the Delta, but we should not try to improve it any longer. It is time to move the people to a place where they can be helped."[58]

Just where people could go to secure stable employment at living wages in the South or the United States was not clear. Contrary to the assumptions held by Ronald Reagan and other policy makers in the late twentieth century, the problems afflicting southern plantation counties did not stem from any inherent deficiencies in the region or its people. They were a consequence of policies that relied too heavily on the imperfect, unpredictable workings of the market to generate growth and distribute its benefits, leaving displaced workers to fend for themselves in the face of global economic forces that eliminated jobs and decimated their communities in the 1980s and 1990s. The FSC/LAF and other social justice activists did what they could to soften the consequences of these developments and advocate alternative courses of action, but they could not coax political leaders into recommitting the resources needed to create the Great Society. Meanwhile, many white Americans joined rural black southerners in "a world of despair" as economic restructuring and laissez-faire approaches to social problems affected other regions in the decades following the civil rights movement.

CHAPTER 8

GOVERNMENT CANNOT SOLVE OUR PROBLEMS

LEGACIES OF DISPLACEMENT

Rural black southerners were not alone in witnessing the economic devastation of their communities in the late twentieth century. Just as the modernization of agriculture disrupted economic and social relationships in the South in the 1950s and 1960s, the next several decades saw similar processes occur in the nation as a whole. As deindustrialization and globalization undermined the comfortable living standards to which Americans were accustomed, social justice activists might have expected to gain support for policies that allowed a bigger role for government in addressing unemployment and poverty. Yet most citizens rejected that approach, opting instead for free market solutions proposed by theorists who argued that economic revival depended on curbing public investments, deregulating businesses, and encouraging individual initiative. In the background lay the racialized debates over the War on Poverty and federal power that colored many people's views on economic policy after the 1960s.

Opponents of government action to solve social problems had long argued that the private sector could do a better job than public agencies in generating employment and ensuring prosperity for all citizens. Misrepresentations of antipoverty programs as ineffective, wasteful, and riddled with corruption helped convince many other Americans that these efforts were misguided. In the 1970s and 1980s, warnings that efforts to ensure racial equality would lead to tyrannical government gained increasing legitimacy in the minds of citizens who felt threatened by attempts to integrate their schools, workplaces, and neighborhoods. From the perspective of many white Americans in the North as well as the South, government appeared as an enemy that needed to be restrained rather than a potential force for enhancing economic security. Antipathy toward federal interference limited the options available to policy makers during a time of economic transformation that subjected millions more people to the same plight faced by displaced sharecroppers in the civil rights era. The ideological battles between supporters and opponents of government intervention in the southern plantation regions thus helped set the stage for the national response to the transition from industrial capitalism to finance capitalism in later decades.

Beginning in the late 1960s, the strong economic growth and widespread prosperity that Americans enjoyed after World War II faltered as other nations revived their industrial capacity and competed more strongly with American manufacturers in global markets. Free trade agreements that facilitated the movement of goods, services, and capital across national borders opened American markets to foreign businesses and encouraged domestic corporations to look beyond the United States for labor and other resources. Increasing competition and the need to keep up with the newer technology being used by foreign manufacturers inspired many companies to modernize plants and machinery, further reducing the need for labor. A DOL study conducted in the mid-1980s found that, nationwide, 112,067 manufacturing plants shut down between 1963 and 1982 and another 146,943 reduced the number of workers they employed, for a total loss of 18.3 million jobs. Although new factories were built and new jobs created in the same period, most of this growth occurred in the South and West. Other parts of the country stagnated or went into decline. The industrial northeastern and midwestern states were hardest hit, recording net losses in manufacturing jobs in every census period after 1967. New York City alone lost around 300,000 factory jobs in the 1970s, a story that was repeated in many other cities. Detroit shed 180,000 positions between 1978 and 1984, leaving one-fifth of its workforce unemployed. Dozens of steel mills closed their doors between 1966 and 1986, laying off hundreds of thousands of workers. By 1987, corporate giant U.S. Steel was producing as much steel with 18,000 employees as it had once produced with 48,600.[1]

Changes in the structure of the economy attended by the rise of finance capitalism also affected workers' prospects. President Nixon's decision to devalue the dollar in 1971 by abandoning the system of stable currency exchange rates that most nations had adhered to since 1944 introduced a level of volatility into the global economy that had unforeseen consequences. Companies involved in international trade began stockpiling foreign currencies in case they were needed and traded currencies as prices went up or down, creating new sources of profits that did not depend on building factories and hiring workers to produce goods. Over the next few decades, deregulation of the banking industry in the United States generated more opportunities for corporations to enrich themselves through financial investments and services that required little labor to maintain. The lucrative business generated by these activities encouraged a shift in focus away from manufacturing, making finance the fastest growing sector of the American economy.[2] By the mid-1980s, finance accounted for 30 percent of total profits (up from 10–15 percent in the 1950s and 1960s) but employed only about 7 percent of the nation's workers. The percentage of the labor force working in finance declined slightly even as the proportion of profits generated grew to 45 percent by 2001. Concurrently, the percentage of American workers employed in manufacturing declined steadily, from 31 percent in 1959, to 23 percent in 1979, and down to 14 percent by 1999.[3]

A white working class that achieved unprecedented levels of prosperity and economic security through a combination of collective organizing efforts, government assistance, and racial exclusion in the mid-twentieth century faced a much more precarious future in later decades. Like the southern sharecroppers who were laid off from their jobs and evicted from their homes, factory laborers across the nation found that they too were expendable as manufacturers shut down their operations or moved them overseas. Cities such as Detroit, Cleveland, and Chicago, as well as smaller industrial towns in the Northeast and Midwest, lost hundreds of thousands of well-paid positions, leaving unemployed workers scrambling to make ends meet. An analysis of corporate data undertaken by scholars Barry Bluestone and Bennett Harrison in 1982 estimated that in all sectors, "somewhere between 32 and 38 *million* jobs were lost during the 1970s as the direct result of private disinvestment in American business."[4]

Reports of hardship and despair from such states as Indiana and Ohio rivaled those that emanated from Mississippi and Alabama in an earlier era. Laid-off steel worker Larry Koker told an interviewer that watching a factory that once employed 20,000 people in Gary, Indiana, reduce its workforce to 7,500 was "like watching a very bad movie, and you can't turn the movie off. . . . You have no control." Sharon Harmon, who was five months pregnant when her husband lost his job at the plant, recalled, "His job was gone, but the bills kept coming. We lost our house, car, and . . . the gas company shut off our gas." By 1985 the city's unemployment rate was higher than 20 percent, one-fifth of the city's residents lived below poverty level, and criminal activity was on the rise. When the cash-strapped municipal government announced plans to cut social services, one resident observed: "We've already been designated the murder capital and now we are headed on the road toward becoming the hunger capital." In the Youngstown-Warren region of Ohio, once known for its skilled workers, good jobs, and high rates of home ownership, plant closings eliminated 50,000 positions after 1977. By the turn of the century, Youngstown was synonymous with unemployment, poverty, population losses, home foreclosures, bankruptcies, and crime.[5]

The consequences of deindustrialization extended beyond workers and their families to encompass entire communities. Businesses that had once thrived by catering to the needs of well-paid factory laborers closed their doors, adding to the problems of depressed areas and sending them into a spiral of decline. Without jobs, workers lacked incomes, businesses lacked customers, and municipal governments lacked tax revenues to fund education, transportation, recreational facilities, and other public services. The deteriorating infrastructure in turn discouraged new businesses from locating in economically distressed areas, creating a cycle of job losses and disinvestment that was difficult to break. In 1984 musician Bruce Springsteen gave expression to the economic and emotional trauma that afflicted such communities in his song "My Hometown," the melancholy musings of a man who feels compelled to leave the place where he was born and raised because of the lack of jobs. Set in a northern textile mill town, the song makes reference to racial tensions, plant closings, and boarded-up main street stores, ending with a mirror image of the same impetus that drove millions of rural black southerners to migrate from their hometowns in the 1950s and 1960s. In the final stanza, the narrator and his wife contemplate leaving their declining community and moving south to look for work.[6]

Citizens experiencing the loss of local industries, declining employment prospects, and out-migration from their dying towns might have looked to the examples set by social justice activists in the rural South to solve these problems. Investing in education and social services, forming cooperatives, and using government loans to start local businesses had alleviated economic distress and inspired promising self-help initiatives in dozens of impoverished communities that were devastated by agricultural modernization in the 1960s and 1970s. In those same decades, however, federal action to end racial discrimination and eliminate poverty generated intense antipathy toward government, making many Americans less amenable to policies that could enhance the power of bureaucrats they saw as being far too involved in their lives already.

Whereas supporters of the black freedom struggle saw civil rights legislation as a long-overdue correction to racist policies that undermined American ideals, others viewed the new laws as dangerous encroachments on their rights. Irate constituents frequently expressed their fears to congressional representatives and federal agencies, using the language of constitutionality and free enterprise to oppose initiatives designed to enhance equality. Writing to John Sparkman in March 1965, Alabama resident Margaret McPherson asserted that Americans' liberties were "in great danger of being completely destroyed by a ruthless, power mad, Federal Bureaucracy." In 1967, when HEW threatened to withhold federal funds from the school district in Webster County, Mississippi, because of its failure to integrate, administrators responded that the system had been operating under a freedom of choice plan for two years and they could not be blamed if no black parents wanted to send their children to the white schools. Persistent segregation reflected local residents' preferences, they asserted, and forcing schools to integrate through other measures would "be in violation of the parents and childs civil rights." A woman in Alabama expressed her frustration with a new rezoning plan that meant her four children had to attend three different schools by advocating an end to the public school system. "If we can't have freedom of choice and control of our own schools, we don't need them," she stated. "I THINK MY CONSTITUTIONAL RIGHTS ARE BEING VIOLATED!!!!"[7]

Federal efforts to end discrimination in housing markets and open all-white neighborhoods to black residents elicited similar objections from opponents. Real estate industry leaders lobbied strongly against fair housing legislation that they perceived as undermining Americans' cherished ideals. The president of the Eufaula Board of Realtors in Alabama urged Senator Sparkman to do everything in his power to defeat the open-housing initiatives being debated in Congress in 1966. "The Board feels that this is a direct threat to the traditional freedom of choice that goes with property ownership," he stated. Russell Long in Louisiana received the same message from Louisiana Realtors Association president Frank Grigsby. Denying home owners "freedom of choice in contracting for the sale or rental of their property . . . erodes the right of all the people," Grigsby stated. Although his organization supported voluntary efforts to ensure equal housing opportunities, its members thought coercive legislation that "tramples on a fundamental right" was counterproductive. Businessman L. Heidel Brown expressed fears that open-housing legislation would destroy the real estate industry by exposing brokers to expensive lawsuits. Although he recognized the need to address racial inequities, he stated, "The way to do it is not to take away private individual rights of a much larger segment of the population and to, in effect, legislate out of business a numerically large and important segment of our business community."[8]

Concern that improving conditions for African Americans came at the expense of the nation's white majority permeated discussions of equal employment opportunity initiatives as well. Affirmative action policies that encouraged federal contractors, government agencies, public universities, and some private employers to actively recruit and hire nonwhite people came in for some harsh criticism from opponents who viewed them as a form of discrimination against white people.[9] John Edgar complained to Russell Long that such efforts had created a situation where employers now hired "4 blacks to 1 white," leaving white job seekers at a disadvantage. In a letter to John Sparkman, college graduate Arthur James Elliott expressed frustration with businesses that hired black applicants "whether they are qualified or not before the average middle-class white man can even be considered." Elliott was not opposed to black people getting good jobs but stated, "I have civil rights too. . . . I feel that I am being discriminated against and I think that it is time the Federal Government take a realistic view at what is happening." Echoing the arguments against oppressive government made in the context of school and housing integration, Martin Broderick Jr. of Louisiana argued that equal employment policies were unconstitutional. "Since when did it become the right of any Government to tell any employer who he must hire?" he asked Congressman John Rarick.[10]

White families feeling hard pressed to make ends meet and laboring under the misperception that black Americans benefited from overly generous social welfare programs were particularly resentful of the government's efforts to address racial disparities. A resident of St. Landry Parish in Louisiana mailed a news item about welfare rights activists to Russell Long along with a note complaining that hardworking, middle-class mothers like herself had to "moon-lite to keep body and soul together" and pay their bills without any help from the government. A couple in Lafayette were similarly angered by a notice they spotted in a local newspaper encouraging African Americans to set up small businesses with government financing. "To say I almost burst a blood vessel when I read it is putting it mildly," wrote Mrs. A. E. Huckabay in a letter to the senator. "*I*, as a *white*, am sick of being 'discriminated' against!" Huckabay and her husband both had to work to support their household, and it galled them to see "the young blacks use Federal food stamps and drive new cars which we cannot afford." In 1974, a local television news show reinforced white Louisianans' sense of injustice by examining the effects of inflation on middle-class and poor families in New Orleans. The story spotlighted a policeman and his wife who had two children and wanted a third but could not afford it, contrasting their situation with that of an unmarried mother on welfare who was pregnant again and whose every need seemed taken care of by the government. "She did not seem compelled to seek employment. She had free rent, food stamps, spending money, and more money to come with the other child," wrote Leroy Cooper in a letter describing the report to Long.[11]

Perceptions that African Americans were receiving special treatment at the expense of other Americans rested on a fair amount of misinformation and elision. Claims that middle-class white families achieved success solely through hard work and individual effort failed to acknowledge the help these citizens received from government programs such as agricultural subsidies, Social Security, and federal mortgage guarantees that made home ownership easier to achieve. This assistance aided white Americans far more than African Americans, many of whom were excluded from participation by racism.[12] Millions of white people also benefited from the War on Poverty, despite its reputation as an effort that was targeted mainly at black families. Between 1959 and 1975 the number of white Americans living in poverty fell from 28.5 million to 17.8 million, a decline of 38 percent. In the same period, black poverty was reduced by a slightly lesser amount, from 11 million to 7.5 million, or 32 percent. At the end of the 1970s, black people still lagged behind white people in key indicators of social well-being. The median income for white families was $20,254, compared with $12,358 for nonwhite families. Thirty-one percent of African Americans had incomes below poverty level compared with only 9 percent of white Americans, and the black unemployment rate of 11 percent was double the 5 percent for white workers.[13] The numbers suggested that, far from being pampered or privileged, African Americans continued to encounter obstacles in their quest for equal access to education, housing, and economic opportunities.

Despite such evidence, the idea that African Americans were now a privileged class and white people were oppressed gained wide acceptance, and not just in the South. White residents of cities such as Detroit, Chicago, and Los Angeles frequently resisted efforts to integrate their schools, neighborhoods, and workplaces just as strongly as the most blatant segregationists in Birmingham, Jackson, or New Orleans. Like their southern counterparts, they crafted arguments based on constitutional principles and concerns about government overreach to deflect accusations of racism while defending policies that perpetuated inequality. The leaders of a movement to protest a court-ordered busing plan in Boston emphasized that they were not seeking to deny equal education to black children but wanted to preserve their system of neighborhood schools and local control. Like the school officials in Webster County who argued that racially concentrated schools were a product of free choice rather than racism, Boston antibusing spokeswoman Louise Day Hicks claimed there was no discrimination in the public school system and that "forced busing" violated people's rights. Echoing the concerns of southern parents regarding rezoning plans that required children to attend school farther from their homes, a white suburban father in Detroit asserted, "I'm not going to pay big high school taxes and pay more for a home so that somebody can ship my son 30 miles away to get an inferior education."[14]

Opponents of federal civil rights enforcement also cited financial considerations as reasons for concern. Parents in a white neighborhood in Brooklyn, New York, who staged a sit-in to protest the reassignment of thirty-one black students to their local school stressed that their motivations were economic, not racial. The school was already overcrowded and 30 percent African American, they pointed out. They feared that allowing more black children to attend would push it over the tipping point that made schools and the surrounding neighborhoods less desirable for prospective home buyers, causing property values to plummet. Regardless of their own views about black people, the racism embedded in the nation's housing markets meant that white residents of integrating neighborhoods felt "forced" to leave when African Americans moved in. Ralph Vitol, an Italian American who had experienced prejudice against southern and eastern Europeans when he started work in a subway yard 40 years earlier, told reporters that his opposition to integration was "not racism" and simply reflected concern for his family and community. "We've got to think about our grandchildren," he stated. "We've built up this neighborhood; why should we leave now?"[15]

White northerners as well as southerners believed they were the victims of government policies that focused too heavily on the plight of black Americans at their expense. Seventy percent of voters who supported Barry Goldwater for president in 1964, described by pollster Louis Harris as people who saw the civil rights movement as "one vast power play, designed to take over the reins of government," lived outside the South. Among white ethnic Americans like Ralph Vitol, there was a growing sense that African Americans were receiving more assistance than their own immigrant ancestors had received in the early twentieth century, coupled with fears that black people were after their jobs. At a conference examining the problems facing working-class people of European descent held in Washington, D.C., in June 1970, Barbara Mikulski of Southeast Community Organization in Baltimore asserted that these citizens were "overtaxed and underserved at every level of government" and received "no help" from federal programs. The National Confederation of American Ethnic Groups made similar observations in its 1972 convention report. Most government programs were administered by leftist bureaucrats who viewed white workers as racists and bigots, the organization claimed. Consequently, federal officials were interested in helping only nonwhite people, and white ethnic Americans were "systematically excluded from all the antipoverty, housing, equal employment and economic betterment programs made available in profusion to other minorities" even though they bore "the major portion of the nation's tax burden." Other grievances expressed in the report included rising crime rates, unemployment, and busing. At the same time, the group praised the achievements of a joint manpower training project that it operated in conjunction with the DOL and expressed goals that were similar to those of social justice activists in the South, including improved education, health care, and economic opportunities.[16]

Nixon administration officials knew the root causes of problems confronting working-class Americans were economic, not racial. A panel convened by the president to study the problems of blue-collar workers noted that upward mobility was proving impossible for millions of Americans affected by stagnating wages, higher living costs, and the lack of health insurance, pensions, or other benefits. As Assistant Secretary of Labor Jerome Rosow explained in a lengthy memorandum that became the basis for the panel's final report, 40 percent of the nation's families, including 34 percent of nonwhite families, earned modest incomes between $5,000 and $10,000 per year. Although they were struggling financially, they were not eligible for welfare, Medicaid, public housing, and other programs that helped the nation's poorest citizens. "As taxpayers, they support these programs with no visible relief—no visible share," Rosow noted. To alleviate the frustrations felt by this group, Rosow suggested several measures the government could take, including expanding job training programs, enhancing access to higher education through loans and grants, and providing tax subsidies to help working parents pay for transportation and child care. In October 1970 Rosow called on private industry leaders to help address working people's problems. Too many Americans were employed in low-wage, dead-end jobs that had no provisions for sick leave, vacations, retirement, or medical insurance, he argued in a speech to the American Compensation Association. By offering blue-collar workers more opportunities for upward mobility and the same level of respect and dignity that white-collar workers enjoyed, businesses could do much to overcome feelings of anger and alienation that afflicted the nation's working class.[17]

Rosow's appeal to private employers was significant and reflected the administration's ambivalence regarding the government's role in dealing with these issues. Some officials expressed concerns that initiatives proposed to extend government assistance to working families living just above the poverty line represented an expansion of the welfare state that the nation could not afford. Nixon aide Tom Huston complained that such measures were too costly and counseled developing ways to appeal to blue-collar Americans that did not involve promises of federal programs to raise living standards. Other analysts argued that increasing people's incomes was incompatible with bringing inflation under control—more spending money meant more demand for goods, which only led to more price increases. In the next decade, under Presidents Nixon and Ford and continuing under President Carter, the economic plight of working-class families receded into the background as political leaders came to see inflation as the biggest problem facing the nation and one that could not be solved without some sacrifice on the part of wage earners.[18]

As historian Jefferson Cowie has shown, the Nixon administration pursued a strategy of drawing white working-class voters away from the Democratic Party by legitimizing their cultural conservatism rather than offering solutions to their economic problems. Facing off against George McGovern in the 1972 presidential election, Nixon realized that the Democrat's voting record on labor issues established him as a staunch defender of workers' interests. Nonetheless, he argued, his own campaign could appeal to a broad spectrum of the electorate through other means. "The real issues of the election are the ones like patriotism, morality, religion—not the material issues," he told his advisers. "If the issues were prices and taxes, they'd vote for McGovern. We've done things labor doesn't like. We've held wages down. But they'll support us for these other reasons."[19] In addition to emphasizing McGovern's ties to student radicals and the antiwar movement, Nixon worked to undermine his opponent by exploiting divisions over racially charged issues such as busing, crime, affirmative action, and welfare policies.[20]

Polls conducted in the run-up to the election found a significant correlation between voters' racial views and their favored candidate. In response to a question asking whether they thought minority groups were receiving "too much, too little or just about the right amount of attention," 40 percent of the people surveyed answered "too much," and of those almost 80 percent said they planned to vote for Nixon. One-third of respondents who identified as Democrats stated that they were switching sides to support the Republican candidate in this election, and issues that many Americans understood as proxies for race—"welfare, job quotas, education, crime"—influenced this shift. In October, a Harris survey indicated a dramatic falloff in support for the Democratic candidate among Italian Americans compared with the previous presidential election. Having supported Hubert Humphrey over Nixon by 57 to 37 percent in 1968, these voters were leaning 62 to 27 percent in favor of Nixon in 1972. "They are deeply affected by concern over the thrust by blacks for equality," the report stated, noting the strong opposition of Italian Americans to busing and support for tough measures to combat crime.[21]

Nixon won the election convincingly, securing 61 percent of the popular vote and taking the electoral college votes of every state except for Massachusetts. Some of his strongest support came from the Deep South: the president won 78 percent of the vote in Mississippi, 72 percent in Alabama, 65 percent in Louisiana, and 92 percent of the overall southern rural white vote. Significantly, support from voters in the Northeast and Midwest was strong as well.[22] At a time of economic transition that imperiled the jobs and incomes of white as well as black Americans, a majority of voters sided with the party of big business against the party of the New Deal and the Great Society, even though a strong social safety net and government action to soften the impact of these shifts seemed more necessary than ever. Their choice sent a clear message to political leaders and emboldened efforts to cut funding for social programs and roll back the federal government's role in addressing economic problems. When Nixon announced his plans to dismantle the OEO in 1973, he argued that the election returns of the previous November indicated a demand from voters for this "change of direction." Democratic Party leaders also backed off their support for a social justice agenda and tried to distance themselves from issues that white voters perceived as "black" problems, such as poverty and urban decay. In an influential book titled *The Real Majority*, Richard Scammon and Ben Wattenberg argued that social issues were becoming a more powerful influence on voting patterns than economic concerns in the 1970s. Candidates who focused too heavily on minorities and failed to appeal to the more conservative sensibilities of the white, middle-class Americans who made up the biggest chunk of the electorate could not hope to win power. Strikingly, the authors found a broad consensus among voters "regardless of age, region, sex, education, occupation, religion, politics, unions, community size" or other factors. Success lay in the ability to appeal to a national, not just southern, population that cared little about the problems of the poor and black.[23]

This was a recipe for neglecting impoverished communities in both the North and the South. Even after Democrats regained dominance over the federal government in the late 1970s, social justice activists were unable to persuade policy makers to renew the national commitment to issues that concerned them in the 1960s. President Carter sympathized with the plight of poor people but ultimately decided that their needs were not as important as balancing the federal budget and taming inflation. In his State of the Union address in January 1978, Carter warned Americans not to look to the government to address their woes. "We really need to realize that there is a limit to the role and the function of government," he stated. "Government cannot solve our problems, it can't set our goals, it cannot define our vision. Government cannot eliminate poverty or provide a bountiful economy or reduce inflation or save our cities or cure illiteracy or provide energy." Sounding much like opponents of the War on Poverty, Carter suggested allowing the private sector to act as the engine of economic growth, asserting: "We know that in our free society, private business is still the best source of new jobs." To that end, the president proposed initiatives such as tax cuts for corporations and families and promised a "lean and tight" federal budget for 1979 that eliminated wasteful spending.[24]

Administration officials did not seem very interested in addressing the problems of displaced factory workers, and some of Carter's actions worsened their plight. The president's cabinet included twenty members of the Trilateral Commission, an organization of business and political leaders from Europe, North America, and Japan that promoted free trade and international investment as keys to a prosperous future for the United States and the world. These advisers and other influential theorists argued that deregulation and tax cuts were more effective ways to stimulate economic activity than was government action to create jobs or soften the effects of unemployment, and they pushed successfully for policies that favored investors over labor. Reduced tax rates on investment income replaced the targeted tax credits previously used to nudge corporate activity in directions desired for the public good, essentially transferring millions of dollars to corporations and wealthy individuals to spend as they liked. Hopes that this would inspire them to create new businesses and hire workers in the United States turned out to be misguided. Instead, they invested the money overseas. American banks and corporations sent $530 billion abroad during the Carter administration, while working- and middle-class families faced higher taxes to make up for the lost revenue. These burdens only intensified many people's antagonism toward government and fueled grassroots movements in California and dozens of other states to cap further tax increases. The success of these efforts created significant gaps between the costs of public services and what citizens in many communities were prepared to pay, generating budget deficits at all levels of government. Not wanting to face the wrath of taxpayers by trying to raise the needed revenue, political leaders chose instead to cut spending, making it less likely than ever that the investments needed to adequately deal with labor displacement would materialize.[25]

Candidates for public office frequently obscured the real causes of the nation's economic decline by blaming African Americans' alleged aversion to work and preference for government assistance. In his campaign for the Republican presidential nomination in 1976, Ronald Reagan deployed the same racialized depictions of welfare recipients that appeared with such frequency in the *Citizen* and other segregationist literature, including references to black unmarried mothers who supposedly lived large on their government checks and reports of able-bodied, young black men using food stamps to purchase T-bone steaks and other culinary luxuries. Government spending on social programs and overregulation of businesses by federal bureaucrats were the cause of rising inflation and the slowing economy, he argued, reinforcing white voters' sense that they were being victimized by a system that was too focused on helping black people.[26] With disturbing symbolism, Reagan began his 1980 presidential campaign by proclaiming his support for states' rights and promising to "restore to state and local governments the power that properly belongs to them" in a speech delivered to a mostly white crowd in Neshoba County, Mississippi, a community that gained national notoriety in 1964 as the site where Klan members and county law enforcement officials colluded to murder three civil rights workers.[27]

Reagan consistently responded to critics of such tactics by saying he held no prejudice toward black people and expressing bewilderment at suggestions that he was a racist. At the same time, campaign operatives were fully aware of how framing economic issues in racial rather than class terms contributed to their candidate's appeal among white voters. Reagan's calls for limiting the government's role in the economy could not have succeeded by targeting popular programs that disproportionately benefited white families, such as Social Security or Medicare. Antigovernment sentiment was much more easily sown on ground that was already prepared by the racial conflicts and debates over the War on Poverty in the 1960s. Thus, Mississippi Republicans organized the Neshoba County event to cast Reagan in the same mold as George Wallace and Barry Goldwater, while campaign workers in Alabama presented potential voters with a fact sheet that emphasized Reagan's opposition to "forced busing," plans to eliminate welfare fraud, and support for free enterprise against Carter's agenda of using government to ensure continued busing, expansion of food stamp programs, and "make-work jobs." Reflecting on the party's manipulation of racial divisions several years later, Republican operative Hastings Wyman Jr. admitted that he and others "consciously encouraged" racist voters to align with their party by denouncing busing and linking Democratic candidates to integration efforts.[28]

As with earlier campaigns that deployed racial tactics, these messages played well nationwide, not just in the South. The *New York Times* reported in April 1980 that many working-class Democrats supported Reagan in the primary elections and seemed likely to vote for him in the presidential election as well. Although dissatisfaction with President Carter more than affinity for Reagan motivated many of these voters, some of those interviewed expressed positive views of the Republican candidate. One man who worked as an awning hanger thought Reagan understood how burdensome federal income taxes were on families like his and hoped for some relief after the election. Another potential defector stated, "Reagan knows who should be on welfare and who shouldn't."

These supporters understood Reagan's "tough stand against welfare as a tough stand against black demands," the report noted. A grocer from South Philadelphia openly expressed fears that black people were "taking over" the neighborhood and predicted racial violence if the situation was allowed to continue.[29]

In the minds of these and other voters, racial and economic concerns intertwined with real and fabricated fears as financial security slipped away, programs for poor people sapped their tax dollars, and government morphed from ally to enemy in the decades after the 1960s. A study of the "Reagan Democrats" who contributed to the candidate's victory in 1980 and his reelection in 1984 found that they associated government assistance with African Americans and had no sense of how they benefited from it themselves. These voters were convinced that white people were being systematically blocked from educational and economic opportunities by affirmative action programs and scoffed at suggestions that these initiatives were necessary to address lingering inequality. "There is no historical memory of racism and no tolerance for present efforts to offset it," the report stated. "There is no sense of personal or collective responsibility that would support government anti-discrimination and civil rights policies. . . . The special status of blacks is perceived by almost all of these individuals as a serious obstacle to their personal advancement. Indeed, discrimination against whites has become a well-assimilated and ready explanation for their status, vulnerability and failures." None of the participants could identify any tangible benefits they received from paying taxes. This money, they believed, was generally misappropriated by corrupt politicians or spent on the most undeserving elements of the population rather than hardworking people like themselves.[30]

Although Reagan made good on his promises to cut taxes and social spending, these actions did not address the underlying causes of working people's problems, and the administration pursued other policies that only worsened their distress. Free trade agreements and deregulation empowered corporations to continue their search around the globe for new production sites offering cheap labor and minimal government interference. Job losses in manufacturing proceeded unchecked, and cuts in federal aid meant declining communities were left to deal with the consequences on their own. Labor unions saw their ability to negotiate favorable wages and conditions for workers deteriorate as management responded to their requests by threatening to close down plants and move them overseas. Reagan and his advisers were indifferent to workers' economic disempowerment, viewing lower wages and unemployment as tools to fight inflation. Reagan's own response to a strike by the nation's air traffic controllers in August 1980 indicated that he was no friend of organized labor. Noting that the strike by federal employees was illegal and arguing that it endangered the nation, the president fired everyone who refused to return to work, banned them from federal employment, and jailed their union representatives. These actions traumatized union leaders and emboldened employers in the private sector, further weakening labor's ability to preserve the gains made in the New Deal and postwar eras. Reflecting on the damage inflicted on his working-class community in the 1980s, Detroit autoworker Dewey Burton told an interviewer that "Reagan blindsided us" and his policies "basically devastated the workingman."[31]

Despite their social costs, laissez-faire approaches to the economy gained greater acceptance among theorists and policy makers as inflation subsided and the nation experienced stronger economic growth. The final decades of the twentieth century saw Democratic and Republican administrations alike promoting ideas and actions that liberals in both parties had once strongly contested. In the 1960s President Johnson and his supporters viewed the persistence of poverty in the United States as a national embarrassment. In contrast, Democratic Party leaders in the 1980s and 1990s appeared to accept widening inequality as a natural consequence of a vibrant capitalist economy.[32] Across the aisle, their Republican colleagues denied there was a need for government measures to ensure citizens had incomes that met their basic needs, whether working or unemployed. Rejecting arguments in favor of raising the minimum wage, Texas representative Tom DeLay asserted: "Emotional appeals about working families trying to get by on $4.25 an hour are hard to resist. Fortunately, such families don't really exist." Similarly, in response to news reports that unemployed workers experienced longer periods of joblessness and often ended up taking jobs that paid less than their previous positions, Congressman John Duncan Jr. of Tennessee ignored the role that economic restructuring played in these developments and attributed the problem to overtaxation and government regulations that hindered small businesses. When critics of free trade agreements raised concerns about the impact these policies had on American workers, legislator Philip Crane of Illinois accused them of engaging in "political demagoguery" and referred his colleagues to a *Washington Times* article that called deindustrialization a "myth."[33]

Poverty and unemployment only reemerged as national political issues in the context of proposals for reforming the welfare system that attributed these problems to government dependency rather than a lack of jobs. In 1992 Democratic presidential candidate Bill Clinton campaigned successfully on a promise to "end welfare as we know it," proposing $10 billion in funding for job training and child care to help recipients of public assistance move into private sector employment. Two years later, after Republicans gained control over the House and Senate in the midterm elections, they presented alternative solutions that cast welfare recipients as miscreants deserving of punishment rather than economic casualties entitled to aid. Proponents of the measures frequently expressed the same contempt for poor people and the same reasons for withdrawing government support that were presented by political leaders in southern plantation counties during the agricultural crisis of earlier decades. Representative Roger Wicker of Mississippi highlighted the need to reduce the federal role in people's lives and to "emphasize individual responsibility and State and local control." Others explained increases in the number of families receiving support from AFDC in terms of recipients' moral failures, such as laziness and promiscuity, and stated that the reforms aimed to discourage this behavior. Capping benefits and imposing time limits on aid would encourage single mothers to find jobs, get married, and stop having illegitimate babies, they argued. Asked what would happen to the children of women who were unable to find employment before the time limit ran out, Louisiana congressman Jim McCrery suggested they could be given up for adoption. "Will some people have a hard time? Yes," he acknowledged, but went on to argue that the existing system condemned children to "lives of hopelessness and desperation" by allowing lifelong welfare dependency.[34]

Opponents of the welfare reform bill presented alternative explanations for these problems, citing plant closings, layoffs, the declining availability of unionized jobs with benefits, and disincentives to work created by restrictive eligibility requirements for public assistance. One mother in Chicago told sociologist William Julius Wilson that she much preferred working to living on welfare but feared falling into worse poverty and losing access to health care if she took a job. "I was working and then I had two kids," she explained. "I was making, like, close to $7 an hour. . . . I had to pay a baby-sitter. . . . And I couldn't even afford medical insurance." Having once been turned away from a hospital with her sick child because she did not have health insurance, she thought it was more prudent to stay on government assistance than seek employment in the private sector. "I don't like being on public aid and stuff right now," she stated. "But what do I do with my kids when the kids get sick?" Other residents recalled that in the 1950s, when Chicago was home to large manufacturing plants that employed tens of thousands of people, jobs were plentiful and families were more likely to be intact. The disappearance of work, Wilson argued, was the most significant cause of the social problems that concerned policy makers, not the inherent immorality or other cultural deficiencies of poor people. Government action to improve education, housing, and social services, along with public works projects to create jobs, would do more to encourage economic independence than the punitive measures proposed in Congress.[35]

Progressive representatives such as Bernie Sanders of Vermont and Marcy Kaptur of Ohio made similar arguments in Congress. Noting that the federal minimum wage was not enough to keep families out of poverty, they argued it was no wonder that people sometimes chose welfare over work. A full-time employee making $4.25 an hour earned only $8,500 a year, usually in jobs that offered no health or retirement benefits. Kaptur reported that women in her district who labored in restaurants, bakeries, laundries, and other service sector jobs frequently moved back and forth between welfare and work, using public assistance as a way to "gain their footing again" when their poverty grew too severe. She went on to contrast the lives of these women with those of her mother and older relatives who lived and worked in Toledo when jobs were plentiful and within walking distance. "Champion Sparkplug is no longer in Toledo," she explained. "Chase Bank, that was right up the street where my aunt worked, closed its door, moved offshore. The glove factory that my cousin worked at isn't there anymore. Dana Corporation moved 3,500 jobs to Mexico and out of our city. Bostwick Brown. Durwick Corporation. Swift and Armour. All the bicycle manufacturing capacity of the country was moved to Taiwan. When you think about what has happened to people, it isn't easy for them to find good-paying jobs."[36]

Such arguments failed to sway the majority in Congress or in the nation at large. Public opinion polls taken in the mid-1990s showed that voters aligned more with Republicans than Democrats on how best to reform the welfare system, reduce the nation's deficits, and ensure prosperity. Observers noted that compassion for poor people seemed largely absent from the thinking of most citizens as well as their representatives in government.[37] Although President Clinton twice vetoed bills passed by

Congress that he considered too extreme, in August 1996 he finally signed legislation that radically overhauled the welfare system along essentially the same lines proposed in earlier versions. The Personal Responsibility and Work Opportunity Act cut funding for welfare by $55 billion and ended the federal guarantee of assistance for poor children provided through AFDC. Instead, the federal government distributed block grants to the states and allowed them to set their own rules within some general guidelines for eligibility. In addition, the new law required welfare recipients to find employment within two years and imposed a five-year lifetime limit on aid.[38]

Critics of the legislation wondered what would happen to people who simply could not find work and noted that it did nothing to solve a fundamental problem: the difficulty of securing stable, well-paid jobs in communities decimated by industrial decline and union busting. A *New York Times* article observed, "Jobs in the inner city are scarce even when the economy thrives, and most are low-wage or part-time or both," so recipients who gained employment often earned poverty-level incomes that failed to move them off the welfare rolls. A welfare office administrator in Oakland, California, reported that out of 885 people on her case load who found jobs in June 1995, only 28 earned enough to make them ineligible for assistance. The same month, 204 people started new jobs, while 72 others lost theirs. Given the precarious nature of local job markets like these, the authors noted, it was not certain that the reforms would have their intended impact, "and no one knows what will happen in the economy's next recession, when tens of thousands of former welfare recipients lose their jobs."[39]

An opportunity to find out came a decade later, when the global financial meltdown of 2008 sent countless businesses into bankruptcy and displaced millions of workers. The crisis had roots in the economic policies pursued since the 1970s, including deregulation of the banking system, predatory lending practices that targeted poor communities of color, and overborrowing by middle-class Americans who were earning less but shouldering more of the costs for health care, college tuition, and retirement savings. The speculation- and debt-fueled bubble of easy credit, rising home values, and consumer spending was unsustainable, and its collapse had catastrophic effects on the economy. Between October 2008 and March 2009, job losses averaged 712,000 per month. The Bureau of Labor Statistics placed the total number of positions eliminated during the recession at 8.8 million, noting that mass layoffs affected every

LEGACIES OF DISPLACEMENT

sector of the economy.[40] Although a slow recovery began in June 2009, in December that year 15 million Americans (10 percent of the labor force) remained unemployed. Six million of them had been out of work for more than six months, and 3 million for over a year. As home foreclosure rates skyrocketed, home values and consumer spending plummeted, giving businesses little incentive to expand or hire workers. Economic hardship reached into every corner of the nation, afflicting middle-class as well as poor people, white and nonwhite, skilled and unskilled workers, cities and formerly wealthy suburbs as well as depressed rural communities. News media carried stories about people who had once held professional, highly paid jobs being laid off and foreclosed upon, forcing them to seek help from public assistance programs and private charities "for the first time in their lives." In November 2009, the USDA reported that hunger was on the rise in the United States, with an estimated 49 million households facing "difficulty obtaining food for all their members due to a lack of resources."[41]

Now more than at any time since the 1930s, Americans might have looked to their government to intervene rather than waiting for market forces to correct the situation. The initial onset of the crisis did help elect the nation's first black president, Barack Obama, a Democrat who ran on a progressive agenda promoting a role for government as well as private enterprise in getting Americans back to work. The Democratic Party platform promised "immediate relief to working people who have lost their jobs" and enhanced investments in public education, infrastructure, and renewable energy to "generate the good, high-paying jobs of the future." Upon taking office in 2009, however, Obama repeatedly found his efforts to revitalize economic activity stymied by obstructionists in Congress who were determined not to allow anything resembling the New Deal or Great Society initiatives of the past. At hearings of the Joint Economic Committee of Congress held in December, Representative Kevin Brady of Texas argued that the United States was at an "economic crossroads" and outlined the choices the nation faced in familiar language: "The road to the right is a free market economy in which the decisions of Americans acting as entrepreneurs, consumers, workers, investors, and savers are determinative, while the road to the left is a social market economy in which the Federal Government plays a controlling role." Arguing that federal deficits and the national debt were bigger threats to the nation than mass unemployment, conservative politicians and their supporters in the antigovernment Tea Party movement used the crisis to promote further shredding of the social safety net. These "deficit hawks" ignored the role that tax cuts and two unfunded wars in Afghanistan and Iraq played in racking up the nation's $13 trillion debt, blaming government spending on social programs and pushing for cuts in Social Security and Medicare.[42]

Debates over efforts to make health insurance more affordable, extend time limits on unemployment benefits, and expand access to food stamps revived the demonic imagery of overbearing government and lazy, undeserving poor people that permeated similar discussions in the 1960s. When Obama proposed legislation to expand access to health care by making the private insurance market more competitive, critics labeled it a government takeover and falsely claimed that it empowered federal bureaucrats to make life-or-death decisions regarding patient care. In 2010, South Carolina's lieutenant governor Andre Bauer opposed government assistance for poor people by comparing them to stray animals that would only multiply if they were fed. Speaking at a town hall meeting, Bauer stated: "You're facilitating the problem if you give an animal or a person ample food supply. They will reproduce, especially ones that don't think too much further than that. And so what you've got to do is you've got to curtail that type of behavior. They don't know any better." Coverage by media outlet Fox News of outreach programs that encouraged eligible people to sign up for food stamps echoed the sentiments expressed decades earlier in the *Citizen*. One report highlighted a "blissfully jobless California surfer who expects taxpayers to underwrite his life of beaches and booze." In other segments, commentators asserted that fraud was rampant in the program and expressed outrage that recipients could buy food deemed appropriate only for wealthier people, such as fresh fish and organic produce. The racial coding of earlier decades also persisted in some of the attacks on the administration's policies. Radio commentator Rush Limbaugh, for example, referred to Obama's economic reforms as "reparations," implying that they were ploys to take money away from white people and give it to black people rather than attempts to enhance the well-being of all Americans.[43]

The legacies of debates over race and rights in the rural South during the civil rights era lived on and shaped policy responses to mass unemployment in the early twenty-first century. Like the displaced sharecroppers in the plantation regions, millions of discarded workers faced poverty, hunger, and homelessness resulting from economic transformations that rendered their labor obsolete. This time, however, national leaders proposed no innovative antipoverty measures to address the crisis, and other Americans seemed to accept that there was nothing they could do. In the transformed political climate generated by decades of rhetoric that blamed overbearing government for the nation's problems and promoted free markets as the solution, it was difficult to revive a fundamental tenet that had once seemed obvious to a majority of citizens: that some regulation and other mechanisms to ensure a fair distribution of wealth were needed for capitalism to work at its best and meet basic human needs. Without a strong social safety net to catch those who were periodically jolted out of the labor force by volatile markets and technological change, many more people were poised to discover what the South's displaced persons knew in the 1960s: that political liberties unmoored from economic security were mere shadows of freedom, incapable of delivering on their promises.

CONCLUSION

In July 2014 the FSC/LAF's Ben Burkett was among five winners of the James Beard Foundation's Leadership Awards recognizing "visionaries in the world of food politics and sustainable agriculture." The other honorees were community organizers Karen Washington and Navina Khanna, both active in efforts to enhance access to nutritious food for low-income people, and writers Michael Pollan and Mark Bittman, known for their critiques of corporate agriculture and advocacy of locally grown, organic food. Meanwhile, the United Nations promoted 2014 as the International Year of Family Farming with initiatives designed to draw attention to the part small farms played in fighting hunger and poverty, improving living conditions, managing natural resources, and strengthening local economies in the world's poorest regions. By encouraging cross-cultural discussions and increasing awareness of the challenges these enterprises faced, the organization hoped to "reposition family farming at the centre of agricultural, environmental and social policies . . . to promote a shift towards a more equal and balanced development."[1]

In the United States and around the world, the technology- and market-driven agribusiness model that American policy makers had long held up as the most efficient means of production was called into question as analysts exposed its detrimental effects, including environmental degradation, concentration of landownership, disrupted communities, involuntary migration, growing inequality, poor nutrition and health, and human rights violations. In its place, reformers sought to create more direct relationships between the land, farmers, and consumers that aimed to protect the environment and ensure a decent standard of living for all. Organic produce, farmers' markets, and cooperatives gained in popularity as people voted with their dollars against corporate practices that threatened the well-being of people and the planet.[2]

Although the interest in supporting family farms and restoring local food systems seemed like a new phenomenon, its roots lay in the social justice movements that emerged in the South after the passage of civil rights legislation in the 1960s. As Burkett explained after the

FSC/LAF received an award from the U.S. Food Sovereignty Alliance in September 2015, "Our view is local production for local consumption. . . . Everything we're about is food sovereignty, the right of every individual on earth to wholesome food, clean water, clean air, clean land, and the self-determination of a local community to grow and eat what they want. . . . It's what we've always done."[3]

In the 1960s activists faced with a humanitarian crisis created by economic restructuring, politically motivated reprisals, and government inaction organized local communities to resist the pressures being placed on African Americans to leave. Taking advantage of resources made available by the War on Poverty and with the support of sympathetic federal officials, they forged creative solutions to the problems facing displaced workers in the plantation regions. Antipoverty projects employed the jobless while offering needed social services and injecting money into local economies. Cooperative enterprises provided work, income, and dignity to individual participants and helped generate broader economic gains in rural communities. These businesses, along with the training and technical assistance provided by the FSC, enabled small farmers to stay on the land and created new employment options for people whose jobs were replaced by machines. By allowing member-owners to make decisions for themselves, helping to maintain black voting majorities, and encouraging people to exercise the rights they had won through the Civil Rights and Voting Rights Acts, cooperatives fostered political as well as economic empowerment for black southerners. Plans for a coordinated regional development effort to expand on these achievements represented a promising way forward to a more prosperous, equitable, and democratic society.

Large landowners, business leaders, and public officials who believed black out-migration was the best solution to the unemployment problem reacted strongly against activists' suggestions that alternative paths existed. Fearing the financial costs of equalizing education and employment opportunities, providing adequate social services, and retraining workers for other jobs, opponents of these initiatives portrayed them as wasteful and misguided attempts to interfere with market forces that naturally allocated labor and resources in accordance with the laws of supply and demand. These arguments ignored the role that political decisions played in organizing the economy and the ways the southern social order was rigged to channel a disproportionate share of the region's wealth to a small number of white residents. Although critics of the War on Poverty used the language of freedom and individual rights to gain wide support for rolling back federal intervention and restoring limited government, the policies pursued after the 1970s enhanced liberty only for those with the means to provide for their own material needs. Americans' sense of collective responsibility for ensuring adequate incomes and decent living conditions for all citizens dissipated in the late twentieth century, leaving white as well as black workers to weather the economic turbulence associated with global capitalist restructuring largely on their own.

The political and ideological struggles that played out in the South during these decades occurred in the context of a racialized class system that had exploited black people's labor for centuries and attributed the resulting inequities to African Americans' inherent deficiencies. When agricultural modernization transformed black workers from essential to marginal participants in the region's economy, racism came to serve new purposes as plantation owners sought to avoid responsibility for assisting displaced tenants and sharecroppers. White residents' racial prejudices conditioned them to accept arguments against government intervention that framed antipoverty efforts as threats to white supremacy and an unjust transfer of wealth from hardworking taxpayers to undeserving African Americans. Conservative politicians stoked voters' racial fears to gain control over the national government in the 1970s and 1980s and justify laissez-faire economic policies that abandoned displaced workers to their fate. Consequently, deindustrializing towns and cities in the North suffered along with rural poor communities in the plantation South as jobs disappeared, public services declined, and businesses invested more in financial speculation than in producing goods. When economic catastrophe on a global scale revealed the underlying fault lines of finance capitalism, some Americans once again began to seek alternative paths to prosperity grounded in support for local farmers and businesses, living wage campaigns, cooperatives, and socially responsible entrepreneurship.

Ben Burkett and other veterans of the FSC/LAF who lived to see the dawn of a new century could point proudly to their role in keeping the organization's founding ideals alive and inserting them into the national dialogue. At sixty-two years old, Burkett still farmed the land that had been in his family since 1889, growing 16 types of vegetables on just over 300 acres and selling them through his co-op to national grocery chains as well as at local farmers' markets. In an interview conducted in Mozambique while he was attending a conference of Via Campesina, an international organization representing the interests of small farmers, Burkett credited the cooperative model with helping him and his fellow member-owners remain in business. "We try to work with each other and see what we can do to support each other," he stated, contrasting this with the exploitative practices of large corporations that seemed bent on paying farmers "as little as possible." Similarly, Wendell Paris outlined the FSC/LAF's long-standing struggles for a fairer economy and the opposition this provoked from more powerful constituencies in a speech delivered at a staff meeting of the organization in 2009. "You're talking about empowering people that is poor, and that never was supposed to take place, because when you empower people, it's hard to steal from them," he stated. "That's what we represented and that's what we still represent."[4]

In the early twenty-first century, the dilemmas and debates over how to ensure racial equality and economic justice remained as salient as they were in the 1960s. Americans and others around the globe pondered whether capitalist restructuring and technological advances that reduced the need for workers across a broad spectrum of professions must consign a proportion of humanity to lives of joblessness, poverty, and despair or if alternatives could be developed that asserted the inherent value of human beings regardless of their employment status or ability to generate profits for multinational corporations. Those seeking answers to these questions could look to the responses of displaced agricultural workers in the plantation South, whose experiences foreshadowed those of an ever-widening segment of the labor force. Mid-twentieth-century policy makers might have dismissed small farms, cooperatives, and locally owned businesses as anachronistic vestiges of an earlier era, but for rural black southerners, these enterprises represented political empowerment and economic autonomy. The social justice experiments of those decades are worth remembering as new generations of workers grapple with the possibility that they may someday find themselves converted from free labor to displaced persons.

APPENDIX

Table 1. Agricultural and nonagricultural employment in the plantation counties, 1950–1990

County	Number employed in agricultural work					Number employed in nonagricultural work				
	1950	1960	1970	1980	1990	1950	1960	1970	1980	1990
ALABAMA										
Barbour	4,578	1,697	716	430	292	5,753	5,954	7,177	8,212	10,021
Bullock	3,240	1,347	710	345	340	2,557	2,541	2,756	2,919	3,413
Dallas*	6,402	2,906	1,083	694	659	12,774	13,923	15,569	18,393	15,971
Greene	3,666	1,697	470	197	124	1,978	2,336	2,267	2,761	3,122
Hale	3,646	2,099	606	393	289	2,506	3,523	3,657	4,348	5,153
Henry	3,440	1,699	686	544	428	2,480	3,505	4,099	5,156	6,085
Lowndes	4,344	2,032	472	412	249	1,983	2,327	2,826	3,343	3,951
Macon	3,715	1,674	292	261	287	5,988	6,146	6,827	7,703	8,236
Marengo	4,888	1,921	617	352	281	5,226	6,143	6,705	8,067	8,487
Montgomery*	4,562	2,564	1,268	1,155	1,046	47,173	54,541	59,866	78,356	91,568
Perry	3,492	1,076	651	371	325	3,230	4,062	3,963	4,251	3,929
Russell*	3,194	1,207	479	387	255	11,733	14,248	15,472	17,268	19,443
Sumter	4,011	2,100	477	254	214	3,478	3,606	4,118	4,976	5,094
Wilcox	4,951	1,925	491	189	160	3,359	3,234	3,690	3,611	3,512
Total	58,129	25,944	9,018	5,984	4,949	110,218	126,089	138,992	169,364	187,985
LOUISIANA										
Avoyelles	4,982	2,812	1,435	1,191	680	5,659	7,320	8,424	11,360	11,183
Bossier*	2,569	1,083	558	443	674	7,854	13,210	17,321	31,250	34,408
Caddo*	4,979	2,433	1,368	1,143	1,470	61,923	77,546	81,208	108,045	97,409
Catahoula	1,739	739	596	656	484	1,540	1,900	2,495	3,299	3,135
Claiborne	2,971	664	269	220	121	5,127	5,131	4,732	5,705	5,269
Concordia	1,874	842	701	853	527	2,607	4,746	6,106	7,101	6,404
De Soto	2,833	1,104	563	460	468	4,333	5,622	5,876	8,515	8,065
East Carroll	2,811	1,560	867	575	505	1,945	2,221	2,200	2,820	1,966
East Feliciana	2,193	906	309	259	230	2,892	3,547	4,110	5,727	6,004
Franklin	5,453	2,792	1,360	1,123	967	2,902	4,128	4,959	6,276	6,392
Madison	2,208	1,202	750	606	497	3,153	3,032	3,265	4,020	3,294
Morehouse	3,440	1,561	971	818	754	6,413	7,586	8,067	9,700	9,594
Natchitoches	4,064	1,594	779	757	571	5,958	7,708	9,302	13,115	12,046
Ouachita*	1,731	876	692	679	817	25,253	32,718	38,648	53,233	57,283
Pointe Coupee	3,356	1,410	844	500	540	3,242	3,760	4,666	7,199	7,110
Rapides*	3,207	1,716	1,505	1,125	1,245	24,312	29,929	33,848	46,890	47,543
Red River	1,868	630	340	276	132	1,477	1,922	2,375	3,268	2,992
Richland	4,386	2,149	1,037	1,060	909	3,341	4,002	4,812	5,718	6,110
St. Landry	9,923	5,496	2,362	1,277	912	12,231	16,182	18,207	26,664	24,088
Tensas	2,306	1,084	707	599	621	1,689	1,824	1,681	1,935	1,591
Webster	1,646	638	265	241	284	9,066	11,779	13,104	15,543	14,794
West Carroll	3,104	1,671	768	736	678	1,512	1,985	2,460	2,862	3,358
West Feliciana	1,000	573	137	57	68	1,107	1,682	1,608	2,830	2,987
Total	74,643	35,535	19,183	15,654	14,154	195,536	249,480	279,474	383,075	373,025

MISSISSIPPI

Adams	1,457	476	310	237	296	11,040	12,098	11,791	14,030	12,599
Amite	3,496	1,311	525	283	244	2,662	3,324	3,423	4,269	4,182
Attala	4,321	1,529	467	327	218	4,180	4,581	5,721	6,226	6,535
Benton	2,097	826	355	225	97	651	1,396	1,896	2,571	2,707
Bolivar	12,576	6,828	2,401	1,533	1,146	6,773	8,279	11,541	12,766	13,138
Carroll	3,406	1,666	547	366	262	1,399	1,621	2,275	2,818	3,281
Chickasaw	3,475	1,436	498	423	172	2,620	4,237	5,226	6,605	7,644
Claiborne	1,767	700	210	176	123	2,283	2,267	2,555	3,715	2,955
Clay	2,290	1,269	384	231	188	3,239	4,873	5,947	7,726	8,109
Coahoma	8,857	5,249	1,854	1,372	1,007	7,783	8,639	9,164	9,732	8,871
Copiah	4,819	1,838	657	399	563	5,591	6,400	6,814	8,518	9,517
De Soto	5,458	2,835	905	721	627	2,185	4,097	10,569	21,392	32,501
Franklin	1,158	306	129	81	64	2,372	2,364	2,251	2,613	2,606
Grenada	2,068	964	398	269	179	4,266	5,380	6,724	8,038	8,316
Hinds*	6,934	3,364	1,682	1,241	1,999	49,854	67,341	80,151	109,734	112,762
Holmes	6,449	2,992	1,239	757	649	4,304	4,470	4,728	5,274	4,962
Humphreys	4,750	2,664	1,328	811	1,016	2,150	2,597	2,623	3,053	3,362
Issaquena	1,179	604	396	297	214	270	316	353	457	460
Jefferson	2,341	916	172	173	57	1,574	1,793	1,866	2,552	2,255
Kemper	3,552	1,700	460	157	170	1,362	1,872	2,213	3,033	3,477
Lafayette	3,066	1,398	477	186	343	4,099	5,198	7,470	12,630	13,263
Leflore	8,256	4,816	1,588	1,356	946	9,453	10,426	11,883	12,540	12,136
Lowndes	4,066	1,739	685	582	398	9,434	12,950	15,986	20,724	24,862
Madison	6,411	3,694	851	705	587	4,785	6,429	8,031	14,845	23,270
Marshall	4,946	2,836	889	515	382	2,510	3,669	5,564	9,204	11,007
Monroe	5,202	2,131	778	494	405	5,963	9,829	11,942	13,998	15,518
Montgomery	2,018	966	523	236	197	2,736	3,134	3,754	4,333	4,545
Noxubee	4,390	2,141	872	533	288	2,129	2,647	3,060	3,423	3,878
Oktibbeha	2,971	1,512	593	393	447	4,663	6,766	8,847	13,083	15,796
Panola	5,954	3,615	1,168	891	481	3,613	4,992	7,109	8,671	10,686
Quitman	5,811	3,211	913	699	418	1,904	2,369	3,128	3,149	2,888
Rankin	3,139	1,420	733	697	646	4,962	9,102	14,308	29,916	41,538
Sharkey	2,508	2,017	756	603	610	1,306	1,510	1,676	1,660	1,737
Sunflower	11,583	6,095	2,039	1,700	1,175	5,054	6,480	7,812	8,978	9,118
Tallahatchie	6,541	4,578	1,323	1,001	671	2,778	2,961	3,609	4,022	4,225
Tate	3,814	2,462	864	412	385	1,746	2,981	4,827	6,916	8,758
Tunica	5,966	3,295	774	729	478	1,581	1,701	1,921	1,684	1,882
Warren*	1,678	903	409	465	372	12,843	13,590	15,315	20,123	19,001
Washington*	8,843	4,955	2,154	1,768	1,514	14,294	19,641	19,829	23,522	22,617
Wilkinson	2,443	895	377	111	144	2,499	2,449	2,615	2,992	2,813
Yalobusha	2,591	1,195	369	190	159	2,520	2,611	3,653	4,561	4,390
Yazoo	6,246	2,995	1,474	1,084	1,024	5,814	6,480	6,825	8,068	7,274
Total	190,893	98,342	35,526	25,429	21,361	223,244	285,890	346,995	464,164	511,441

Sources: U.S. Bureau of the Census, *Census of Population, Social and Economic Characteristics, 1950–1990* (Washington, D.C.: GPO, various years). Industry of employed persons information from table 43 (1950), table 85 (1960), table 123 (1970), table 178 (1980), and table 146 (1990).

*Counties with towns or cities of 25,000 or more inhabitants in 1960.

Table 2. Black unemployment and poverty rates in the plantation counties, 1950–1990

County	Percentage of black civilian labor force unemployed					Percentage of black families with incomes below poverty level				
	1950	1960	1970	1980	1990	1950	1960	1970	1980	1990
ALABAMA										
Barbour	2.3	7.9	6.6	12.9	12.5	93.5	85.6	69.0	45.3	36.3
Bullock	1.3	4.8	8.3	13.4	9.4	93.7	90.0	67.9	41.4	40.4
Dallas*	2.7	6.8	7.2	15.6	18.3	90.8	84.3	60.1	46.0	52.5
Greene	1.3	4.8	7.4	19.8	13.8	93.4	88.5	72.2	47.0	50.3
Hale	1.1	4.3	4.9	16.3	11.1	96.3	87.4	65.6	52.2	46.1
Henry	2.0	6.0	3.7	7.6	9.1	93.8	91.7	56.3	–	29.2
Lowndes	0.6	5.9	6.4	16.2	15.5	95.4	87.9	68.8	50.5	43.7
Macon	2.2	4.8	5.4	12.0	15.7	82.1	64.1	42.9	31.8	31.9
Marengo	2.4	6.7	7.5	11.6	14.2	93.6	86.5	70.1	–	43.9
Montgomery*	4.4	7.3	6.3	12.3	13.4	88.5	68.8	45.7	32.9	31.5
Perry	2.1	9.8	6.6	10.3	12.7	92.3	90.7	62.1	47.1	56.1
Russell*	2.6	8.2	7.1	12.8	13.7	88.5	71.5	52.9	34.6	31.3
Sumter	1.1	3.2	8.2	15.5	14.8	92.8	88.6	64.0	41.8	47.4
Wilcox	0.6	5.3	8.9	13.5	22.1	94.6	89.8	70.9	53.1	57.9
Average	1.9	6.1	6.8	13.6	14.0	92.1	84.0	62.0	43.6	42.8
LOUISIANA										
Avoyelles	5.7	7.4	18.5	14.3	27.9	91.5	86.5	68.0	51.3	60.9
Bossier*	3.6	8.0	9.5	14.2	22.4	88.2	77.5	49.4	32.3	40.2
Caddo*	4.2	7.4	8.6	10.2	20.5	85.3	65.0	44.9	30.0	41.0
Catahoula	6.1	6.4	10.6	12.2	28.5	92.9	85.1	70.5	–	54.9
Claiborne	1.9	6.2	8.7	10.4	18.7	90.9	82.6	58.9	–	52.8
Concordia	3.4	15.4	11.3	11.7	26.3	93.3	82.2	65.5	–	53.6
De Soto	2.8	7.5	11.0	12.4	22.3	90.0	78.2	56.2	39.0	49.6
East Carroll	6.3	8.3	15.2	15.9	40.1	92.9	86.5	76.5	53.4	71.6
East Feliciana	1.2	7.6	9.9	10.7	17.6	91.8	80.0	57.1	30.4	39.3
Franklin	3.0	8.4	11.0	15.0	21.4	91.9	89.0	73.1	55.4	57.6
Madison	5.6	15.1	5.2	9.6	25.9	91.8	84.7	65.9	52.0	58.5
Morehouse	5.3	6.2	10.9	12.3	22.2	89.7	78.7	64.6	52.1	50.8
Natchitoches	3.7	13.8	12.7	14.4	23.9	86.4	82.1	67.3	38.0	51.2
Ouachita*	6.2	8.2	6.3	11.6	19.1	87.1	68.3	52.2	41.5	48.8
Pointe Coupee	5.5	10.5	16.8	16.5	23.9	91.4	84.8	56.4	47.8	49.4
Rapides*	8.2	10.3	7.6	11.4	17.6	85.4	70.3	45.9	34.5	42.2
Red River	2.4	7.4	13.7	12.4	20.1	93.4	88.9	71.7	39.0	56.2
Richland	4.1	2.2	8.7	9.5	19.4	91.4	87.1	68.6	59.8	56.4
St. Landry	4.3	10.5	10.6	10.5	24.6	91.8	84.6	65.8	41.9	55.4
Tensas	5.2	6.3	7.9	12.5	22.7	94.4	91.8	73.4	60.6	59.5
Webster	4.7	9.6	10.2	15.8	21.5	89.3	73.3	48.1	37.3	41.8
West Carroll	1.6	6.8	13.6	6.2	17.6	94.8	86.3	77.0	58.7	57.1
West Feliciana	1.2	10.6	15.9	13.7	17.4	92.3	84.9	60.1	46.7	53.7
Average	4.2	8.7	11.1	12.3	22.7	90.8	81.7	62.5	45.1	52.3
MISSISSIPPI										
Adams	7.0	12.0	8.8	14.6	20.9	86.6	71.8	57.5	42.3	43.0
Amite	2.1	4.5	10.4	9.9	15.2	91.4	84.2	69.0	–	45.7
Attala	4.2	5.7	7.7	16.0	12.9	94.3	88.0	68.7	51.9	46.7
Benton	0.1	5.5	9.4	20.0	25.4	92.2	90.6	65.4	33.4	37.3
Bolivar	7.2	11.5	15.5	16.7	23.4	93.1	91.4	68.9	50.7	53.4

Carroll	0.8	3.7	7.6	14.5	21.4	95.9	94.4	72.1	43.6	50.5
Chickasaw	1.9	6.6	8.7	6.2	12.0	95.9	88.1	55.9	31.3	28.9
Claiborne	2.6	7.1	10.0	15.2	25.9	93.5	89.9	61.2	35.8	43.8
Clay	3.1	3.8	9.5	10.3	16.1	94.9	84.0	51.2	33.0	39.2
Coahoma	5.3	9.9	11.6	20.6	21.9	92.2	85.2	68.4	50.3	58.5
Copiah	2.2	9.1	10.5	14.5	15.0	96.7	88.3	57.8	43.0	44.9
De Soto	0.5	4.3	7.5	12.5	12.7	93.4	88.6	61.5	43.9	34.7
Franklin	4.5	5.0	11.7	15.9	22.9	93.7	86.7	72.1	49.6	51.0
Grenada	5.4	7.2	9.8	16.2	18.3	93.7	85.5	51.8	–	37.8
Hinds*	5.7	5.8	6.3	9.9	12.9	86.5	66.9	44.8	29.4	31.0
Holmes	1.6	7.8	10.1	14.9	21.9	95.1	92.3	73.1	54.9	61.3
Humphreys	6.2	8.1	6.1	18.8	10.5	96.6	92.8	77.4	54.9	55.2
Issaquena	1.8	6.1	9.3	12.9	15.3	99.0	98.0	62.8	–	62.8
Jefferson	0.3	10.0	15.9	20.0	28.5	96.0	92.7	73.6	41.9	49.3
Kemper	1.1	2.9	12.3	13.5	16.3	94.8	91.0	74.0	50.8	47.8
Lafayette	2.1	3.5	5.3	8.2	9.7	94.6	84.1	55.9	29.3	36.1
Leflore	7.1	9.2	9.2	15.7	18.3	93.4	87.3	61.6	46.9	51.5
Lowndes	3.9	7.3	7.4	14.9	13.5	94.0	80.9	56.2	39.9	40.5
Madison	4.5	6.0	5.8	12.1	15.7	93.8	86.0	61.9	43.4	43.4
Marshall	1.3	3.2	8.3	15.0	18.7	95.9	84.4	68.4	40.8	38.4
Monroe	3.6	12.0	7.7	8.2	11.6	95.6	83.7	55.3	38.8	39.5
Montgomery	2.8	5.4	10.8	–	16.1	95.5	88.5	67.3	46.8	48.0
Noxubee	1.4	5.7	16.0	18.0	22.4	94.6	92.8	74.3	47.1	49.7
Oktibbeha	2.4	6.5	7.8	16.2	11.9	92.5	84.3	60.2	39.2	41.6
Panola	3.3	3.4	12.2	14.1	14.7	95.8	94.4	65.6	46.1	46.7
Quitman	3.3	5.2	15.9	14.9	20.5	96.1	93.5	81.7	50.1	51.9
Rankin	1.2	5.3	5.2	9.1	8.3	92.7	78.1	43.3	29.8	25.8
Sharkey	15.2	6.7	18.7	11.8	16.0	93.4	90.3	76.6	51.0	60.2
Sunflower	3.1	6.2	12.6	15.0	16.7	94.1	90.8	72.3	49.1	54.7
Tallahatchie	1.6	5.5	9.2	12.9	20.0	94.2	92.7	79.5	49.8	54.2
Tate	1.2	3.9	10.1	13.6	13.9	96.2	92.0	64.7	41.8	35.8
Tunica	1.5	5.6	15.9	21.7	23.8	93.2	93.4	76.7	63.9	68.0
Warren*	9.8	9.2	7.2	11.1	14.9	90.1	78.6	49.0	34.6	42.7
Washington*	12.4	12.1	12.8	12.8	21.1	93.2	80.8	59.4	42.9	46.4
Wilkinson	1.3	8.6	18.7	14.6	25.3	93.0	87.6	68.3	39.7	51.2
Yalobusha	2.0	5.2	7.2	–	11.0	93.2	90.5	63.2	35.1	41.3
Yazoo	6.5	5.8	7.7	13.6	15.9	94.8	89.5	75.7	53.9	54.2
Average	3.7	6.6	10.2	14.2	17.4	93.9	87.5	64.9	43.6	46.3

Sources: Bureau of the Census, *Census of Population, Social and Economic Characteristics, 1950–1990* (Washington, D.C.: GPO, various years). Unemployment rates from table 44 (1950), table 87 (1960), table 126 (1970), table 184 (1980), and table 9 (1990). Poverty rates from table 45a (1950), table 88 (1960), table 128 (1970), table 187 (1980), and table 9 (1990).

Note: Dashes (–) indicate counties and categories for which no data were provided in the 1980 census. Standard poverty measures were not developed until the 1970 census, so poverty rates for 1950 and 1960 are not entirely comparable with those from 1970 to 1990. Data for 1960 represents the percentage of families earning less than $3,000 per year, the same threshold that federal officials used as a rough measure for poverty in the 1960s. Data for 1950 represents the percentage of families earning less than $2,500 per year, which is comparable in purchasing power with $3,000 in 1960 (determined using the Bureau of Labor Statistics' Consumer Price Index Calculator at http://www.bls.gov/data/inflation_calculator.htm). The figures for 1950 may be slightly inflated by the inclusion of unrelated individuals along with families in the census data, since these were not separated out in 1950 as they were in later censuses.

*Counties with towns or cities of 25,000 or more inhabitants in 1960.

NOTES

Abbreviations Used in the Notes

AC	Alabama Collection, Special Collections, Hoole Library, University of Alabama, Tuscaloosa.
AECC	Allen Eugene Cox Collection, Special Collections Department, Mississippi State University Libraries, Starkville.
AFBFR	Alabama Farm Bureau Federation Records, Special Collections and Archives Department, Draughon Library, Auburn University, Alabama.
CDP	Charles Davis Papers, McCain Library and Archives, University of Southern Mississippi, Hattiesburg.
CFC, RG 403	Chronological Files, 1969–1979, Office of the Chairman, Equal Employment Opportunity Commission, Record Group 403, National Archives, Washington, D.C.
COREP	*Papers of the Congress of Racial Equality, 1941–1967.* Sanford, N.C.: Microfilming Corporation of America, 1980. Microfilm.
CORER	Congress of Racial Equality Records, 1941–1967, Wisconsin Historical Society, Madison.
DCC	Delta Council Collection, Charles W. Capps Jr. Archives and Museum, Delta State University, Cleveland, Mississippi.
DHCR	Delta Health Center Records, Southern Historical Collection, Wilson Library, University of North Carolina, Chapel Hill.
DMP	Delta Ministry Papers, Special Collections Department, Mississippi State University Libraries, Starkville.
DRBC	David R. Bowen Collection, Congressional and Political Research Center, Mississippi State University Libraries, Starkville.
FISR	Freedom Information Service Records, Wisconsin Historical Society, Madison.
FSCR	Records of the Federation of Southern Cooperatives, Amistad Research Center, Tulane University, New Orleans, Louisiana.
GC, RG 16	General Correspondence, 1906–1975, General Records, Office of the Secretary of Agriculture, Record Group 16, National Archives, Washington, D.C.
GFMD, RG 381	Grant Files, 1966–1971, Migrant Division, Office of Operations, Office of Economic Opportunity, Community Services Administration, Record Group 381, National Archives, Washington, D.C.
GPS, RG 174	Records of Secretary of Labor George P. Shultz, 1969–1970, Office of the Secretary of Labor, General Records of the Department of Labor, Record Group 174, National Archives, Washington, D.C.
GRPR, RG 381	General Records Relating to Public Reaction to OEO Programs, 1965–1971, Office of Public Affairs, Office of Economic Opportunity, Community Services Administration, Record Group 381, National Archives, Washington, D.C.

GRSF, RG 381   General Records ("Subject File"), 1976–1981, Office of the Director, Community Services Administration, Record Group 381, National Archives, Washington, D.C.

GSCF, RG 378   General Subject and Chronological Files, 1965–1966, Office of the Assistant Secretary for Economic Development, Economic Development Administration, Record Group 378, National Archives, Washington, D.C.

GWAP   George W. Andrews Papers, Special Collections and Archives Department, Draughon Library, Auburn University, Alabama.

HCP   Hodding Carter III Papers, Special Collections Department, Mississippi State University Libraries, Starkville.

HOEO, RG 381   History of OEO during the Nixon Administration, Office of Public Affairs, Office of Economic Opportunity, Community Services Administration, Record Group 381, National Archives, Washington, D.C.

IIF, RG 381   Inspection and Investigation Files, 1969–1974, General Counsel, Office of Economic Opportunity, Community Services Administration, Record Group 381, National Archives, Washington, D.C.

JAS, RG 16   Records of Under Secretary John A. Schnittker, 1961–1969, Records of the Under Secretary and Assistant Secretary, General Records, Office of the Secretary of Agriculture, Record Group 16, National Archives, Washington, D.C.

JCSC   John C. Stennis Collection, Congressional and Political Research Center, Mississippi State University Libraries, Starkville.

JDH, RG 174   Records of Secretary of Labor James D. Hodgson, 1970–1972, Office of the Secretary of Labor, General Records of the Department of Labor, Record Group 174, National Archives, Washington, D.C.

JHP   James Hand Jr. Papers, Charles W. Capps Jr. Archives and Museum, Delta State University, Cleveland, Mississippi.

JJSSP   John J. Sparkman Senate Papers, Special Collections, Hoole Library, University of Alabama, Tuscaloosa.

JTD, RG 174   General Subject Files, Records of Secretary of Labor John T. Dunlop, 1975–1976, Office of the Secretary of Labor, General Records of the Department of Labor, Record Group 174, National Archives, Washington, D.C.

JWHP   John W. Hatch Papers, Southern Historical Collection, Wilson Library, University of North Carolina, Chapel Hill.

JZP   John Zippert Papers, Wisconsin Historical Society, Madison.

LBP   Lee Bankhead Papers, Wisconsin Historical Society, Madison.

LMDDCF   Lower Mississippi Delta Development Commission Files, Charles W. Capps Jr. Archives and Museum, Delta State University, Cleveland, Mississippi.

MBC   Marjorie Baroni Collection, Archives and Special Collections, University of Mississippi, Oxford.

MFDPR   Mississippi Freedom Democratic Party Records, 1962–1971, Wisconsin Historical Society, Madison. Microfilm.

NPR, RG 381   Narrative Progress Reports, 1966–1967, Community Action Program, Office of Economic Opportunity, Community Services Administration, Record Group 381, National Archives, Washington, D.C.

PBJFP   Paul B. Johnson Family Papers, McCain Library and Archives, University of Southern Mississippi, Hattiesburg.

PFDD, RG 381   Project Files, 1965–1970, Deputy Director, Office of Economic Opportunity, Community Services Administration, Record Group 381, National Archives, Washington, D.C.

PJB, RG 174   Records of Secretary of Labor Peter J. Brennan, 1973–1975, Office of the Secretary of Labor, General Records of the Department of Labor, Record Group 174, National Archives, Washington, D.C.

PR, RG 381   Press Releases, 1976–1981, Community Services Administration, Record Group 381, National Archives, Washington, D.C.

PRADCR, RG 381

        Program Records of the Assistant Director for Civil Rights, 1965–1968, Office of Civil Rights, Office of Economic Opportunity, Community Services Administration, Record Group 381, National Archives, Washington, D.C.

RBFA   Rockefeller Brothers Fund Archives, Rockefeller Archives Center, Sleepy Hollow, New York.

RBLC   Russell B. Long Collection, Hill Memorial Library, Louisiana State University, Baton Rouge.

RJD, RG 174   Records of Secretary of Labor Raymond J. Donovan, 1981–1984, Office of the Secretary of Labor, General Records of the Department of Labor, Record Group 174, National Archives, Washington, D.C.

RM, RG 174   Records of Secretary of Labor Ray Marshall, 1977–1980, Office of the Secretary of Labor, General Records of the Department of Labor, Record Group 174, National Archives, Washington, D.C.

SEDFREP   Papers of the Scholarship, Education and Defense Fund for Racial Equality, Wisconsin Historical Society, Madison.

SFDD, RG 381 Subject Files, 1966–1973, Deputy Director, Office of Economic Opportunity, Community Services Administration, Record Group 381, National Archives, Washington, D.C.

SFES, RG 378 Subject Files, 1965–1969, Office of the Executive Secretariat, Office of Administration, Economic Development Administration, Record Group 378, National Archives, Washington, D.C.

SFFCD, RG 381 Subject File, 1968–1972, Field Coordination Division, Office of Field Operations, Office of Economic Opportunity, Community Services Administration, Record Group 381, National Archives, Washington, D.C.

SFPP, RG 378 Subject Files Relating to Program Planning, 1961–1969, Office of the Deputy Assistant Secretary for Economic Development Planning (Robert M. Rauner), Economic Development Administration, Record Group 378, National Archives, Washington, D.C.

StFDCAP, RG 381

        State Files, 1965–1968, Records of the Director, Community Action Program Office, Office of Economic Opportunity, Community Services Administration, Record Group 381, National Archives, Washington, D.C.

SuFDCAP, RG 381
        Subject Files, 1965–1969, Records of the Director, Community Action
        Program Office, Office of Economic Opportunity, Community Services
        Administration, Record Group 381, National Archives, Washington, D.C.

TCHRC   Tombigbee Council on Human Relations Collection, Special Collections
        Department, Mississippi State University Libraries, Starkville.

TGAP   Thomas G. Abernethy Papers, Archives and Special Collections, University of
        Mississippi, Oxford.

VGAP   Victoria Gray Adams Papers, McCain Library and Archives, University of
        Southern Mississippi, Hattiesburg.

WFNP   William F. Nichols Papers, Special Collections and Archives Department,
        Draughon Library, Auburn University, Alabama.

WJU, RG 174 Office Files of William J. Usery, 1976–1977, Office of the Secretary of Labor,
        General Records of the Department of Labor, Record Group 174, National
        Archives, Washington, D.C.

WSP   Walter Sillers Jr. Papers, Charles W. Capps Jr. Archives and Museum, Delta
        State University, Cleveland, Mississippi.

WWJC   William Walter Jones Collection of the Papers of Sam Houston Jones,
        1939–1973, Tulane University Special Collections, New Orleans, Louisiana.

WWW, RG 174 Records of Secretary of Labor W. Willard Wirtz, 1962–1969, Office of the
        Secretary of Labor, General Records of the Department of Labor, Record
        Group 174, National Archives, Washington, D.C.

Introduction

1. Fields, *Slavery and Freedom*, 193.
2. For analyses of Reconstruction-era struggles over land, labor, and the meaning of freedom, see Du Bois, *Black Reconstruction*, 431–636, 670–710; Woodward, *Origins of the New
   South*, 205–34; Foner, *Nothing but Freedom*, 39–73; Fields, *Slavery and Freedom*, 167–93;
   Saville, *Work of Reconstruction*, 5–31, 102–41; and Ortiz, *Emancipation Betrayed*, 9–32.
   Black southerners' experiences in the Jim Crow era are examined in McMillen, *Dark Journey*; Daniel, *Shadow of Slavery*; Litwack, *Trouble in Mind*; and Woodruff, *American Congo*.
3. Daniel, *Breaking the Land*, 168–83, 239–55; Aiken, *Cotton Plantation South*, 119–32, 228;
   Kirby, *Rural Worlds Lost*, 51–79, 334–48; de Jong, "Staying in Place," 388–90.
4. Ezra Cunningham quoted in Bethell, *Sumter County Blues*, 5.
5. Cunningham interview, 1–7, 10–11, 30, 32; John Zippert, "Inspiring Histories of Two Black
   and White Civil Rights Heroes in Alabama," 15 Feb. 2007, FSC/LAF website, http://www
   .federationsoutherncoop.com/press/feb1507.htm (last modified 15 Feb. 2007).
6. Bureau of the Census, *Statistical Abstract: 1960*, 216 (table 278); Bureau of the Census,
   Statistical Abstract: 1970, 236 (table 353). Census statistics for the South include the
   District of Columbia and the following states: Alabama, Arkansas, Delaware, Florida,
   Georgia, Kentucky, Louisiana, Maryland, Mississippi, Oklahoma, North Carolina, South
   Carolina, Tennessee, Texas, Virginia, and West Virginia.
7. Lawrence Guyot quoted in Key List Mailing No. 7, 5 Feb. 1966, 6, item 2, reel 2, MFDPR;
   Robert Patterson quoted in "Reverse Freedom Ride Impact Told," *Jackson Daily News*, 14
   June 1962, 2.

8. See Department of Labor, *Economic Adjustment and Worker Dislocation*, 145 (Appendix C, p. 1); Esposito, "Evaluating the Displaced-Worker/Job-Tenure Supplement," 1; and the glossary of terms on the Bureau of Labor Statistics website at www.bls.gov/bls/glossary .htm.

9. For background on the political economy of the plantation South before the 1960s, see Mandle, *Roots of Black Poverty*, 16–51; Wright, *Old South, New South*, 81–123, 156–97; Cohen, *At Freedom's Edge*, 23–43, 201–47; Woodman, *New South—New Law*, 95–115; McMillen, *Dark Journey*, 111–53; Aiken, *Cotton Plantation South*, 29–62; Woods, *Development Arrested*, 40–71, 88–120; and Woodruff, *American Congo*, 8–37. Useful overviews of the struggle for racial equality in Alabama, Louisiana, and Mississippi include Meier and Rudwick, *CORE*; Carson, *In Struggle*; Dittmer, *Local People*; Payne, *I've Got the Light of Freedom*; Fairclough, *Race and Democracy*; Eskew, *But for Birmingham*; and de Jong, *A Different Day*.

10. Definitions of the South's cotton plantation regions vary across sources and changed over time with the transformations in the agricultural system that occurred between the 1930s and 1970s. The shaded areas on Maps 1, 2, and 3 represent those counties that historically had significant black populations (typically 40 percent or more) and economies based on plantation agriculture and cotton production, according to census data from the early to mid-twentieth century. Statistical data for the plantation regions cited in this book refer to these counties. The archival research for the book focused primarily (though not exclusively) on counties that retained black majorities in 1960 and became centers for social justice activism in the decades after 1965. Because the archival sources sometimes refer to the Mississippi Delta, a subset of Mississippi's larger plantation region, counties making up that area are also indicated on the map for Mississippi. All of the Delta counties had black majorities in 1960.

11. Crosby, *A Little Taste of Freedom*; Moye, *Let the People Decide*; Fleming, *In the Shadow of Selma*; Jeffries, *Bloody Lowndes*; Hamlin, *Crossroads at Clarksdale*.

12. Crespino, *In Search of Another Country*; Kruse, *White Flight*; Lassiter, *Silent Majority*; Bobo, Kluegel, and Smith, "Laissez-Faire Racism"; Bonilla-Silva, *Racism without Racists*; de Jong, *Invisible Enemy*.

13. Peake, *Keeping the Dream Alive*; Newman, *Divine Agitators*; Tuck, *We Ain't What We Ought to Be*; Danielson, *After Freedom Summer*; Minchin, *Hiring the Black Worker*; Minchin and Salmond, *After the Dream*; de Jong, "From Votes to Vegetables"; de Jong, "Scholarship, Education and Defense Fund for Racial Equality."

14. Wilson, *Communities Left Behind*, 103–20; Schulman, *From Cotton Belt to Sunbelt*, 185.

15. Orleck, *Storming Caesars Palace*; Ashmore, *Carry It On*; Clayson, *Freedom Is Not Enough*; Korstad and Leloudis, *To Right These Wrongs*; de Jong, "Staying in Place." See also Orleck and Hazirjian, *War on Poverty*, and Bailey and Danziger, *Legacies of the War on Poverty*.

16. See, for example, Crosby, *A Little Taste of Freedom*, xv, 155–57, 258–62; Sokol, *There Goes My Everything*, 1, 304–8; and Asch, *Senator and the Sharecropper*, 66–73.

17. As discussed in later chapters of this book, the idea that these developments were inevitable was promoted by plantation owners and accepted by many other people outside the South in the late twentieth century. It is also suggested in Asch, *Senator and the Sharecropper*, xiv, 225–30.

Chapter 1

1. Johnson, *Public Papers, 1965*, bk. 2, 840, 842.

2. "Eviction Victims Holiday Cheerless," *Louisiana Weekly*, 8 Jan. 1966, sec. 2, p. 5; George Lardner Jr., "Negro Tenants Lose Cotton Farms; Wouldn't Surrender Federal Checks," *Washington Post*, 20 June 1966, A1; Dorsey interview, 12.

3. Plantation owner quoted in Robert Sherrill, "It Isn't True That Nobody Starves in America," *New York Times Sunday Magazine*, 4 June 1967, 107.

4. Bureau of the Census, *Fifteenth Census, Agriculture: 1930*, vol. 2, pt. 2, pp. 1004–9 (Alabama), 1242–47 (Louisiana), 1083–89 (Mississippi) (county table 5); Bureau of the Census, *Census of Agriculture: 1959*, vol. 1, pt. 32 (Alabama), pp. 206–11; pt. 33 (Mississippi), pp. 215–21; pt. 35 (Louisiana), pp. 232–37 (county table 11).

5. Wright, *Old South, New South*, 244; Heinicke and Grove, "'Machinery Has Completely Taken Over,'" 70.

6. Schulman, *From Cotton Belt to Sunbelt*, 153, 156; Asch, *Senator and the Sharecropper*, 229.

7. Bonnen, "Distribution of Benefits," 461, 483–86, 501–4; Commission on Civil Rights, *Equal Opportunity in Farm Programs*, 99–108, and *Decline of Black Farming*, iii–iv, 1–13, 175–81 (land loss statistic on p. 2); "The Mess in Agriculture," clipping from unknown source, 6 Mar. 1965, 1, encl. in Thomas R. Hughes to Heads of Department Agencies, memorandum, 10 Mar. 1965, file "Civil Rights Jan. 1–Apr. 2, 1965," box 4255, GC, RG 16 (quotation). For a comprehensive account of how racist assumptions and practices permeated federal farm programs, see Daniel, *Dispossession*.

8. Roger Beardwood, "Southern Roots of Urban Crisis," *Fortune*, Aug. 1968, 84; Statement of Orville L. Freeman, in *Hunger and Malnutrition in America*, 140.

9. Bureau of the Census, *Historical Statistics*, pt. 1, 95; "State's Loss by Migration Shown in Census Study," *Bolivar County Democrat*, 18 Nov. 1965, 2; Hodding Carter III, "The Negro Exodus from the Delta Continues," *New York Times Sunday Magazine*, 10 Mar. 1968, 119; Brown interview, 4; Greene County Economic Development Commission, "A Proposal for Funding the Comprehensive Economic Development of Greene County, Alabama," 2 Oct. 1972, 1, cons. with Spiver W. Gordon to Leslie Dunbar, 29 Nov. 1972, file "Scholarship, Education and Defense Fund, Inc., 1970–1972," box 433, series 3, RBFA.

10. Bureau of the Census, *Fifteenth Census, Population: 1930*, vol. 3, pt. 1, pp. 99–103 (Alabama), 980–84 (Louisiana), 1282–87 (Mississippi) (table 13); Bureau of the Census, *Census of the Population: 1960*, vol. 1, pt. 2 (Alabama), pp. 24–25; pt. 20 (Louisiana), pp. 24–25; pt. 26 (Mississippi), pp. 24–25 (table 13).

11. Bureau of the Census, *Census of the Population: 1950*, vol. 2, pt. 2 (Alabama), pp. 73–83; pt. 18 (Louisiana), pp. 67–77; pt. 24 (Mississippi), pp. 60–73 (table 41); Bureau of the Census, *Census of the Population: 1970*, vol. 1, pt. 2 (Alabama), pp. 109–25; pt. 20 (Louisiana), pp. 103–18; pt. 26 (Mississippi), pp. 87–107 (table 35); "Old farmer" quoted in "Evaluation—SWAFCA Board of Director [*sic*] Workshop Conducted at Selma, Alabama, June 7 and 9, 1969," 26 June 1969," 1, file 11, box 18, SEDFREP.

12. Southeastern Area Office, "Area Policy Paper for Lowndes County, Alabama," 1 June 1967, 1–3, 6–7, file "1967—EDA Area Policy Papers," box 5, SFPP, RG 378.

13. Southeastern Area Office, "EDA Strategy Paper for Wilcox County," [1967], 1, 3, encl. in Robert M. Rauner to Assistant Secretary, memorandum, 7 Apr. 1967, file "1967—EDA Area Policy Papers," box 5, SFPP, RG 378.

14. Southeastern Area Office, "EDA Strategy Paper for Sunflower County, Mississippi," 17 Apr. 1967, 1, 4, file "1967—EDA Area Policy Papers," box 5, SFPP, RG 378; Carol Stevens, "Hope in Sunflower," *Southern Patriot*, Mar. 1966, 4.

15. Bureau of the Census, *Fifteenth Census, Population: 1930*, vol. 3, pt. 1, pp. 1299–1309 (table 20); Bureau of the Census, *Census of the Population: 1970*, vol. 1, pt. 26 (Mississippi), pp. 297–303 (table 123); Hodding Carter III, "The Negro Exodus from the Delta Continues," *New York Times Sunday Magazine*, 10 Mar. 1968, 119.

16. Wofford, *Preliminary Report*, 1141; W. P. Smith, "Site Visit Report, Anti-Poverty Coordinating Committee, Camden, Alabama," 7 Sept. 1968, 7, file "Evaluations Alabama 8539," box 3, GFMD, RG 381. For job loss statistics see table 1 in the appendix of this book.

17. Schulman, *From Cotton Belt to Sunbelt*, 88; Bolivar County Area Development Association, *Bolivar County Development Plan (OEDP)*, 1967, 118–19, file 3, box 1, LBP; W[illiam] J. Nagle to Mr. Harvey, Dr. Nixon, Mr. Eaton, Mr. Jeffers, Mr. Coss, Mr. Williams, and Miss Conway, memorandum, 17 Mar. 1966, 1, cons. with Eugene P. Foley to [name unreadable], 21 Mar. [1966], file "Mississippi," box 6, SFES, RG 378; Theo. James Pinnock, Site Visit Report, 11–17 June 1968, 2, file "Huntsville-Madison Co. CAC—Evaluations," box 2, GFMD, RG 381.

18. Dorsey interview, 12; "Briefing Memorandum on Employment Agencies and Equal Employment Opportunity," n.d. [ca. 1964], 4, file "1965—Commission—Equal Employment Opportunity (November–December)," box 237, WWW, RG 174; "Progress against Discrimination Reported by Labor Department," DOL news release, 2–3, file "Equal Opportunity in MA Programs (Title VI—CRA) 1968," box 628, WWW, RG 174. For a thorough examination of persistent employment discrimination and black activists' efforts to integrate southern industry, see Minchin, *Hiring the Black Worker*.

19. Monroe E. Price to Secretary [Willard Wirtz], memorandum, 20 Dec. 1965, 1, file "1965—Conference—White House Conference on Civil Rights," and Carl Holman, Berl Bernhard, and Harold Fleming to Lee C. White, memorandum, 3 Dec. 1965, 9, file "1965—Conference—White House Conference To Fulfill These Rights," both in box 240, WWW, RG 174; "Eviction Victims Holiday Cheerless," *Louisiana Weekly*, 8 Jan. 1966, sec. 2, p. 5; Commission on Civil Rights, *Cycle to Nowhere*, 12 (Sadie Allen quotation), 29 (Shambray).

20. "'Inferior' Education Barring Negroes from 'Good' Jobs," *Louisiana Weekly*, 26 Feb. 1966, 1, 7; Eric Blanchard, "Negro Seen Hindered by Job Aptitude Tests," *Washington Post*, 2 Jan. 1967, B5; Unidentified source quoted in William H. Brown III, "The '64 Civil Rights Act: A Promise Unrealized?," Jan. 1972, reprinted in *EEOC Newsletter*, 15 Feb. 1972, 5, file "Clippings 1971," box 6, CFC, RG 403.

21. "Report from Mississippi," 29 Oct. 1965, 4, item 2, reel 2, MFDPR; "New School Desegregation Order," *Louisiana Weekly*, 14 Jan. 1967, sec. 2, 4. Efforts to desegregate rural southern schools and the fierce opposition this generated are examined in Fleming, *In the Shadow of Selma*, 187–281; Moye, *Let the People Decide*, 171–99; Crespino, *In Search of Another Country*, 173–204; and Jeffries, *Bloody Lowndes*, 81–116.

22. James E. Allen Jr. to Garvin H. Johnston, 9 July 1969, 2–3, file "State Department of Education—Title I School Funds—School Compliance," box 169, TGAP; Cascio and Reber, "K–12 Education Battle," 66–67, 71–73; Rims Barber, "A Report to the Commission on the Delta Ministry," June 1968, 3–4, file 2, box 4, DMP; Jake Ayers Sr. and Rims Barber, "Title I as Remedial Education," 13 Dec. 1969, 1–2, file 14, box 11, DMP.

23. Wilson, *Communities Left Behind*, 103–20. Cobb also discusses white opposition to industrial employment for black workers in *Selling of the South*, 115–17.

24. "Council Drops Plans for Expanding Farm Machinery Training Program," *Delta Council News*, Jan. 1962, 1; H. L. Mitchell to Daniel L. Goldy, 27 Mar. 1962, 1, file 11, box 3A, AECC. For more on the Delta Council and planters' responses to labor problems, see Woodruff, "Mississippi Delta Planters."

25. John D. Pomfret, "First Projects to Retrain Unemployed Approved," *New York Times*, 9 Sept. 1962, 1, 67.

26. "Negro Group Hits U.S. Job Training," *New York Times*, 6 May 1963, 29; Carl Holman, Berl Bernhard, and Harold Fleming to Lee C. White, memorandum, 3 Dec. 1965, 7, file "1965—Conference—White House Conference To Fulfill These Rights," box 240, WWW, RG 174; Kenneth W. Munden, "The Office of Economic Opportunity in the Nixon Administration," unpublished manuscript, 1973, 188–89, unfoldered, box 107, HOEO, RG 381; Theodore James Pinnock to Tom Karter, 16 Feb. 1967, 1, cons. with Theodore James Pinnock, Progress Report, Lowndes and Wilcox Counties, Alabama, 15 Nov. 1966–15 Jan. 1967, file "Lowndes Co. Christ. Mvmt.," box 6, GFMD, RG 381; "Staff Report on Employment," [1968], 2, encl. in Robert W. Saunders to Maurice A. Dawkins, 6 May 1968, file "Saunders—Civil Rights Commission Hearings, Montgomery, Ala.," box 9, PRADCR, RG 381.

27. Segalman and Basu, *Poverty in America*, 91–108, 317; Slesinger and Pfeffer, "Migrant Farm Workers," 138–39, 153 (n. 2); Statement of Orville L. Freeman, in *Hunger and Malnutrition in America*, 121.

28. See, for example, Gordon, *Pitied but Not Entitled*, 253–306; Quadagno, *Color of Welfare*, 8–15, 19–25; and Neubeck and Cazenave, *Welfare Racism*, 41–65.

29. Ida Mae Lawrence quoted in "We Ain't Got Nothin' but Needs," *Delta Ministry Reports*, Feb. 1966, 6, file 7, box 142, PBJFP; "Statement of Mississippi Freedom Labor Union Members, Supporting Minimum Wage Coverage of Farm Laborers and Sharecroppers before the House Subcommittee on Education and Labor," 15 July 1965, 3, file 18, box 1, MFDPR (Jessie Atkins quotation); Mrs. X (2 of 2) to Orville Freeman, affidavit, Sept. 1965, 1, cons. with William M. Seabron to Lawrence Guyot, 3 Dec. 1965, file "Civil Rights Nov. 24–Dec. 7, 1965," box 4254, GC, RG 16; Key List Mailing No. 5, 7 Jan. [1966], 3, item 2, reel 2, MFDPR; Statement of Raymond M. Wheeler, in *Hunger and Malnutrition in America*, 10.

30. "Welfare Cut Hits All Parts of La.," *Louisiana Weekly*, 30 July 1960, 1, 7; "Example of States Rights . . . Southern Style," ibid., 17 Sept. 1960, 11; "Starving Tots No Distortion of Fact—Kerns," ibid., 1 Oct. 1960, 1, 7; "Child Welfare League Asks Probe of La. Welfare Laws," ibid., 1 Oct. 1960, 2.

31. Morris J. Priebatsch to Fred A. Ross, 30 Oct. 1962, 1, memorandum, file 3, box 42, WSP.

32. Walter Goodman, "The Case of Mrs. Sylvester Smith," *New York Times Sunday Magazine*, 25 Aug. 1968, 29, 62 (Alabama substitute father law); Joseph Brenner, Robert Coles, Alan Mermann, Milton J. E. Senn, Cyril Walwyn, and Raymond Wheeler, "Children in Mississippi: A Report to the Field Foundation," June 1967, 7, encl. in William Ling to Jule Sugarman, memorandum, 27 June 1967, file "Administrative—Mississippi—1967," box 16, StFDCAP, RG 381. For more on the ways racism shaped southern (and national) welfare policies, see Cobb, "'Somebody Done Nailed Us on the Cross,'" 914–20; Quadagno, *Color of Welfare*, 8–15, 19–25, 117–34; and Neubeck and Cazenave, *Welfare Racism*, 41–65, 117–44.

33. "Staff Report on Public Assistance in Alabama," [1968], 8, encl. in Robert W. Saunders to Maurice A. Dawkins, 6 May 1968, file "Saunders—Civil Rights Commission Hearings, Montgomery, Ala.," box 9, PRADCR, RG 381; Arundell, "Welfare Rights," 94; Garland L. Bonin to N. P. Himbert, 9 Oct. 1968, 1–2, file 1, box 371, RBLC.

34. Department of Health, Education, and Welfare, *A Constructive Public Welfare Program*, 3; Hosek, *AFDC-Unemployed Fathers Program*, 2; Robert B. Choate, "Summary Statement to the House Agriculture Committee," 27 Sept. 1967, 10–11, cons. with W. Willard Wirtz to Mrs. Roberts B. Owen, 5 Oct. 1967, file "Agriculture 1967," box 499, WWW, RG 174.

35. Commission on Civil Rights, *Cycle to Nowhere*, 7; Walter Rugaber, "In the Delta, Poverty Is a Way of Life," *New York Times*, 31 July 1967, 1.

36. Schulman, *From Cotton Belt to Sunbelt*, 112–34; "Rich Farmers Get Huge Handouts while the Poor Go Hungry," *Rural Advance*, Summer 1968, 3 (Abernethy); Bolivar County Area Development Association, *Bolivar County Development Plan (OEDP)*, 1967, 106–7, file 3, box 1, LBP; Bureau of the Census, *Census of the Population: 1970*, vol. 1, pt. 26 (Mississippi), p. 332 (table 128).

37. Subcommittee on Employment, Manpower and Poverty to President, 27 Apr. 1967, 2, file "Mississippi—Clark Sub-cte," box 3, GRPR, RG 381; Joseph Brenner, Robert Coles, Alan Mermann, Milton J. E. Senn, Cyril Walwyn, and Raymond Wheeler, "Children in Mississippi: A Report to the Field Foundation," June 1967, 3–6, encl. in William Ling to Jule Sugarman, memorandum, 27 June 1967, file "Administrative—Mississippi—1967," box 16, StFDCAP, RG 381; "The Agricultural Co-operative as a Possible Means of Providing Food for Needy Persons," n.d. [ca. 1966], 1–2, file 16, box 1, LBP (Bolivar County). Other studies of the hunger crisis included *Hunger and Malnutrition in America*; Citizens' Board of Inquiry, *Hunger, U.S.A.*; and Commission on Civil Rights, *Cycle to Nowhere*.

38. Supplemental Statement of Raymond M. Wheeler, in *Hunger and Malnutrition in America*, 62; "NAACP: Starvation Fighter," [fund-raising pamphlet, 1968], 1, file "59th Annual NAACP Convention, Atlantic City, New Jersey, June 24 1968," box 10, PRADCR, RG 381.

39. Charlotte Devree, "Draft for a Fact Sheet, for CORE SEDF Education Project in Mississippi," 24 Oct. 1963, 2, file 1, box 74, series 5, CORER; "The People Who Make History," *Southern Patriot*, Feb. 1963, Special Supplement, 2 (Delta town); Dorsey interview, 31, 32–33.

40. "What's New in Mississippi," *Delta Ministry*, Jan. 1966, [3], file 6, box 2A, AECC; "Notes on the Condition of the Mississippi Negro—1966," 3, file 5, box 1, FISR ("final solution" quotation); Frank Millspaugh, "Black Power," *Commonweal*, 5 Aug. 1966, 502 (Lowndes County); Percy McShan quoted in J. M. McFadden, "U.S. Official Denies Farm Bias in Ala.," *Washington Post*, 28 May 1967, A2; Theo. James Pinnock, Site Visit Report, 11–17 June 1968, 2, file "Huntsville-Madison Co. CAC—Evaluations," box 2, GFMD, RG 381.

41. Nan Robertson, "Stennis and Eastland Reject 'Libel' on Mississippi," *New York Times*, 12 July 1967, 22; Charles C. Jacobs Jr. to William Colmer, 13 July 1967, 1, cons. with Thomas Abernethy to Jacobs, 20 July 1967, file "Poverty in Mississippi," box 182, TGAP; George H. Lipscomb Jr. to Paul B. Johnson, 24 July 1967, 1, file "Poverty Hearings, 1967," box 7, series 25, JCSC; Erle Johnston Jr., form letter, n.d. [ca. 1967], 1, file 6, box 141, PBJFP.

42. Lonnie Hudkins and O. D. Wilson, "Delta in Distress," *Houston Post*, 8 Mar. 1964, 1; Statement of Raymond M. Wheeler, in *Hunger and Malnutrition in America*, 11; Robert Sherrill, "It Isn't True That Nobody Starves in America," *New York Times Sunday Magazine*, 4 June 1967, 103, 107.

43. Wofford, *Preliminary Report*, 1095, 1097; National Education Association, *Wilcox County, Alabama*, 78, 82; Southeastern Area Office, "Area Policy Paper for Tunica County Mississippi," 25 Aug. 1967, 9, encl. in Edwin W. Webber to Area Directors, Deputy Assistant Secretaries, and Office Directors, memorandum, 20 Oct. 1967, file "1967—EDA Area Policy Papers," box 9, SFPP, RG 378.

44. Development official quoted in Cobb, *Selling of the South*, 116; "Resolutions Adopted at Meeting of Citizens' Councils of America in New Orleans, May 19, 1962," and "Negro Surplus or Deficit for Each State," *Citizen*, May 1962, 4, 8.

45. Paul Harvey, "Living in Glass Houses," *Citizen*, May 1962, 2; "Reverse Freedom Ride Impact Told," *Jackson Daily News*, 14 June 1962, 2 (Patterson quotation); *Congressional Record*, 88th Cong., 2nd sess., 1964, 110, pt. 4: 5338, 5578.

46. Shirley Till Russell to John Sparkman, 31 Mar. 1965, 5, cons. with Eleanor Ballentine to Sparkman, 3 Apr. 1965, and Mrs. A. P. Brooks to John Sparkman, 1 Apr. 1965, 2, cons. with Sparkman to Aklin Lwmmond [*sic*], 9 Apr. 1965, both in file "Robo Civil Rights," box 9, 1963–64 series, JJSSP; Ellett Lawrence to Friend, n.d. [1960s], 1, file 2, box 105, WSP.

47. Annie Denman to Governor [Paul] Johnson, 29 Mar. 1965, 1, file 7, box 110, PBJFP; C. R. Singletary to Russell Long, 21 Feb. 1968, 1, file 8, box 110, RBLC; Joseph Miller to John Sparkman, 12 Apr. 1965, 1, cons. with Sparkman, form letter, 14 Apr. 1965, file "CR Voting Bill," box 16, 1965 series, JJSSP.

48. Mrs. Merritt quoted in Al From to Bob Emond, memorandum, 23 Jan. 1968, 29, file "Anti-Poverty Coordinating Committee (Wilcox County)" (2 of 2), box 6, GFMD, RG 381; Fred Ross, "Racial Amalgamation Propaganda versus Segregation and Racial Cooperation," 16 Apr. 1963, 4, 6, file 11, box 134, PBJFP.

49. Thomas G. Abernethy, "In the News," 12 Mar. 1964, 1, file "Newsletters, 1964," box 128, TGAP; Mrs. Robert L. Jefferson Sr. to W. R. Poage, 17 June 1968, 1, cons. with John Sparkman to Jefferson, 20 June 1968, file "Health and Welfare (Poverty Programs)," box 6, 1968 series, JJSSP; Janet Williams to Bill Nichols, 25 June 1974, cons. with Nichols to Williams, 12 July 1974, 1, file "22-Q Pensions and Security (Ruben King)," box 19, series 81-1, WFNP.

50. Charles B. Shuman, "What Kind of Poverty?," clipping from *Nation's Agriculture*, n.d. [ca. Nov. 1966], 6, file 20, box 229, RBLC; Bolivar County Area Development Association, *Bolivar County Development Plan (OEDP)*, 1967, 132–33 (quotations), 138, file 3, box 1, LBP; American Farm Bureau Federation, *Farm Bureau Policies for 1967*, 8 Dec. 1965, 48, unfoldered, box 2, series 86-97, AFBFR; Louisiana Department of Public Welfare, news release, 24 Apr. 1968, 1–2, file 1, box 371, RBLC.

51. Mrs. B. G. Burton to John Sparkman, 13 Sept. 1965, 2, cons. with Sparkman to Burton, 18 Sept. 1965, file "States and Human Rights" (1 of 2), box 7, 1965 series, JJSSP; Roger Samson to Russell Long, 3 Oct. 1966, 2, file 46, box 97, RBLC; Robert Norman McKnight to R. B. Long, 24 Sept. 1967, 1, file 4, box 103, RBLC; Bill Nichols to J. H. Robison, 10 May 1968, 1, file "7-B Civil Rights, Riots, etc.," box 15, series 81-4, WFNP.

52. Hamner Cobbs quoted in Ashmore, *Carry It On*, 131; Sam H. Jones, "Louisiana, The Optimistic View," speech to Rotary Club, New Orleans, Louisiana, 31 Mar. 1965, 11, file "Speeches—January–May 21, 1965," box 57, WWJC.

53. Donald C. Mosley and D. C. Williams Jr., "An Analysis and Evaluation of a Community Action Anti-Poverty Program in the Mississippi Delta," July 1967, 31–32, file "Community Action Program" (1 of 6), box 150, GFMD, RG 381; "Sims Lockett" [Semmes Luckett] quoted in Howell, *Freedom City*, 18.

54. "DP's in the Delta," *Newsweek*, 14 Feb. 1966, 28.

55. American Taxpayers Association, "E.D.A.: Something Borrowed, Nothing New," Tax Information Series No. 65-11, 30 Nov. 1965, 2, encl. in B. Parrette to Gene Foley, memorandum, 8 Dec. [1965], file "Clippings," box 5, SFES, RG 378; American Farm Bureau Federation, *Farm Bureau Policies for 1964*, 12 Dec. 1963, 24–25, unfoldered, box 2, series 86-97, AFBFR.

56. Aaron Shirley quoted in Homer Bigart, "Hunger in America: Mississippi Delta," *New York Times*, 18 Feb. 1969, 18.

Chapter 2

1. George Lardner Jr., "Negro Tenants Lose Cotton Farms; Wouldn't Surrender Federal Checks," *Washington Post*, 20 June 1966, A1.

2. Unknown author to John F. Kennedy, 1 Mar. 1961, 2, file 3, box 1, 1974 Addendum, AECC; Brown interview, 4, 6; Lonnie Hudkins and O. D. Wilson, "Delta in Distress," *Houston Post*, 8 Mar. 1964, 19; John Bradford quoted in Victor Ullman, "In Darkest America," *Nation*, 4 Sept. 1967, 180; Commission on Civil Rights, *Cycle to Nowhere*, 47.

3. Theo. James Pinnock and G. W. Taylor, "Tuskegee Institute–OEO Seasonally Employed Agricultural Workers Educational Project, Summary of Accomplishments and Disappointments," 1 Nov. 1966–31 Oct. 1967, 4, 23, file "Miscellaneous Alabama 8539," box 3, GFMD, RG 381. For studies of the challenges that racism posed for African Americans in the North, see Grossman, *Land of Hope*; Massey and Denton, *American Apartheid*; and Sugrue, *Origins of the Urban Crisis*.

4. Hatch interview, 31, 33, 34; "Proposal Submitted by Southern Rural Action Incorporated for a Comprehensive Enterprise and Community Development Program for the United States Southeast," n.d. [1968], 11, cons. with Maurice A. Dawkins to Harding, Perrin and Templeton, memorandum, 29 Aug. 1968, file "Rural Affairs Proposal Project 1968 w/ Civil Rights Implications (SCLC)," box 13, SFDD, RG 381; James Joliff Jr. quoted in Phyl Garland, "A Taste of Triumph for Black Mississippi," *Ebony*, Feb. 1968, 32.

5. "The People Who Make History," *Southern Patriot*, Feb. 1963, 2; [Stephen Arons], "Memorandum Re: Thanksgiving Fast for Freedom, 1964–65," 1, cons. with Ben Steele to John V. Lindsay, 12 Nov. 1965, file "Food Stamp Program Nov. 9–12, 1965," box 4300, GC, RG 16; Newman, *Divine Agitators*, 95–97; Guyot and Thelwell, "Toward Independent Political Power," 252.

6. Joseph Wheatley, Sue Geiger, and Robert Strickland quoted in Nick Kotz, "In the Deep South, the Enemy Is Poverty," *Minneapolis Tribune*, 14 May 1967, 1B (Wheatley and Strickland), 4B (Geiger).

7. Southwest Alabama Self-Help Housing, Inc., Application for Community Action Program, n.d. [ca. 1966], 2, file "Southwest Alabama Self-Help Housing, Inc.—Miscellaneous" (1 of 2), and Southwest Alabama Self-Help Housing, Application for Community Action Program, n.d. [1968], Attachment CAP 7, 1–2, file "Southwest Alabama Self-Help Housing, Inc.—Miscellaneous" (2 of 2), both in box 7, GFMD, RG 381.

8. [SCDP], "Small Farmers Increased Income Program," n.d. [ca. 1966], 6–7, file 1, box 29, SEDFREP; R. M. Stevens quoted in Kotz, "In the Deep South, the Enemy Is Poverty," *Minneapolis Tribune*, 14 May 1967, 4B.

9. Unita Blackwell and Annie Devine, "Congressman Resnick's Visit to Mississippi," n.d. [Dec. 1965], 1–2, cons. with Thomas Abernethy to Joe T. Patterson, 16 Dec. 1965, file "Freedom Democratic Party," box 272, TGAP; Joseph Y. Resnick to Orville L. Freeman, 4 Dec. 1965, cons. with William M. Seabron to Resnick, 17 Dec. 1965, 2, file "Civil Rights Dec. 8, 1965–," box 4254, GC, RG 16; Ben Steele to John V. Lindsay, 12 Nov. 1965, 1, file "Food Stamp Program Nov. 9–12, 1965," box 4300, GC, RG 16 (identical letters to other congressional representatives who expressed interest in the issue are in the same file).

10. "We Ain't Got Nothin' but Needs," *Delta Ministry Reports*, Feb. 1966, 3, 5, file 7, box 142, PBJFP; Ora D. Wilson quoted in Howell, *Freedom City*, 67.

11. "We Ain't Got Nothin' But Needs," *Delta Ministry Reports*, Feb. 1966, 1–3, file 7, box 142, PBJFP; Howell, *Freedom City*, 29–30 (quotations).

12. Key List Mailing No. 7, 5 Feb. 1966, 5, item 2, reel 2, MFDPR; "Government's 'No' to Squatters," *New York Times*, 6 Feb. 1966, E2; Victoria J. Gray to Friends and Supporters of the MFDP, 10 Feb. 1966, 2, item 2, reel 2, MFDPR; Ida Mae Lawrence quoted in "We Ain't Got Nothin' but Needs," *Delta Ministry Reports*, Feb. 1966, 6, file 7, box 142, PBJFP. For more on the Greenville protest, see Cobb, "'Somebody Done Nailed Us on the Cross,'" 928–31; Dittmer, *Local People*, 366–68; and Newman, *Divine Agitators*, 104–5.

13. "DP's in the Delta," *Newsweek*, 14 Feb. 1966, 28, 30; "'Secret' Crisis in the Delta," *Newsweek*, 7 Mar. 1966, 28; Thomas Karter to Noel H. Klores, 21 Feb. 1966, 1–2, file "Mississippi Food Demonstration Project 1966" (2 of 3), box 28, SuFDCAP, RG 381; Orville Freeman quoted in Wayne D. Rasmussen and Gladys L. Baker, "The Department of Agriculture during the Administration of President Lyndon B. Johnson, Volume II," 1969, 119, unfoldered, box 8, JAS, RG 16.

14. Foster Davis, "Kennedy and Clark Tour Anti-Poverty Facilities," *Delta Democrat-Times*, 11 Apr. 1967, 1; Comment by Jacob Javits, in *Hunger and Malnutrition in America*, 4.

15. *The Delta Ministry*, Aug. 1965, 3, file 6, box 2A, AECC; "Food Assistant Program in All Counties of State," *Madison County Herald*, 17 Mar. 1966, sec. 3, p. 4; Orville L. Freeman to Edith Green, 7 Dec. 1965, 1, file "Civil Rights Nov. 10–Nov. 23, 1965," box 4254, GC, RG 16.

16. "USDA Food Programs Expanding to All 1,000 Lowest Income Counties," USDA news release, 8 July 1968, 1, file "Civil Rights May 14, 1969," box 4949, GC, RG 16; "USDA Family Food Programs Aided 10.4 Million Needy Persons in June," USDA news release, 3 Aug. 1970, 1, in "USDA Civil Rights Report, August 1970," encl. in Joseph M. Robertson to Robert J. Brown, 4 Sept. 1970, file "Civil Rights August 24–September 30, 1970," box 5160, GC, RG 16; "Statement by Secretary of Agriculture Orville L. Freeman on Recommendations of the Board of Inquiry into Hunger and Malnutrition in the United States," 23 Apr. 1968, 1, file 3, box 1, JHP.

17. "What Happens to All the Surplus Food?" n.d. [1965/66], 1, file 5, box 1, FISR; Brown interview, 18.

18. Hatch interview, 52; Lucille Dukes, "Marion County News," *Freedom Information Service Mississippi Newsletter*, 5 Apr. 1968, 4, file 21, box 3, VGAP; Marjorie Baroni, Daily Journal entry, 20 July 1966, no page numbers, file 1, box 7, MBC.

19. Dorothy Beith, "Hopes of Migrant Workers Overflow Tunica Meeting," clipping from *Memphis Commercial Appeal*, [12 Apr. 1967], file "Mid-State Oppor., Inc." (1 of 2), box 153, GFMD, RG 381; Geiger interview, 76–77 (Bolivar County); South Delta Community Action Association, "CAP Narrative Progress Report," 1 Oct.–30 Dec. 1966, 3, file "5156 La.," box 836, NPR, RG 381.

20. W. Willard Wirtz to Mrs. D. O'Reilly, 5 July 1967, 2, file "Intergration [*sic*] and Civil Rights July–September 1967," box 530, WWW, RG 174; Office of Economic Opportunity, *As the Seed Is Sown*, 15; "Statement of Reverend Ralph David Abernathy to the Secretary of Labor," n.d. [2 June 1967], 1–2, cons. with George P. Shultz to Ralph D. Abernathy, 17 June 1969, file "Integration, Civil Rights, Voting Rights and Negro Family April–May (Except May 13) 1969," box 123, GPS, RG 174.

21. "OEO, Labor Join in Mississippi Job Training," OEO news release, 21 Feb. 1966, 1, file "Mississippi—Clark Sub-cte," box 3, GRPR, RG 381; "Discussions with William Seabron of the Dept. of Agriculture," 25 Mar. [1966], 1, file 5, box 1, MFDPR.

22. Dick Hausler to Theodore M. Berry, routing slip, 16 Mar. 1966, 1, cons. with Eugene P. Foley to [name unreadable], 21 Mar. [1966]; "Mississippi Progress Report," n.d. [9 Mar. 1966], encl. in W[illiam] J. Nagle to Emanuel Boasberg, 9 Mar. 1966, cons. with Eugene P. Foley to [name unreadable], 21 Mar. [1966], 1–2; and W[illiam] J. Nagle to Eugene P. Foley, memorandum, 29 Mar. 1966, 4, all in file "Mississippi," box 6, SFES, RG 378.

23. *Congressional Record*, 88th Cong., 2nd sess., 1964, 110, pt. 4: 5578; SCLC, "Poor People in America," 1968, 2–5, file 31, box 5, VGAP.

24. *Congressional Record*, 88th Cong., 2nd sess., 1964, 110, pt. 4: 5197.

25. United States Department of Agriculture, Office of the Secretary, "Agriculture in the Sixties," Oct. 1966, 11, cons. with Secretary of Labor [W. Willard Wirtz] to Orville Freeman, 25 Oct. 1966, file "Farm Labor, October 1966," box 372, WWW, RG 174; "U.S. Seeks to Cut Negro Migration," *Washington Post*, 12 Nov. 1966, A4 (Foley); Maurice Dawkins to Sargent Shriver and Bertrand Harding, memorandum, 11 May 1967, 2, file "Civil Rights" (4 of 4), box 2, PFDD, RG 381 (OEO officials); Economic Opportunity Amendments of 1967, Pub. L. No. 90–222, *Statutes at Large* 81 (1967): 691; President's National Advisory Committee on Rural Poverty, *People Left Behind*, xiii.

26. Marshall interview, 22; Wilfred C. Leland to John B. Morris, memorandum, 7 Dec. 1965, 2, file "Minority Groups," box 2, GSCF, RG 378; A. J. Foster to Orville L. Freeman, 4 Apr. 1966, 2, cons. with John Stennis to Foster, 4 May 1966, file "Agriculture—Farmers Home Administration, 1966," box 9, series 8, JCSC.

27. Jennie T. Burrell to John Sparkman, Mar. 1968, 1–2, cons. with Sparkman to Burrell, 8 Mar. 1968; Claire L. Benjamin to John Sparkman, 9 Apr. 1968, 1, cons. with Sparkman to Benjamin, 18 Apr. 1968; and Charles S. Watson to John Sparkman, 7 Apr. 1968, cons. with Sparkman to Watson, 10 Apr. 1968, all in file "Civil Rights, Jan. thru April, 1968," box 1, 1968 series, JJSSP; J. F. Ingram to John Sparkman, 17 Feb. 1965, 1–2, cons. with Wiley Messick to Ingram, 26 Feb. 1965, file "Vocational Education," box 8, 1965 series, JJSSP.

28. Paul B. Johnson, manuscript of article written for *American Banker*, n.d. [mid-1960s], [4], file 3, box 108, PBJFP; "Mississippi Progress Report," n.d. [9 Mar. 1966], 1, encl. in W[illiam] J. Nagle to Emanuel Boasberg, 9 Mar. 1966, cons. with Eugene P. Foley to

[name unreadable], 21 Mar. [1966], 1, and William J. Nagle to Eugene P. Foley, memorandum, 29 Mar. 1966, 1, both in file "Mississippi," box 6, SFES, RG 378; "Mississippi Tries to Narrow the Gap," *Business Week*, 29 June 1968, 80–82 (quotation on p. 82).

29. Crespino, *In Search of Another Country*, 135–36; Hamlin, *Crossroads at Clarksdale*, 214–22; Ben A. Franklin, "Race Issue Snags Aid to Louisiana," *New York Times*, 5 Mar. 1965, 1; Jack Gonzales to Bill Haddad, 5 Mar. 1965, 1, cons. with Haddad to Sargent Shriver, memorandum, 14 Mar. 1965, file "Mississippi—Personnel—1965," box 5, StFDCAP, RG 381.

30. Frederick O'R. Hayes to Theodore M. Berry, memorandum, 20 Mar. 1965, 1–2, and "Conclusions," 1, encl. in Jack Gonzales to Bill Haddad, memorandum, 9 Mar. 1965 (quotation), both in file "Alabama—Personnel—1965" (1 of 2), box 1, StFDCAP, RG 381.

31. Robert L. Martin to Edgar May, memorandum, 4 Aug. 1966, 3–4, file "Lowndes County, Alabama 1966 (Inactive)" (3 of 5), box 27, SuFDCAP, RG 381; Reginald Albritton quoted in Al From to Bob Emond, memorandum, 5 Feb. 1968, 16, file "Anti-Poverty Coordinating Committee (Wilcox County)" (2 of 2), box 6, GFMD, RG 381.

32. Dorsey interview, 3; Steve Reed to Sargent Shriver, 17 Nov. 1966, 1, file "Administrative Mississippi 1966" (1 of 2), box 12, StFDCAP, RG 381; Hazel Brannon Smith, "The War on Poverty," excerpt from editorial in *Lexington Advertiser*, 24 Nov. 1966, in Saints Junior College Migrant Farmers Educational Project, "Project Report to the Office of Economic Opportunity: Second Start 1967," Apr. 1968, [Preface], file "Migrant Farmers Educational Project (Publication)," box 149, GFMD, RG 381.

33. Bennie Gooden and Andrew Carr quoted in Kotz, "In the Deep South, the Enemy Is Poverty," 5B; Hamlin, *Crossroads at Clarksdale*, 215; Donald C. Mosley and D. C. Williams Jr., "An Analysis and Evaluation of a Community Action Anti-Poverty Program in the Mississippi Delta," July 1967, 8, 36 (quotation), file "Community Action Program" (1 of 6), box 150, GFMD, RG 381.

Chapter 3

1. Johnson, *Public Papers, 1963–64*, bk. 1, 113–15 (quotation on p. 114).

2. *Congressional Record*, 88th Cong., 2nd sess., 1964, 110, pt. 13: 16743 (Magnuson quotation); Moynihan, *Maximum Feasible Misunderstanding*, 83–87, 90–91 (Kennedy quotation on p. 90); "President's War on Poverty Seen as Boon to 'Poor Folks,'" *Louisiana Weekly*, 28 Mar. 1964, 10. For general background on the origins, achievements, and limits of the War on Poverty, see Levine, *The Poor Ye Need Not Have with You*; Quadagno, *Color of Welfare*; Clark, *The War on Poverty*; and Cazenave, *Impossible Democracy*.

3. Katz, *Undeserving Poor*, 98–101; National Advisory Council on Economic Opportunity, "Perspectives on Poverty: First Draft of the 1968 Report to the President," 5 Jan. 1968, 49–50, file "National Advisory Council" (1 of 2), box 3, PFDD, RG 381.

4. Jordan, "Fighting for the Child Development Group of Mississippi," 290; Dorsey interview, 33–34, 36–37 (quotations on p. 36); Andrews, "Social Movements and Policy Implementation," 80 (Bernice Johnson); Jeffries, *Bloody Lowndes*, 117–25, 134–39; Al From to Bob Emond, memorandum, 23 Jan. 1968, 2, 13, file "Anti-Poverty Coordinating Committee (Wilcox County)" (2 of 2), box 6, GFMD, RG 381.

5. Lillian McGill quoted in Al From to Bob Emond, memorandum, 23 Jan. 1968, 13, file "Anti-Poverty Coordinating Committee (Wilcox County)" (2 of 2), box 6, GFMD, RG 381; Dorsey interview, 14; "CORE Summer Project Orientation—Educational Program

Workshop," June 1965, frame 00826, reel 124, pt. 5, COREP; Marian McBride, "Fear Is for Real in Ferriday, La.," *Milwaukee Sentinel*, 25 Aug. 1965, pt. 3, p. 3.

6. Black, *People and Plows against Hunger*, 23–24; Geiger, "Community Control," 139; Miller, *Light on the Hill*, 355; Hatch, "Community Shares in Policy Decisions," 109; Geiger, "A Life in Social Medicine," 15 (quotation).

7. Geiger, "A Life in Social Medicine," 16 (quotation); Geiger interview, 50–54.

8. Simpson, *Sister Stella's Babies*, 87.

9. L. C. Dorsey, "Dirt Dauber Nests, Socks Nailed over Doorways, Salts, Prayer and OTC's: Space Age Medicine in the Poor Community," n.d. [1990], 10–12, 14, file 252, box 12, JWHP; Dorsey interview, 36–37; Nelson, "Hold Your Head Up," 104–5; Williams interview.

10. Leon E. Kruger, "The Role of the Comprehensive Health Center in Social Change," n.d. [1969], 5, file 10, box 1, LBP; Kelly, "Health Care in the Mississippi Delta," 760.

11. Sandra Blakeslee, "To Rural Negroes, Health Center Is Hope," *New York Times*, 28 Aug. 1970, 30; "Progress Report," Feb. 1970, [14], file "Health Assoc. Council Progress Reports etc. 1969–70," box 39, DHCR; Geiger, "A Life in Social Medicine," 17.

12. "The Agricultural Co-operative as a Possible Means of Providing Food for Needy Persons," n.d. [ca. 1967], 1–3 (quotations on p. 1), file 16, box 1, LBP.

13. Black, *People and Plows against Hunger*, 2–3; H. Jack Geiger, "Statement Presented to the Subcommittee on Employment Manpower and Poverty, United States Senate," 21 May 1969, 14–15, file 15, box 1, LBP; Geiger interview, 59–61; John Hatch, "My Experience and Feeling toward O.E.O. Health Center," 6 May 1971, 2, file 69, box 3, JWHP.

14. John Hatch, "My Experience and Feeling toward O.E.O. Health Center," 6 May 1971, 3, file 69, box 3, JWHP; Hatch, "Community Shares in Policy Decisions," 111; "Negroes Urged to Stay on Delta Farms," *New York Times*, 10 Nov. 1968, 120 (OEO grant); "Tufts-Delta Health Center," n.d. [1969], 7–8, file 10, box 1, LBP (employment and production statistics).

15. John Hatch, "Historical Sketch and Progress Report on the North Bolivar County Farm Cooperative AAL," n.d. [1969], 6–8, cons. with "Tufts-Delta Health Center," n.d. [1969], file 10, box 1, LBP; Black, *People and Plows against Hunger*, 75; L. C. Dorsey, "1969 Progress Report," 4–6, 9 (quotation), file "Farm Coop—1969 Progress Report—L. C. Dorsey," box 39, DHCR.

16. Simpson, *Sister Stella's Babies*, 121; "Progress Report," Feb. 1970, [4], file "Health Assoc. Council Progress Reports etc. 1969–70," box 39, DHCR; Geiger interview, 56, 73.

17. Geiger interview, 64, 85–86; Simpson, *Sister Stella's Babies*, 79, 100.

18. Rosedale Black Community to Merchants of Rosedale, 25 Aug. 1970, 1–2, encl. in Rosedale Health Association to Tufts-Delta Center Staff, n.d., file "Rosedale, Town of," box 22, DHCR; Minutes, North Bolivar County Health Council Meeting, 27 Sept. 1970, 2, file "North Bolivar County Health and Improvement Council" (1 of 2), box 13, DHCR; Theodore Parrish to Andrew B. James, memorandum, 16 Mar. 1971, 1, file "1971—January–June," box 25, DHCR; [John Hatch], "Mound Bayou Revisited," n.d. [Aug. 1990], 9, file 68, box 3, JWHP; Geiger interview, 98–99.

19. "Sad Nurse" to A. B. Albritton, 31 July 1972, 2, file "March–December 1972," box 25, DHCR.

20. Geiger interview, 77–81, 88. For more on the TDHC's impact on class relationships within the black community, see de Jong, "Plantation Politics," 267–75.

21. Joseph F. Mooney Jr. to Gus Roessler, 2 Oct. 1967, 1, cons. with Thomas G. Abernethy to Roessler, 12 Oct. 1967, file "Office of Economic Opportunity—General, 1967–," box 161,

TGAP; Chickasaw County Board of Supervisors to Thomas G. Abernethy, telegram, 6 June 1972, 1, cons. with Clair Stevens to DeVan Hill, 13 June 1972, file "Manpower Development and Training Act, Department of Labor," box 135, TGAP.

22. Donald C. Mosley and D. C. Williams Jr., "An Analysis and Evaluation of a Community Action Anti-Poverty Program in the Mississippi Delta," July 1967, 41, 45–46, 49, file "Community Action Program" (1 of 6), box 150, GFMD, RG 381; Thomas L. Threadgill to Sargent Shriver, 10 June 1967, 1–2, file "Wilcox County SCLC" (1 of 2), box 6, GFMD, RG 381; G. T. Dowdy, "A Descriptive Study of Extra Activities in Conjunction with an Educational Program for Seasonally Employed Agricultural Workers," 1966, 1, 7–8, encl. in G. T. Dowdy to Don Derman, 19 Apr. 1967, file "Administrative Alabama 1967," box 14, StFDCAP, RG 381.

23. National Education Association, *Wilcox County, Alabama*, 80; Geiger interview, 63; Donald C. Mosley and D. C. Williams Jr., "An Analysis and Evaluation of a Community Action Anti-Poverty Program in the Mississippi Delta," July 1967, 35, file "Community Action Program" (1 of 6), box 150, GFMD, RG 381 (COI); Bill Nagle to Gene Foley, memorandum, 31 Mar. 1966, 1, file "Mississippi," box 6, SFES, RG 378 (Greenville); Fred E. Romero, "Position Paper," [Mar. 1976], 3, cons. with Robert O. Aders to John Read, memorandum, 2 Apr. 1976, file "Farm Labor, Feb–April 1976," box 51, WJU, RG 174.

24. Unita Blackwell quoted in National Advisory Council on Economic Opportunity, "Perspectives on Poverty: First Draft of the 1968 Report to the President," 5 Jan. 1968, 59, file "National Advisory Council" (1 of 2), box 3, PFDD, RG 381; "Office of Economic Opportunity Response to Poor People's Campaign," n.d. [3 May 1968], 1, file "PPC: Demands on OEO, May 1, 1968," box 11, PRADCR, RG 381.

25. "OEO: A Self-Evaluation," n.d. [1969], section titled "Community Action—Overview," [2–4], and section titled "The Community Action Agency," [5] (quotation), file "OEO—Self-Evaluation 1969," box 3, GRPR, RG 381; Coahoma Opportunities, Inc., "Adult Basic Education [Grant Application]," n.d. [late 1960s], 16, file "Office of Economic Opportunity," box 148, GFMD, RG 381.

26. Irving Lazar, "A Report of Consultation of the STAR Centers," 22–28 May 1966, 26, encl. in Robert L. Martin to Edgar May, memorandum, 5 Aug. 1966, file "Proposals—Related Papers" (2 of 2), box 151, GFMD, RG 381.

27. Bill Nagle to Gene Foley, memorandum, 31 Mar. 1966, 1, file "Mississippi," box 6, SFES, RG 378; Mid-State Opportunity Inc., Application for Community Action Program, n.d. [ca. 1967], [4], cons. with Mid-State Opportunity Inc., Adult Education and Prevocational Training, file "Community Action Program" (4 of 4), box 152, GFMD, RG 381; "Excerpt from FY 1968 Appropriation Hearings," 12 Dec. 1967, 49, file "Mary Holmes Junior College: Board of National Mission, Jackson, Mississippi" (1 of 2), box 9, IIF, RG 381.

28. Louis H. Anderson, "Narrative," 7 Nov. 1967, 2, file "Lowndes Co. Christ. Mvmt.," box 6, GFMD, RG 381; Quarterly Narrative Report, OEO-SEAW, Tuskegee Institute, Alabama, Jan.–Mar. 1968, Attachment A, 5, encl. in G. W. Taylor to CAP Headquarters, 7 May 1968, file "Correspondence Alabama 8539," box 3, GFMD, RG 381.

29. Saints Junior College Migrant Farmers Educational Project, "Project Report to the Office of Economic Opportunity: Second Start 1967," Apr. 1968, 38, file "Migrant Farmers Educational Project (Publication)," box 149, GFMD, RG 381; Wilmer Hunt, "Trip Report—Counties in Mississippi June 6 through 8, 1967," 8, file "D/T Mississippi June 6, 7, 8, 1967," box 10, PRADCR, RG 381 (Bolivar and Sunflower CAPs).

30. "Can Our Children Grow Healthfully," n.d. [ca. 1966/1967], 1–2, file 12, box 1, LBP.

31. Bureau of the Census, *Census of the Population: 1950*, vol. 2, pt. 24 (Mississippi), p. 60 (table 41); *Census of the Population: 1960*, vol. 1, pt. 26 (Mississippi), p. 62 (table 27); *Census of the Population: 1970*, vol. 1, pt. 26 (Mississippi), p. 88 (table 35); *Census of the Population: 1980*, vol. 1, pt. 26 (Mississippi), chap. C, p. 29 (table 59); H. Jack Geiger, Statement Presented to the Subcommittee on Employment Manpower and Poverty, United States Senate, 21 May 1969, 17, file 15, box 1, LBP; Al From to Bob Emond, memorandum, 5 Feb. 1968, 4, 29 (quotation), file "Anti-Poverty Coordinating Committee (Wilcox County)" (2 of 2), box 6, GFMD, RG 381.

32. Thurman Sensing, "Patronage Pork-Barrel: The Poverty Political," *Sensing the News*, *Madison County Herald*, 2 Sept. 1965, sec. 1, p. 6; American Farm Bureau Federation, *Farm Bureau Policies for 1967*, 8 Dec. 1965, 48, unfoldered, box 2, series 86-97, AFBFR; Leon Bramlett quoted in Donald C. Mosley and D. C. Williams Jr., "An Analysis and Evaluation of a Community Action Anti-Poverty Program in the Mississippi Delta," July 1967, 26–27, file "Community Action Program" (1 of 6), box 150, GFMD, RG 381; Mr. and Mrs. C. H. Grimes to John Sparkman, 26 June 1966, 1–2, cons. with Sparkman to Grimes, 30 June 1966, file "Health and Welfare—Poverty Program," box 6, 1966–67 series, JJSSP.

33. George Andrews to G. P. Brock, 28 July 1964, 1, file "Correspondence, July 28, 1964," box 27, GWAP; Thomas G. Abernethy to C. B. Curlee, 29 July 1965, 1, cons. with Abernethy to Curlee, 2 Aug. 1965, file "Office of Economic Opportunity, General, 1965–1966," box 161, TGAP; Joseph A. Loftus, "South Is Lagging in Requests for Federal Antipoverty Money," *New York Times*, 2 Jan. 1966, 48; Mrs. N. E. Roberts to Russell Long, 27 Aug. 1966, 1, file 46, box 97, RBLC; Neil Maxwell, "Rural Dixie's Plight: Poor Southern Negroes' Life Worsens Despite the War on Poverty," *Wall Street Journal*, 8 Oct. 1968, 1.

34. "The Leader," anonymous flyer included in "Harassment and Negative Attitudes," n.d., 1, unfoldered, box 1, 1998 Addition, HCP; Germany, "Poverty Wars," 234–37; "St. Helena School Aud. Burned Down," *Louisiana Weekly*, 11 June 1966, sec. 1, p. 7; Selma Inter-Religious Project, Newsletter, 12 Apr. 1967, 2, file "Southwest Ala. Farmers Co-op (Shirley Mesher)," box 12, series 81-4, WFNP.

35. Robert L. Martin to Edgar May, memorandum, 4 Aug. 1966, 1, file "Lowndes County, Alabama 1966 (Inactive)" (3 of 5), box 27, SuFDCAP, RG 381; Theo. James Pinnock and G. W. Taylor, Tuskegee Institute–OEO Seasonally Employed Agricultural Workers Educational Project, Summary of Accomplishments and Disappointments, 1 Nov. 1966–31 Oct. 1967, 20, file "Miscellaneous Alabama 8539," box 3, GFMD, RG 381.

36. Robert Hoskins and Joe D. Edmondson to Theodore Berry, 26 July 1965, 1, file "Mississippi—Correspondence—1965," box 5, StFDCAP, RG 381; Al From to Edgar May, memorandum, 6 Sept. 1967, 2, cons. with Theodore M. Berry to Director [Sargent Shriver], memorandum, 29 Sept. 1967, file "Administrative Alabama 1967," box 14, StFDCAP, RG 381 (Wilcox County problems); Nick Kotz, "In the Deep South, the Enemy Is Poverty," *Minneapolis Tribune*, 14 May 1967, 1B (Francis X. Walter).

37. Chambers-Tallapoosa Community Action Agency, "Narrative Progress Report," 1 Jan.–31 Mar. 1967, 3, unfoldered, box 825, NPR, RG 381; South Delta Community Action Association, "CAP Narrative Progress Report," 1 Oct.–30 Dec. 1966, 3, file "5156 La.," box 836, NPR, RG 381; "Rose Hill Center," *CDGM Newsletter*, 28 Aug. 1967, 8, file "Child Development

Groups of Mississippi," box 1, TCHRC; National Education Association, *Wilcox County, Alabama*, 81.

38. Robert W. Saunders to Frank K. Sloan, memorandum, 5 Apr. 1967, 1, file "CR Robert W. Saunders—1967" (1 of 2), box 8, PRADCR, RG 381; [Minutes], General Staff Meeting, Mississippi Action for Progress, 5 June 1967, 1–2, unfoldered, box 2, 1998 Addition, HCP (Leflore County).

39. Robert W. Saunders to Maurice A. Dawkins, memorandum, 6 June 1967, 2, file "CR Robert W. Saunders—1967" (1 of 2), box 8, PRADCR, RG 381; "All-Negro City Set in Alabama," *Baltimore Sun*, 29 May 1967, A4; Kenneth Vallis to Fran Scott, memorandum, 5 June 1967, 1, file "Southwest Alabama Self-Help Housing," box 7, GFMD, RG 381.

40. Lee Bandy, "Anti-Poverty Blasted by John Bell," *Jackson Daily News*, 7 Apr. 1966, 1, 16A; Edwin Strickland to [William F. Nichols], 21 Mar. 1967, 1–2, file "Office of Economic Opportunity, General, March–June 1967," box 10, series 81-4, WFNP; Thurman Sensing, "Watching the Poverty Warriors," Sensing the News, *Madison County Herald*, 31 Mar. 1966, sec. 1, 6; Vant Neff, "The American Taxpayer: Casualty in the War on Poverty," Comment from the Capital, *Bolivar County Democrat*, 20 Jan. 1966, 4.

41. Thomas W. Herren to George Andrews, 11 Aug. 1967, 1, cons. with Andrews to Herren, 14 Aug. 1967, file "Correspondence, August 10–14, 1967," box 39, GWAP; Unknown author to Bill [Nichols], n.d., file "OEO 1969 General," box 26, series 81-4, WFNP; John D. Morrow to John Sparkman, 25 May 1966, 1, and Sargent Shriver to Sparkman, 24 June 1966, 1, both cons. with Sparkman to Morrow, 8 July 1966, file "Health and Welfare—Poverty Program," box 6, 1966–67 series, JJSSP.

42. Sargent Shriver to John R. Rarick [draft], n.d. [ca. Mar. 1967], 1, encl. in Peter Spruance and Ed Terrones to C. B. Patrick, memorandum, 24 Mar. 1967, file "Administrative—Louisiana—1967," box 15, StFDCAP, RG 381; "Myths and Facts about OEO," n.d., 7–8 (taxpayer savings quotation and alcohol/tobacco comparisons), 10–12 (return on investment, agency size comparisons, and Job Corps costs), cons. with Damon Holmes to Ken Sparks, memorandum, 11 July 1968, file "Public Affairs," box 4, PFDD, RG 381.

43. Bradley H. Patterson Jr., cover letter for National Advisory Council on Economic Opportunity, "Perspectives on Poverty: First Draft of the 1968 Report to the President," 5 Jan. 1968, 2–3, and Morris I. Leibman to President, 15 Aug. 1967, 1–2, both in file "National Advisory Council" (1 of 2), box 3, PFDD, RG 381.

44. National Advisory Council on Economic Opportunity, "Perspectives on Poverty: First Draft of the 1968 Report to the President," 5 Jan. 1968, 10, 81 (quotation), file "National Advisory Council" (1 of 2), box 3, PFDD, RG 381.

45. Comptroller General of the United States, *Review of Economic Opportunity Programs*, 5–7; John Herbers, "Congress Is Told Drive on Poverty Is Badly Managed," *New York Times*, 19 Mar. 1969, 1, 25; Attorney General to George P. Shultz, 30 Jan. 1969, 2, file "1969—Justice Department," box 17, GPS, RG 174.

46. Kenneth W. Munden, "The Office of Economic Opportunity in the Nixon Administration," unpublished manuscript, 1973, 55, unfoldered, box 107, HOEO, RG 381; Thomas Abernethy to Dorothy E. Fanyo, 22 Mar. 1966, 1, file "Office of Economic Opportunity, General, 1965–1966," box 161, TGAP; John Stennis, "Address to Joint Session of Mississippi Legislature," 27 Jan. 1966, 8, file 10, box 119, PBJFP; Jack Raymond, "Budget, Too, Feels the Impact of the Growing War in Vietnam," *New York Times*, 26 Dec. 1965, E4.

47. Carter, *Music Has Gone Out of the Movement*, 133–63; McKee, "'This Government Is with Us,'" 54.

48. Cazenave, *Impossible Democracy*, 166–69; Al From to Bob Emond, memorandum, 23 Jan. 1968, 35, file "Anti-Poverty Coordinating Committee (Wilcox County)" (2 of 2), box 6, GFMD, RG 381.

49. "Statement by Sargent Shriver before the House Appropriations Committee," 28 Nov. 1967, 2–3, encl. in Maurice A. Dawkins to Friend, 15 Dec. 1967, file "Mailings to CR Leaders 1967," box 10, PRADCR, RG 381; Sargent Shriver to President, memorandum, 25 Jan. 1968, 2, file "Reports: Bi-Weekly Report to the President—April '67–April '69," box 12, SFDD, RG 381.

50. "CAA Closings," 1, encl. in William H. Bozman to Record, memorandum, 8 Oct. 1968, cons. with "FY 1970 Budget, Office of Economic Opportunity," file "Regional Directors Conf. NYC—10/24–25/68" (1 of 3), box 4, PRADCR, RG 381; Clark, *War on Poverty*, 59; William H. Bozman to Record, memorandum, 8 Oct. 1968, 1, cons. with "FY 1970 Budget, Office of Economic Opportunity," file "Regional Directors Conf. NYC—10/24–25/68" (1 of 3), box 4, PRADCR, RG 381; Aaron W. Crawford Jr. to Lyndon B. Johnson, n.d. [1967], 1, file "Southwest Ala. Farmers Co-op (Shirley Mesher)," box 12, series 81-4, WFNP.

51. Comptroller General of the United States, *Review of Economic Opportunity Programs*, 27; Richard W. Boone, "Reflections on Citizen Participation and the Economic Opportunity Act," paper prepared for the National Academy of Public Administration Conference on Crisis, Conflict and Creativity, n.d. [1970], 15–16, encl. in Joe P. Maldonado to Donald Rumsfeld, Wes Hjornevik, and Frank Carlucci, 23 June 1970, file "Citizen Participation in EO Act Program—Richard Boone Comments—1970," box 1, SFDD, RG 381.

52. STAR, Inc., "CAP Narrative Progress Report," 1 Oct.–31 Dec. 1966, [7], unfoldered, box 811, NPR, RG 381; Gustave T. Roessler to [Participants], 13 Mar. 1967, 1, cons. with Stanley H. Ruttenberg to Theodore M. Berry, 21 Mar. 1967, file "Administrative—Mississippi—1967," box 16, StFDCAP, RG 381; Quarterly Narrative Report, OEO-SEAW, Tuskegee Institute, Alabama, Jan.–Mar. 1968, 3–4, encl. in G. W. Taylor to CAP Headquarters, 7 May 1968, file "Correspondence Alabama 8539," box 3, GFMD, RG 381; H. Jack Geiger, Statement Presented to the Subcommittee on Employment Manpower and Poverty, United States Senate, 21 May 1969, 20, file 15, box 1, LBP; National Advisory Council on Economic Opportunity, "Perspectives on Poverty: First Draft of the 1968 Report to the President," 5 Jan. 1968, 84, file "National Advisory Council" (1 of 2), box 3, PFDD, RG 381.

53. Erika Duncan, "Long After '65, Still Fighting to Overcome," *New York Times*, 10 Sept. 1995, LI17; Dittmer, *Local People*, 371–82; Dunbar interview, 25; A. C. Krumlauf to Edgar May, memorandum, 16 Nov. 1966, 2, 4, encl. in May to Jule Sugarman and Ted Berry, memorandum, 19 Nov. 1966, file "Mississippi—Administrative—1965," box 5, StFDCAP, RG 381; Clay Salvant and Social Service Staff, "Parent Participation," 1, unfoldered, box 2, 1998 Addition, HCP (quotation).

54. Al From to Bob Emond, memorandum, 23 Jan. 1968, 6, file "Anti-Poverty Coordinating Committee (Wilcox County)" (2 of 2), box 6, GFMD, RG 381; "Revised Draft of Mr. Shriver's Statement on Wilcox and Lowndes Counties, Alabama," 12 Aug. 1966, 2, file "Wilcox County SCLC" (1 of 2), box 6, GFMD, RG 381.

55. "Minutes of the Director's Executive Staff Meeting," 30 Aug.1968, 2, file "Executive Staff Meetings," box 3, SFDD, RG 381; Mississippi Council on Human Relations, "Meeting on Poverty," 24 Feb. 1970, 1, file 56, box 8, DMP.

56. John Zippert, "Report on Conference for a Southwide Co-op Training Program," 9–11 June 1966, [2], file 1, box 1, JZP; Francis X. Walter to Sargent Shriver, 19 Sept. 1966, 2, cons. with Shriver to Walter, 10 Oct. 1966, file "CAP—Lowndes County and Wilcox County," box 3, GRPR, RG 381; Robert W. Saunders to Maurice A. Dawkins, memorandum, 6 June 1967, 3, file "CR Robert W. Saunders—1967" (1 of 2), box 8, PRADCR, RG 381; C. Erskine Smith (CCR chairman) quoted in Commission on Civil Rights, *Cycle to Nowhere*, 45.

Chapter 4

1. Lawrence Guyot, Arthur Thomas, and Isaac Foster to President Lyndon Baines Johnson, 29 Jan. 1966, 1, item 2, reel 2, MFDPR.
2. Cowling and Warbasse, *Co-Operatives in America*, 34–40, 45–47; Voorhis, *American Cooperatives*, 18–22; Charles O. Prejean to Bryant George, 4 Aug. 1971, 2, file 23, box 17, FSCR. For a useful overview of cooperative efforts among African Americans from the nineteenth century to the present, see Nembhard, *Collective Courage*.
3. Cunningham interview, 2; Nannette Sachs to Society of Brothers, 2 July 1963, 1, and Nannette Sachs to Lynn Rohrbaugh, 12 July 1963, 1, both in file 2, box 14, SEDFREP.
4. Bob Bass quoted in "Poor People's Coop," *As Is*, [July 1967], 3, file 33, box 5, VGAP.
5. Minutes, Special Meeting of the Board of the Directors, CORE Scholarship, Education and Defense Fund Incorporated, 12 Sept. 1963, 3, and Minutes, Special Meeting of the Board of the Directors, CORE Scholarship, Education and Defense Fund Incorporated, 7 Oct. 1963, 2, both in file 5, box 1, SEDFREP; Charlotte Devree, "Draft for a Fact Sheet, for CORE SEDF Education Project in Mississippi," 24 Oct. 1963, 3, file 1, box 74, series 5, CORER; Charlotte Devree to Ezra Levin, Fay Bennett, Andrew Norman, Nanette Sachs, and Marvin Rich, 7 Nov. 1963, 1–3 (quotation on p. 3), file 1, box 7, SEDFREP; Nannette Sachs to Members of the Board, memorandum, n.d. [1963], 1, file 1, box 74, series 5, CORER.
6. CORE Scholarship, Education and Defense Fund to James N. Mays, memorandum, 15 May 1964, 1–2; James N. Mays, Application for the Job of Rural Field Worker, 10 Mar. [1964], 1–3; Scholarship Education and Defense Field Representative [James Mays], "A Summary of Four Months Work," n.d. [Nov. 1964], 1–6, all in file 9, box 10, SEDFREP.
7. "Panola County Okra Co-op," reprint from *Vicksburg Citizens' Appeal*, n.d. [1966], [1]–[4] (quotations on pp. [2] and [4]), file 5, box 1, FISR.
8. "In Canton: A New Business," *Vicksburg Citizens' Appeal*, 20 Sept. 1965, 3.
9. "The Story of Freedomcrafts," n.d. [ca. 1970], 1–2, file 9, box 6, DMP; "How 'Freedom-crafts' Came to Be," n.d., 1, file 5, box 6, DMP.
10. William A. Carhart to Irving Jay Fain, 24 Oct. 1966, 1, file 2, box 13, SEDFREP; [Delta Ministry], *This Land Is Our Land . . .* , n.d. [early 1967], 1, file 10, box 2, SEDFREP; Ida Mae Lawrence quoted in "Radio Delta Reporting, This Week in Mississippi," [draft of transcript], n.d. [July 1966], 1, file 7, box 1, FISR.
11. Gene Roberts, "Negro Co-op Opens Jobs in Mississippi," *New York Times*, 5 Mar. 1967, 78; "Minutes of the First Membership Meeting of the Poor People's Corp.," 29 Aug. 1965, 1, cons. with Wilfred C. Leland to Jesse Morris, 2 Nov. 1965, file "Minority Groups," box 2, GSCF, RG 378 (quotation); Lucy Komisar, "Poor People's Corporation Lets the Poor Speak Out," *Village Voice*, 22 July 1965, 3.

12. "Minutes of the First Membership Meeting of the Poor People's Corp.," 29 Aug. 1965, 1–4, cons. with Wilfred C. Leland to Jesse Morris, 2 Nov. 1965, file "Minority Groups," box 2, GSCF, RG 378; Elizabeth Sutherland, "Mississippi: Summer of Discontent," *Nation*, 11 Oct. 1965, 214.

13. Poor People's Corporation, Application for Community Action Program, 15 Mar. 1966, 1–2, cons. with D. S. Rosen to Community Action Program, 2 Mar. 1966, file "Mississippi Housing" (2 of 2), box 28, SuFDCAP, RG 381; Gene Roberts, "Negro Co-op Opens Jobs in Mississippi," *New York Times*, 5 Mar. 1967, 78; Phillip H. Wiggins, "Poor People's Corporation Builds Jobs for Negroes in Rural Mississippi," *New York Times*, 21 July 1968, F16.

14. "The Selma Inter-Religious Project," *Alabama Council Bulletin*, 30 June 1966, 2 (quotations), AC; Selma Inter-Religious Project, Newsletter, 12 Apr. 1967, 4, file "Southwest Ala. Farmers Co-op (Shirley Mesher)," box 12, series 81-4, WFNP.

15. "Green-Hale Sewing Cooperatives," 23 Aug. 1971, 1–2, encl. in Dorothy Bryant to SCDP, 9 Nov. 1971, file 89, box 49, FSCR; "History and Background of the Cooperative," 1–2, encl. in Lewis Black to Episcopal Church, 26 Dec. 1977, file 89, box 49, FSCR.

16. Cunningham interview, 2–4; William Chapman, "$1-a-Bushel Bright Spot in Poverty War," *Washington Post*, 20 Aug. 1967, B5; "SWAFCA Membership Education," n.d. [1969], 1, cons. with "Evaluation—SWAFCA Board of Director Workshop Conducted at Selma, Alabama, June 7 and 9, 1969," 26 June 1969, file 11, box 18, SEDFREP; SWAFCA to Sargent Shriver, n.d. [1967], 1–2, 6 (quotation on p. 1), file "Orrville Cooperative (SNCC) 1967," box 10, series 81-4, WFNP.

17. Southwest Alabama Farmers Cooperative Association, *The SWAFCA Story*, pamphlet, n.d. [1969/1970], 3, file 11, box 18, SEDFREP; "The Southwest Alabama Farmers Cooperative Association (SWAFCA)," n.d. [1967], 1–3, file "Orrville Cooperative (SNCC) 1967," box 10, series 81-4, WFNP; "What Ye Sow—Ye Shall Reap!," *Alabama Council Bulletin*, 29 Apr. 1967, 3, AC.

18. "Farm Cooperative Grant to Ten Alabama Counties," OEO news release, 11 May 1967, 1, file "SWAFCA (Southwest Alabama Cooperative Association 5–11–67," box 6, GRPR, RG 381; Comptroller General of the United States, "Review of Certain Activities of the Southwest Alabama Farmers Cooperative Association under a Grant from the Office of Economic Opportunity," 27 Jan. 1969, 5, file "SWAFCA 1969," box 27, series 81-4, WFNP.

19. Zippert interview (quotation); "History of Grand Marie Co-op," n.d., 1–3, file 3, box 1, JZP; John Zippert to Marvin Rich, 2 Aug. 1966, 1–2, file 11, box 23, SEDFREP; "Sweet Potato Alert Proposal, Progress Report, 30 May–3 July 1966," 2, file 3, box 1, JZP.

20. McKnight, *Whistling in the Wind*, 21–22; "The Quiet Revolution of a Parish Priest," *Ebony*, May 1968, 52–53, 57 (quotation on p. 57).

21. McKnight, *Whistling in the Wind*, 24–27 (quotation on p. 24).

22. John Zippert to Ed Schwartz, 2 Feb. 1968, 1, file 8, box 68, FSCR; "The Quiet Revolution of a Parish Priest," *Ebony*, May 1968, 54.

23. "The Quiet Revolution of a Parish Priest," *Ebony*, May 1968, 52–54; Zippert interview.

24. McKnight, *Whistling in the Wind*, 29, 32.

25. Zippert interview; Charles O. Prejean to Robert Brown, 14 Nov. 1969, 1, file 12, box 28, FSCR; John Zippert to Norman Hill, 6 July 1967, 1, file 12, box 42, FSCR; "A Proposal for the Development of a Cooperative Education Program in the South," 1, encl. in A. J. McKnight to Ronnie Moore, 6 Oct. 1967, file 1, box 29, SEDFREP.

26. "Southern Groups Get Ford Foundation Grants," *Southwest Louisiana Register*, 14 Sept. 1967, 2.

27. John Zippert to SCDP Field Staff, memorandum, n.d. [Aug. 1967], 2, file 1, box 29, SEDFREP; David L. Noflin, "Organizer's Report Form, West Feliciana, Louisiana," n.d. [June 1968], cons. with A. J. McKnight to Noflin, 18 June 1968, file 8, box 68, FSCR; Cunningham interview, 9; Henry Hatches, "'It's New!' Southern Consumers," *Hinds County FDP News Letter*, 6 Oct. 1967, 2, item 12, reel 3, MFDPR.

28. "Field Perspective, Southern Cooperative Development Program," n.d. [Nov. 1967], 7–11, file 1, box 29, SEDFREP.

29. Ibid., 2, 8.

30. Mike Piere to Mr. [Jac] Wasserman, 10 Sept. 1964, 1–2, cons. with Jac [Wasserman] to Ann [Singer], 18 Sept. 1964, and Scholarship Education and Defense Field Representative [James Mays], "A Summary of Four Months Work," n.d. [Nov. 1964], 9–10, both in file 9, box 10, SEDFREP.

31. Guillory interview; Frank P. Graham to Friend, 29 Mar. 1967, 1, file 1, box 2, series 29, JCSC; John Zippert to Hilary Feldstein, 19 Sept. 1969, 3, file 10, box 68, FSCR.

32. Margaret Lauren to [Wilfred C.] Leland, 7 Oct. 1965, cons. with Leland to Jesse Morris, 2 Nov. 1965, file "Minority Groups," box 2, GSCF, RG 378; "Fact, Fiction Fill West Point Fish Pot; But Which Is Which?," *Mississippi Freelance*, Feb. 1970, 1.

33. "The Quiet Revolution of a Parish Priest," *Ebony*, May 1968, 57; McKnight, *Whistling in the Wind*, 27–28.

34. Citizens' Council newsletter quoted in "The Quiet Revolution of a Parish Priest," *Ebony*, May 1968, 57; McKnight, *Whistling in the Wind*, 32–33.

35. "Sweet Potato Alert Program Progress Report," 1 June 1966, 2, and GMVPC newsletter, 16 Apr. 1966, 1, both in file 3, box 1, JZP; Burt Schorr, "Tapping the Green Side of Black Power," *Wall Street Journal*, 4 June 1968, 20; "Chronology of Events in the Formation and Development of the Grand Marie Vegetable Producers Cooperative," n.d. [ca. June 1966], 2, file 11, box 23, SEDFREP.

36. John Zippert, "Memo on the Necessity of Immediate Operating Capital for the Grand Marie Vegetable Producers Cooperative, Inc., Pending Processing of Farmers Home Administration Loan," n.d. [July 1966], 1–2, file 3, box 1, JZP; Joseph Lee Marlbrough to Marvin Rich, 19 July 1966, file 11, box 23, SEDFREP.

37. Guillory interview; Schorr, "Tapping the Green Side of Black Power," *Wall Street Journal*, 4 June 1968, 20; John Zippert to Howard Moore, 19 Sept. 1969, 1, file 13, box 42, FSCR; John Zippert to [Marvin] Rich, 20 July 1966, 2, file 11, box 23, SEDFREP.

38. Selma Inter-Religious Project, Newsletter, 12 Apr. 1967, 2, and Walter C. Givhan to Bill Nichols, 24 Mar. 1967, 1, both in file "Southwest Ala. Farmers Co-op (Shirley Mesher)," box 12, series 81-4, WFNP; "Notes on Shirley Mesher," n.d. [early 1967], 1, 3 (quotation), file "SWAFCA," box 22, series 81-4, WFNP.

39. L. B. Whitfield Jr. to John [Sparkman], 2 June 1967, 1, file "Fed. Gov—Agri." (2 of 4), box 3, 1965–68 series, JJSSP; Orzell Billingsley Jr. to Ira Kaye, 3 Apr. 1967, 1, file "CR Robert W. Saunders—1967" (1 of 2), box 8, PRADCR, RG 381; Joe T. Smitherman, B. A. Reynolds, and Leigh Pegues to John Sparkman, telegram, 28 Apr. 1967, 1–2, cons. with Sparkman to Smitherman, 2 May 1967, file "Fed. Gov—Agri." (2 of 4), box 3, 1965–68 series, JJSSP.

40. Mary Y. Grice and Taylor Wilkins to Whom It May Concern, 28 Apr. 1967, 1–2, file "Fed. Gov—Agri." (2 of 4), and Mary Y. Grice to John Sparkman, 22 May 1967, 1, cons. with Sparkman to Grice, 25 May 1967, file "Fed. Gov—Agri." (2 of 4), both in box 3, 1965–68 series, JJSSP; Roy Reed, "Leaders of Negro Farm Co-op in Alabama Go to Washington to Seek Funds," *New York Times*, 13 Apr. 1967, 30.

41. Walt Robbins to Maurice Dawkins, memorandum, 11 May 1967, 1–2, file "CVR: Robbins' Corres. (Gen.) 1967–July 1968" (1 of 2), box 7, PRADCR, RG 381; "Cooperative Funded after NAACP Protest," *Crisis*, May 1967, 211; Selma Inter-Religious Project, Newsletter, 12 Apr. 1967, 3, file "Southwest Ala. Farmers Co-op (Shirley Mesher)," box 12, series 81-4, WFNP.

42. Selma Inter-Religious Project, Newsletter, 12 Apr. 1967, 4, file "Southwest Ala. Farmers Co-op (Shirley Mesher)," box 12, series 81-4, WFNP; "Statement by Miss Mary Grice, Program Director, Little River Community Action Program, Daphne, Ala.," 18 May 1967, 1, cons. with John Sparkman to Grice, 25 May 1967, file "Fed. Gov—Agri." (2 of 4), box 3, 1965–68 series, JJSSP; Bertrand M. Harding to Joseph S. Knight, 9 May 1967, 1–5 (quotation on p. 5), file "Civil Rights Leaders—June 1 Mtg [1967]," box 1, PRADCR, RG 381.

43. Ethel Overby to Mr. Berry, Don Hess, John Clark, and Gerson Green, memorandum, 17 Jan. 1968, 1, file "Alabama—SWAFCA—1968" (3 of 3), box 70, SuFDCAP, RG 381; Bill Nichols to Orville Freeman, 9 Feb. 1968, 1–2, file "SWAFCA," box 22, series 81-4, WFNP.

44. Bill Nichols to Ernest Johnson, 6 Mar. 1968, 1, file "SWAFCA," box 22, series 81-4, WFNP; John A. Baker to Theodore H. Berry, 15 Feb. 1968, 1, file "Memo of Understanding Re: SWAFCA 1968," box 70, SuFDCAP, RG 381; Gerson M. Green to Theodore M. Berry, memorandum, 19 Jan. 1968, 2–3, and Gerson M. Green to Theodore M. Berry, memorandum, 10 Jan. 1968, 1, both in file "Alabama—SWAFCA—1968" (3 of 3), box 70, SuFDCAP, RG 381.

45. Howard Bechel to Bill Nichols, 24 Jan. 1969, 1, cons. with "SWAFCE [*sic*] Expenditures from June 1967–June 1968," n.d., file "SWAFCA," box 22, series 81-4, WFNP; Edward A. Tenenbaum to Kate Jackson, 8 May 1968, 1–2, cons. with Richard M. Saul to [no name given], n.d. [May 1968], and Olga Boikess and William Kopit to Theodore M. Berry, memorandum, 3 Apr. 1968, 1–3, 7, 12 (quotation on p. 2), both in file "Alabama—SWAFCA—1968" (3 of 3), box 70, SuFDCAP, RG 381.

46. Southwest Alabama Farmers Cooperative Association, "SWAFCA Stalled by the Department of Agriculture," n.d. [May 1968], 6–7, encl. in Stanley Zimmerman to Theodore Berry, 31 May 1968, file "Alabama—SWAFCA—1968" (2 of 3), box 70, SuFDCAP, RG 381.

47. William H. Harrison and Calvin S. Orsborn to Orville L. Freeman, 13 May 1968, 1, file "Alabama—SWAFCA—1968" (3 of 3), box 70, SuFDCAP, RG 381.

48. John A. Baker to William H. Harrison and Calvin S. Orsborn, 28 May 1968, 1–2, ibid.; William Steif, "Black Farm Co-op Is Making Solid Progress," clipping from *Washington D.C. News*, 14 June 1968, [16], file "Alabama—SWAFCA—1968" (2 of 3), ibid.; Roger Beardwood, "Southern Roots of Urban Crisis," *Fortune*, Aug. 1968, 151; Stanley Zimmerman quoted in "$852,000 Loan to SWAFCA Sets Major Precedent," *Rural Advance*, Summer 1968, 5.

49. Bill Nichols to George Andrews, 14 Mar. 1968 (2 of 2), 1, file "SWAFCA," box 22, series 81-4, WFNP; Comptroller General of the United States, "Review of Certain Activities of the Southwest Alabama Farmers Cooperative Association under a Grant from the Office of Economic Opportunity," 27 Jan. 1969, 3, file "SWAFCA 1969," box 27, series 81-4,

WFNP; Bill Nichols to Ross D. Davis, telegram, [6 May 1968], 1, cons. with Mary Elva Rice to R. C. Bamberg, 3 May 1968, and Arnold H. Leibowitz to Bill Nichols, 7 May 1968, 1, both in file "SWAFCA," box 22, series 81-4, WFNP.

50. Gerald J. Stout to Tom [Theodore] Berry, 4 Jan. 1968, 3, 5–6, file "Alabama—SWAFCA—1968" (3 of 3), box 70, SuFDCAP, RG 381; "$852,000 Loan to SWAFCA Sets Major Precedent," *Rural Advance*, Summer 1968, 5 (vegetable spoilage); Theodore Berry to Bob Emond, memorandum, 20 May 1968, 1, file "SWAFCA—Alabama Inspection Reports 1968," box 70, SuFDCAP, RG 381.

51. Continental-Allied Co., "Monthly Evaluation Report on SWAFCA," 24 June 1968, 27–28, file "Alabama—SWAFCA—1968" (2 of 3), box 70, SuFDCAP, RG 381.

52. *Selma Times Journal*, 31 Mar. 1967, quoted in SWAFCA, *The SWAFCA Story*, pamphlet, n.d. [1969/1970], 3, file 11, box 18, SEDFREP; "*Barron's Weekly* Article on SWAFCA," 21 Apr. 1969, 3, file "SWAFCA (Southwest Alabama Cooperative Association 5-11-67," box 6, GRPR, RG 381.

53. George D. McCarthy to Bill Nichols, 20 Mar. 1968, 1, file "SWAFCA," box 22, series 81-4, WFNP; Jerry Hornsby to Calvin Orsborn, 25 Mar. 1968, 1–3, file "Alabama—SWAFCA—1968" (3 of 3), box 70, SuFDCAP, RG 381.

54. Al From to Bob Emond, memorandum, 25 Mar. 1968, 2, encl. in Bob Emond to Acting Director, memorandum, 26 Mar. 1968, file "SWAFCA—Alabama Inspection Reports 1968," box 70, SuFDCAP, RG 381.

55. Comptroller General of the United States, "Review of Certain Activities of the Southwest Alabama Farmers Cooperative Association under a Grant from the Office of Economic Opportunity," 27 Jan. 1969, 10, file "SWAFCA 1969," box 27, series 81-4, WFNP; Gerson M. Green to Acting Director, 30 Sept. 1968, 1–2, file "Alabama—SWAFCA—1968" (1 of 3), box 70, SuFDCAP, RG 381.

56. "Negroes in Alabama Appeal Court Order Blocking Farm Aid," *New York Times*, 31 October 1968, 78; "*Barron's Weekly* Article on SWAFCA," 21 Apr. 1969, 2, file "SWAFCA (Southwest Alabama Cooperative Association 5-11-67," box 6, GRPR, RG 381.

57. Gerson M. Green to Theodore M. Berry, memorandum, 19 Jan. 1968, 1, file "Alabama—SWAFCA—1968" (3 of 3), box 70, SuFDCAP, RG 381 (inexperienced board members); Comptroller General of the United States, "Review of Certain Activities of the Southwest Alabama Farmers Cooperative Association under a Grant from the Office of Economic Opportunity," 27 Jan. 1969, 34, file "SWAFCA 1969," box 27, series 81-4, WFNP (Orsborn's other interests); K. D. English to D. L. Chewning, memorandum, 29 May 1968, 2–4, encl. in Theodore M. Berry to John A. Baker, memorandum, 12 June 1968, file "Alabama—SWAFCA—1968" (2 of 3), box 70, SuFDCAP, RG 381 (Orsborn's deficiencies and farmers hedging bets).

58. Gerson M. Green to Theodore M. Berry, memorandum, 15 Aug. 1968, 1, cons. with Berry to Robert Perrin, memorandum, 16 Aug. 1968, file "Alabama—SWAFCA—1968" (2 of 3), box 70, SuFDCAP, RG 381; Milo Dakin, "Federal Audit Questions SWAFCA's Use of Funds," *Montgomery Advertiser*, 6 Nov. 1968, 17.

59. Comptroller General of the United States, "Review of Certain Activities of the Southwest Alabama Farmers Cooperative Association under a Grant from the Office of Economic Opportunity," 27 Jan. 1969, 34, file "SWAFCA 1969," box 27, series 81-4, WFNP; "*Barron's Weekly* Article on SWAFCA," 21 Apr. 1969, 2–3, file "SWAFCA (Southwest Alabama

Cooperative Association 5-11-67," box 6, GRPR, RG 381; "SWAFCA Training Evaluation," 15 Mar. 1969, 2, 7–9, file 11, box 18, SEDFREP.

60. John Zippert, "Report on Alabama Co-op Trip: December 3–9, 1966," 1, 3, cons. with John Zippert to [Ronnie] Moore, 11 Nov. 1966, file 4, box 20, SEDFREP; Unknown author, [Notes on sewing cooperative], n.d. [Dec. 1968], file 2, box 1, LBP.

61. Rudy Frank to Girson [Gerson] Green, memorandum, 30 July 1969, 2, file "Coop," box 3, DHCR; Black, *People and Plows against Hunger*, 33, 35, 58.

62. Black, *People and Plows against Hunger*, 37–38; Mohamed A. Mohamed to Ronald Thornton, 12 July 1975, 3, file 29, box 60, FSCR.

63. Minutes, Delta Ministry Staff Meeting, 23–24 Feb. 1967, 6, file 35, box 3, DMP.

64. McKnight, *Whistling in the Wind*, 35; "Background Information on Cooperative Development Financial Institution," 1, cons. with Charles Prejean, form letter, n.d. [ca. Feb./Mar. 1969], file 11, box 28, FSCR; Jake Ayers, "Preliminary Proposal from Freedomcrafts to the Presbyterian Inter-racial Council," n.d. [1967], 1, file 8, box 6, DMP.

65. "Full Board Meeting," 28 June 1968, 3, file "Alabama—SWAFCA—1968" (2 of 3), box 70, SuFDCAP, RG 381; "Evaluation—SWAFCA Board of Director Workshop Conducted at Selma, Alabama, June 7 and 9, 1969," 26 June 1969, 5, 8–9, file 11, box 18, SEDFREP; Cunningham interview, 14.

66. "Wanted: Manager for Coop," *Alabama Council Bulletin*, 29 Mar. 1967, 4, AC; Ronnie Moore to Child Development Group of Mississippi, 31 Aug. 1967, 4, file 19, box 22, SEDFREP.

Chapter 5

1. A. Q. Weaver to George W. Andrews, 12 Sept. 1963, 1, cons. with Andrews to Weaver, 18 Sept. 1963, file "Correspondence, September 17–20, 1963," box 23, GWAP; G. M. Ogle to John Sparkman, 6 Sept. 1965, 1, cons. with Sparkman to Ogle, 9 Sept. 1965, file "States and Human Rights" (1 of 2), box 7, 1965 series, JJSSP; Martha L. Kilgore to Russell Long, 18 May 1966, 1–2, file 47, box 97, RBLC.

2. Carter, *Politics of Rage*, 202–22 (quotation on p. 207).

3. Editorial, "Let's Don't Play With Fire!," *Jackson Clarion-Ledger*, 4 Nov. 1963, 1; W[illiam] B. Alexander to Walter Sillers, 28 Mar. 1964, 1, file 5, box 41, WSP.

4. Strom Thurmond quoted in Charles Mohr, "Thurmond Joins Goldwater Drive," *New York Times*, 18 Sept. 1964, 1, 16; Scammon and Wattenberg, *Real Majority*, 309; Roy V. Harris, "What Does the Election Prove?," *Citizen*, Nov. 1964, 6.

5. Thomas O'Neill, "Two-Party System in South of Little Help to Negroes," *Newark Sunday News*, 18 Sept. 1966, sec. 2, p. C1; Novak, *Agony of the G.O.P.*, 179, 201; William Miller quoted in Thurber, *Republicans and Race*, 184. For more on the Republican Party's "southern strategy," see Phillips, *Emerging Republican Majority*, 203–32, 461–74; Edsall, *Chain Reaction*, 3–31; Carter, *Politics of Rage*, 326–34; and Wyman, Review of *The Two-Party South*, 30–31. Debates within the party over the use of racism to win elections are discussed in Crespino, *In Search of Another Country*, 205–22, and Thurber, *Republicans and Race*, 241–54.

6. See, for example, Crespino, *In Search of Another Country*, 235–66; Lassiter, *Silent Majority*, 3–7, 251–75; Shafer and Johnston, *End of Southern Exceptionalism*, 2–3, 11–18, 92–133; Nash and Taggart, *Mississippi Politics*, 7; Asch, *Senator and the Sharecropper*, xiii–xiv, 74, 90–95, 241–42; and Thurber, *Republicans and Race*, 32, 77, 122, 144.

7. *Christian Conservative Communique*, 27 May 1965, 2, file 4, box 19, WSP; James T. Wooten, "Private Schools Thrive in South, but Finances Restrict Quality," *New York Times*, 1 Feb. 1970, 1, 34 (private school student quotation); "Notes from the State Office," *Council Newsletter*, Jan. 1971, 3, file "Mississippi Council on Human Relations—Newsletters, 1970–1972," box 4, TCHRC. Crespino analyzes the racist motivations behind the private school movement in *In Search of Another Country*, 240–48.

8. News Release, 6 Sept. 1966, 1, file "Press Releases, Statements and Speeches, 1965–1966," box 127, TGAP; "Award for Abernethy," 1, n.d., file "News Releases, 1971–1972," box 127, TGAP; "Notes for Speech before National Association of Real Estate Boards," 17 Nov. 1966, 1, file 29, box 559, RBLC; Henry Brisbay to Strom Thurmond, 18 Sept. 1971, 1–2, file 17, box 136, RBLC; Robert B. Patterson, "Right to Bear Arms Not Just for Rabbit-Hunters," *Citizen*, Jan. 1977, 4–6.

9. "Resolutions Adopted at Meeting of Citizens' Councils of America in New Orleans, May 19, 1962," *Citizen*, May 1962, 1; Medford Evans, "The Future of Private Education," *Citizen*, Apr. 1966, 14.

10. See, for example Robert B. Patterson, "Right to Bear Arms Not Just for Rabbit-Hunters," *Citizen*, Jan. 1977, 4–6; George W. Shannon, "U.S. Blacks on Relief Shun Work; Jamaicans Take Jobs," *Citizen*, Nov. 1977, 11–12; and George W. Shannon, "New Welfare Queen's Story Spotlights National Fraud," *Citizen*, May 1979, 4–6.

11. "Random Glances at the News," *Citizen*, May 1972, 12 (hospital robbery); June 1972, 28 (rape); and Dec. 1973, 26–27 (food stamp fraud); "Integration in Housing," *Citizen*, Nov. 1972, 2; Editorial, "Where We Stand," *Citizen*, Dec. 1979, 2.

12. James E. Perkins to Thomas G. Abernethy, 19 June 1968, 1, cons. with Abernethy to Perkins, 24 June 1968, file "Poor People's March," box 309, TGAP; Robert P. Griffin to Bill Nichols, 14 Mar. 1973, 1, cons. with Nichols to Griffin, 4 Apr. 1973, file "O.E.O. 32-B-4," box 26, series 81-4, WFNP; W. C. Watson to Dear Sir, 10 Feb. 1970, 1, and Thomas G. Abernethy to Watson, 24 Feb. 1970, 1, both in file "Civil Rights," box 272, TGAP.

13. American Farm Bureau Federation, *Farm Bureau Policies for 1967*, 8 Dec. 1965, 48, and American Farm Bureau Federation, *Farm Bureau Policies for 1968*, Dec. 1967, 44 (quotations), 48, both unfoldered in box 2, series 86-97, AFBFR; Walter Flowers, "1970 Legislation and Inflation," *Greene County Democrat*, 5 Feb. 1970, 1.

14. Ben A. Franklin, "Agnew Makes Bid for 'Protest' Vote," *New York Times*, 8 Oct. 1968, 33; Richard Nixon quoted in "Nixon Raps Government Renewal Aid," *Pittsburgh Post-Gazette*, 7 Oct. 1968, 4; "Republican Platform 1968," 752–56; Richard S. Franzen to Conference Body, memorandum, 17 Oct. 1968, 6, cons. with Harold R. Sims to Executive Staff and Regional Directors, 21 Oct. 1968, file "Regional Directors Conf. NYC—10/24–25/68" (1 of 3), box 4, PRADCR, RG 381.

15. Alabama politician quoted in Frady, *Wallace*, 6–7. See also Carter, *Politics of Rage*, 10–12, 195–225, 324–70.

16. Lassiter, *Silent Majority*, 234; white man quoted in "At the Crossroads," *Newsweek*, 6 Oct. 1969, 45; Scammon and Wattenberg, *Real Majority*, 167 (polls).

17. "Minutes of the Commission on the Delta Ministry," 5–6 Mar. 1969, 3, file 5, box 4, DMP; Skrentny, *Ironies of Affirmative Action*, 189–91; "Excerpts from Speech by N.A.A.C.P. Head Calling Administration Anti-Negro," *New York Times*, 30 June 1970, 25; "The Black Caucus in Congress Protests Nixon's Indifference to 'The Black Nation,'" *Voice*, 31 Aug.–15

Sept. 1970, 2; Mrs. Jack F. Patton to John Stennis, 21 Mar. 1972, 1, cons. with Stennis to Mr. and Mrs. John Sharp, 18 Apr. 1972, file 3, box 3, series 29, JCSC.

18. "Why Mayors Complain They Can't Do Business with Washington," *U.S. News and World Report*, 27 Mar. 1967, 64–66; National Governors' Conference, [Resolution] VI, 20 Oct. 1967, 1, encl. in Ross D. Davis to Deputy Assistant Secretaries and Office Heads, memorandum, 29 Nov. 1967, file "National Governor's Conference," box 9, SFES, RG 378; Robert Perrin to Donald Rumsfeld, memorandum, 19 May 1969, 1–2, file "Donald Rumsfeld," box 5, PFDD, RG 381; John Stennis to Holace Morris, 18 July 1966, 1, file "Economic Opportunity, General Correspondence," box 2, series 25, JCSC; Matthew C. Coller to Bill Nichols, 19 Mar. 1969, 1, file "SWAFCA 1969," box 27, series 81-4, WFNP ("responsible people" quotation).

19. "Transcript of Nixon's Address to Nation Outlining Proposals for Welfare Reform," *New York Times*, 9 Aug. 1969, 10.

20. Robert Perrin to Donald Rumsfeld, memorandum, 19 May 1969, 2, file "Donald Rumsfeld," box 5, PFDD, RG 381; "Federal-State Employment Service Called 'High on Rhetoric, Low on Performance,'" *EEOC News Digest*, 2 June 1970, 15, file "News Digest May 1970 to June 1970," box 4, CFC, RG 403 (Urban League concerns); Roy Batchelor (regional director) quoted in Harold M. Bailin to Record, 4 Feb. 1971, 4, file "Regional Directors of CAP Directors Meeting," box 5, SFFCD, RG 381; John Zippert to FSC Membership and Staff, 30 Jan. 1973, 3, file 2, box 43, FSCR; Gerald LaBrie to John Zippert, 5 Apr. 1972, 2, file 24, box 21, FSCR.

21. Thurber, *Republicans and Race*, 363; F. C. Doyal Jr. to George P. Shultz, 4 Aug. 1969, 1, cons. with Shultz to Doyal, 7 Aug. 1969, file "1969—State Correspondence, Alabama-Louisiana," box 18, GPS, RG 174; "North Bolivar," encl. in Charles O. Prejean to Robert J. Brown, 16 Jan. 1970, 1, file 16, box 28, FSCR.

22. John Iglehart, "Poverty Units Facing Pressures," clipping from *Newark News*, 25 Nov. 1970, 1, file "Head Start," box 7, SFFCD, RG 381 (Carlucci); "Statement by Frank Carlucci, Director of Operations and Assistant Director of the Office of Economic Opportunity, before the House of Representatives Committee on Education and Labor," 2 Dec. 1970, 1, file "Head Start," box 7, SFFCD, RG 381 (CAA reviews); Harold M. Bailin to Ted Jones, memorandum, 3 Dec. 1970, 1, file "Head Start," box 7, SFFCD, RG 381 (regional director complaints).

23. Ray Collins to Donald Rumsfeld, memorandum, 14 Jan. 1970, 1–2, file "Office of Program Development" (2 of 3), box 8, SFDD, RG 381; H. Jack Geiger to Andrew James, 26 Jan. 1971, 3, file "OEO Grant Correspondence 1971–72," box 43, DHCR.

24. "FY 74 Budget Proposes End to OEO, Community Action," *Economic Opportunity Report*, 29 Jan. 1973, 1, file "Memos from Mr. Owen Brooks," box 2, DHCR; John Berbers, "Budget Chief Affirms Plan to Abolish Poverty Office," *New York Times*, 27 Jan. 1973, 1, 26; Jack Rosenthal, "Poverty Agency Faces More Cuts," *New York Times*, 13 Jan. 1973, 14 (Phillips's background); Howard Phillips quoted in "Acting O.E.O. Chief Discerns Marxism in Poverty Agency," *New York Times*, 4 Feb. 1973, 37.

25. "Report for the President: An Assessment of the Community Services Administration," n.d. [early 1977], 1, encl. in Joseph W. Aragon, "Report for the President on the Community Services Administration: An Overview and Six Recommendations," n.d. [early 1977], file "Arragon [*sic*] Report on CSA," box 5, GRSF, RG 381 ("staff vacancies" quotation);

Wilbert C. Russell and Cleveland Gilcrease to Joseph Aragon, 4 Feb. 1977, 2, file "National Center for Community Action," box 10, GRSF, RG 381 ("dumping ground" quotation).

26. Ben A. Franklin, "Suits to Oppose O.E.O. Dispersal," *New York Times*, 26 Feb. 1973, 18; Philip Shabecoff, "4 Senators Seek to Oust Head of O.E.O.," *New York Times*, 15 Mar. 1973, 29; Marjorie Hunter, "House and Nixon Act to Aid O.E.O.," *New York Times*, 27 June 1973, 27; William E. Farrell, "Poverty Agency Is Seen as Entity," *New York Times*, 23 Apr. 1975, 25; "Report for the President: An Assessment of the Community Services Administration," n.d. [early 1977], 1, encl. in Joseph W. Aragon, "Report for the President on the Community Services Administration: An Overview and Six Recommendations," n.d. [early 1977], file "Arragon [*sic*] Report on CSA," box 5, GRSF, RG 381.

27. "Report for the President: An Assessment of the Community Services Administration," n.d. [early 1977], 2, encl. in Joseph W. Aragon, "Report for the President on the Community Services Administration: An Overview and Six Recommendations," n.d. [early 1977], file "Arragon [*sic*] Report on CSA," box 5, GRSF, RG 381; John Macomber quoted in William L. Chaze, "After 15 Years of 'Great Society' Spending," *U.S. News and World Report*, 30 June 1980, 36.

28. Gerson Green to Dick Blumenthal, memorandum, 26 May 1969, 5, file "OEO Review Task Force, 1969—General Comments, Reports, Correspondence—'Working Notes'" (2 of 4), and L. S./B. K., "Delegation Strategy," 15 June 1969, 1, file "OEO Review Task Force, 1969—General Comments, Reports, Correspondence—'Working Notes'" (3 of 4), both in box 7, SFDD, RG 381.

29. Daniel, *Dispossession*, 231–32; "Farmers Home Administration Discriminates against Blacks," *ELF Newsletter*, Nov. 1976, 1–2, file 12, box 14, MBC; Unknown author to Art Campbell, 22 Mar. 1979, 1, file 53, box 9, FSCR; [Fred Romero to Ray Marshall, memorandum, 6 Feb. 1977], 2, file "Memo 2/6/77 to the Secretary from Fred Romero regarding Meeting with Farmworker Representatives," box 84, RM, RG 174 ("generally ignored" quotation); Wilbert C. Russell and Cleveland Gilcrease to Joseph Aragon, 4 Feb. 1977, 6, file "National Center for Community Action," box 10, GRSF, RG 381.

30. ["A New Life for the Country: Report of the Presidential Task Force on Rural Development," 4 Jan. 1970], chap. IV, p. 1, cons. with John R. Price to Members of Rural Affairs Council, memorandum, 26 Feb. 1970, file "White House—Rural Affairs Council—1970," box 154, GPS, RG 174; Office of Economic Opportunity, "Actions and Plans Directed toward Cooperation and Coordination with Local Governments," June 1970, title page (Rumsfeld quotation), 1–2, file "State Involvement in Poverty Programs," box 7, GRPR, RG 381; "OEO's Efforts to Increase State Involvement in Fiscal Year 1970," June 1970, 1, ibid.

31. "OEO Testimony on Department of Community Development," n.d. [ca. May/June 1971], 22, file "Proposed Reorganization—Dept. of Human Resources—OEO/Dept. of Community Development—1971" (1 of 3), box 10, SFDD, RG 381 (SEOO budget); Department of Labor, *Manpower Technical Exchange*, 18 May 1973, 1, file "Departmental Releases May 1973," box 68, PJB, RG 174; Charles Culhane, "Manpower Report/Revenue Sharing Shift Set for Worker Training Programs," *National Journal Reports*, 12 Jan. 1974, 51, file "Administration of State Programs December 1975," box 66, JTD, RG 174 (CETA).

32. Huttie, "New Federalism," 25; "Minority Elected Officials Learn to Play the New Federal Game: A Report on the Economic Development Conference, Atlanta, Georgia, June

29–July 1, 1973," 3–6, file "Scholarship, Education and Defense Fund, Inc., Sept. 1973–Dec. 1974," box 433, series 3, RBFA.

33. Danny Mitchell quoted in Huttie, "New Federalism," 26.

34. William E. Farrell, "Poverty Agency Is Seen as Entity," *New York Times*, 23 Apr. 1975, 25; Southeast Region Equal Opportunity Association, Resolution, 2nd Annual Session, 19–22 Feb. 1975, 1–2, encl. in Olan Faulk to John T. Dunlop, 18 Apr. 1975, file "Equal Employment Opportunity 1975," box 64, JTD, RG 174; Hubert H. Humphrey and Dick Clark to John Dunlop, 28 Mar. 1975, 1, 5, cons. with Dunlop to Humphrey, 5 May 1975, file "Farm Labor March–August 1975," box 69, JTD, RG 174.

35. Fred E. Romero, "Position Paper," [Mar. 1976], 1–8, cons. with Robert O. Aders to John Read, memorandum, 2 Apr. 1976, file "Farm Labor, Feb–April 1976," box 51, WJU, RG 174.

36. John F. Adams, Vernon M. Briggs Jr., Brian Rungeling, Lewis H. Smith, and Roosevelt Steptoe, "Labor Markets in the Rural South: A Study Based on Four Rural Counties," 31 Mar. 1977, 335–37 (quotation on p. 335), file "Articles about and by the Secretary, Labor Markets in the Rural South: A Study Based on Four Rural Southern Counties, 1977," box 122, RM, RG 174. The counties studied were Dodge County, Georgia; Natchitoches Parish, Louisiana; Starr County, Texas; and Sunflower County, Mississippi.

37. William H. Harrison, "Progress Report for March, April, May, and June 1972," 13 July 1972, 2–4 (quotation on p. 4), and William H. Harrison to Bill Nichols, 6 Dec. 1972, 1–2, cons. with Nichols to Willie J. Williams, 15 Nov. 1972, both in file "12-T Office of Economic Opportunity—SWAFCA—Community Action," box 10, series 85-1, WFNP.

38. Black, *People and Plows against Hunger*, 76–78 (L. C. Dorsey quoted on p. 76 and Brenton Creelman on p. 78).

39. Rudy Frank to Girson [Gerson] Green, memorandum, 30 July 1969, 2, file "Coop," box 3, DHCR; "Minutes of Meeting at OEO Called by Rudy Frank," 6 Aug. 1969, 11, file "Mtg. Minutes w/ R. Frank OEO and Farm Coop Board about Cannery," box 38, DHCR.

40. Rutherford Associates, "Food-Processing in the Mississippi Delta," 1 Oct. 1970, Part II, Continental-Allied Study (no page numbers), file "Rutherford and Continental Reports: Farm Coop Cannery," box 39, DHCR; Black, *People and Plows against Hunger*, 58.

41. Herbert Black to Charles O. Prejean, 7 May 1974, 1, cons. with Prejean to Black, 15 May 1974, file 11, box 29, FSCR; Geiger interview, 74.

42. "Sad Nurse" to A. B. Albritton, 31 July 1972, 2–3, file "March–December 1972," box 25, DHCR.

43. Geiger interview, 90–93; Huttie, "New Federalism," 21.

44. Richard Polk quoted in Huttie, "New Federalism," 23.

45. Center for Community Change, "Revitalizing the Nation's Anti-Poverty Programs," n.d. [November/December 1976], 3, 6–7, 20, file "Anti-Poverty Program," box 5, GRSF, RG 381; John F. Adams, Vernon M. Briggs Jr., Brian Rungeling, Lewis H. Smith, and Roosevelt Steptoe, "Labor Markets in the Rural South: A Study Based on Four Rural Counties," 31 Mar. 1977, 293–96, file "Articles about and by the Secretary, Labor Markets in the Rural South: A Study Based on Four Rural Southern Counties, 1977," box 122, RM, RG 174; [Problem Analysis prepared by Human Services Study Staff], n.d. [before Apr. 1978], 1, encl. in Patricia A. Gwaltney to Grace Olivarez, memorandum, 19 Apr. 1978, file "President's Reorganization Project" (1 of 2), box 13, GRSF, RG 381.

46. Senate Committee on Agriculture and Forestry, *Rural Development Act of 1972*, ix–xii; Cunningham interview, 29; Woodrow Keown, Statement to the Subcommittee on Rural Development, United States Senate, 6 Mar. 1975, 4, file 15, box 43, FSCR.

47. Robert A. Levine to Leon Sullivan, 14 July 1967, 1, cons. with Ira Kaye, Elmer Moore, and Maurice Dawkins to Director, memorandum, 1 Aug. 1967, file "Civil Rights—thru FY 1967," box 1, IIF, RG 381; "Inventory of Actions Taken to Implement the Intent of the Recommendations of the President's Commission on Rural Poverty," section listing recommendations and agency responses, 1, cons. with W. Willard Wirtz to Orville L. Freeman, 19 June 1968, file "1968—Commission—National Advisory Commission on Rural Policy," box 581, WWW, RG 174.

48. Ross Davis (official) quoted in "Minutes of Sub-Committee Meeting on Internal Migration," 31 Jan. 1969, 4, file "1969—White House—Sub-Committee on Internal Migration," box 28, GPS, RG 174; "Internal Migration," n.d. [Mar. 1969], 8–11, cons. with Memorandum for the Record, 10 Mar. 1969, file "1969—White House—Sub-Committee on Internal Migration," box 28, GPS, RG 174; Lynn M. Daft to Albert E. Abrahams, memorandum, 21 Dec. 1970, 1–3, encl. in Wesley L. Hjornevik to Joe Maldonado, memorandum, 22 Dec. 1970, file "Office of Program Development" (2 of 3), box 8, SFDD, RG 381.

49. Delta Ministry report quoted in "City Development Controlled," *Center Light*, 26 Jan. 1973, 1, 8, file "Revenue Sharing," box 6, TCHRC.

50. John B. Mitrisin, "The Economic Adjustment Act—A Discussion and Analysis of the President's Economic Adjustment Program," 25 Feb. 1974, 25–27, 31, file 4, box 83, RBLC.

51. Elbert Jones Jr. to Executive Staff, memorandum, 12 July 1973, 1, file 19, box 38, FSCR.

52. "Background on Office of Economic Opportunity Relations with Regional Economic Development Commissions," 26 Jan. 1970, 2, encl. in Carol Khosrovi to Donald Rumsfeld, memorandum, 10 Apr. 1970, 2, file "Interagency and White House Related—Boards, Panels, Committees, Task Forces (1967–1970)" (1 of 2), box 4, SFDD, RG 381.

53. Henry Rogers to Secretary of Labor, 15 Feb. 1971, 4–6, file "Committee—Interagency Committee on Minority Business Enterprise, 1971," box 106, JDH, RG 174; "The Freeze," *The Drummer*, 2 Dec. 1971, 14–15, file 3, box 2, LBP (Pat Patterson); William E. Simon to Pete [Brennan], 26 Apr. 1973, 1, cons. with Pete [Brennan] to Simon, 10 May 1973, file "Integration, Civil Rights, Voting Rts, Negro Family, Poor People's Campaign, Viet Nam, Student Riots, Moratorium, 1973," box 80, PJB, RG 174.

54. Jeanne McFarland, "The Relationship between Minority Business Enterprise and Minority Economic Development," 8 Feb. 1978, 2–4 (quotation on p. 2), file "Interagency Council for Minority Business Enterprise Participation," box 9, GRSF, RG 381.

Chapter 6

1. Charles O. Prejean to Robert Brown, 14 Nov. 1969, 1–2, file 12, box 28, FSCR; Charles O. Prejean to Member Cooperatives, memorandum, 23 Jan. 1969, 1, file 11, box 28, FSCR.

2. Prejean interview, 1–9 (quotation on p. 7).

3. "Excerpts from the Minutes of the Board of Directors Meeting of October 11, 1969," 1, encl. in Howard Moore Jr. to Charles Collins, 11 June 1970, file 51, box 19, FSCR; FSC, *Annual Report, 1978*, 5, file 13, box 83, FSCR; Prejean interview, 14–17, 28–30 (quotation on p. 17).

4. Ruth P. Field, Morris B. Abram, and Leslie W. Dunbar to Wilbur D. Mills, 9 June 1969, 1–3, encl. in Dunbar to Charles Prejean, 9 June 1969, 1–3, file 2, box 48, FSCR; "Undermining the Foundations," *New York Times*, 14 June 1969, 32; James M. Naughton, "Foundations Gain

in Fight against Curbing Tax-Free Status," *New York Times*, 13 Oct. 1969, 28; M. A. Farber, "Foundation Tax Plan Is Attacked," *New York Times*, 21 Sept. 1969, 66; McGeorge Bundy to Ford Foundation Grantees, 31 Dec. 1969, 1–2, file 49, box 48, FSCR.

5. Charles O. Prejean to Leslie W. Dunbar, 10 July 1968, 1–2, file 9, box 28, FSCR.

6. "Background Information on Cooperative Development Financial Institution," cons. with Charles Prejean, form letter, n.d. [ca. Feb./Mar. 1969], 1–3 (quotation on p. 3), file 11, box 28, FSCR.

7. McKnight, *Whistling in the Wind*, 35–36; John Zippert to State Supervisors, Department Heads, Etc., memorandum, 1 Oct. 1971, 1–2, file 18, box 42, FSCR (loan details); "The Southern Cooperative Development Fund, Inc.," encl. in Michael Darnell to Sir/Madam, n.d., 1, file 20, box 68, FSCR (loan amounts).

8. Charles O. Prejean to Grant Revels, 22 Apr. 1968, 1, and Prejean to Jacob M. Kaplan, 29 Apr. 1968, 1 (quotation), both in file 9, box 28, FSCR; Charles O. Prejean to James Henry, 26 June 1972, 1, file 6, box 29, FSCR.

9. "Executive Director's Report on Staff Activities," FSC Annual Meeting, 19–20 Apr. 1969, 2, and "Executive Director's Report," [Apr. 1969], 2–7 (quotation on p. 7), both in file 3, box 83, FSCR.

10. Charles O. Prejean to FSC Membership, 10 June 1969, 3, file 11, box 28, FSCR; Charles O. Prejean to James Henry, 26 June 1972, 1–2, file 6, box 29, FSCR.

11. Prejean interview, 18–19; Charles O. Prejean, *Annual Report to the Board and Membership of FSC*, 1971, 1–2, file 6, box 83, FSCR; FSC, "Report to the Ford Foundation," [Oct. 1971], 9, 11–12, 25 (quotation on p. 25), encl. in Charles Prejean to Mitchell Sviridoff, 15 Oct. 1971, file 26, box 28, FSCR.

12. Charles O. Prejean to John Price, 11 Nov. 1970, 1, file 18, box 28, FSCR; Guillory interview; Daniel, *Dispossession*, 156–95; Charles O. Prejean to J. M. Kaplan, 16 Nov. 1970, 2, file 16, box 28, FSCR (quotation).

13. Charles O. Prejean, *Annual Report to the Board and Membership of FSC*, 1971, 4, 7–9 (quotation on pp. 8–9), file 6, box 83, FSCR.

14. John Zippert to Herb Calender, 8 July 1968, 1–2, file 12, box 42, FSCR.

15. Lewis Black to Rev. St. Paul Epps, 11 June 1971, 1, file 7, box 62, FSCR; Allen J. Dunn to Virginia H. Knever, 2 May 1972, 2, file 1, box 29, FSCR; FSC, *Annual Report, 1972*, 5, file 7, box 83, FSCR.

16. Allen J. Dunn to Virginia H. Knever, 2 May 1972, 1, file 1, box 29, FSCR; "Overview of FSC Membership Success in 1971–1972," 1, file 7, box 83, FSCR (quotation); Charles O. Prejean to James O. Jones, 6 July 1972, 2, file 6, box 29, FSCR (self-sufficiency); Prejean interview, 22 (white southerners see value).

17. Charles O. Prejean to Leslie W. Dunbar, 7 May 1968, 1, file 9, box 28, FSCR; Lillie Dunn Johnson to Howell Heflin, 16 Feb. 1980, 1, cons. with John Zippert to Johnson, 21 Feb. 1980, file 2, box 76, FSCR; John Perkins to Charles Prejean, 6 Apr. 1971, 1, file 23, box 19, FSCR; George M. Paris to Alfred Brooks, 2 Feb. 1973, 1, file 9, box 40, FSCR.

18. Michael Depp, "The Legacy of a Family Farm," 9 Sept. 2001, *American Profile*, http://americanprofile.com/articles/ben-burkett-family-farm-legacy/ (last modified 2015); Nic Paget-Clarke, "Interview with Ben Burkett of the National Family Farm Coalition in the U.S.," *In Motion Magazine* online, 25 May 2009, http://www.inmotionmagazine.com/global/b_burkett_int.html (last modified 2015).

19. Heather Gray, "Melbah Smith Inducted into the Cooperative Hall of Fame in May 2009," 26 May 2009, FSC/LAF website, http://www.federationsoutherncoop.com/press/pr2009/may2609.htm (last modified 26 May 2009); "Melbah Smith," [May] 2009, FSC/LAF website, http://www.federationsoutherncoop.com/press/pr2009/Melbahbio.pdf (last modified 26 May 2009). (McAfee married in 1985 and became Melbah McAfee Smith.)

20. "History from the 35th Annual Report (2002)," 1, FSC/LAF website, http://www.federationsoutherncoop.com/files%20home%20page/fschistory/fsc35hist.pdf (last modified 25 May 2015); Nic Paget-Clarke, "Interview with Ben Burkett of the National Family Farm Coalition in the U.S.," *In Motion Magazine* online, 25 May 2009, http://www.inmotionmagazine.com/global/b_burkett_int.html (last modified 2015).

21. Jerry Voorhis quoted in John Zippert to Cooperative Foundation, 20 Sept. 1972, 1, file 22, box 42, FSCR; Leslie Dunbar to Charles O. Prejean, 16 Dec. 1971, 1, file 2, box 48, FSCR; Timothy Halnon to Charles Prejean, 3 Feb. 1972, 1, file 29, box 74, FSCR; FSC, *Annual Report, 1972*, 4, 6, file 7, box 83, FSCR.

22. Charles O. Prejean to Roger Wilkins, 5 May 1970, 1, file 17, box 28, FSCR; B. P. Atterbury to Charles O. Prejean, 20 Dec. 1968, 1, file 49, box 48, FSCR; Hilary S. Feldstein to Mitchell Sviridoff, memorandum, 11 Feb. 1969, 8, cons. with Charles O. Prejean to Feldstein, 10 July 1969, file 20, box 17, FSCR.

23. Charles O. Prejean to Roger Wilkins, 5 May 1970, 2, file 17, box 28, FSCR.

24. Charles O. Prejean to McGeorge Bundy, 14 June 1971, 1–2, and Prejean to Bryant George, 1 June 1971, 1, both in file 23, box 17, FSCR; Prejean interview, 56–57.

25. Charles O. Prejean to McGeorge Bundy, 14 June 1971, 1–2 (quotation on p. 2), file 23, box 17, FSCR.

26. A. J. McKnight to Mitchell Sviridoff, 24 June 1971, 1, ibid.

27. McGeorge Bundy to [Charles] Prejean, 1 July 1971, 1, file 51, box 48, FSCR; Charles O. Prejean to Bryant George, 15 July 1971, 1, and Prejean to George, 4 Aug. 1971, 1, both in file 23, box 17, FSCR.

28. Charles O. Prejean, A. J. McKnight, and John Zippert to Individuals and Organizations Who Support the Activities of the Federation of Southern Cooperatives, memorandum, 3 Dec. 1969, 1–2, file 10, box 68, FSCR; Charles O. Prejean to Robert Brown, 14 Nov. 1969, 3, file 12, box 28, FSCR (quotation).

29. Elmer J. Moore to Joseph A. Kershaw, memorandum, 1 Mar. 1966, 1, encl. in Kershaw to Eugene P. Foley, memorandum, 12 Mar. 1966, and Kershaw to Foley, memorandum, 12 Mar. 1966, 1, both in file "Mississippi," box 6, SFES, RG 378; "Conclusion" [to Ford Foundation study, encl. in Bryant George to Charles Prejean, 24 July 1971], [1], file 51, box 48, FSCR.

30. Charles O. Prejean to Bryant George, 5 Aug. 1971, 1, file 23, box 17, FSCR; "Southern Rural Cooperative Economic Development," n.d. [1971], 1, cons. with Gene Bradford to Carol Khosrovi, memorandum, 10 Sept. 1971, file "Office of Program Development" (1 of 3), box 8, SFDD, RG 381; William H. Peace III to All Co-op Managers, memorandum, 5 Nov. 1971, 2, file 28, box 28, FSCR.

31. Charles O. Prejean to FSC Membership, 26 May 1970, 1–2, file 51, box 19, FSCR.

32. John M. Brazzel to Charles O. Prejean, 17 Aug. 1971, 1, file 53, box 61, FSCR; John Brown Jr. to William H. Peace III, 22 Oct. 1971, 2, file 43, box 22, FSCR.

33. "Southern Rural Cooperative Economic Development," n.d. [1971], 2, cons. with Gene Bradford to Carol Khosrovi, memorandum, 10 Sept. 1971, and William H. Peace III to Hubert H. Humphrey, 23 Aug. 1971, 1, encl. in Bradford to Khosrovi, memorandum, 10 Sept. 1971, both in file "Office of Program Development" (1 of 3), box 8, SFDD, RG 381.

34. Carol Khosrovi to Charles O. Prejean, 9 Nov. 1971, 1, and Phillip V. Sanchez and Carol Khosrovi to John Brown Jr., 20 Dec. 1971, 1–2, both in file 53, box 61, FSCR.

35. A. J. McKnight to Charles O. Prejean, 20 Jan. 1972, 1–2, file 13, box 68, FSCR; Charles O. Prejean to Carol Khosrovi, 22 Dec. 1971, 1, and Prejean to Phillip V. Sanchez, 22 Dec. 1971, 1, both in file 52, box 19, FSCR.

36. Charles O. Prejean to Phillip V. Sanchez, 11 Jan. 1972, 1–2, and Prejean to Carol Khosrovi, 11 Jan. 1972, 1, both cons. with Prejean to FSC Staff Members, memorandum, 11 Jan. 1972, file 3, box 29, FSCR.

37. Carol M. Khosrovi to Robert Freeman Jr., 8 June 1972, 1, file 54, box 61, FSCR; A. J. McKnight to Charles O. Prejean, 3 Apr. 1972, 1–2, file 13, box 68, FSCR.

38. Bryant George to Charles O. Prejean, 26 Apr. 1972, 1, file 52, box 48, FSCR.

39. Lewis Black to McGeorge Bundy, 22 July 1972, 1–2, file 24, box 17, FSCR; Charles O. Prejean to Bryant George, 26 Apr. 1972, 1–3 (quotation on p. 2), file 24, box 17, FSCR.

40. Mitchell Sviridoff to Charles O. Prejean, 15 June 1972, 1–2, file 52, box 48, FSCR.

41. Prejean interview, 56–57.

42. Charles O. Prejean to Mrs. J. A. Blakslee, 28 July 1972, 1, file 6, box 29, FSCR; FSC, *Annual Report, 1972*, unnumbered page titled "Gratitude," file 7, box 83, FSCR.

43. FSC, *Annual Report, 1972*, 6–7, file 7, box 83, FSCR; Charles O. Prejean to Andrew Young, 10 Apr. 1974, 2, file 11, box 29, FSCR (BDO information); Charles O. Prejean to Paul Adkins, 4 Mar. 1974, 1, file 10, box 29, FSCR.

44. "Tennessee-Tombigbee Inland Waterway Project," news release, 15 July 1959, 1, file "Tennessee-Tombigbee Waterway 1959," box 67, TGAP; Pat Broocks-Ross, "Tenn-Tom: Water-Borne Potential," *Mainstream Mississippi*, Winter 1982–83, 5, file 2, box 1, DCC.

45. "A Statement to the President of the United States by Tennessee-Tombigbee Waterway Development Authority in Support of a Budget Allocation to Allow Construction of the Tennessee-Tombigbee Waterway," Nov. 1967, 3–4, cons. with "Joint Statement to the President of the United States by Members of the United States Senate and House Representatives in Support of a Budget Allocation to Allow Construction of the Tennessee-Tombigbee Waterway," Nov. 1967, file 4, box 120, PBJFP (quotation); "Why Tennessee-Tombigbee Now," [1967], 1, file 4, box 120, PBJFP; Pat Broocks-Ross, "Tenn-Tom: Water-Borne Potential," *Mainstream Mississippi*, Winter 1982–83, 5, file 2, box 1, DCC.

46. John Zippert to James O. James, memorandum, 16 Nov. 1973, 1–2, file 5, box 43, FSCR.

47. Lamond Godwin quoted in Donna Myhre, "Notes on First Peoples Conference on the Tennessee-Tombigbee Waterway," 19 Jan. 1974, 3, file "Tennessee-Tombigbee Waterway," box 6, TCHRC; MPC, "Report of the Committee Goals and Objectives," cons. with Wendell Paris to Members, memorandum, 19 Mar. 1974, 1–4, file "Tennessee-Tombigbee Waterway," box 6, TCHRC.

48. Anthony Griggs, "How Blacks Lost 9,000,000 Acres of Land," *Ebony*, Oct. 1974, 98, 102 (quotation); Wolfgang Saxon, "Robert S. Browne, 79, Dies; Economist and Advocate," *New York Times* online, 15 Aug. 2004, http://www.nytimes.com/2004/08/15/

us/robert-s-browne-79-dies-economist-and-advocate.html (last modified 2015); MPC, Minutes of Meeting, 31 Aug. 1974, 2–3, cons. with Wendell Paris to Council Members, memorandum, 18 Sept. 1974, file "Tennessee-Tombigbee Waterway," box 6, TCHRC; FSC, *Annual Report, 1974–75*, 37, file 10, box 83, FSCR.

49. Wendell Paris to Committee Members, memorandum, 17 May 1974, file "Tennessee-Tombigbee Waterway," box 6, TCHRC; MPC, Minutes of Meeting, 31 Aug. 1974, 3, cons. with Wendell Paris to Council Members, memorandum, 18 Sept. 1974, ibid.; FSC, *Annual Report, 1974–75*, 36–37, file 10, box 83, FSCR; "Training Men for a Better Life," *Ebony*, Dec. 1973, 94–100 (quotation on p. 100).

50. "Stennis Hosts Meeting on Area-Wide Affirmative Action Plan," *MPC TTW Newsletter*, Oct. 1975, 1, file "Tennessee-Tombigbee Waterway," box 6, TCHRC; MPC, Minutes of Meeting, 26 Apr. 1975, 1, ibid.

51. "Stennis Hosts Meeting on Area-Wide Affirmative Action Plan," *MPC TTW Newsletter*, Oct. 1975, 1, 3, file "Tennessee-Tombigbee Waterway," box 6, TCHRC; Lamond Godwin to Bryant George, Robert Schrank, Ernest Osbourne, Tom Wahman, and Hugh Burroughs, memorandum, 20 Sept. 1976, 1–2, encl. in John Zippert to Charles Prejean, memorandum, 4 Oct. 1976, file 2, box 30, FSCR; "Management Report to FSC Membership," n.d. [1976], [10], file 11, box 83, FSCR.

52. Pat Broocks-Ross, "Tenn-Tom: Water-Borne Potential," *Mainstream Mississippi*, Winter 1982–83, 8, file 2, box 1, DCC; Wilbur O. Colom to Franklin Thomas, 5 Oct. 1983, cons. with Franklin A. Thomas to Pearl G. Long, 20 Oct. 1983, file 53, box 48, FSCR ("important voice" quotation); FSC, *Annual Report, 1984–85*, 28, file 20, box 83, FSCR (MPC contribution recognized).

53. Lamond Godwin to Bryant George, Robert Schrank, Ernest Osbourne, Tom Wahman, and Hugh Burroughs, memorandum, 20 Sept. 1976, 2, encl. in John Zippert to Charles Prejean, memorandum, 4 Oct. 1976, file 2, box 30, FSCR; John Zippert to Ernest Green, 8 Aug. 1975, 1–2, file 22, box 15, FSCR (TTW training project); Charles O. Prejean to Jack Ravan, 16 July 1976, 1, file 5, box 30, FSCR.

54. Ramon E. Tyson Jr. to Reginald L. Dunn, 30 Dec. 1974, 1–2, file 16, box 31, FSCR.

55. Charles O. Prejean to Parren Mitchell, 7 May 1975, 1–2, file 21, box 29, FSCR.

56. [Fred Romero to Ray Marshall, memorandum, 6 Feb. 1977], 2–4, file "Memo 2/6/77 to the Secretary from Fred Romero regarding meeting with Farmworker Representatives," box 84, RM, RG 174.

57. Marshall interview, 1–3, 21–22, 39, 51, 55; Gordon Cavanaugh to National Office Staff, State Directors, District Directors, and County Supervisors, memorandum, 18 Sept. 1978, 1–2, encl. in Karl S. Wright to Extension Specialists, memorandum, 3 Nov. 1978, file 27, box 22, FSCR.

58. Robert C. Altman quoted in FSC, *Annual Report, 1978*, 7, file 13, box 83, FSCR; Charles O. Prejean to Mitchell Sviridoff, 13 Mar. 1979, 1, file 26, box 17, FSCR.

59. Charles O. Prejean to Robert Smith, 7 Mar. 1978, 2, file 18, box 15, FSCR (CSA grant); John Zippert to William McKinley Branch, 4 May 1978, 1, file 57, box 17, FSCR (CETA project); John Zippert to Freddie Washington, 14 Oct. 1977, 1, file 17, box 15, FSCR (VISTA volunteers); Charles O. Prejean to Leslie Dunbar, 9 Aug. 1978, 1, file 10, box 30, FSCR (total federal funding).

60. Cunningham interview, 17, 30.

61. FSC, *Annual Report, 1972,* 11, file 7, box 83, FSCR; Harold Turner to Alex Armendaris, 27 Dec. 1974, 1, and Adell Williams to Armendaris, 31 Dec. 1974, 1, both cons. with Ramon E. Tyson Jr. to Reginald L. Dunn, 30 Dec. 1974, file 16, box 31, FSCR.

62. Gordon Crowe to Gene Sally, 7 Feb. 1969, 1, file 51, box 19, FSCR.

63. Charles O. Prejean to John Price, 23 Apr. 1971, 1, file 23, box 28, FSCR.

64. Charles O. Prejean to Thomas K. Goines, 6 Dec. 1971, 2, file 27, box 28, FSCR.

65. Frank Cook and Annie B. Williams to James F. Neville, 8 Feb. 1973, 1–2, file 26, box 22, FSCR; John Zippert to Supporters of PLBA, memorandum, 16 Apr. 1973, 1–3, file 8, box 62, FSCR; Frank L. Cook to Gordon Cavanaugh, 17 Jan. 1980, 1–2, file 9, box 62, FSCR; John Zippert to Art Collings, 4 Feb. 1981, 1, file 2, box 46, FSCR.

66. Charles O. Prejean to Larry Tyner, 20 Jan. 1977, 2, file 6, box 30, FSCR; Bethell, *Sumter County Blues,* 9, 12–13 (John Neel quoted on p. 9).

67. Bethell, *Sumter County Blues,* 12–14 (*Home Record* quoted on p. 12); John Zippert to Michael Darnell, 1 Nov. 1979, 1–2, file 4, box 10, FSCR.

68. Wilbur O. Colom to Thad Cochran, 21 Jan. 1980, 1, file 1, box 76, FSCR.

69. Charles O. Prejean to Friends, 31 Jan. 1980, 1–2, file 1, box 76, FSCR.

70. Bethell, *Sumter County Blues,* 15.

71. FSC, *Annual Report, 1980–81,* 6, file 16, box 83, FSCR; Charles O. Prejean to Vernon Jordan, 4 Dec. 1980, 1, file 14, box 30, FSCR; Bethell, *Sumter County Blues,* 16; FSC, *Annual Report, 1980–81,* 6, file 16, box 83, FSCR.

72. Charles O. Prejean to Carl Holman, 5 Aug. 1980, 1, file 4, box 76, FSCR.

73. Leslie W. Dunbar, Tom Wahman, George Patterson, Elridge McMillan, David Ramage, Diane Leslie, and Patricia Hewitt to Benjamin Civiletti, 25 Mar. 1980, 1, file 3, box 76, FSCR; Howard Moore Jr. to J. R. Brooks, 9 Jan. 1981, 1, 5–6, file 6, box 76, FSCR.

74. John Paul Dalsimer to Howard Moore Jr., 2 Feb. 1981, 1–3, and John Paul Dalsimer to Howard Moore Jr., 2 Feb. 1981 (private note), 1, cons. with Dalsimer to Moore and Others, 2 Feb. 1981, both in file 15, box 30, FSCR.

75. Charles Prejean and Leslie Dunbar quoted in Bethell, *Sumter County Blues,* 16; J. R. Brooks to Howard Moore [Jr.], 20 May 1981, 1, encl. in Moore to Charles Prejean, 27 May 1981, file 7, box 76, FSCR.

Chapter 7

1. Untitled, CSA news release 78-17, n.d. [1978], 1, file "Press Releases, 1978," box 1, PR, RG 381.

2. Berman, *America's Right Turn,* 21–22; Bernard Sloan quoted in Dorothy Gilliam, "Is Recession Society Mean toward Poor?," *Washington Post,* 13 Sept. 1980, C1.

3. Charles Evers, "When Elected Officers Must Be Trained First," *Washington Sunday Star,* 30 Nov. 1969, D2; Wilbert C. Russell and Cleveland Gilcrease to Joseph Aragon, 4 Feb. 1977, 13, file "National Center for Community Action," box 10, GRSF, RG 381; Gilliam, "Is Recession Society Mean toward Poor?," *Washington Post,* 13 Sept. 1980, C1.

4. "Attention: Inflation, Budget Cuts, and the Rural Poor," *Rural Coalition Update,* Mar. 1980, 3, and "Review: The Carter Administration's Small Community and Rural Development Policy," *Rural Coalition Update,* July 1980, 2, both in file "Rural Coalition," box 14, GRSF, RG 381.

5. Governor's Office of Human Resources, "Annual Report, State Office of Economic Opportunity," 1973, 5, file "Miss. Governor's Office of Human Resources," box 12, DHCR;

"Mississippi Children," *Council Newsletter*, June 1977, 3, and "Ten Years Later," *Council Newsletter*, May 1977, 1–2, both in file "Mississippi Council on Human Relations—Newsletters, 1975–1978," box 9, TCHRC.

6. Robert Bamberg quoted in "The Seven Fat Years of Red," *Alabama Magazine*, July 1978, 2, file "22-B Alabama Development Office 1978," box 1, series 82-2, WFNP; William L. Chaze, "After 15 Years of 'Great Society' Spending," *U.S. News and World Report*, 30 June 1980, 36; William Raspberry, "What Would We Do without Poverty?," *Washington Post*, 11 July 1980, A13.

7. Paul Delaney, "Black Supporters of President under Fire," *New York Times*, 17 Oct. 1972, 29; "McKissick Calls on Blacks to Join Two-Party Politics," *New York Times*, 10 Aug. 1972, 25; Howell Raines, "Reagan Suggests Ban on Soviet Trade," *New York Times*, 23 Oct. 1980, B12 (Evers's endorsement of Reagan); "Evers and the IRS," *Newsweek*, 26 Aug. 1971, 21–22; "Will This Man Be Mississippi's Next Senator?," *People*, 25 Sept. 1978, 32–34; George Goodman, "Mayor Evers Visits College Here Named for Brother," *New York Times*, 13 May 1973, 51 (quotation). For some analysis of Evers's political philosophy and the controversial role he played in the freedom movement, see Crosby, *A Little Taste of Freedom*, 189–223.

8. Edsall, *Chain Reaction*, 137–39; 189; Thurber, *Republicans and Race*, 261; Ronald Reagan, "A Time for Choosing," national television address, 27 Oct. 1964, in Balitzer, *A Time for Choosing*, 43, 46.

9. Ronald Reagan, "Government and the Family," national television address, 6 July 1976, in Balitzer, *A Time for Choosing*, 169, 171; George Wallace quoted in Sokol, *There Goes My Everything*, 252; O'Reilly, *Nixon's Piano*, 350, 357 (Klan endorsement); Editorial, "New Hope for America," *Citizen*, Dec. 1980, 2. For more on the ways Reagan manipulated white voters' racial resentments, see Klinkner, *Unsteady March*, 300–305, and Marable, *Crisis of Color*, 134–36.

10. Ronald Reagan quoted in O'Reilly, *Nixon's Piano*, 359; Marable, *Crisis of Color*, 135; Sloan, *Reagan Effect*, 104–18.

11. Sloan, *Reagan Effect*, 139; Robert Pear, "U.S. Welfare Plan to Require Check on Family Assets," *New York Times*, 4 Sept. 1981, A1, A7 (public assistance); Edsall, *Chain Reaction*, 192 (food and nutrition); Sara Rosenbaum, "Administration 'Testament' to Children's Poverty," Letter to the Editor, *New York Times*, 25 Feb. 1984, 22 (Medicaid).

12. Commission on Civil Rights, *Civil Rights*, 77–81, 83–88, 90–93, 101–2; Aaron E. Henry to Delegates, *Program, 36th Annual Convention, Mississippi State Conference NAACP*, 5–7 Nov. 1981, 4, file 2, box 4, CDP; Charles O. Prejean to Frederic Walls, 2 July 1981, 2, file 17, box 30, FSCR.

13. "Statement of Alabama Department of Pensions and Security on the Administration's Public Assistance Policies," n.d. [Aug. 1983], 2, 4, cons. with Bill Nichols to Leon Frazier, 1 Sept. 1983, file "22Q Pensions and Security," box 5, series 89-10, WFNP.

14. Charles Austin, "U.S. Budget Cuts Strain Church Aid Programs," *New York Times*, 2 Jan. 1982, 1 (quotation), 9; David Shribman, "Death Comes to a Federal Agency," *New York Times*, 19 Sept. 1981, 7.

15. Department of Labor, "Information Sheet: National Rural Development Strategy," 1, encl. in Raymond J. Donovan to John R. Block, 8 Sept. 1982, and Donovan to Block, 8 Sept. 1982, 1, both in file "Rural Development," box 125, RJD, RG 174; Gerald Hambleton to Russell B. Long, 21 Apr. 1983, 1–2, file 18, box 471, RBLC.

16. Southern Growth Policies Board, *Halfway Home*, 7.

17. Colclough, "Uneven Development," 73, 84; George Howard (Industrial Development director) quoted in Commission on Civil Rights, *Fifteen Years Ago*, 14.

18. Eckes, "The South and Economic Globalization," 55–57; Southern Growth Policies Board, *Halfway Home*, 7–8, 23; Friedman, "'Trail of Ghost Towns,'" 43 (Schwinn and Boeing examples); William Harrison to Bill Nichols, 9 Apr. 1984, 4, cons. with Nichols to Harrison, 15 May 1984, file "2-B Economic Development Administration," box 12, series 89-10, WFNP; William E. Schmidt, "Rural Southern Towns Find Manufacturing Boom Fading," *New York Times*, 21 Mar. 1985, A1, A20 (quotation).

19. Speech by William F. Winter in The Mississippi River Delta: Its People, Its Problems, Its Potential, proceedings of a symposium sponsored by the East Arkansas Higher Education Economic Development Consortium, 24 Oct. 1988, 14, unfoldered, box 4, LMDDCF; Lower Mississippi Delta Development Commission, *Body of the Nation*, 12.

20. George Paris and John Zippert, "State Coordinators Meeting Summary," 16 Mar. 1981, 1, encl. in Paris and Zippert to FSC State Coordinators, memorandum, 17 Mar. 1981, file 16, box 30, FSCR; George Paris to Alabama CETA Title VI Employees, 15 Apr. 1981, 1, file 32, box 15, FSCR.

21. John Zippert to Robert L. Paterson, 27 Apr. 1981, 1–2, file 4, box 15, FSCR; John Zippert to Karl N. Stanber, 23 Dec. 1981, 1–2, file 5, box 46, FSCR.

22. FSC, *Annual Report, 1980–81*, 6–8, 10–11, 13 (quotation on p. 8), file 16, box 83, FSCR.

23. John Zippert to Karl N. Stanber, 23 Dec. 1981, 2, file 5, box 46, FSCR; FSC, *Annual Report, 1980–81*, 8, file 16, box 83, FSCR; Charles O. Prejean to Franklin Thomas, 23 Sept. 1983, 2–3, file 21, box 30, FSCR; J. D. Brown to John Hatch, 5 Feb. 1986, file 254, box 12, JWHP; [Ezra Cunningham] to Henry Sanders and SWAFCA Board Members, 9 Aug. 1986, 1–2, encl. in Ezra Cunningham to SWAFCA Board Members, 1 Aug. 1986, file 9, box 35, FSCR.

24. Melbah McAfee to John Zippert, 19 July 1982, 1–2, file 28, box 21, FSCR; Bill Peace to Joseph Brooks, Charles Prejean, and A. T. [A. J.] McKnight, 1 Mar. 1979, 2–5, file 11, box 30, FSCR.

25. Karl S. Wright to Julius Robinson, 8 Apr. 1980, 1, file 4, box 16, FSCR; FSC, *Annual Report, 1981–82*, 6, file 17, box 83, FSCR; John Zippert to Janet Michaud, 13 July 1983, 2, file 20, box 30, FSCR.

26. John Zippert and Jerry Pennick to Joe Brooks and Charles O. Prejean, memorandum, 9 Nov. 1981, 1–3, file 36, box 13, FSCR; FSC, *Annual Report, 1984–85*, 21, file 20, box 83, FSCR; "Federation/LAF History from the 25th Annual Report (1992)," 15–16, Federation of Southern Cooperatives/Land Assistance Fund website, http://www.federationsoutherncoop .com/fschistory/FSC25hist.pdf (last modified 8 Apr. 2015); John Zippert to Jack Litzenberg, 8 Nov. 1985, 1, file 3, box 47, FSCR.

27. FSC, *Annual Report, 1984–85*, 13–14, file 20, box 83, FSCR; FSC/LAF, *Annual Report, 1990–91*, 2, 12, 14–16, file 3, box 84, FSCR.

28. FSC, *Annual Report, 1984–85*, 30, file 20, box 83, FSCR; FSC/LAF, *Annual Report, 1990–91*, 4, 15, 17 (quotation), file 3, box 84, FSCR.

29. FSC, *Annual Report, 1984–85*, 21–23, file 20, box 83, FSCR; C. Scott Graber, "A Blight Hits Black Farmers," *Nation*, 11 Mar. 1978, 269–72.

30. Richard Porter, "The Emergency Land Fund," *40 Acres and a Mule*, Dec. 1979, 2, file "Black Community, 1979," box 1, series 5, DRBC; Ralph Paige quoted in FSC/LAF, *Annual Report, 1990–91*, 28, file 3, box 84, FSCR.

31. FSC, *Annual Report, 1984–85*, 21–23, file 20, box 83, FSCR; FSC/LAF, *Annual Report, 1990–91*, 25, file 3, box 84, FSCR; FSC/LAF, *Annual Report, 1987–88*, 46, file 23, box 83, FSCR (land losses reduced).

32. FSC, *Annual Report, 1984–85*, 24–25, file 20, box 83, FSCR.

33. FSC/LAF, *Annual Report, 1990–91*, 26–27, file 3, box 84, FSCR.

34. FSC, *Annual Report, 1984–85*, 29, file 20, box 83, FSCR.

35. FSC/LAF, *Annual Report, 1987–88*, 4, 35, file 23, box 83, FSCR; FSC/LAF, *Annual Report, 1990–91*, 33, file 3, box 84, FSCR.

36. "Letter of Intent, Targeted Jobs Demonstration Program for Greene County and Selected Adjoining Areas in Pickens County, Alabama Impacted by the Tennessee-Tombigbee Waterway," n.d. [July 1979], 1, encl. in John Zippert to Jack Dickinson, 2 July 1979, file 18, box 15, FSCR; Charles O. Prejean to Franklin Thomas, 10 Feb. 1984, 2, file 26, box 17, FSCR.

37. Charles O. Prejean to Franklin Thomas, 23 Sept. 1983, 2, file 21, box 30, FSCR; FSC, *Annual Report, 1984–85*, 26, file 20, box 83, FSCR; FSC/LAF, *Annual Report, 1987–88*, 31, file 23, box 83, FSCR.

38. FSC/LAF, *Annual Report, 1990–91*, 1, file 3, box 84, FSCR.

39. FSC, *Annual Report, 1984–85*, 7–10, file 20, box 83, FSCR; FSC/LAF, *Annual Report, 1990–91*, 1, file 3, box 84, FSCR (quotation); Aiken, *Cotton Plantation South*, 327–39; Austin, *Transformation of Plantation Politics*, 61–94.

40. Newman, *Divine Agitators*, 216; Lower Mississippi Delta Development Commission, *Body of the Nation*, 1, Appendixes, ii, xxxiv.

41. LMDDC Public Hearing, Human Services Section, Monroe, Louisiana, 24 Jan. 1990, 79–80, 84, file 45, box 2, LMDDCF ("world of despair" quotation p. 79; Joseph George quotation p. 84).

42. LMDDC Public Hearing, Education Section, Monroe, Louisiana, 24 Jan. 1990, 58–61 (quotation on pp. 59–60), file 44, box 2, LMDDCF.

43. LMDDC Mississippi Public Hearing, Itta Bena, Mississippi, 28 Nov. 1989, 118–20 (quotation on p. 120), unfoldered, box 4, LMDDCF.

44. LMDDC Public Hearing, Economic Development Section, Monroe, Louisiana, 24 Jan. 1990, 2–3, file 46, box 2, LMDDCF.

45. Ibid., 89–90.

46. LMDDC Public Hearing, Education Section, Monroe, Louisiana, 24 Jan. 1990, 64–71, 75, file 44, box 2, LMDDCF.

47. Ibid., 69.

48. LMDDC Agriculture/Environmental Hearings, Baton Rouge, Louisiana, 23 Jan. 1990, 5–6, 11, file 4, box 1, LMDDCF (quotations); Guillory interview.

49. LMDDC Mississippi Public Hearing, Itta Bena, Mississippi, 28 Nov. 1989, 72–77, unfoldered, box 4, LMDDCF.

50. LMDDC Hearing, Baton Rouge, Louisiana, 23 Jan. 1990, 5 (Arnold Lincove), 115–20 (Dewitt Jones, quotation on p. 119), file 21, box 1, LMDDCF.

51. LMDDC Agriculture/Environmental Hearings, Baton Rouge, Louisiana, 23 Jan. 1990, 8, file 4, box 1, LMDDCF (Webb Franklin); LMDDC Hearing, Baton Rouge, 23 Jan. 1990, 123–24, file 21, box 1, LMDDCF (tax incentives).

52. LMDDC Agriculture/Environmental Hearings, Baton Rouge, Louisiana, 23 Jan. 1990, 11–14, file 4, box 1, LMDDCF; LMDDC Public Hearing, Education Section, Monroe,

Louisiana, 24 Jan. 1990, 70–73, file 44, box 2, LMDDCF; LMDDC Mississippi Public Hearing, Itta Bena, Mississippi, 28 Nov. 1989, 11–15 (quotation on p. 15), unfoldered, box 4, LMDDCF.

53. Lower Mississippi Delta Development Commission, *Delta Initiatives*, 4 ("Handbook for Action" quotation), 24–25 (health care), 34 (Head Start), 75, 77, 121 (small farms and economic development).

54. Newman, *Divine Agitators*, 216; Joan I. Duffy, "Center to Help Delta Sinks into Poverty," *Memphis Commercial Appeal*, 29 July 1991, A1 ("little interest" quotation); L. G. Brooks quoted in Christopher Sullivan, "Plan Has Brought Only Hope to the Delta," *Baton Rouge Advocate*, 7 July 1991, 14A.

55. James W. Brosnan, "Clinton Owes Delta Two Things: Apology, and Help," *Memphis Commercial Appeal*, 4 July 1999, B5; Roland Klose, "Bluer Blues," *Memphis Commercial Appeal*, 8 Nov. 2009, V1.

56. Eckes, "The South and Economic Globalization," 56–60.

57. Chris Frink and Steven Ward, "Lake Providence 'Dwindling Away,'" *Baton Rouge Advocate*, 25 Aug. 2002, 10A.

58. Klose, "Bluer Blues," *Memphis Commercial Appeal*, 8 Nov. 2009, V1.

Chapter 8

1. Department of Labor, *Economic Adjustment and Worker Dislocation*, 123, 134–37 (Appendix B, pp. 8, 19–22, tables 6 and 7); Sassen, *Global City*, 200 (New York); High, *Industrial Sunset*, 115 (Detroit), 122 (steel mill closings); O'Hara, "Envisioning the Steel City," 229 (U.S. Steel).

2. Stiglitz, *Globalization and Its Discontents*, 10–12; Schaeffer, *Understanding Globalization*, 53–57, 68–72, 217–50; Sassen, *Global City*, 2–15; Krippner, *Capitalizing on Crisis*, 27–57.

3. Krippner, *Capitalizing on Crisis*, 30–33 (figs. 1 and 3); Bluestone, Foreword, xii.

4. Bluestone and Harrison, *Deindustrialization of America*, 9.

5. Larry Koker, Sharon Harmon, and Gary resident quoted in O'Hara, "Envisioning the Steel City," 229–30; Russo and Linkon, "Collateral Damage," 202 (Youngstown).

6. Bruce Springsteen, "My Hometown," *Born in the USA* (Columbia Records, 1984).

7. Margaret McPherson to John Sparkman, 31 Mar. 1965, 1, cons. with Eleanor Ballentine to Sparkman, 3 Apr. 1965, file "Robo Civil Rights," box 9, 1963–64 series, JJSSP; F. E. Lucius and W. C. Butler to John C. Stennis, 1 Dec. 1967, 1, file 3, box 2, series 29, JCSC; Janet Williams to George W. Andrews, 4 Feb. 1970, cons. with Andrews to Mr. and Mrs. Walter Chesser, 12 Feb. 1970, file "Correspondence, February 10–12, 1970," box 51, GWAP.

8. Young Johnston to John Sparkman, 26 May 1966, 1, cons. with Sparkman to Johnston, 4 June 1966, file "Civil Rights—Discrimination," box 1, 1966–67 series, JJSSP; "Statement of Frank W. Grigsby, President, Louisiana Realtors Association," n.d. [ca. 1966], 1, and L. Heidel Brown to Russell B. Long, 19 July 1966, 1, both in file 47, box 97, RBLC.

9. For analyses of the origins and impact of affirmative action policies, see Davies, *From Opportunity to Entitlement*; Skrentny, *Ironies of Affirmative Action*; Anderson, *Pursuit of Fairness*; MacLean, *Freedom Is Not Enough*; and Yuill, *Richard Nixon and the Rise of Affirmative Action*.

10. John L. Edgar to Russell B. Long, 13 Dec. 1971, 1, file 36, box 136, RBLC; Arthur James Elliott to John Sparkman, 6 Sept. 1972, 1, cons. with Stephen C. Blakeslee Jr. to Sparkman,

9 Nov. 1972, file "Civil Rights," box 6, 1972 series, JJSSP; Martin P. Broderick Jr. to John R. Rarick, 22 May 1972, 1, file 31, box 146, RBLC.

11. Mrs. Enos Cormier to Senator [Russell] Long, 8 Sept. 1969, 1, file 27, box 115, RBLC; Mr. and Mrs. A. E. Huckabay to Russell B. Long, 2 Nov. 1971, 1–2, file 1, box 135, RBLC; Leroy J. Cooper to Senator [Russell] Long, 10 Dec. 1974, 1, file 21, box 164, RBLC.

12. For a helpful overview of racial discrimination in federal programs, see Katznelson, *When Affirmative Action Was White*.

13. Bureau of the Census, *Statistical Abstract: 1980*, 407 (table 682) (unemployment rates), 451 (table 745) (incomes), 465 (table 773) (poverty rates).

14. Hillson, *Battle of Boston*, 13, 29, 35–36, 54; Dewey Burton quoted in Cowie, *Stayin' Alive*, 4.

15. Iver Peterson, "Parents of Whites Believe Homes Are at Stake," *New York Times*, 22 Oct. 1972, 95 (Ralph Vitol quotation). For more on the ways that racism permeated housing policies and home valuation practices, see Jackson, *Crabgrass Frontier*, 195–218; Massey and Denton, *American Apartheid*, 26–59; and Freund, "Marketing the Free Market."

16. Louis Harris, "The 'Backlash' Issue," *Newsweek*, 13 July 1964, 25; Jack Rosenthal, "Angry Ethnic Voices Decry a 'Racist and Dullard' Image," *New York Times*, 17 June 1970, 49; National Confederation of American Ethnic Groups, *'72 Convention Report*, [June 1972], 1–4 (quotations on pp. 2 and 4), file "PI-6-3-6, 1972," box 240, JDH, RG 174.

17. Jack Rosenthal, "U.S. Urged to Aid Blue-Collar Man," *New York Times*, 30 June 1970, 1, 20; Rosow, "Problem of the Blue Collar Worker," 2–4, 8, 11–13 (quotation on p. 8); Jack Rosenthal, "U.S. Aide Asks Blue-Collar Gains," *New York Times*, 30 Oct. 1970, 69.

18. Cowie, *Stayin' Alive*, 133–34, 146–51, 220–27; Stein, *Pivotal Decade*, 111–17, 219–20, 227–37.

19. Richard Nixon quoted in Cowie, *Stayin' Alive*, 124.

20. Cowie, *Stayin' Alive*, 97; Frank Lynn, "Many Unions in the State Expected to Support Nixon," *New York Times*, 21 July 1972, 18; Tom Wicker, "Maybe the Voters Are Overlooking Some Things," *New York Times*, 5 Nov. 1972, E15; Paul Delaney, "Nixon Held Likely to Drop Program of Minority Jobs," *New York Times*, 4 Sept. 1972, 1, 16.

21. Jack Rosenthal, "The 'Secret' Key Issue," *New York Times*, 6 Nov. 1972, 47; Louis Harris, "Two Ethnic Groups Indicate Shift from Dem. Column in '72," Harris Survey news release, 12 Oct. 1972, 1, The Harris Poll online archive, http://media.theharrispoll.com/documents/Harris-Interactive-Poll-Research-TWO-ETHNIC-GROUPS-INDICATE-SHIFT-FROM-DEM-COLUMN-IN-72-1972-10.pdf (last modified 2015).

22. "Presidential General Election, All States, 1972 Summary," *CQ Voting and Elections Collection* (Website), Washington, D.C.: CQ Press, 2003, retrieved from http://library.cqpress.com.unr.idm.oclc.org/elections/avg1972–1us1 (last modified 2015); Thurber, *Republicans and Race*, 358.

23. Richard Nixon quoted in Kenneth W. Munden, "The Office of Economic Opportunity in the Nixon Administration," unpublished manuscript, 1973, 369, unfoldered, box 107, HOEO, RG 381; Scammon and Wattenberg, *Real Majority*, 20–22, 37–40, 207–9 (quotation on p. 207); Thurber, *Republicans and Race*, 345.

24. Carter, *Public Papers, 1978*, bk. 1, 91, 93.

25. Stein, *Pivotal Decade*, 158–59, 200–204; Edsall, *Chain Reaction*, 18, 130–31.

26. "'Welfare Queen' Becomes Issue in Reagan Campaign," *New York Times*, 15 Feb. 1976, 51; Jon Nordheimer, "Reagan Is Picking His Florida Spots," *New York Times*, 5 Feb. 1976, 29;

Ronald Reagan, "Rebuilding a Prosperous America," speech to the American Trucking Association Board of Directors, 16 Oct. 1974, in Balitzer, *Time for Choosing*, 154–56.

27. Douglas E. Kneeland, "Reagan Campaigns at Mississippi Fair," *New York Times*, 4 Aug. 1980, A11; Crespino, *In Search of Another Country*, 1.

28. O'Reilly, *Nixon's Piano*, 357, 377; Crespino, *In Search of Another Country*, 1; John Herbers, "Cracks in No-Longer-Solid South Could Cause a Carter Defeat in Close Election," *New York Times*, 16 Oct. 1980, B8; Wyman, Review of *The Two-Party South*, 30–31.

29. Steven V. Roberts, "Blue-Collar Democrats Slipping to Reagan," *New York Times*, 20 Apr. 1980, 30.

30. Greenberg Research Inc., *Democratic Defection*, 13–22 (quotation on pp. 14 and 16).

31. Stein, *Pivotal Decade*, 267; "Statement of Alabama Department of Pensions and Security on the Administration's Public Assistance Policies," n.d. [August 1983], 3, cons. with Bill Nichols to Leon Frazier, 1 Sept. 1983, file "22Q Pensions and Security," box 5, series 89-10, WFNP; Cowie, *Stayin' Alive*, 17 (Dewey Burton first quotation), 311 (Dewey Burton second quotation), 362–63.

32. Phillips-Fein, *Invisible Hands*, 264–65.

33. *Congressional Record*, 104th Cong., 2nd sess., 1996, 142, no. 53—Daily Edition: H3705 (Tom DeLay), and no. 73—Daily Edition: H5386 (John Duncan Jr.); *Congressional Record*, 105th Cong., 1st sess., 1997, 160, no. 160—Daily Edition: E2363–64 (Philip Crane).

34. Todd S. Purdum, "Clinton Recalls His Promise, Weighs History, and Decides," *New York Times*, 1 Aug. 1996, A1, A22; *Congressional Record*, 104th Cong., 2nd sess., 1996, 142, no. 124—Daily Edition: H11220 (Roger Wicker); Jim McCrery quoted in Celia W. Dugger, "Displaced by the Welfare Wars," *New York Times*, 26 Feb. 1995, E1.

35. William Julius Wilson, "Work: Work Work," *New York Times Sunday Magazine*, 18 Aug. 1996, 27–31, 40, 48, 52–54 (quotation on p. 30).

36. *Congressional Record*, 104th Cong., 1st sess., 1995, 141, no. 54—Daily Edition: H3723–27 (quotation on H3724).

37. R. W. Apple Jr., "Poll Shows Disenchantment with Politicians and Politics," *New York Times*, 12 Aug. 1995, 1, 8; Editorial, "The Quality of Mercy in 1995," *New York Times*, 1 Jan. 1995, E8; Russell Baker, "Those Vital Paupers," Observer, *New York Times*, 17 Jan. 1995, A19.

38. Todd S. Purdum, "Clinton Recalls His Promise, Weighs History, and Decides," *New York Times*, 1 Aug. 1996, A1; Peter T. Kilborn and Sam Howe Verhovek, "Clinton's Welfare Shift Ends Tortuous Journey," *New York Times*, 2 Aug. 1996, A1, A18, A19; Robert Pear, "Overhauling Welfare: A Look at the Year Ahead," *New York Times*, 7 Aug. 1996, A8; Mink and Solinger, "1990–2002," 536.

39. Peter T. Kilborn and Sam Howe Verhovek, "Clinton's Welfare Shift Ends Tortuous Journey," *New York Times*, 2 Aug. 1996, A1, A18, A19 (quotations on pp. A19 and A18). For scholarly analyses of the ambiguous impacts of welfare reform, see Marchevsky and Theoharis, *Not Working*, and Brush, "Impacts of Welfare Reform."

40. Stiglitz, *Freefall*, 1–26; ACORN Fair Housing, *Impending Rate Shock*, 3–5; Keeley and Love, *From Crisis to Recovery*, 18–28; Goodman and Mance, "Employment Loss and the 2007–09 Recession," 3, 5.

41. Opening Statement of Carolyn B. Maloney, in *Challenge of Creating Jobs*, 1–2; Bureau of Labor Statistics, *BLS Spotlight on Statistics: The Recession of 2007–2009*, Feb. 2012, 2, http://

www.bls.gov/spotlight/2012/recession/pdf/recession_bls_spotlight.pdf (last modified Feb. 2012); Public Broadcasting Service, *NewsNite*, 26 Nov. 2010, http://video.pbs.org/video/1661498782/ (last modified 2015); Jason DeParle, "Hunger in U.S. at a 14-Year High," *New York Times* online, 16 Nov. 2009, http://www.nytimes.com/2009/11/17/us/17-hunger.html (last modified 2009); Anna Shoup, "USDA: 1 in 7 U.S. Households Struggle for Food," *PBS NewsHour*, 17 Nov. 2009, http://www.pbs.org/newshour/updates/health-july-dec09-hungerreport_11-17/ (last modified 2015) (quotation).

42. "Renewing America's Promise," 2008 Democratic Party Platform, 25 Aug. 2008, The American Presidency Project website, http://www.presidency.ucsb.edu/ws/?pid=78283 (last modified 2015); Opening Statement of Kevin Brady, in *Challenge of Creating Jobs*, 3; Thomas B. Edsall, "The War on Entitlements," *New York Times* online, 6 Mar. 2013, http://opinionator.blogs.nytimes.com/2013/03/06/the-war-on-entitlements/ (last modified 2015).

43. Jim Rutenberg and Jackie Calmes, "False 'Death Panel' Rumor Has Some Familiar Roots," *New York Times* online, 13 Aug. 2009, http://www.nytimes.com/2009/08/14/health/policy/14panel.html (last modified 2009); Brian Montopoli, "S.C. Lt. Gov. Andre Bauer Compares Helping Poor to Feeding Stray Animals," *CBS News*, 25 Jan. 2010, CBSNews.com, http://www.cbsnews.com/news/sc-lt-gov-andre-bauer-compares-helping-poor-to-feeding-stray-animals/ (last modified 2015); "Fox News Reporting: The Great Food Stamp Binge," The Daily Bret Blog, 8 Aug. 2013, http://www.foxnews.com/on-air/special-report-bret-baier/blog/category/food+stamps/ (last modified 24 June 2015); "What Not to Buy," *The Daily Show*, 4 Mar. 2014, http://thedailyshow.cc.com/videos/elvsf4/what-not-to-buy (last modified 2014); Rush Limbaugh, "Trouble Brews on Sharpton Show," 22 July 2009, transcript, http://www.rushlimbaugh.com/daily/2009/07/22/trouble_brews_on_sharpton_show (last modified 2015). For more examples and analysis of the racist attacks on the Obama administration, see McCamey and Murty, "A Paradigm Shift in Political Tolerance," and Fishman, "Racial Attacks on President Obama."

Conclusion

1. Maria Newman, "Beard Foundation Presents Leadership Awards," *New York Times* online, 17 July 2014, http://www.nytimes.com/2014/07/17/dining/beard-foundation-presents-leadership-awards.html (last modified 2015); Food and Agriculture Organization of the United Nations, *2014 International Year of Family Farming*, 1.

2. See, for example, Schaeffer, *Understanding Globalization*, 153–90; Global Campaign for Agrarian Reform, *Working Document*, 4–9; Lyson, *Civic Agriculture*, 2–7, 30–83; and Merrett and Walzer, *Cooperatives and Local Development*.

3. Ben Burkett quoted in "And the 2015 Winners Are . . . ," 2 Sept. 2015, U.S. Food Sovereignty Alliance website, http://usfoodsovereigntyalliance.org (last modified 30 Sept. 2015).

4. Maria Newman, "Beard Foundation Presents Leadership Awards," *New York Times* online, 17 July 2014, http://www.nytimes.com/2014/07/17/dining/beard-foundation-presents-leadership-awards.html (last modified 2015); Nic Paget-Clarke, "Interview with Ben Burkett of the National Family Farm Coalition in the U.S.," *In Motion Magazine* online, 25 May 2009, http://www.inmotionmagazine.com/global/b_burkett_int.html (last modified 2015); Wendell Paris, Speech to Staff Meeting of FSC/LAF, video recording, 2009, https://www.youtube.com/watch?v=22rSvRAGQq8#t=63 (last modified 2014).

BIBLIOGRAPHY

Manuscript Collections

Auburn, Ala.

    Special Collections and Archives Department, Draughon Library, Auburn University

        Alabama Farm Bureau Federation Records

        George W. Andrews Papers

        William F. Nichols Papers

Baton Rouge, La.

    Hill Memorial Library, Louisiana State University

        Russell B. Long Collection

    T. Harry Williams Center for Oral History, Louisiana State University

        Civil Rights Series

Chapel Hill, N.C.

    Southern Historical Collection, Wilson Library, University of North Carolina

        Delta Health Center Records

        John W. Hatch Papers

Cleveland, Miss.

    Charles W. Capps Jr. Archives and Museum, Delta State University

        Delta Council Collection

        James Hand Jr. Papers

        Lower Mississippi Delta Development Commission Files

        Walter Sillers Jr. Papers

Hattiesburg, Miss.

    McCain Library and Archives, University of Southern Mississippi

        Victoria Gray Adams Papers

        Charles Davis Papers

        Paul B. Johnson Family Papers

Madison, Wisc.

    Wisconsin Historical Society

        Lee Bankhead Papers

        Congress of Racial Equality Records, 1941–1967

        Freedom Information Service Records

        Mississippi Freedom Democratic Party Records, 1962–1971. Microfilm.

        Papers of the Scholarship, Education and Defense Fund for Racial Equality

        John Zippert Papers

New Orleans, La.

    Amistad Research Center, Tulane University

        Records of the Federation of Southern Cooperatives

    Tulane University Special Collections

        William Walter Jones Collection of the Papers of Sam Houston Jones, 1939–1973

Oxford, Miss.

    Archives and Special Collections, University of Mississippi

        Thomas G. Abernethy Papers

        Marjorie Baroni Collection

Sleepy Hollow, N.Y.

    Rockefeller Archives Center

        Rockefeller Brothers Fund Archives

Starkville, Miss.

    Congressional and Political Research Center, Mississippi State University Libraries

        David R. Bowen Collection

        John C. Stennis Collection

    Special Collections Department, Mississippi State University Libraries

        Hodding Carter III Papers

        Allen Eugene Cox Collection

        Delta Ministry Papers

        Tombigbee Council on Human Relations Collection

Tuscaloosa, Ala.

    Special Collections, Hoole Library, University of Alabama

        Alabama Collection

        John J. Sparkman Senate Papers

Washington, D.C.

    National Archives

        General Records of the Department of Labor, Record Group 174

        Records of the Community Services Administration, Record Group 381

        Records of the Economic Development Administration, Record Group 378

        Records of the Equal Employment Opportunity Commission, Record Group 403

        Records of the Office of the Secretary of Agriculture, Record Group 16

Microform Collections

Papers of the Congress of Racial Equality, 1941–1967. Sanford, N.C.: Microfilming Corporation of America, 1980. Microfilm.

Interviews

Brown, John H., Jr. Interview by Robert Korstad. Transcript, 14 May 1992. Southern Rural Poverty Collection, DeWitt Wallace Center for Media and Democracy, Duke University, Durham, N.C. http://dewitt.sanford.duke.edu/rutherfurd-living-history/southern-rural-poverty-collection.

Cunningham, Ezra. Interview by Susan Youngblood. Transcript, 7 May 1992. Copy in author's possession.

Dorsey, L. C. Interview by Robert Korstad and Neil Boothby. Transcript, 22 April 1992. Southern Rural Poverty Collection, DeWitt Wallace Center for Media and Democracy, Duke University, Durham, N.C. http://dewitt.sanford.duke.edu/rutherfurd-living-history/southern-rural-poverty-collection.

Dunbar, Leslie W. Interview by Robert Korstad and Neil Boothby. Transcript, 5 February 1992. Southern Rural Poverty Collection, DeWitt Wallace Center for Media and

Democracy, Duke University, Durham, N.C. http://dewitt.sanford.duke.edu/
rutherfurd-living-history/southern-rural-poverty-collection.

Geiger, H. Jack. Interview by Robert Korstad. Transcript, 22 April 1992. Southern
Rural Poverty Collection, DeWitt Wallace Center for Media and Democracy, Duke
University, Durham, N.C. http://dewitt.sanford.duke.edu/rutherfurd-living-history/
southern-rural-poverty-collection.

Guillory, Wilbert. Interview by author. Tape recording, 25 June 1998. Civil Rights Series,
T. Harry Williams Center for Oral History, Louisiana State University, Baton Rouge.

Hatch, John W. Interview by Robert Korstad and Neil Boothby. Transcript, 23 April
1992. Southern Rural Poverty Collection, DeWitt Wallace Center for Media and
Democracy, Duke University, Durham, N.C. http://dewitt.sanford.duke.edu/
rutherfurd-living-history/southern-rural-poverty-collection.

Marshall, F. Ray. Interview by Robert Korstad. Transcript, n.d. [1992 or 1993]. Southern
Rural Poverty Collection, DeWitt Wallace Center for Media and Democracy, Duke
University, Durham, N.C. http://dewitt.sanford.duke.edu/rutherfurd-living-history/
southern-rural-poverty-collection.

Prejean, Charles. Interview by Robert Korstad. Transcript, n.d. [1992 or 1993]. Southern
Rural Poverty Collection, DeWitt Wallace Center for Media and Democracy, Duke
University, Durham, N.C. http://dewitt.sanford.duke.edu/rutherfurd-living-history/
southern-rural-poverty-collection.

Williams, Irene. Interview by John Hatch. Tape recording, 18 July 1992. Delta Health Center
Records, Southern Historical Collection, Wilson Library, University of North Carolina,
Chapel Hill.

Zippert, John. Interview by author. Tape recording, 28 June 1998. Civil Rights
Series, T. Harry Williams Center for Oral History, Louisiana State University,
Baton Rouge.

Newspapers and Periodicals

Alabama Council Bulletin

Baltimore Sun

Baton Rouge Advocate

Bolivar County Democrat

Business Week

Citizen

Commonweal

Crisis

Delta Council News

Delta Democrat-Times

Ebony

Fortune

Greene County Democrat

Houston Post

Jackson Clarion-Ledger

Jackson Daily News

Louisiana Weekly

Madison County Herald

Memphis Commercial Appeal

Milwaukee Sentinel

Minneapolis Tribune

Mississippi Freelance

Montgomery Advertiser

Nation

Newark Sunday News

Newsweek

New York Times

People

Pittsburgh Post-Gazette

Rural Advance

Southern Patriot

Southwest Louisiana Register

U.S. News and World Report

Vicksburg Citizens' Appeal

Village Voice

The Voice

Wall Street Journal

Washington Post

Washington Sunday Star

Government Documents

Bureau of the Census. *Census of Agriculture: 1959.* Vol. 1, *Counties.* Pt. 32, *Alabama.* Pt. 33,
Mississippi. Pt. 35, *Louisiana.* Washington, D.C.: GPO, 1961.

———. *Census of the Population: 1950.* Vol. 2, *Characteristics of the Population.* Pt. 2,
　Alabama. Pt. 18, *Louisiana.* Pt. 24, *Mississippi.* Washington, D.C.: GPO, 1952.

———. *Census of the Population: 1960.* Vol. 1, *Characteristics of the Population.* Pt. 2,
　Alabama. Pt. 20, *Louisiana.* Pt. 26, *Mississippi.* Washington, D.C.: GPO, 1963.

———. *Census of the Population: 1970.* Vol. 1, *Characteristics of the Population.* Pt. 2,
　Alabama. Pt. 20, *Louisiana.* Pt. 26, *Mississippi.* Washington, D.C.: GPO, 1973.

———. *Census of the Population: 1980.* Vol. 1, *Characteristics of the Population.* Pt. 26,
　Mississippi. Washington, D.C.: GPO, 1982.

———. *Fifteenth Census of the United States, Population: 1930.* Vol. 3, *Reports by States.* Pt. 1,
　Alabama–Missouri. Washington, D.C.: GPO, 1932.

———. *Fifteenth Census of the United States, Agriculture: 1930.* Vol. 2, *Reports by States.* Pt. 2,
　The Southern States. Washington, D.C.: GPO, 1932.

———. *Historical Statistics of the United States, Colonial Times to 1970.* Washington, D.C.:
　GPO, 1975.

———. *Statistical Abstract of the United States: 1960. 1970. 1980.* Washington, D.C.: GPO,
　1960–80.

Carter, Jimmy. *Public Papers of the Presidents of the United States: Jimmy Carter, 1978.* Bk. 1,
　January 1 to June 30, 1978. Washington, D.C.: GPO, 1979.

*The Challenge of Creating Jobs in the Aftermath of "The Great Recession": Hearing before
　the Joint Economic Committee, Congress of the United States.* 111th Cong., 1st sess., 10
　December 2009. Washington, D.C.: GPO, 2010.

Commission on Civil Rights. *Civil Rights: A National, Not a Special Interest.* Washington, D.C.:
　GPO, 1981.

———. *Cycle to Nowhere.* Clearinghouse Publication No. 14. Washington, D.C.: GPO, 1968.

———. *The Decline of Black Farming in America.* Washington, D.C.: GPO, 1982.

———. *Equal Opportunity in Farm Programs: An Appraisal of Services Rendered by Agencies of
　the United States Department of Agriculture.* Washington, D.C.: GPO, 1965.

———. *Fifteen Years Ago . . . Rural Alabama Revisited.* Washington, D.C.: GPO, 1983.

Comptroller General of the United States. *Review of Economic Opportunity Programs: Report
　to the Congress of the United States.* Washington, D.C.: GPO, 1969.

Congressional Record. Washington, D.C.: GPO, 1873–.

Department of Health, Education, and Welfare. *A Constructive Public Welfare Program.*
　Washington, D.C.: GPO, 1965.

Department of Labor. *Economic Adjustment and Worker Dislocation in a Competitive Society.*
　Washington, D.C.: [GPO], December 1986.

*Hunger and Malnutrition in America: Hearings before the Subcommittee on Employment,
　Manpower, and Poverty of the Senate Committee on Labor and Public Welfare.* 90th Cong.,
　1st sess., 11–12 July 1967. Washington, D.C.: GPO, 1967.

Johnson, Lyndon B. *Public Papers of the Presidents of the United States: Lyndon B. Johnson,
　1963–64.* Bk. 1, *November 22, 1963, to June 30, 1964.* Washington, D.C.: GPO, 1965.

———. *Public Papers of the Presidents of the United States: Lyndon B. Johnson, 1965.* Bk. 2,
　June 1 to December 31, 1965. Washington, D.C.: GPO, 1966.

Lower Mississippi Delta Development Commission. *Body of the Nation: The Interim Report of
　the Lower Mississippi Delta Development Commission.* 16 October 1989. Memphis, Tenn.:
　Lower Mississippi Delta Development Commission, 1989.

————. *The Delta Initiatives: Realizing the Dream . . . Fulfilling the Potential.* 14 May 1990. Memphis, Tenn.: Lower Mississippi Delta Development Commission, 1990.

Office of Economic Opportunity. *As the Seed Is Sown.* 4th Annual Report of the Office of Economic Opportunity. [Washington, D.C.: GPO], 1968.

President's National Advisory Committee on Rural Poverty. *The People Left Behind.* Washington, D.C.: GPO, 1967.

Senate Committee on Agriculture and Forestry. *The Rural Development Act of 1972: Analysis and Explanation.* 92nd Cong., 2nd sess., 3 October 1972. Washington, D.C.: GPO, 1972.

Southern Growth Policies Board. *Halfway Home and a Long Way to Go: The Report of the 1986 Commission on the Future of the South.* Research Triangle Park, N.C.: Southern Growth Policies Board, 1986.

Books and Articles

ACORN Fair Housing. *The Impending Rate Shock: A Study of Home Mortgages in 130 American Cities.* Washington, D.C.: Association of Community Organizations for Reform Now, 2006.

Aiken, Charles S. *The Cotton Plantation South since the Civil War.* Baltimore: Johns Hopkins University Press, 1998.

Anderson, Terry H. *The Pursuit of Fairness: A History of Affirmative Action.* New York: Oxford University Press, 2004.

Andrews, Kenneth T. "Social Movements and Policy Implementation: The Mississippi Civil Rights Movement and the War on Poverty, 1965 to 1971." *American Sociological Review* 66 (Feb. 2001): 71–95.

Arundell, Ronald M. "Welfare Rights as Organizing Vehicle." In *The Mississippi Experience: Strategies for Welfare Rights Action,* edited by Paul A. Kurzman, 84–101. New York: Association Press, 1971.

Asch, Chris Myers. *The Senator and the Sharecropper: The Freedom Struggles of James O. Eastland and Fannie Lou Hamer.* Chapel Hill: University of North Carolina Press, 2008.

Ashmore, Susan Youngblood. *Carry It On: The War on Poverty and the Civil Rights Movement in Alabama, 1964–1972.* Athens: University of Georgia Press, 2008.

Austin, Sharon D. Wright. *The Transformation of Plantation Politics: Black Politics, Concentrated Poverty, and Social Capital in the Mississippi Delta.* Albany: State University of New York Press, 2006.

Bailey, Martha J., and Sheldon Danziger, eds. *Legacies of the War on Poverty.* New York: Russell Sage Foundation, 2013.

Balitzer, Alfred, ed. *A Time for Choosing: The Speeches of Ronald Reagan, 1961–1982.* Chicago: Regnery Gateway, 1983.

Berman, William C. *America's Right Turn: From Nixon to Clinton.* 2nd ed. Baltimore: Johns Hopkins University Press, 1998.

Bethell, Thomas N. *Sumter County Blues: The Ordeal of the Federation of Southern Cooperatives.* Washington, D.C.: National Committee in Support of Community Based Organizations, 1982.

Black, Herbert. *People and Plows against Hunger: Self-Help Experiment in a Rural Community.* Boston, Mass.: Marlborough House, 1975.

Bluestone, Barry. Foreword to *Beyond the Ruins: The Meanings of Deindustrialization*, edited by Jefferson Cowie and Joseph Heathcott, vii–xiii. Ithaca, N.Y.: ILR Press of Cornell University Press, 2003.

Bluestone, Barry, and Bennett Harrison. *The Deindustrialization of America: Plant Closings, Community Abandonment, and the Dismantling of Basic Industry*. New York: Basic Books, 1982.

Bobo, Lawrence, James R. Kluegel, and Ryan A. Smith. "Laissez-Faire Racism: The Crystallization of a Kinder, Gentler, Antiblack Ideology." In *Racial Attitudes in the 1990s: Continuity and Change*, edited by Steven A. Tuch and Jack K. Martin, 15–42. Westport, Conn.: Praeger, 1997.

Bonilla-Silva, Eduardo. *Racism without Racists: Color-Blind Racism and the Persistence of Racial Inequality in the United States*. 2nd ed. Lanham, Md.: Rowman and Littlefield, 2006.

Bonnen, James T. "The Distribution of Benefits from Selected U.S. Farm Programs." In *Rural Poverty in the United States: A Report by the President's National Advisory Commission on Rural Poverty*, edited by C. E. Bishop and George L. Wilbur, 461–505. Washington, D.C.: GPO, 1968.

Brush, Lisa D. "Impacts of Welfare Reform." *Race, Gender and Class* 10 (July 2003): 173–192.

Carson, Clayborne. *In Struggle: SNCC and the Black Awakening of the 1960s*. Cambridge, Mass.: Harvard University Press, 1981.

Carter, Dan T. *The Politics of Rage: George Wallace, the Origins of the New Conservatism, and the Transformation of American Politics*. Baton Rouge: Louisiana State University Press, 1995.

Carter, David C. *The Music Has Gone Out of the Movement: Civil Rights and the Johnson Administration, 1965–1968*. Chapel Hill: University of North Carolina Press, 2009.

Cascio, Elizabeth, and Sarah Reber. "The K–12 Education Battle." In *Legacies of the War on Poverty*, edited by Martha J. Bailey and Sheldon Danziger, 66–92. New York: Russell Sage Foundation, 2013.

Cazenave, Noel A. *Impossible Democracy: The Unlikely Success of the War on Poverty Community Action Programs*. Albany: State University of New York Press, 2007.

Citizens' Board of Inquiry into Hunger and Malnutrition in the United States. *Hunger, U.S.A.* Boston: Beacon Press, 1968.

Clark, Robert F. *The War on Poverty: History, Selected Programs and Ongoing Impact*. Lanham, Md.: University Press of America, 2002.

Clayson, William S. *Freedom Is Not Enough: The War on Poverty and the Civil Rights Movement in Texas*. Austin: University of Texas Press, 2010.

Cobb, James C. *The Selling of the South: The Southern Crusade for Industrial Development, 1936–1990*. 2nd ed. Urbana: University of Illinois Press, 1993.

———. "'Somebody Done Nailed Us on the Cross': Federal Farm and Welfare Policy and the Civil Rights Movement in the Mississippi Delta." *Journal of American History* 77 (Dec. 1990): 912–36.

Cohen, William. *At Freedom's Edge: Black Mobility and the Southern White Quest for Racial Control, 1861–1915*. Baton Rouge: Louisiana State University Press, 1991.

Colclough, Glenna. "Uneven Development and Racial Composition in the Deep South: 1970–1980." *Rural Sociology* 53 (Spring 1988): 73–86.

Cowie, Jefferson. *Stayin' Alive: The 1970s and the Last Days of the Working Class*. New York: New Press, 2010.

Cowie, Jefferson, and Joseph Heathcott, eds. *Beyond the Ruins: The Meanings of Deindustrialization*. Ithaca, N.Y.: ILR Press of Cornell University Press, 2003.

Cowling, Ellis, and J. P. Warbasse. *Co-Operatives in America: Their Past, Present and Future*. New York: Coward-McCann, 1938.

Crespino, Joseph. *In Search of Another Country: Mississippi and the Conservative Counterrevolution*. Princeton, N.J.: Princeton University Press, 2006.

Crosby, Emilye. *A Little Taste of Freedom: The Black Freedom Struggle in Claiborne County, Mississippi*. Chapel Hill: University of North Carolina Press, 2005.

Daniel, Pete. *Breaking the Land: The Transformation of Cotton, Tobacco, and Rice Cultures since 1880*. Urbana: University of Illinois Press, 1985.

———. *Dispossession: Discrimination against African American Farmers in the Age of Civil Rights*. Chapel Hill: University of North Carolina Press, 2013.

———. *The Shadow of Slavery: Peonage in the South, 1901–1969*. Illini Books ed. Urbana: University of Illinois Press, 1990.

Danielson, Chris. *After Freedom Summer: How Race Realigned Mississippi Politics, 1965–1986*. Gainesville: University Press of Florida, 2011.

Davies, Gareth. *From Opportunity to Entitlement: The Transformation and Decline of Great Society Liberalism*. Lawrence: University Press of Kansas, 1996.

de Jong, Greta. *A Different Day: African American Struggles for Justice in Rural Louisiana, 1900–1970*. Chapel Hill: University of North Carolina Press, 2002.

———. "From Votes to Vegetables: Civil Rights Activism and the Low-Income Cooperative Movement in Louisiana after 1965." In *Louisiana beyond Black and White: New Interpretations of Twentieth-Century Race and Race Relations*, edited by Michael S. Martin, 145–61. Lafayette: University of Louisiana at Lafayette Press, 2011.

———. *Invisible Enemy: The African American Freedom Struggle after 1965*. Malden, Mass.: Wiley-Blackwell, 2010.

———. "Plantation Politics: The Tufts-Delta Health Center and Intraracial Class Conflict in Mississippi, 1965–1972." In *The War on Poverty: A New Grassroots History, 1964–1980*, edited by Annelise Orleck and Lisa Gayle Hazirjian, 256–79. Athens: University of Georgia Press, 2011.

———. "The Scholarship, Education and Defense Fund for Racial Equality and the African American Organizing Tradition in the Era of Black Power." *Journal of Contemporary History* 48 (July 2013): 597–616.

———. "Staying in Place: Black Migration, the Civil Rights Movement, and the War on Poverty in the Rural South." *Journal of African American History* 90 (Fall 2005): 387–409.

Dittmer, John. *Local People: The Struggle for Civil Rights in Mississippi*. Urbana: University of Illinois Press, 1994.

Du Bois, W. E. Burghardt. *Black Reconstruction in America: An Essay toward a History of the Part Which Black Folk Played in the Attempt to Reconstruct Democracy in America, 1860–1880*. New York: Russell and Russell, 1935.

Eckes, Alfred E. "The South and Economic Globalization, 1950 to the Future." In *Globalization and the American South*, edited by James C. Cobb and William Stueck, 36–65. Athens: University of Georgia Press, 2005.

Edsall, Thomas Byrne, with Mary D. Edsall. *Chain Reaction: The Impact of Race, Rights, and Taxes on American Politics*. New York: W. W. Norton and Company, 1992.

Eskew, Glenn T. *But for Birmingham: The Local and National Movements in the Civil Rights Struggle*. Chapel Hill: University of North Carolina Press, 1997.

Esposito, James L. "Evaluating the Displaced-Worker/Job-Tenure Supplement to the CPS: An Illustration of Multimethod Quality Assessment Research." Paper presented at the Conference of the Federal Committee on Statistical Methodology, 1999. http://www.bls.gov/osmr/abstract/st/st990070.htm (last modified 19 July 2008).

Fairclough, Adam. *Race and Democracy: The Civil Rights Struggle in Louisiana, 1915–1972*. Athens: University of Georgia Press, 1995.

Fields, Barbara Jeanne. *Slavery and Freedom on the Middle Ground: Maryland during the Nineteenth Century*. New Haven, Conn.: Yale University Press, 1985.

Fishman, Darwin. "Racial Attacks on President Obama and the White Nationalist Legacy." *Western Journal of Black Studies* 37 (Winter 2013): 236–48.

Fleming, Cynthia Griggs. *In the Shadow of Selma: The Continuing Struggle for Civil Rights in the Rural South*. Lanham, Md.: Rowman and Littlefield, 2004.

Foner, Eric. *Nothing but Freedom: Emancipation and Its Legacy*. Baton Rouge: Louisiana State University Press, 1983.

Food and Agriculture Organization of the United Nations. *2014 International Year of Family Farming*. Rome, Italy: Food and Agriculture Organization of the United Nations, 2014. http://www.fao.org/3/a-as281e.pdf.

Frady, Marshall. *Wallace*. New York: World Publishing, 1968.

Freund, David M. P. "Marketing the Free Market: State Intervention and the Politics of Prosperity in Metropolitan America." In *The New Suburban History*, edited by Kevin M. Kruse and Thomas J. Sugrue, 11–32. Chicago: University of Chicago Press, 2006.

Friedman, Tami J. "'A Trail of Ghost Towns across Our Land': The Decline of Manufacturing in Yonkers, New York." In *Beyond the Ruins: The Meanings of Deindustrialization*, edited by Jefferson Cowie and Joseph Heathcott, 19–43. Ithaca, N.Y.: ILR Press of Cornell University Press, 2003.

Geiger, H. Jack. "A Life in Social Medicine." In *The Doctor-Activist: Physicians Fighting for Social Change*, edited by Ellen L. Bassuk with assistance from Rebecca W. Carman, 11–27. New York: Plenum Press, 1996.

———. "Community Control—or Community Conflict?" In *Neighborhood Health Centers*, edited by Robert M. Hollister, Bernard M. Kramer, and Seymour S. Bellin, 133–42. Lexington, Mass.: Lexington Books, 1974.

Germany, Kent B. "Poverty Wars in the Louisiana Delta: White Resistance, Black Power, and the Poorest Place in America." In *The War on Poverty: A New Grassroots History, 1964–1980*, edited by Annelise Orleck and Lisa Gayle Hazirjian, 231–55. Athens: University of Georgia Press, 2011.

Global Campaign for Agrarian Reform. *Working Document: Commentary on Land and Rural Development Policies of the World Bank*. N.p.: Global Campaign for Agrarian Reform, n.d. [ca. 2003]. http://viacampesina.net/downloads/PDF/Global_Campain_WB_policies_factsheet.en.pdf.

Goodman, Christopher J., and Steven M. Mance. "Employment Loss and the 2007–09 Recession: An Overview." *Monthly Labor Review*, April 2011, 3–12. http://www.bls.gov/opub/mlr/2011/04/art1full.pdf.

Gordon, Linda. *Pitied but Not Entitled: Single Mothers and the History of Welfare, 1890–1935*. New York: Free Press, 1994.

Greenberg Research Inc. *Democratic Defection: A Report*. Washington, D.C.: Greenberg Research, 1985. Copy provided by Bentley Historical Library, University of Michigan.

Grossman, James R. *Land of Hope: Chicago, Black Southerners, and the Great Migration*. Chicago: University of Chicago Press, 1989.

Guyot, Lawrence, and Mike Thelwell. "Toward Independent Political Power." *Freedomways* 6 (Summer 1966): 246–55.

Hamlin, Françoise N. *Crossroads at Clarksdale: The Black Freedom Struggle in the Mississippi Delta after World War II*. Chapel Hill: University of North Carolina Press, 2012.

Hatch, John. "Community Shares in Policy Decisions for Rural Health Center." *Hospitals* 43 (1 July 1969): 109–12.

Heinicke, Craig, and Wayne A. Grove. "'Machinery Has Completely Taken Over': The Diffusion of the Mechanical Cotton Picker, 1949–1964." *Journal of Interdisciplinary History* 39 (Summer 2008): 65–96.

High, Steven. *Industrial Sunset: The Making of North America's Rust Belt, 1969–1984*. Toronto: University of Toronto Press, 2003.

Hillson, Jon. *The Battle of Boston*. New York: Pathfinder Press, 1977.

Hosek, James R. *The AFDC-Unemployed Fathers Program and Welfare Reform*. Santa Monica: Rand, 1979.

Howell, Leon. *Freedom City: The Substance of Things Hoped For*. Richmond, Va.: John Knox Press, 1969.

Huttie, Joseph J., Jr. "New Federalism and the Death of a Dream in Mound Bayou, Mississippi." *New South* 28 (Fall 1973): 20–29.

Jackson, Kenneth L. *Crabgrass Frontier: The Suburbanization of the United States*. New York: Oxford University Press, 1985.

Jeffries, Hasan Kwame. *Bloody Lowndes: Civil Rights and Black Power in Alabama's Black Belt*. New York: New York University Press, 2009.

Jordan, Amy. "Fighting for the Child Development Group of Mississippi: Poor People, Local Politics, and the Complicated Legacy of Head Start." In *The War on Poverty: A New Grassroots History, 1964–1980*, edited by Annelise Orleck and Lisa Gayle Hazirjian, 280–307. Athens: University of Georgia Press, 2011.

Katz, Michael B. *The Undeserving Poor: From the War on Poverty to the War on Welfare*. New York: Pantheon Books, 1989.

Katznelson, Ira. *When Affirmative Action Was White: An Untold History of Racial Inequality in Twentieth-Century America*. New York: W. W. Norton, 2005.

Keeley, Brian, and Patrick Love. *From Crisis to Recovery: The Causes, Course and Consequences of the Great Recession*. Paris, France: OECD Publishing, 2010. http://www.oecd.org/insights/46156144.pdf.

Kelly, Cynthia. "Health Care in the Mississippi Delta." *American Journal of Nursing* 69 (April 1969): 758–63.

Kirby, Jack Temple. *Rural Worlds Lost: The American South, 1920–1960*. Baton Rouge: Louisiana State University Press, 1987.

Klinkner, Philip A., with Rogers M. Smith. *The Unsteady March: The Rise and Decline of Racial Equality in America*. Chicago: University of Chicago Press, 1999.

Korstad, Robert R., and James L. Leloudis. *To Right These Wrongs: The North Carolina Fund and the Battle to End Poverty and Inequality in 1960s America*. Chapel Hill: University of North Carolina Press, 2010.

Krippner, Greta R. *Capitalizing on Crisis: The Political Origins of the Rise of Finance*. Cambridge, Mass.: Harvard University Press, 2011.

Kruse, Kevin M. *White Flight: Atlanta and the Making of Modern Conservatism*. Princeton, N.J.: Princeton University Press, 2005.

Lassiter, Matthew D. *The Silent Majority: Suburban Politics in the Sunbelt South*. Princeton, N.J.: Princeton University Press, 2006.

Levine, Robert A. *The Poor Ye Need Not Have with You: Lessons from the War on Poverty*. Cambridge, Mass.: MIT Press, 1970.

Litwack, Leon F. *Trouble in Mind: Black Southerners in the Age of Jim Crow*. New York: Alfred A. Knopf, 1998.

Lyson, Thomas A. *Civic Agriculture: Reconnecting Farm, Food, and Community*. Medford, Mass.: Tufts University Press, 2004.

MacLean, Nancy. *Freedom Is Not Enough: The Opening of the American Workplace*. New York: Russell Sage Foundation, 2006.

Mandle, Jay R. *The Roots of Black Poverty: The Southern Plantation Economy after the Civil War*. Durham, N.C.: Duke University Press, 1978.

Marable, Manning. *The Crisis of Color and Democracy: Essays on Race, Class, and Power*. Monroe, Maine: Common Courage Press, 1992.

Marchevsky, Alejandra, and Jeanne Theoharis. *Not Working: Latina Immigrants, Low-Wage Jobs, and the Failure of Welfare Reform*. New York: New York University Press, 2006.

Massey, Douglas S., and Nancy A. Denton. *American Apartheid: Segregation and the Making of the Underclass*. Cambridge, Mass.: Harvard University Press, 1993.

McCamey, Jimmy D., Jr., and Komanduri S. Murty. "A Paradigm Shift in Political Tolerance since President Obama Was Elected." *Race, Gender and Class* 20 (2013): 80–97.

McKee, Guian A. "'This Government Is with Us': Lyndon Johnson and the Grassroots War on Poverty." In *The War on Poverty: A New Grassroots History, 1964–1980*, edited by Annelise Orleck and Lisa Gayle Hazirjian, 31–62. Athens: University of Georgia Press, 2011.

McKnight, A. J. *Whistling in the Wind: The Autobiography of the Rev. A. J. McKnight*. Edited by Ronnie M. Moore. Opelousas, La.: Southern Development Foundation, 1994.

McMillen, Neil R. *Dark Journey: Black Mississippians in the Age of Jim Crow*. Urbana: University of Illinois Press, 1989.

Meier, August, and Elliott Rudwick. *CORE: A Study in the Civil Rights Movement, 1942–1968*. New York: Oxford University Press, 1973.

Merrett, Christopher D., and Norman Walzer, eds. *Cooperatives and Local Development: Theory and Applications for the 21st Century*. Armonk, N.Y.: M. E. Sharpe, 2004.

Miller, Russell E. *Light on the Hill*. Vol. 2, *A History of Tufts University since 1952*. Cambridge, Mass.: MassMarket Books, 1986.

Minchin, Timothy J. *Hiring the Black Worker: The Racial Integration of the Southern Textile Industry, 1960–1980*. Chapel Hill: University of North Carolina Press, 1999.

Minchin, Timothy J., and John A. Salmond. *After the Dream: Black and White Southerners since 1965*. Lexington: University Press of Kentucky, 2011.

Mink, Gwendolyn, and Rickie Solinger. "1990–2002." In *Welfare: A Documentary History of U.S. Policy and Politics*, edited by Gwendolyn Mink and Rickie Solinger, 535–37. New York: New York University Press, 2003.

Moye, J. Todd. *Let the People Decide: Black Freedom and White Resistance in Sunflower County, Mississippi, 1945–1986*. Chapel Hill: University of North Carolina Press, 2004.

Moynihan, Daniel P. *Maximum Feasible Misunderstanding: Community Action in the War on Poverty*. New York: Free Press, 1969.

Nash, Jere, and Andy Taggart. *Mississippi Politics: The Struggle for Power, 1976–2006*. Jackson: University Press of Mississippi, 2006.

National Education Association, Commission on Professional Rights and Responsibilities. *Wilcox County, Alabama: A Study of Social, Economic, and Educational Bankruptcy*. Washington, D.C.: National Education Association, 1967.

Nelson, Jennifer. "'Hold Your Head Up and Stick Out Your Chin': Community Health and Women's Health in Mound Bayou, Mississippi." *NWSA Journal* 17 (Spring 2005): 99–118.

Nembhard, Jessica Gordon. *Collective Courage: A History of African American Cooperative Economic Thought and Practice*. University Park: Pennsylvania State University Press, 2014.

Neubeck, Kenneth J., and Noel A. Cazenave. *Welfare Racism: Playing the Race Card against America's Poor*. New York: Routledge, 2001.

Newman, Mark. *Divine Agitators: The Delta Ministry and Civil Rights in Mississippi*. Athens: University of Georgia Press, 2004.

Novak, Robert D. *The Agony of the G.O.P. 1964*. New York: Macmillan, 1965.

O'Hara, S. Paul. "Envisioning the Steel City: The Legend and Legacy of Gary, Indiana." In *Beyond the Ruins: The Meanings of Deindustrialization*, edited by Jefferson Cowie and Joseph Heathcott, 219–36. Ithaca, N.Y.: ILR Press of Cornell University Press, 2003.

O'Reilly, Kenneth. *Nixon's Piano: Presidents and Racial Politics from Washington to Clinton*. New York: Free Press, 1995.

Orleck, Annelise. *Storming Caesars Palace: How Black Mothers Fought Their Own War on Poverty*. Boston: Beacon Press, 2005.

Orleck, Annelise, and Lisa Gayle Hazirjian, eds. *The War on Poverty: A New Grassroots History, 1964–1980*. Athens: University of Georgia Press, 2011.

Ortiz, Paul. *Emancipation Betrayed: The Hidden History of Black Organizing and White Violence in Florida from Reconstruction to the Bloody Election of 1920*. Berkeley: University of California Press, 2005.

Payne, Charles M. *I've Got the Light of Freedom: The Organizing Tradition and the Mississippi Freedom Struggle*. Berkeley: University of California Press, 1995.

Peake, Thomas R. *Keeping the Dream Alive: A History of the Southern Christian Leadership Conference from King to the Nineteen-Eighties*. New York: Peter Lang, 1987.

Phillips-Fein, Kim. *Invisible Hands: The Businessmen's Crusade against the New Deal*. New York: W. W. Norton, 2009.

Phillips, Kevin P. *The Emerging Republican Majority*. New Rochelle, N.Y.: Arlington House, 1969.

Quadagno, Jill. *The Color of Welfare: How Racism Undermined the War on Poverty*. New York: Oxford University Press, 1994.

"Republican Platform 1968." In *National Party Platforms, 1840–1972*, compiled by Donald Bruce Johnson and Kirk H. Porter, 748–63. Urbana: University of Illinois Press, 1973.

Rosow, Jerome M. "The Problem of the Blue Collar Worker: Memorandum for the Secretary." N.d. [1970]. Copy provided by the University of Illinois at Urbana-Champaign Library.

Russo, John, and Sherry Lee Linkon. "Collateral Damage: Deindustrialization and the Uses of Youngstown." In *Beyond the Ruins: The Meanings of Deindustrialization*, edited by Jefferson Cowie and Joseph Heathcott, 201–18. Ithaca, N.Y.: ILR Press of Cornell University Press, 2003.

Sassen, Saskia. *The Global City: New York, London, Tokyo*. Princeton, N.J.: Princeton University Press, 1991.

Saville, Julie. *The Work of Reconstruction: From Slave to Wage Labor in South Carolina, 1860–1870*. Cambridge, U.K.: Cambridge University Press, 1994.

Scammon, Richard M., and Ben J. Wattenberg. *The Real Majority*. New York: Coward-McCann, 1970.

Schaeffer, Robert K. *Understanding Globalization: The Social Consequences of Political, Economic, and Environmental Change*. 2nd ed. Lanham, Md.: Rowman and Littlefield, 2003.

Schulman, Bruce J. *From Cotton Belt to Sunbelt: Federal Policy, Economic Development, and the Transformation of the South, 1938–1980*. New York: Oxford University Press, 1991.

Segalman, Ralph, and Asoke Basu. *Poverty in America: The Welfare Dilemma*. Westport, Conn.: Greenwood Press, 1981.

Shafer, Byron E., and Richard Johnston. *The End of Southern Exceptionalism: Class, Race, and Partisan Change in the Postwar South*. Cambridge, Mass.: Harvard University Press, 2006.

Simpson, Mary Stella. *Sister Stella's Babies: Days in the Practice of a Nurse-Midwife*. New York: American Journal of Nursing, 1978.

Skrentny, John David. *The Ironies of Affirmative Action: Politics, Culture, and Justice in America*. Chicago: University of Chicago Press, 1996.

Slesinger, Doris P., and Max J. Pfeffer. "Migrant Farm Workers." In *Rural Poverty in America*, edited by Cynthia M. Duncan, 135–53. New York, Auburn House, 1992.

Sloan, John W. *The Reagan Effect: Economics and Presidential Leadership*. Lawrence: University Press of Kansas, 1999.

Sokol, Jason. *There Goes My Everything: White Southerners in the Age of Civil Rights, 1945–1975*. New York: Alfred A. Knopf, 2006.

Stein, Judith. *Pivotal Decade: How the United States Traded Factories for Finance in the Seventies*. New Haven: Yale University Press, 2010.

Stiglitz, Joseph E. *Freefall: America, Free Markets, and the Sinking of the World Economy*. New York: W. W. Norton, 2010.

———. *Globalization and Its Discontents*. New York: W. W. Norton, 2002.

Sugrue, Thomas J. *Origins of the Urban Crisis: Race and Inequality in Postwar Detroit*. First Princeton Classics ed. Princeton, N.J.: Princeton University Press, 2005.

Thurber, Timothy N. *Republicans and Race: The GOP's Frayed Relationship with African Americans, 1945–1974*. Lawrence: University Press of Kansas, 2013.

Tuck, Stephen. *We Ain't What We Ought to Be: The Black Freedom Struggle from Emancipation to Obama*. Cambridge, Mass.: Belknap Press of Harvard University Press, 2010.

Voorhis, Jerry. *American Cooperatives: Where They Come From, What They Do, Where They Are Going*. New York: Harper and Row, 1961.

Wilson, Gregory S. *Communities Left Behind: The Area Redevelopment Administration,*
  1945–1965. Knoxville: University of Tennessee Press, 2009.
Wofford, Harris. *A Preliminary Report on the Status of the Negro in Dallas County, Alabama*
  (January 1953). In *We Shall Overcome: The Civil Rights Movement in the United States in*
  the 1950s and 1960s, vol. 3, edited by David J. Garrow, 1063–1150. Brooklyn, N.Y.: Carlson
  Publishing, 1989.
Woodman, Harold D. *New South—New Law: The Legal Foundations of Credit and Labor*
  Relations in the Postbellum Agricultural South. Baton Rouge: Louisiana State University
  Press, 1995.
Woodruff, Nan E. *American Congo: The African American Freedom Struggle in the Delta.*
  Cambridge, Mass.: Harvard University Press, 2003.
———. "Mississippi Delta Planters and Debates over Mechanization, Labor, and Civil Rights
  in the 1940s." *Journal of Southern History* 60 (May 1994): 263–84.
Woods, Clyde. *Development Arrested: The Blues and Plantation Power in the Mississippi Delta.*
  London: Verso, 1998.
Woodward, C. Vann. *Origins of the New South, 1877–1913.* Baton Rouge: Louisiana State
  University Press, 1951; reprint, with a new preface, 1971.
Wright, Gavin. *Old South, New South: Revolutions in the Southern Economy since the Civil*
  War. New York: Basic Books, 1986.
Wyman, Hastings, Jr. Review of *The Two-Party South,* by Alexander P. Lamis. *Election Politics:*
  A Journal of Political Campaigns and Elections 2 (Summer 1985): 30–31.
Yuill, Kevin L. *Richard Nixon and the Rise of Affirmative Action: The Pursuit of Racial Equality*
  in an Era of Limits. Lanham, Md.: Rowman and Littlefield, 2006.

INDEX

Aaron E. Norman Foundation, 104

Abbeville, La., 100

Abbey, R. I., 76

Abernathy, Ralph, 55

Abernethy, Thomas, 32, 39, 76, 81, 120, 122

Acadian Delight Bakery, 98, 103

Acadia Parish, 104

Affirmative action, 164, 179, 189, 190, 192–93, 205, 210, 214

Africa, 32, 38, 66, 121, 122, 150, 155

Agnew, Spiro, 123

Agricultural Adjustment Act, 155

Agricultural workers: desire for jobs, 52, 53–55, 58; displacement of, 2–5, 11–13, 16, 18–25, 33–34, 41–42, 43, 65, 197, 222–23, 225; exploitation of, 1–2, 19, 44–45, 70–71, 89; and federal agencies, 55–56, 129–30, 132, 147–48, 181, 186; and out-migration, 44–52; protests by, 51–52; retraining needs of, 58, 59; training programs for, 34, 35, 54, 55–56, 92, 186, 196; and War on Poverty, 66–69, 71–72, 74–75, 84–85, 86. *See also* Cooperatives: agricultural

Agriculture: corporate, 1, 155, 189, 193, 222; and federal policy, 15, 19–21, 36, 90, 106–8, 136, 147–48, 154–55, 175, 189–90, 193–94, 206; mechanization of, 2–4, 11–12, 23, 56, 61, 200, 203, 216, 223; sustainable, 17, 147–48, 167, 193–94, 196, 222. *See also* Agricultural workers; Cooperatives: agricultural; Small farmers

Aid to Families with Dependent Children (AFDC), 29, 31–32, 39, 216, 218

Alabama: antipoverty programs in, 65, 71–72, 74, 75, 76–77, 78, 79–80, 82, 85, 86, 104–5; civil rights activism in, 3, 5–6, 46, 65, 161–62, 164, 167–68; cooperatives in, 93–95, 99, 100, 104–12, 114, 141, 142, 148; cotton plantation region of, 5–6; economic development policies in, 24, 34, 36, 58–59, 177, 183, 197; employment discrimination in, 26, 28–29; FSC activities in, 15, 141, 142, 147–48, 160, 161–65, 167–68, 169–73, 185, 189, 190–91; labor displacement in, 20, 23, 24, 46; mechanization of agriculture in, 20, 23; opposition to antipoverty efforts in, 39, 41, 75, 76–77, 78, 79–80, 84, 86, 121–22, 125–26, 177; opposition to cooperatives in, 104–12, 114, 168, 169–73; opposition to racial equality in, 38–39, 60, 104–12, 204, 205; out-migration from, 21, 22, 23, 34, 41, 94–95; plantation owners in, 18, 44; political leadership in, 60, 76, 82, 104–5, 107, 108–9, 110–11, 112, 122, 168, 169–73, 190–91; and presidential campaigns, 210, 213; social justice activism in, 48, 50, 58–59, 60, 65; unemployment in, 181; welfare policy in, 31, 32, 39, 181

Alabama Coalition Against Hunger, 181

Alabama Council Bulletin, 94

Alabama Department of Pensions and Security, 31, 181

Alabama Development Office, 177

Alabama Industrial Development Training Institute, 183

Alabama Legislative Commission to Preserve the Peace, 79

Alabama New South Coalition, 168

Alabama Water Improvement Commission, 169

Albritton, Reginald, 60

Alexander, William, 118

Allen, Sadie, 26

Altman, Robert C., 166

American Farm Bureau Federation (AFBF), 28, 40, 42, 75, 122

American Friends Service Committee, 105
American Independent Party, 123
American Institute of Cooperatives, 151
Americans for Constitutional Action, 120
American Taxpayers Association, 42
Andrews, George, 76, 79, 108, 117
Andrews Brothers Plantation. 48, 51, 60
Antigovernment sentiment. *See* Federal
    government: antipathy toward
Antipoverty programs. *See* War on Poverty
Appalachian Regional Commission, 197
Area Development Associations, 25, 40
Area Redevelopment Administration,
    10–11, 28
Arkansas, 142, 168, 191
Asia, 32, 66, 150, 155, 184
Atkins, Jessie, 30
Atlanta, Ga., 138, 142, 158, 166
Auburn University, 106

Baines, Bruce, 100
Baker, John, 108
Baltimore, Md., 78, 208
Baltimore Sun, 78
Bamberg, Robert, 177
Bank for Cooperatives, 147
Bank of Bolivar County, 72
Barber, Rims, 27
Barnes, Thelma, 113–14
Baroni, Marjorie, 54
Bauer, Andre, 220
Benjamin, Claire, 59
Billingsley, Orzell, Jr., 105
Birmingham, Ala., 110, 171, 172, 207
Birmingham News, 110
Bittman, Mark, 222
Black, Herbert, 134
Black, Lewis, 94, 143, 158–59
Black, Mildred, 100, 143
Black Belt Community Health Center,
    160, 185
Black elected officials, 10, 19, 70,
    167–68, 190
Black Enterprise, 139
Black landowners, 150, 162, 187, 188–90

Black-owned businesses, 15, 87, 98, 138–39,
    160, 178, 192–93. *See also* Cooperatives
Black Panther Party, 82, 110
Black power, 79, 81, 86, 134
Blackwell, Unita, 51, 64, 73
Block grants, 125, 181, 182, 185, 193, 218
Boeing Company, 184
Boligee, Ala., 167
Bolivar County, Miss.: civil rights activism
    in, 33–34, 69–70; economic development
    in, 25; labor displacement in, 20, 45, 55;
    poverty in, 32, 40, 65–66, 75; War on
    Poverty in, 55, 65–71, 72, 74–75, 79, 127,
    133–35
Bolivar County Democrat, 22, 79
Bonin, Garland, 40
Boston, Mass., 46–47, 66, 133, 134, 164, 207
Boston Globe, 134
Bradford, John, 46
Brady, Kevin, 219
Bramlett, Leon, 75
Brewer, Albert, 110
Brisbay, Henry, 120
Britton, Donald, 192–93
Broderick, Martin, Jr., 205
Brooks, A. P. (Mrs.), 38
Brooks, J. R., 170–73
Brooks, L. G., 196
Brooks, Owen, 134
Brosnan, James, 196–97
Brown, John, 113
Brown, John, Jr., 22, 45, 54, 100, 156
Brown, L. Heidel, 205
Browne, Robert, 162
Brown v. Board of Education, 120, 121
Bundy, McGeorge, 152, 153
Bureau of Labor Statistics, 5, 218
Bureau of the Budget, 84
Burkett, Ben, 150, 222–23, 224–25
Burrell, Jennie, 58–59
Burton, B. G. (Mrs.), 40
Burton, Dewey, 215
Bush, George W., 197
Business Development Offices (BDOs), 160,
    165–66, 168

Business Week, 59

Busing, 120, 121, 124, 179, 207, 208, 210, 213

California, 47, 178, 212, 218, 220

Camden, Ala., 60

Canton, Miss., 91, 93

Capitalism: agrarian, 1–2; alternatives to,
12, 14, 17, 88–89, 194; finance, 5, 16–17,
201–2, 218–19, 224, 225; industrial, 1,
5, 201; transformations in, 1–5, 11–12,
19–20, 201–3, 220–21, 223–25. *See also*
Free market economics

Carlucci, Frank, 127

Carr, Andrew, 59, 61

Carr, Oscar, 61

Carroll County, Miss., 22

Carter, Hodding, III, 24

Carter, Jimmy: economic policies of,
176–77, 183, 209, 211–12, 213; and rural
development, 166–67, 175, 176–77, 182,
185; voters' disillusionment with, 174,
178, 213

Chamber of Commerce, 73, 80

Chicago, Ill., 46, 47, 89, 90, 150, 184, 202,
207, 216–17

Chickasaw County, Miss., 71, 78

Child Development Group of Mississippi
(CDGM), 64, 77, 85, 91, 106

Choctaw County, Ala., 95

Christian Conservative Communique, 119

Churches: burnings of, 76–77, 101; support
for cooperative movement, 102, 103,
145, 160, 174, 186, 188; support for social
justice efforts, 93–94, 97–98, 162, 182

Ciscel, David, 198

Citizen, 36, 120–21, 212, 220

Citizens Crusade Against Poverty, 80

Citizens' Council, 4, 28, 38, 103, 120–21, 179

Civil Rights Act, 3, 10, 18, 25, 26, 36, 121, 223

Civil rights activism: and agricultural
labor displacement, 2–4, 12, 33–34; and
cooperative movement, 88–92, 95, 115,
143, 169; opposition to, 4, 14, 27, 31–32,
33–34, 36–39, 76, 117, 121, 144, 208, 214;
and out-migration, 22, 36; persistence

after 1960s, 10, 15; reprisals for, 18–19,
30–31, 33–34, 38–39, 89–90, 91, 94, 148,
213; and social justice, 3; and War on
Poverty, 11, 51, 61, 64–65, 76, 82, 86, 131

Civil rights legislation: impact of, 3, 12, 56,
57, 64; limits of, 2–3, 6, 10, 13, 16, 26–27,
43, 44, 139, 221, 222–23; opposition to,
6, 10, 117–22, 179, 204–7; white southern
support for, 58–59, 94

Civiletti, Benjamin, 172

Clark, Dick, 131–32

Clarksdale, Miss., 59, 133

Clay County, Miss., 22, 102

Cleveland, Ohio, 202

Clinton, Bill, 191, 195, 196, 216, 217–18

Coahoma County, Miss., 41, 55, 61, 71, 72, 73

Coahoma Opportunities Inc. (COI), 61, 71,
72, 75, 84

Cobbs, Hamner, 41

Cochran, Thad, 197

Colclough, Glenna, 183

Commission on Civil Rights (CCR), 21, 26,
34, 46, 105, 181, 189

Community action agencies/Community
action programs (CAAs/CAPs):
achievements of, 71–75, 81; and black
freedom struggle, 11, 61, 64–65, 71–72,
82, 195; contested control over, 59–60,
82, 105–6, 125–26, 130; decentralization
of, 125–26, 128, 181–82; deradicalization
of, 82–87, 129, 130, 131, 135; and
funding cuts, 82–85, 127, 131–32, 176;
opposition to, 76–80, 85–86, 121–23,
128, 144; white support for, 60–61. *See
also* Office of Economic Opportunity;
War on Poverty

Community health centers, 62, 135, 181, 185.
See also Black Belt Community Health
Center; Tufts-Delta Health Center

Community Services Administration (CSA),
129, 167, 175, 176, 181, 185. *See also* Office
of Economic Opportunity

Comprehensive Employment Training Act
(CETA), 130–31, 132, 165, 167, 180, 185

Concordia Parish, La., 22, 65, 77

Congressional Black Caucus, 124

Congress of Racial Equality (CORE), 5, 10, 33, 65, 89, 90, 94, 97, 100, 143, 178

Conservatism: Christian, 119–20; of Congress, 15–17; and economic theory, 147, 219–20; and racism, 6, 117–20, 123–24, 176, 178–79, 224; of Republican Party, 15, 116, 123–24, 128, 174, 219–20; of southern political and business leaders, 118, 161, 168–69, 181; of voters, 81, 210–11

Consortium for the Development of the Rural Southeast, 186

Continental Allied, 133–34

Cooper, Leroy, 206

Cooperative movement: achievements of, 99–101, 148–51, 159, 191, 194, 203, 222–23, 224–25; and civil rights movement, 89–96, 100, 101–2, 105–6, 115, 142–43; and federal government, 86, 104–8, 110–11, 126, 132–34, 136–37, 140, 143–44, 153–58, 165–67, 184–86; financing of, 92–93, 99, 140, 141–42, 151–55, 159–60; opposition to, 89, 101–11, 142, 168–73; origins of, 88–99; overview of, 14–16. See also Cooperatives; Federation of Southern Cooperatives

Cooperatives: achievements of, 68–69, 90–92, 93–94, 97–99; agricultural, 68–69, 89–91, 94–95, 97, 100–102, 103–12, 113–14, 132–34, 146, 147–48, 150, 154–55, 187–88; in Alabama, 93–95, 99, 100, 104–12, 114, 141, 142, 148; and black freedom struggle, 14, 88–89, 91–92, 93–94, 101–2, 115, 146, 149, 150–51, 167–68, 173; capitalization of, 68–69, 92–93, 99, 114, 145, 166–67, 185; consumer, 97–98, 100, 150, 166–67; financial, 71–72, 98, 100, 102, 143, 147, 166–67, 168, 187; handcraft, 89, 92, 93, 94, 98, 100, 103, 148; housing, 92, 148, 169, 190; in Louisiana, 95–99, 100, 141, 142, 150, 193–94; manufacturing, 91–92, 93, 94, 101, 146, 148–49; marketing, 93, 95, 97, 100–101, 102, 103–12, 150; in Mississippi, 89–93, 99, 100, 101–2, 113–14, 141, 142, 150, 186, 188; opposition

to, 14, 15, 89, 101–11, 142; problems of, 92, 111–15, 132–34, 136–37, 142, 144, 154, 155–56, 159–60, 169; and rural development, 90, 95, 99–101, 150; technical assistance to, 93, 99–101, 112, 141–42, 143, 145–48, 160, 165, 185–88; viability of, 133, 134, 147, 151, 153, 154–55, 159–60. See also Cooperative movement; Federation of Southern Cooperatives

Council of Economic Advisers, 137

Cowan, Berton, 192

Crane, Philip, 215

Credit unions, 71–72, 98, 100, 102, 143, 147, 167, 168, 187

Creelman, Brenton, 133

Crime, 57, 121, 122, 123–24, 191, 203, 208, 210

Cummings, Henry, 18

Cunningham, Ezra, 3, 89, 94, 100, 136, 143, 167–68

Daft, Lynn, 137

Dallas County, Ala., 18, 22, 24, 35–36, 44, 95, 105

Dallas-Selma Community Action Agency, 105

Dalsimer, John Paul, 172

Dan River Mills, Ala., 26

Davis, F. C., 198

Deep South, 5, 28, 31, 34, 102, 118, 210

Deindustrialization, 2, 16, 29, 200–203, 214–15, 216–17, 224

DeLay, Tom, 215

Delta and Pine Land Company, 20

Delta Community Hospital and Health Center (DCHHC), 135

Delta Council, 28

Delta Ministry, 10, 27, 34, 46, 48, 51, 53, 56, 64, 92, 99, 113, 124, 131, 137

Delta Regional Authority, 197

Democratic Party: black disillusionment with, 178; and conservative policies, 180, 211–12, 215; defections from, 116, 117–19, 209–11, 213–14, 217; and social justice, 124, 166, 175, 215, 219; and War on Poverty, 82, 105, 123

Denman, Annie, 38

Department of Agriculture (USDA): and
cooperatives, 107–8, 109, 114, 147–48,
154–55, 169; food programs of, 29, 30,
50–51, 53–54, 58, 62, 67, 68, 73, 121, 177,
180, 188, 206, 212, 213, 219, 220; local
control over programs of, 21, 50–51, 90,
101, 107, 108; and plantation owners, 32,
155, 193; racism of, 20–21, 90, 97, 101,
147–48, 189; and rural poverty, 55, 57, 58,
73, 129–30, 136, 137, 154–55, 175, 189–90;
and small farmers, 15, 20–21, 136, 147–48,
155, 193–94. *See also* Farmers Home
Administration; Federal Extension Service

Department of Commerce, 11, 138

Department of Defense, 80

Department of Health, Education, and
Welfare (HEW), 27, 28, 73, 127, 130, 135,
151, 160, 204

Department of Housing and Urban
Development (HUD), 73, 121, 137, 139,
181, 185

Department of Justice, 81, 111, 172

Department of Labor (DOL): and
antipoverty efforts, 73, 130, 132, 160;
and employment discrimination, 25,
164; and job training programs, 127,
130–31, 139, 167, 168–69, 208; and labor
displacement, 5, 28–29, 55, 182, 186, 201

Deregulation, 16, 179, 184, 202, 212, 214, 218

Desegregation. *See* Integration

De Soto County, Miss., 22

De Soto Parish, La., 22

Detroit, Mich.: black migration to, 22, 45, 89,
150; deindustrialization in, 46, 201, 202,
215; desegregation in, 207; as market for
cooperatives, 68, 93; uprisings in, 57

Displacement: of agricultural workers, 2–5,
11–13, 16, 18–25, 33–34, 41–42, 43, 65,
197, 222–23, 225; of black landowners,
20–21, 187, 188–89, 193, 198; defined,
4–5; government responses to, 17, 19,
55–58, 62–64, 88, 136–38, 198–99,
211–12, 214–15, 219–21, 223–24, 225; of
industrial workers, 17, 183–84, 199,

201–3, 211–12, 214–15, 218–19; liberal
white southerners' responses to, 58–61;
of middle-class professionals, 17, 197–98,
199, 218–19, 225; planter responses to,
4, 19, 23, 24–25, 28, 42–43, 50–51; social
justice activists' responses to, 44–56,
61, 68–69, 74–75, 88–90, 92, 94–95, 101,
144–46, 148, 149, 160, 160–65, 167–68,
173, 222–23, 224–25

Donovan, Raymond, 182

Dorsey, L. C.: activism of, 33–34, 60, 64, 65;
career of, 67, 113, 133; displacement of,
19, 25

Douglass, Maggie, 91

Dunbar, Leslie, 151, 172, 173

Duncan, John, Jr., 215

Dunlop, John, 132

Dunne, Pat, 59

Eastland, James, 20, 34

Ebony, 164

Economic Development Administration
(EDA): and antipoverty efforts, 55–56,
57, 58, 59, 181, 193; and cooperatives,
108–9, 145; creation of, 11; criticisms of,
42; and out-migration, 137; reports on
conditions in rural South, 23–24, 25, 36,
58, 59, 132, 139

Economic development initiatives: failures
of, 24–25, 136, 182–84, 193–94, 195–98;
of federal government, 10–11, 15, 55–58,
62, 73, 90, 108–9, 124–25, 131, 136–40,
166–67, 193, 195–97; inadequate funding
for, 127, 139–40, 194, 195, 196–97;
opposition to, 23, 24, 36, 41–42, 132, 197;
of social justice activists, 14–15, 45, 52–53,
68–69, 99–101, 193–94; of state and
local governments, 12–13, 15, 23–25, 40,
56, 58–61, 73–74, 132, 166, 194. *See also*
Cooperative movement; Federation of
Southern Cooperatives; War on Poverty

Economic Opportunity Act: amendments to,
57, 82, 130, 132, 157; debates over, 63–64,
76; impact of, 29, 62–64, 84; passage
of, 11, 62

Edgar, John, 205

Education: adult, 19, 52, 54–55, 58, 59,
66–67, 71–72, 73–74, 84–85, 97, 132;
desegregation of, 16, 27–28, 76–78, 91,
117, 119–20, 121, 123, 170, 179, 200, 204,
207, 223; private, 27, 119–20; public, 13,
27–28, 35–36, 40, 62, 68, 119–20, 123,
170, 179, 182, 191, 192, 195, 196, 203, 207,
219; racial discrimination in, 1, 3, 19, 21,
23–24, 26, 27–28, 35–36, 44, 46, 64, 114,
170, 195, 207, 223. *See also* Head Start
program

Edwards, Miss., 92

Elementary and Secondary Education
Act, 27

Elliott, Arthur James, 205

Emergency Land Fund (ELF), 162, 186–87

Epes, Ala., 148, 150, 158, 160, 161, 164, 169

Eufaula Board of Realtors, 204

Eutaw, Ala., 190

Evers, Charles, 176, 178

Family farms. *See* Small farmers

Farmers Home Administration (FmHA):
and cooperatives, 90, 97, 104, 106–8, 111,
147, 148, 169, 190; racism of, 21, 130; and
rural poverty, 129–30, 166, 189, 190, 193

Federal Bureau of Investigation (FBI),
170–71, 172, 190

Federal Extension Service (FES), 21, 102,
147, 154, 193–94

Federal government: agricultural policies
of, 2, 19–21, 32, 34, 36, 50–51, 90, 167,
189–90, 193–94, 222; antipathy toward,
16–17, 28, 34, 38, 39, 42–43, 63, 75–76,
81, 86, 116, 117–22, 123, 125, 173, 175–78,
197, 200–201, 204–8, 210–11, 213–14;
civil rights policies of, 1, 6, 10, 16, 18,
24, 27–28, 164; conservatism of, 14–17,
174, 175–77, 179–81; and cooperative
movement, 89, 95, 98, 99, 104–8, 110–11,
112, 115, 141, 143–44, 146–47, 154–58;
168–69, 170–73; economic policies of,
16–17, 28–29, 42, 45, 50–51, 52–54, 55–58,
61, 116–17, 124–28, 130–32, 136–40, 161,

165–67, 180–82, 183–85, 191, 193–94,
196–98, 201–2, 208–12, 214–18, 223–24;
perceived tyranny of, 6, 38, 117–18,
119, 120, 121, 122, 123, 179, 200, 204–8,
219–20; social welfare policies of, 29–32,
38, 39–40, 50–51, 59–60, 81–82, 84,
122–23, 216–18, 219–21; subsidization
of plantation owners, 21, 32, 36, 155;
subsidization of white middle class, 2,
36, 182, 206. *See also* U.S. Congress; War
on Poverty

Federation of Southern Cooperatives (FSC):
and black freedom struggle, 15, 142–43,
149–51, 169–70, 173, 175, 188–91; and
black-owned businesses, 160, 165–66,
168; and displaced workers, 144–46, 148,
149, 160, 160–65, 167–68, 173, 222–23,
224–25; financial struggles of, 16,
141–42, 143–44, 146–47, 151–54, 155, 158,
165–66, 173, 174, 185–86, 199; and Ford
Foundation, 141, 145, 146–47, 151–53,
154, 158–60; formation of, 14, 141, 142;
formation of FSC/LAF, 187; foundation
support for, 141, 143, 144, 145, 146–47,
151, 155, 172; and global development,
150; government support for, 141, 144,
145, 146–47, 151, 155, 157, 166–67, 189,
190–91; grand jury investigation of,
170–73, 174; housing programs of,
167, 169, 190; impact of, 17, 150–51,
195–96, 222–23, 224–25; land retention
programs of, 162, 188–90; and OEO, 141,
142, 143–44, 145, 146–47, 148, 153–54,
155, 156–58; and OMBE, 160, 165–66;
opposition to, 15, 146, 147, 168–73;
political activism of, 161–65, 167–68,
189–90; and Reagan administration, 181,
185–86, 187; rural development efforts
of, 15, 141, 145–46, 148–51, 154, 160–65,
167, 168–69, 174, 186–88, 190–91; Rural
Training and Research Center (RTRC)
of, 15, 147–48, 160, 162, 164, 169, 170;
and SCDF, 145, 153, 157–58, 160; services
to cooperatives, 15, 141, 145–48, 148–51,
153, 175, 187–88; and small farmers, 15,

147–48, 149–50, 162, 167, 188–90, 222–23, 224–25; staff of, 142–43, 145, 149–51, 169; and sustainable agriculture, 15, 147–48, 150, 167, 188, 222–23, 224–25; and Tennessee-Tombigbee Waterway (TTW) project, 161–65

Federation of Southern Cooperatives/ Land Assistance Fund (FSC/LAF). *See* Federation of Southern Cooperatives

Field Foundation, 144, 151, 172, 177

Fields, Elvadis, Jr., 193

Financial crisis of 2008, 16–17, 218–20

Florida, 28, 142, 191

Flowers, Walter, 122

Foley, Eugene, 57

Food Stamp Act, 29

Food stamp program. *See* Department of Agriculture: food programs of

Food, Agriculture, Conservation, and Trade Act, 189

Ford, Gerald, 116, 135, 166, 209

Ford Foundation: and civil rights, 144; and cooperatives, 68, 99, 143, 145; and FSC, 14, 141, 146–47, 151–53, 154, 158–60

Fordice, Kirk, 197

Forkland, Ala., 167

Foster, A. J., 58

Foster, Isaac, 51–52

Foundations: and cooperative movement, 99, 102, 104, 141, 145, 148, 151, 160, 165, 172–73, 174, 186, 222; restrictions on funding from, 114, 144, 167, 171, 173. *See also* Field Foundation; Ford Foundation

Fox News, 220

Frank, Rudy, 134

Franklin, Webb, 194

Free, James, 110

Freedom City, 92, 113–14

Freedomcrafts, 92, 114

Freedom Information Service, 53

Freedom of choice plans, 27, 204

Freedom Quilting Bee, 94, 100, 115

Freedom Rides, 36

Freedom Summer, 5

Freeman, Orville, 21, 51, 52, 53, 58, 98, 107–8

Free market economics: debates over, 16–17, 50–51, 56–57, 61, 137–38, 219–21, 223–24, 225; and federal government, 125, 138–40, 174, 180–84, 215; limits of, 5, 14, 15–17, 50, 55, 116–17, 138–40, 181–84, 197–99, 219–21, 222, 223–25; promotion of, 5, 6, 15–17, 19, 41–43, 50, 63, 75–76, 116–17, 118, 119, 122–23, 138, 154, 173, 178–81, 182, 200–202, 204–5, 211–13, 223–24; and working class, 16–17, 198–99, 201–3, 214–15, 223–24, 225

Free trade. *See* Globalization

From, Al, 82

Gainesville, Ala., 161

Gary, Ind., 202

Geiger, H. Jack, 65–66, 67, 70, 72, 75, 85, 128, 134

Geiger, Sue, 48

General Accounting Office (GAO), 81, 84, 108, 110, 111–12, 170, 171

George, Bryant, 152, 155, 158–59

George, Joseph, 192

Georgia, 28, 90, 142, 166, 168, 187, 189, 191

Gibson, Count, 66

Gilliam, Dorothy, 176

Givhan, Walter, 105

Globalization: and economic inequality, 194, 197–98, 199, 200, 225; and financial crisis of 2008, 218–19, 224; and labor displacement, 2, 16–17, 183–84, 197–98, 199, 200, 201–2, 214–15, 218–19, 224; promotion of, 212

Godwin, Lamond, 157, 161–62, 164

Goldwater, Barry, 118, 208, 213

Good, Paul, 46

Gooden, Bennie, 61

Good Morning America, 179

Government. *See* Federal government; Local governments; State governments

Grand Marie Vegetable Producers Cooperative (GMVPC), 97, 98, 100, 102, 103–4, 193

Gray, Floyd, 192

Green, Edith, 53

Green, Gerson, 129

Greene County, Ala., 22, 34, 94, 95, 167, 169, 170, 190

Greene County Commission, 190

Greene County Democrat, 122

Greene-Hale Sewing Cooperative, 94, 100, 146

Greensboro, Ala., 94, 190

Greenville, Miss., 51–52, 55, 56, 59, 72, 92, 184

Greenville Air Force Base sit-in, 51–52, 55, 92

Greenwood, Miss., 100, 192

Griffin, Robert, 121

Grigsby, Frank, 204

Guillory, Wilbert, 100, 101–2, 193–94

Gulf Coast, Miss., 48

Guyot, Lawrence, 4, 48

Hale County, Ala., 94, 95, 112

Hambleton, Gerald, 182

Harding, Bertrand, 106

Harlem, N.Y., 57

Harmon, Sharon, 202

Harris, Louis, 208, 210

Harrison, William, 107–8, 112, 132–33, 184

Hartfield, James, 51

Hatch, John, 46–47, 54, 68, 134

Hattiesburg, Miss., 138

Head Start, Economic Opportunity and Community Partnership Act, 129

Head Start program: achievements of, 71, 177, 196; and civil rights activism, 64–65, 99; inadequate funding for, 84, 85; integration of, 76, 77–78; opposition to, 76–78, 85; origins of, 62

Health care: expansion of access to, 13, 35, 55, 62, 195, 220; inadequacies of, 16, 23, 33, 40, 57, 180, 181, 182, 191, 208, 216–17, 222; and social justice activism, 95, 146, 154, 176, 187, 208. *See also* Black Belt Community Health Center; Tufts-Delta Health Center

Heflin, Howell, 170

Hendrix, James, 193

Herren, Thomas, 79

Hicks, Louise Day, 207

Hinds County, Miss., 100

Holmes County, Miss., 64–65, 101

Hornsby, Jerry, 110

Housing: costs of, 175, 176; desegregation of, 58, 120, 123, 204–5, 207; low-income, 3, 44, 46–47, 48, 50, 52, 62, 66, 78, 90, 92, 93, 121, 150, 169, 180, 185, 187, 190, 192, 209, 217; rehabilitation, 66, 72, 101, 167, 190, 191; segregation of, 46, 206, 207; self-help, 48, 50, 62, 78, 92, 100, 148, 169; substandard, 16, 23, 40, 51, 65, 66, 69, 72, 101, 146, 167, 192; white control over, 2, 3

Houston Post, 35, 45–46

Huckabay, A. E., 206

Hulett, John, 65

Humphrey, Hubert, 123–24, 131–32, 156, 210

Hunger: attempts to combat, 29, 32, 47–48, 50–54, 55–56, 67–69, 181–82, 222; investigations of, 33–36, 41–42, 177; persistence of, 177, 181–82, 203, 219, 220; political leaders' denial of, 34–35, 39, 40, 51; publicizing of, 13, 33–34, 44–45, 50–52

Huston, Tom, 209

Indian Springs Farmers Co-op, 150

Individualism: and explanations for poverty, 39–40, 42–43, 44, 75–76, 179, 181, 197, 198–99, 200, 206, 216, 224; in segregationist rhetoric, 6, 16, 75–76, 117–18, 119, 120, 204–5

Inflation: attempts to combat, 175–76, 209, 215; concerns about, 137, 174, 175, 206, 209, 211; and local governments, 131; War on Poverty blamed for, 39, 75, 120, 122, 175, 212

Integration: and antigovernment sentiment, 16, 117–18, 119–22, 200–201, 204–5, 207–8, 213; and antipoverty programs, 73–74, 76, 77–78; and cooperatives, 91, 109; opposition to, 6, 16, 27–29, 76, 77–78, 109, 117–18, 119–21, 204–5, 207–8, 213–14

Internal Revenue Service, 171
International Union of Operating Engineers, 162
International Year of Family Farming, 222
Itta Bena, Miss., 192, 195

Jackson, Miss., 35, 52, 59, 86, 93, 100, 118, 194, 207
Jackson Clarion-Ledger, 118
Jacobs, Charles, Jr., 34
James, Andrew, 128
James, Bob, 91
James, James E.. 164
James Beard Foundation, 222
Javits, Jacob, 53, 56
Jim Crow system: demise of, 2, 6, 11, 12, 18–19, 120, 172; and labor control, 1–2, 4, 20, 113; legacies of, 5, 6, 10, 19, 25, 40, 43, 44, 58–59, 61, 114, 143, 172, 181
Job Corps, 55, 79, 80, 84
Job training programs: decentralization of, 125, 126, 130–32; discrimination in, 23–24, 25, 28–29, 132; of federal government, 10–11, 28–29, 55–56, 67, 72, 73–74, 84–85, 131–32, 208, 216; of FSC, 142, 148, 151, 162, 164–65, 167, 185, 191; and funding cuts, 84–85, 127, 180–81, 185; need for, 10, 13, 52, 53–55, 59, 90, 92, 194, 196, 216; opposition to, 28–29, 33, 34, 76, 86
Johnson, Bernice, 64
Johnson, Lillie Dunn, 149
Johnson, Lyndon B.: and antipoverty efforts, 11, 52, 57, 62–63, 82, 84, 125, 215; and labor displacement, 88, 92; opposition to policies of, 75–76, 82, 116, 117–18; and Vietnam War, 81, 82; and Voting Rights Act, 18–19
Johnson, Paul, 34, 59, 60, 118
Johnson, Percy, 110
Johnston, Erle, Jr., 34–35
Joliff, James, Jr., 47
Jones, Dewitt, 194
Jones, Jim, 159
Jones, Nolan, Sr., 18
Jones, Sam, 41

Kaptur, Marcy, 217
Kemper County, Miss., 22
Kennedy, John F., 45
Kennedy, Robert F., 64
Keown, Woodrow, 136
Kershaw, Joseph, 154
Khanna, Navina, 222
Khosrovi, Carol, 157
Kilgore, Martha, 117
King, Martin Luther, Jr., 105
Klose, Roland, 198
Kochtitzky, Bob, 194
Koker, Larry, 202
Kosciusko, Miss., 56
Ku Klux Klan, 50, 63, 179, 213

Labor unions, 2, 28, 48, 51, 92, 145, 162, 164, 202, 214–15, 216, 218
LaBrie, Gerald, 126
Lafayette, La., 80, 97, 103, 104, 142–43, 158, 205
Laissez-faire economics. *See* Free market economics
Lake Charles, La., 98, 102–3
Lake Providence, La., 168, 198
Latin America, 66, 184
Lawrence, Ellett, 38
Lawrence, Ida Mae, 30, 51–52, 92
Leadership Conference on Civil Rights, 105
Leflore County, Miss., 22, 78, 192
Leland, Wilfred, 58
Levine, Robert, 137
Lexington, Miss., 50, 61, 74
Limbaugh, Rush, 220
Lincove, Arnold, 194
Little River Community Action Program, 105
Livingston Home Record, 169, 170
Local governments: and antipoverty efforts, 48, 50–51, 53, 59, 60–61, 77, 78, 82, 128, 132, 135–36, 177; control over federal programs, 10, 15, 28–32, 82, 90, 116, 122, 123, 124–26, 130–32, 134–35, 177, 181–82, 191–92, 216, 218; and cooperative movement, 104–5, 106, 110–11, 150–51, 167, 168–70, 190; and economic

development, 184, 190, 193, 194, 195; failure of leadership, 13, 23–24, 34, 64, 132; racism of, 10–11, 23–24, 27–31, 33–34, 35–36, 63–64, 69–70, 77, 78, 101, 131–32, 213; and War on Poverty, 10–11, 13, 29, 45, 53, 56, 59–61, 63–64, 69–71, 73–74, 81, 135–36, 181–82

London, Edna, 18

Long, Russell, 38, 40, 117, 120, 182, 204, 205–6

Los Angeles, Ca., 207

Lott, Trent, 197

Louisiana: antipoverty programs in, 55, 64, 65, 76, 77, 99, 103; civil rights activism in, 5, 18, 31, 95, 97, 143, 168; cooperatives in, 95–99, 100, 141, 150, 193; cotton plantation region of, 4, 5; economic development policies in, 127, 182, 184, 193, 194; education in, 27, 192; employment discrimination in, 26–27; FSC activities in, 141, 142, 150, 160, 165, 168; labor displacement in, 20, 41, 193; mechanization of agriculture in, 20; opposition to antipoverty efforts in, 76, 77, 103, 117, 205–6; opposition to cooperatives in, 102–4, 114, 168; opposition to racial equality in, 18, 27, 30–31, 55, 120, 192–93, 204–5; out-migration from, 21, 22, 41, 58, 193, 198; political leadership in, 30, 31–32, 40, 41, 60, 80, 168, 182, 216; poverty in, 97, 191–92, 198; and presidential campaigns, 210; social justice activism in, 50, 65, 95–99, 100, 143, 193; unemployment in, 55, 127, 191–92, 198; welfare policy in, 30, 31–32, 40, 191–92

Louisiana Department of Employment Security, 127

Louisiana Realtors Association, 204

Louisiana Un-American Activities Committee, 103

Louisiana Weekly, 26, 27, 64

Lower Mississippi Delta Development Commission (LMDDC), 191–97

Lowndes County, Ala: poverty in, 23, 25; racism in, 34, 39, 76–77; social justice activism in, 48, 50, 65, 86, 95; War on Poverty in, 65, 74, 86, 121–22

Lowndes County Christian Movement for Human Rights, 86

Lowther, Murphy, 78

Lucas, Earl, 134

Luckett, Semmes, 41

Madison County Sewing Firm, 91, 93

Madison Parish, La., 100, 165

Magnuson, Warren, 64

Mainstream Mississippi, 164

Manpower Development and Training Act (MDTA), 28–29, 72, 74, 130

Manufacturing: employment discrimination in, 26–27; job creation in, 24, 72, 91–92, 93, 94, 148–49; job losses in, 46, 183–84, 197–98, 199, 200, 201–3, 214–15, 216–17; planter discouragement of, 24–25; unionization of, 2

Marengo County, Ala., 22, 95

Marion, Ala., 190

Marlbrough, Joseph Lee, 104

Marshall, Ray, 58, 157, 166

Massachusetts, 93, 156, 210

Massengill, Sam, 170

Maxwell, Neil, 76

Mays, James, 90, 101

McAfee, Melbah, 150, 186

McComb, Miss., 56, 93

McCrery, Jim, 216

McGill, Lillian, 65

McGovern, George, 209, 210

McKissick, Floyd, 178

McKnight, A. J., 97–100, 102–3, 142, 143, 145, 153, 157, 158

McLain, Rufus, 195

McMullens, Ala., 190

McPherson, Margaret, 204

McShan, Percy, 34

Mechanization, 2–4, 11–12, 23, 56, 61, 200, 203, 216, 223

Media: attention to plantation regions, 6, 45, 98; and hunger crisis, 35, 41–42, 45, 50, 52; reporting on antipoverty efforts, 75, 78–79, 81, 103, 110, 111–12, 206, 220; reporting on displacement, 41–42, 52, 61, 219

Medicaid, 180, 209

Medical Committee for Human Rights, 65

Medicare, 213, 220

Melancon, Frank, 103–4

Memphis, Ala., 190

Memphis, Tenn., 90, 196

Memphis Commercial Appeal, 196

Mesher, Shirley, 94, 105

Mid-State Opportunity, Inc., 74

Migrant and Seasonal Farm Workers Program, 61

Mikulski, Barbara, 208

Miles, Frank, Jr., 65

Miles, Robert, 91, 100, 101

Milestone Farmers Cooperative, 149

Miller, Joseph, 38

Miller, William, 119

Minimum wage, 21, 62, 215, 217

Minneapolis, Minn., 123

Minority Peoples Council on the Tennessee-Tombigbee Waterway Project (MPC), 162–64

Minter, James, 18, 44

Minus, Preston, 170

Mississippi: antipoverty programs in, 50, 54–56, 59, 60–61, 64–65, 65–71, 72, 73–74, 84, 85, 128, 138; civil rights activism in, 4, 6, 10, 33–34, 64–65, 69–70, 85, 162–64, 181; cooperatives in, 68–69, 75, 89–93, 100–101, 113–14, 127, 133–34, 141, 149, 186, 188; cotton plantation region of, 4, 5, 33–34; economic development policies in, 25, 28, 32, 36, 40, 59, 124, 126, 131, 138, 161, 166, 183, 184, 194, 196–98; education in, 24, 27–28, 66–67, 119–20, 204; employment discrimination in, 92; FSC activities in, 141, 142, 149–50, 186, 188, 191; health care in, 33, 65–68, 70–71, 75, 85, 128, 134–35, 138, 160, 195; labor displacement in, 20, 24, 33–34, 35, 41–42, 43, 50–52, 89–90, 198; mechanization of agriculture in, 19, 20, 45; opposition to antipoverty efforts in, 39–40, 41, 75, 76, 77–78, 79, 81, 86, 121, 122; opposition to cooperatives in, 101–2; opposition to racial equality in, 4, 6, 33–34, 36, 38, 119–20, 121, 192, 204; out-migration from, 21–22, 34, 36, 38–39, 50, 75, 198; plantation owners in, 30, 59, 60, 61, 76; political leadership in, 32, 34–35, 39–40, 53, 58, 59, 60–61, 76, 79, 81, 85, 118, 134–35, 197, 216; poverty in, 30, 31–35, 41–42, 50–53, 65–66, 67–68, 98, 177, 179, 198, 202; and presidential campaigns, 210, 213; social justice activism in, 46–48, 50–55, 64–65, 69–71, 85, 89–93, 106, 124, 162–64; unemployment in, 24, 25, 196, 198; welfare policy in, 30, 31, 32, 39

Mississippi Action for Progress, 85

Mississippi Council on Human Relations, 86, 119–20, 177

Mississippi Delta: economic development in, 25, 138, 193, 194, 197; labor displacement in, 21, 25, 33–34, 41–42, 50–52, 75; plantations in, 20, 28; political leadership in, 33, 40; poverty and hunger in, 40, 41–42, 184, 196–97, 198; racism in, 61; social justice activism in, 46–53, 55–56, 64–65, 195. *See also* Delta Ministry; Tufts-Delta Health Center

Mississippi Department of Public Welfare, 31, 39, 53

Mississippi Fish Equity, 102

Mississippi Freedom Democratic Party (MFDP), 10, 24, 27, 30, 50, 51–52, 55–56, 64, 91, 100, 101

Mississippi State Sovereignty Commission, 34

Miss-Lou Farmers Cooperative, 100

Mitchell, Danny, 131

Mitchell, H. L., 28

Mitchell, Parren, 166
Mitrisin, John B., 138
Monroe, La., 76, 165, 191–92
Monroe County, Ala., 3, 95, 105
Montgomery, Ala., 5, 105, 112
Montgomery Advertiser, 112
Moore, Elmer J., 154
Moore, Howard, Jr., 172
Morris, Jesse, 92
Morrow, John, 79
Mound Bayou, Miss., 56, 66–67, 70–71,
    72, 134
Mound Bayou Community Hospital
    (MBCH), 70, 134
Mt. Beulah, Miss., 51, 64, 86, 88, 92, 99
Murphy, George, 52–53

Nagle, William, 59
Natchez, Miss., 54
Nation, 93
National Advisory Committee on Rural
    Poverty, 57
National Advisory Council on Economic
    Opportunity, 80–81, 85
National Association for the Advancement
    of Colored People (NAACP), 10, 28, 33,
    47, 55, 65, 105, 124, 143, 148, 181
National Committee in Support of
    Community Based Organizations, 172
National Confederation of American Ethnic
    Groups, 208
National Consumer Cooperative Bank Act,
    166–67, 185
National Council of Churches, 182, 186
National Education Association, 36
National Family Farm Coalition, 150
National Governors' Conference, 125
National League of Cities, 125
National Sharecroppers Fund (NSF), 90,
    94, 102
National Student Association, 47–48, 98
National Urban League, 10, 126
Neel, John, 169, 170
Neff, Vant, 79
Neighborhood Youth Corps, 71, 84

Neshoba County, Miss., 213
New Deal, 2, 29, 58, 101, 125, 155, 210,
    215, 219
New Federalism, 15, 125–26, 134, 182
New Orleans, La., 41, 47, 68, 94, 138, 158,
    188, 191, 206, 207
Newsweek, 41–42, 52, 175–76
New York City, 91, 93, 94, 95, 97, 146, 201,
    207
New York state, 50–51, 67
New York Times, 35, 76, 81–82, 93, 213, 218
Nichols, Bill, 41, 79, 107, 108, 112, 121
Nixon, Richard: and African Americans,
    55, 123–24, 138–40, 160, 165–66, 178;
    and antipoverty efforts, 15, 116–17,
    124–36, 139–40, 143–44, 154, 182; and
    cooperative movement, 154, 166, 169;
    economic policies of, 15, 55, 116–17,
    201–2, 208–11; electoral campaigns of,
    123–24, 178, 209–11; reorganization of
    OEO, 128–30, 211; rural development
    policies of, 136–38; and working-class
    Americans, 208–11
Noflin, David, 100
North Bolivar County Farm Cooperative
    (NBCFC), 68–69, 75, 113, 127, 133–34,
    149, 186
North Bolivar County Health Council
    (NBCHC), 69–70
Northerners: and antigovernment
    sentiment, 200–201, 207–8, 210–11;
    and migration South, 183, 203; racism
    of, 16, 26, 46, 57, 126, 207–8, 210;
    support for social justice, 47–48, 68,
    91, 92, 95, 98; and War on Poverty, 126,
    133, 210; working-class, 1, 52, 57, 201–4,
    211–18, 224

Oakland, Calif., 218
Obama, Barack, 219–20
Office of Economic Opportunity (OEO):
    achievements of, 62–63, 72–75, 80–81;
    and cooperatives, 14, 90, 95, 98, 99,
    103, 104–7, 109–11, 112, 136, 141, 142,
    145, 146–47; creation of, 11; and FSC,

14, 141, 142, 145, 146–47, 148, 153–54, 155, 156–58, 160, 167; and integration of programs, 77–78; and NBCFC, 68, 113, 133–34; Nixon's reorganization of, 125–26, 127–31, 135, 139–40, 143–44, 211; and out-migration, 57, 136–37; political attacks on, 14, 61, 63, 76, 79–80, 81–82, 85–86, 121–23, 168; skepticism of cooperatives, 154; and social justice, 11, 13–14, 47, 53, 55–56, 62–63, 64–65; staff analyses of problems, 24, 29, 52, 55, 57, 60, 77, 107, 138–39; support for, 60–61; and SWAFCA, 104–7, 109–11, 112, 114, 132–33; and TDHC, 66, 68, 70, 134–35; weakening of, 63, 81–87, 102, 116, 127–32, 135, 139–40. *See also* Community action agencies/Community action programs; Community Services Administration

Office of Federal Contract Compliance Programs, 164

Office of Minority Business Enterprise (OMBE), 138–39, 160, 165–66

Office of Program Development (OPD), 127–28, 157

Office of Self-Help and Technical Assistance, 167

Ogle, G. M., 117

Ohio, 93, 202, 203, 217

Olivarez, Graciela, 175

Operation Freedom, 47

Orsborn, Calvin, 107–8, 111–12, 114

Out-migration: encouraged by white southerners, 4, 12–13, 19, 33–34, 35–39, 41, 58, 121, 223; explanations for, 19, 22, 33–34, 36, 40–41, 61, 222; extent of, 21–22, 23, 24, 75, 167–68, 174–75, 184, 188, 198, 203; government policies regarding, 56–57, 59, 61, 95, 136–38, 154; inadequate solution to poverty, 46–47, 50, 57; political implications of, 4, 48, 50, 167–68; resistance to, 4, 13, 16, 44–53, 56–57, 61, 74–75, 89–90, 94–95, 106, 155, 165, 167–68, 187

Oxford, Miss., 138

Paige, Ralph, 149, 187, 189

Panola County, Miss., 22, 90–91, 101

Panola Land Buyers Association (PLBA), 148, 169, 170, 171, 190

PanSco, Inc., 160

PanSco Construction, 190

Paris, George, 149–50

Paris, Wendell, 162, 225

Patman, Wright, 56–57

Patterson, Pat, 139

Patterson, Robert, 4, 36

Peace, William H., III, 155, 156–57

Peck, Leonard, 18

People's Conference on the Tennessee-Tombigbee Waterway, 161

Perkins, James, 121

Perkins, John, 149

Perrin, Robert, 125–26

Perry County, Ala., 95

Personal Responsibility and Work Opportunity Act, 218

Petal, Miss., 150

Philadelphia, Pa., 214

Phillips, Howard, 128–29

Pickens County, Ala., 190

Pinnock, Theodore James, 25, 34

Plantation owners: and civil rights movement, 11, 12, 33–34, 88; and cooperatives, 89, 90, 101, 109; and economic development, 28; and labor control, 1–2, 20, 24–25, 85; and labor displacement, 2, 4–5, 11–13, 18–21, 23, 28, 35, 43, 48, 50–51, 54, 59, 61, 148, 223–24; and mechanization, 2, 19–20, 21, 54; subsidization by government, 20–21, 32; and War on Poverty, 63, 72, 74, 75, 76

Plantation regions: civil rights activism in, 18–19, 33–34; economic development in, 10–11, 24–25, 141, 174–75, 182–84; and national developments, 5, 11–12, 15–17, 200, 201, 216, 220–21, 224–25; out-migration from, 4, 13, 16, 22–23, 41, 50, 136–38; political economy of, 4–6, 11–13, 16, 17, 19–21, 23–25, 33–36, 43, 44–45, 167–68; poverty in, 5, 13,

16, 23–24, 32–35, 44–45, 47–48, 50–53, 65–66, 67–68, 191–92, 198; social justice activism in, 3–4, 13–16, 44–55, 61, 62–75, 141–73, 223; unemployment in, 4–5, 13, 16, 24–25, 26, 41–42, 50–53, 132, 198; War on Poverty in, 13–14, 62–87, 88

Plantation workers, 1–4, 12–13, 30, 44–52, 58, 63, 70–71, 73. *See also* Agricultural workers

Polk, Richard, 135

Pollan, Michael, 222

Poor People's Campaign, 56, 121

Poor People's Conference, 51, 88

Poor People's Corporation (PPC), 92–93, 102, 112–13

Poor white people, 1, 63, 65, 77–78

Poverty: and cooperatives, 92–93, 97–98, 113, 114, 136, 140, 154, 155–56; explanations for, 5, 16–17, 30, 31–32, 33–34, 39–43, 44–45, 54, 70, 179, 181, 195, 216–17, 218; extent of, 13, 16, 21, 23–24, 29–35, 46, 52–53, 65–66, 67–68, 97, 135, 142–43, 165, 174–75, 176–77, 181–82, 191–92, 196–99, 216–19; indifference toward, 33–35, 36, 39–41, 42–43, 63, 64, 70, 75–76, 82, 86–87, 116–17, 175–78, 209–10, 215–16, 217–18, 220–21; moral implications of, 56, 57, 61, 215, 220–21, 225; persistence of, 174–75, 177, 183, 184, 191–92, 196–99, 218–19, 225; racialization of, 29–31, 40–41, 76, 78, 121–22, 124, 166, 203–4, 205–6, 208, 210–11, 212–14, 224; reduction in extent of, 81, 183, 206; in urban North, 46–47, 50, 52, 57, 95, 202–3, 216–17, 218. *See also* Hunger; War on Poverty

Prejean, Charles: biography and career, 142–43, 187; and grand jury investigation of FSC, 170–73; tensions with Ford Foundation, 151–53, 155, 158–60; tensions with OEO, 155–56, 157–58; views on FSC achievements, 149, 160, 190; views on FSC problems, 144, 145–46, 147, 159–60, 165, 166, 168–69, 181, 186

Prendergast, Creelman and Hill, 133

Presidential Task Force on Rural Development, 130

Pruitt, I. Drayton, 170

Public assistance programs, 29–32, 33, 40–41, 64, 179–80, 181, 184, 191–92, 216–18, 219. *See also* Social welfare policies

Quitman County, Miss., 22, 195

Quitman County Delta Foundation, 195

Racism: in agricultural programs, 129–30; and class oppression, 70–71, 78, 117, 118, 119, 121–22, 223–24; color-blind forms of, 8, 10, 120–21, 123–24, 204–5, 207; of Democratic Party, 118; in economic development, 161–62, 164, 166; in education, 1, 3, 21, 23–24, 26, 27–28, 44, 46; in employment, 1, 3, 10, 25–27, 46, 69, 92, 161–62, 164; of federal agencies, 20–21, 155, 166, 188, 192–93, 206; of financial institutions, 71–72, 188–89, 192–93; in housing market, 46, 207; in Jim Crow era, 1–2, 5; in job training, 23–24, 25, 28–29; persistence of, 5, 6, 10, 11, 12–13, 14, 15, 22, 25–31, 33–34, 40–41, 45, 61, 62, 76–78, 89, 101–11, 119–21, 124, 139, 143, 204–8, 224; of political candidates, 123–24, 178–79, 212–14; of Republican Party, 116, 118–19, 179, 213; in social welfare policy, 3, 29–32; of state and local officials, 13–14, 27–32, 41, 62, 76, 131–32, 169–70, 185; and War on Poverty, 73–74; of white northerners, 46, 155, 207–8; of white southerners, 3, 4, 14–15, 19, 22, 40–41, 54, 84, 92, 116, 119–20, 166; of voters, 116, 122–24, 210–11, 213–14

Randolph, A. Phillip, 105

Rankin County, 119, 150

Rapides Parish, La., 182

Rarick, John, 80, 205

Raspberry, William, 178

Reagan, Ronald: and African Americans, 178–79, 181, 212–14; and antipoverty efforts, 181–83; and cooperative movement, 15–16, 174, 185–86, 187, 188; economic policies of, 15–16, 174, 179–82, 183, 196, 198; electoral campaigns of, 174, 178–79, 212–14; elimination of CSA, 181; rural development policies of, 16, 182–83, 184, 198; and working-class Americans, 213–15

Real Majority, The, 211

Republican Party, 82, 124; appeal to racists, 116–19, 212–14; Democratic defections to, 117, 118–19, 210, 213–14; economic policies of, 122–23, 174, 179–82, 215–16, 217–18; electoral victories of, 15, 16, 210–11; southern strategy of, 118–19, 212–13

Resnick, Joseph, 50–51

Revenue-sharing, 125, 126, 131–32

Reverse freedom rides, 36

Rich, Marvin, 104

Riots, 45, 57, 79, 86, 121, 124

Roberts, N. E. (Mrs.), 76

Rochdale, England, 88

Rogers, Nat, 59

Rosedale, Miss., 68, 69, 70

Rose Hill, Miss., 77–78

Rosow, Jerome, 208–9

Ross, Fred A., 35

Rumsfeld, Donald, 127, 130

Rural Coalition, 176

Rural Development Act, 136

Rural Training and Research Center (RTRC), 15, 148, 160, 162–63, 169, 170

Russell, Richard, 36, 38

Russell, Shirley Till, 38

Sachs, Nanette, 89

Samson, Roger, 40

Sanchez, Phillip, 157

Sanders, Bernie, 217

Saunders, Robert, 78, 86

Scammon, Richard, 211

Scholarship, Education and Defense Fund for Racial Equality (SEDFRE), 10, 97, 104, 112, 131

Schwinn Bicycles, 184

Segregation: color-blind defenses of, 6, 10, 117–18, 119–21, 123, 179, 204–5, 207; in education, 21, 27–28, 195, 204; efforts to challenge, 36, 95, 97, 143; efforts to preserve, 1, 4, 36–39, 56, 60, 116, 117–18, 119–21, 123, 207–8; in employment, 25–26; in housing, 204–5; in job training programs, 28–29; in northern cities, 46, 207; persistence of, 191, 195

Self-help initiatives: black southerners' interest in, 14; and cooperative movement, 88, 92, 95, 98, 100, 142, 144, 147–48, 166, 173, 187, 203; and War on Poverty, 48, 50, 62–63, 78, 95, 128, 136, 144, 203

Selma, Ala., 5, 77, 94, 95, 105, 109, 110, 112

Selma Inter-Religious Project, 10, 77, 94, 105

Selma Times Journal, 110

Selma to Montgomery March, 5

Senate Appropriations Committee, 74, 85

Senate Labor and Public Welfare Subcommittee on Employment, Manpower and Poverty, 52–53

Senate Subcommittee on Rural Development, 136

Sensing, Thurmond, 75, 79

Shambray, Bernard, 26

Sharecroppers: displacement of, 2–5, 18–21, 23, 25, 41–42, 201, 202, 220–21, 224, 225; economic dependence of, 1–2, 3, 18–19; exploitation of, 1–2, 102, 142–43; political awareness of, 12; and social justice activism, 12, 13–15, 90, 102; and War on Poverty, 66–69, 71–72. *See also* Agricultural workers

Sharkey County, Miss., 198

Shaw, Miss., 30

Shelby, Miss., 25

Shelby, Richard, 170

Shepherd, John C., 195

Sherrill, Robert, 35

Shirley, Aaron, 43

Shriver, Sargent, 60, 79–80, 84, 85, 103

Simpson, Stella, 66, 69, 70

Singletary, C. R., 38

Slavery, 1, 5, 19, 43, 113, 116, 134, 161

Sloan, Bernard, 175–76

Small Business Administration, 80, 193

Small farmers: federal programs for, 58, 175, 196; FSC programs for, 15, 147–48, 149–50, 167, 186–89; ignored by USDA, 15, 20–21, 136, 147–48, 155, 193–94; resistance to displacement of, 45–46, 50, 89–91, 94–95, 100–101; revival of, 17, 222–23, 224–25; seen as anachronistic, 1, 154

Smith, Hazel Brannon, 61

Smitherman, Joe, 105, 106, 110–11

Social justice activism: and civil rights movement, 3, 12, 15, 64–65, 101–2, 115, 169–70; goals of, 3, 140, 176, 200, 208; impact of, 149–51, 162, 164, 173, 191, 195–96, 203, 222–23, 224–25; and labor displacement, 11–12, 44–52, 61, 160; opposition to, 16, 116, 124, 174, 175, 181, 185, 210–11; persistence of, 17, 85, 186, 195–96, 199; support for, 60–61, 63–64, 98, 105–6, 143. *See also* Cooperative movement; Federation of Southern Cooperatives; War on Poverty

Social Security, 29, 42, 177, 198, 206, 213, 220

Social Security Act, 29

Social welfare programs: antipathy toward, 14, 32, 38–41, 42–43, 54, 55, 63, 75–76, 81–82, 117, 118, 121–22, 135–36, 205–6, 209, 213–14, 216, 217–18, 219–20; benefits for white Americans, 2, 206, 210; debates over reform of, 216–18; efforts to decrease dependence on, 53–56, 71, 72–73, 80, 85, 123, 156, 161–62; efforts to increase access to, 64, 69, 73, 100; expansion of, 45, 53–54; and funding cuts, 16, 63, 81–85, 127, 179–82, 203, 210, 212, 218; inadequacies of, 29–32, 35, 40, 176–77, 181–82, 184, 191–92, 197–98, 203, 208, 216–17, 220–21; racial discrimination in, 3, 12, 18–19, 29–32, 35, 50–51, 64, 69, 191–92; racialization of,

121–22, 123, 179, 205–6, 210, 212–14, 220. *See also* War on Poverty

South Carolina, 28–29, 118, 168, 189, 191, 220

South Delta Community Action Association, 55, 77

Southeast Alabama Self-Help Association (SEASHA), 100, 156

Southeast Community Organization, 208

Southeast Region Equal Opportunity Association, 131

Southern Christian Leadership Conference (SCLC), 10, 55, 56, 60, 90, 94, 121, 143

Southern Consumers Cooperative (SCC), 98–99, 100, 103, 142, 143

Southern Consumers Education Foundation (SCEF), 99, 103, 143

Southern Cooperative Development Fund (SCDF), 145, 153, 156–57, 158, 160, 184, 186

Southern Cooperative Development Program (SCDP), 99–101, 112, 142, 143, 148

Southern Development Foundation, 186, 193

Southern Patriot, 24, 47

Southern Regional Council, 94, 186–87

Southern Rural Action, 47

Southern Rural Alliance, 186–87

Southern strategy, 118–19, 212–13

Southwest Alabama Farmers Cooperative Association (SWAFCA), 94–95, 100, 104–12, 114, 132–33, 156, 168, 186

Southwest Alabama Self-Help Housing, 48, 50

Sparkman, John, 38, 58–59, 75, 79, 117, 204, 205

Springsteen, Bruce, 203

Stans, Maurice, 138–39

Starkville, Miss., 120, 138

State Economic Opportunity Offices (SEOOs), 60, 130, 168, 177

State governments: and antipoverty efforts, 25, 32, 33, 41, 50–51, 59–60, 81, 86, 179, 197, 220; control over federal programs,

15, 25, 29–32, 116, 122, 123, 125–26, 128, 130–31, 135–36, 181–82, 186, 213, 216, 218; and cooperative movement, 110, 168, 185, 186, 188, 190–91; and economic development, 28–29, 36, 59–60, 182, 184, 191, 194–95; failure of leadership, 13, 50–51, 63–64; racism of, 1, 25, 27–28, 33, 135, 166; and War on Poverty, 14, 56, 59–60, 63–64, 73, 80, 82, 124–26, 130–31, 181–82

States' rights, 59, 64, 116, 121, 213

Steagall, Joe, 170

Stennis, John, 34, 36, 37, 81, 85, 124

Steptoe, Roosevelt, 157

Stewart, Donald, 170

St. Landry Parish, La., 50, 95, 97, 184, 193, 205

Strickland, Edwin, 79

Strickland, Robert, 48, 65

Student Nonviolent Coordinating Committee (SNCC), 10, 65, 90, 92, 94, 143

Sumter County, Ala., 15, 95, 147–48, 149, 169–70, 190

Sunflower County, Miss., 6, 20, 24, 51, 74

Surplus commodity distribution program. *See* Department of Agriculture: food programs of

Sutherland, Elizabeth, 93

Sviridoff, Mitchell, 153, 159

Systematic Training and Redevelopment (STAR), 73–74, 84

Taiwan, 184, 217

Tallahatchie County, Miss., 22

Tallulah, La., 160, 165, 168

Tate County, Miss., 22

Taxes: antipathy toward, 36, 38, 81, 105, 122, 182, 207, 208, 209, 212, 213, 214, 215, 220, 224; and black property losses, 162, 188–89, 192; cuts in, 16, 122, 174, 179–80, 196, 212, 214, 220; decentralized control of, 125, 131; exemptions from, 144, 174, 194, 195; inadequate revenues from, 81, 131, 182, 196, 203, 220; increases in, 30,

50, 72, 80, 105, 132, 208, 212; need for, 13, 36, 59, 80, 155; perceived misuse of funds from, 14, 27–28, 42, 56, 63, 75–76, 79–80, 103, 111–12, 122, 132, 155, 175–76, 186, 208, 209

Tax Reform Act, 144

Tea Party, 219–20

Tennessee, 99, 142, 161, 168, 215

Tennessee-Tombigbee Waterway (TTW), 160–65

Tennessee-Tombigbee Waterway Development Authority (TTWDA), 161–62

Tensas Parish, La., 193

Texas, 56, 142, 215, 219

Thanksgiving Fast for Freedom, 48

Threadgill, Thomas, 71–72

Thurmond, Strom, 118, 120

Todd, Johnny, 70

Toledo, Ohio, 217

Tribbett, Miss., 48, 52, 60

Trilateral Commission, 212

Tufts-Delta Health Center (TDHC), 66–71, 72, 75, 85, 128, 134–35, 138, 160, 195

Tufts Medical School, 66

Tufts University, 133, 134

Tunica County, Miss., 22, 36, 76

Turner, Albert, 94, 100

Tuskegee Institute, 100, 106

Tyson, Ramon, 165

Unemployment: attempts to alleviate, 65, 72–73, 101, 165; debates over causes and solutions, 4–5, 16–17, 50–51, 59, 124–25, 179, 200, 211–12, 214–15, 216–19, 219–21, 223–25; inadequate government responses to, 55, 63–64, 137–39, 140, 181–82; in plantation regions, 2–4, 13, 16, 22–25, 32, 51–53, 65, 137, 181, 183–84, 191, 197–99; in United States, 15, 176, 206, 208, 218–19; in urban North, 202–3. *See also* Displacement

Unemployment insurance, 25, 29, 30, 42, 62

United Nations, 222

United States Cooperative League, 99

University of Southwestern Louisiana, 97

Urban uprisings, 45, 57, 79, 86, 121, 124

U.S. Congress: and antipoverty efforts, 16–17, 29, 32, 50–51, 52–53, 57, 61, 62, 63–64, 80–81, 82, 85, 122, 123, 128–29, 156, 175; and budget cuts, 82–84, 127, 175, 176, 179–80, 190; and civil rights, 10, 38, 59, 120, 121, 124, 144, 204; conservatism of, 15–17, 63, 81, 82, 84, 116, 216, 219–20; and economic development, 10–11, 138, 161, 191, 196–97; and labor displacement, 56–57, 138, 219–20; and welfare reform, 216–18. *See also* U.S. House of Representatives; U.S. Senate

U.S. Constitution, 120, 123, 204, 205, 207

U.S. Food Sovereignty Alliance, 223

U.S. House of Representatives, 105, 108, 144, 180, 216

U.S. News and World Report, 178

U.S. Senate, 52–53, 74, 75, 85, 128, 136, 166, 180, 216

U.S. Supreme Court, 27, 31, 119, 120, 124, 179

U.S. Treasury, 72, 79, 123, 132, 139, 166

Vermilion Parish, La., 97

Via Campesina, 224–25

Vietnam War, 56, 63, 81–82, 84, 144, 175

Vitol, Ralph, 207, 208

Voluntary Racial Relocation Commission, 36, 38

Volunteers in Service to America (VISTA), 167, 185, 187, 191

Voorhis, Jerry, 151

Voter Education Project, 186–87

Voter registration, black: and cooperative movement, 100–101, 102, 143, 167–68, 169–70, 186–87, 189, 190, 223; in 1960s, 3, 5, 97, 144; opposition to, 4, 18–19, 22, 27, 38–39, 105, 117; and out-migration, 4, 22; reprisals for, 18–19, 33–34, 47, 77, 88, 94; and southern politics, 179, 190–91; and War on Poverty, 64–65, 69–70, 72

Voting Rights Act, 3, 10, 18, 38, 95, 117, 121, 177, 223

Wagner, Robert, 193

Walker, Ben, 60

Wall, Viola, 51

Wallace, George, 60, 82, 85–86, 117–18, 123, 124, 179, 213

Walter, Francis X., 77, 86, 105–6

War on Poverty: accusations of corruption in, 79–80, 81, 123; achievements of, 71–75, 80–81, 88, 206, 223; and civil rights movement, 10–11, 64–65, 69–70, 76–77; discouragement of white participation in, 76–78; disillusionment of participants in, 14, 54, 63, 86–87; and empowerment of poor people, 13–14, 65–70, 72–73, 74–75, 99, 181–82; and funding cuts, 82–85, 129, 144, 199; neutralization of, 15–16, 63, 82–87, 116, 129, 135–36, 139, 141; opposition to, 14, 15, 16, 63, 66, 75–79, 81–82, 85–86, 87, 117, 120, 123, 125, 175–78, 179, 200, 210, 211, 213, 219, 223–24; origins of, 10–11, 62, 63–64; perceived failure of, 177–78; racialization of, 76–78, 82, 200, 213; radical potential of, 13–14, 62–65, 86–87, 181–82; and southern political economy, 13–14, 59, 63–64, 69–75, 161; support for, 59–61, 71, 73–74, 116. *See also* Community action agencies/Community action programs; Office of Economic Opportunity

Washington, D.C., 80, 98, 106, 108, 109, 121, 189, 208

Washington, Karen, 222

Washington County, Miss., 22, 48, 92

Washington Post, 44, 176, 178

Washington Times, 215

Waterproof, La., 168

Watson, Charles, 59

Watson, W. C., 122

Wattenberg, Ben, 211

Weaver, A. Q., 117

Webster County, Miss., 204, 207

Welfare. *See* Public assistance programs

Welfare rights activism, 30–31, 45, 50–52, 64, 69, 73, 100, 205

West Alabama Health Services, 185

West Batesville Farmers Cooperative (WBFC), 90–91, 100

West Feliciana Parish, La., 18, 26

Wetumpka, Ala., 79

Wheatley, Joseph, 48

White ethnics, 206–7, 210

Whitfield Pickle Company, 105, 106, 109–10, 111

Whitley, Clifton, 102

Wicker, Roger, 216

Wiggins, Phillip, 93

Wilcox County, Ala.: antipoverty efforts in, 60, 71–72, 75, 78, 82, 86; conditions in, 23–24, 36; cooperatives in, 94, 95; opposition to antipoverty efforts in, 36, 77, 78, 86; social justice activism in, 6, 82

Wilkins, Roy, 105

Wilkinson County, Miss., 47, 60

Williams, Adell, 168

Williams, Irene, 67

Williams, J. T., 91

Williams, John Bell, 79

Williams, Willie, 44

Wilson, Ora, 51

Wilson, William Julius, 216–17

Wilson, Woodrow, 124

Winstonville, Miss., 93

Winter, William, 59, 184

Wirtz, Willard, 55

Wofford, Harris, 35–36

Working class: black, 1–3, 5, 25–30, 70–71, 206, 223–25; and capitalist restructuring, 1, 16–17, 183–84, 223–25; white, 16–17, 21, 26, 28–30, 36, 202, 206, 208–12, 213–14. *See also* Displacement

World War II, 2, 3, 46, 201

Wright, Karl, 186

Wyandotte Chemical Corporation, La., 26

Wyman, Hastings, Jr., 213

Yazoo County, Miss., 22

Young Americans for Freedom, 128

Youngstown, Ohio, 203

Zimmerman, Stanley, 108

Zippert, John: biography and career, 95, 97; and formation of FSC/LAF, 287; and FSC, 143, 148, 149, 161, 170, 171, 185; and GMVPC, 97, 102, 104; and SCC, 98–99; and SCDP, 99–100, 112, 115

MIX
Paper from
responsible sources
FSC® C013483